For Reference

Not to be taken from this room

ENCYCLOPEDIA OF

MODERN

AMERICAN

SOCIAL

ISSUES

ENCYCLOPEDIA OF
MODERN
AMERICAN
SOCIAL
ISSUES

MICHAEL KRONENWETTER

ABC-CLIO

Santa Barbara, California
Denver, Colorado
Oxford, England

Library of Congress Cataloging-in-Publication Data

Kronenwetter, Michael.
    Encyclopedia of modern american social issues / Michael Kronenwetter.
        p. cm.
    Includes bibliographical references and index.
    ISBN 0-87436-779-4 (alk. paper)
    1. United States—Social conditions—Encyclopedias. 2. United States—Economic conditions—Encyclopedias. 3. United States—Politics and government—Encyclopedias.
I. Title.
HN57.K73 1997
306′.0973—dc2197-25967

02 01 00 99 98   10 9 8 7 6 5 4 3 2

ABC-CLIO, Inc.
130 Cremona Drive, P.O. Box 1911
Santa Barbara, California 93116-1911

This book is printed on acid-free paper ∞.
Manufactured in the United States of America

Contents

INTRODUCTION

The *Encyclopedia of Modern American Social Issues* is intended as a handy reference source for students and others interested in U.S. social affairs. It deals with issues that have been important to the United States in the twentieth century, concentrating especially on those that are still of concern today and those likely to remain of concern for some time to come.

The overriding purpose of this book is to provide, in a single source, the information and explanations necessary for a basic understanding of the problems and controversies that have faced—and continue to face—the United States. These problems and controversies range across virtually every area of American life, including social welfare and reform, civil rights, politics and government, the environment, media, economics, health, family, religion, education, law, and even sports.

Clearly, a work of this size cannot explore all possible issues, much less explore them in depth. Indeed, each subject covered in this book is worthy of an entire book. Many, in fact, have been the subject of more than one book already. Rather, the *Encyclopedia*'s goal is to provide useful background information about a wide selection of key issues.

Entries are arranged alphabetically by subject. Some entries, such as "Burden of Proof," are essentially definitional. They explain the meaning and significance of a term, concept, or event crucial to an understanding of modern U.S. society. Other entries, such as "Civil Rights Movement" and "Death Penalty (Controversies)," are much longer and more detailed. These longer entries typically provide an overview of the subject as well as pertinent facts and an exploration of the subject's relevance to modern society.

Issues are put into historical context where appropriate. Past and present controversies are aired, and brief summations of the most important positions are taken on every side. Although such pros and cons are central to some subjects, such as abortion and gun control, they are largely irrelevant to others (domestic violence and the Kerner Commission Report, for example). A small but significant selection of entries, such as "Bill of Rights" and "Contract with America," present all or substantial portions of the text of specific documents that have had a significant impact on U.S. society or social thought.

Although the focus of this book is on the twentieth century and the issues that have helped to form and define it, some entries, such as "Gospel of Wealth" and "Social Darwinism," deal with issues, events, or ideas that are identified primarily with previous centuries. These entries are included because of the perspective they provide on more recent issues and controversies.

This book is not intended as a statistical reference. Statistics date quickly, and they are used here primarily to indicate the size of a social phenomenon, or the direction of a trend, rather than as a guide to present conditions.

Because the entries are intended to provide basic rather than specialized or academically advanced information, the effort has been made to present helpful and accurate information in a readable and readily understandable form.

Abortion

An abortion is the ending of a pregnancy with the destruction of the fetus. Abortions can be either spontaneous or induced. Spontaneous abortions, also known as miscarriages, occur in about one-quarter of human pregnancies as a result of natural processes not entirely understood. Induced abortions, on the other hand, are deliberate acts, most often accomplished by expelling the fetus from the womb before it is sufficiently developed to survive. Induced abortion is a bitterly controversial moral and social issue.

Reasons for Induced Abortions

More than 1.5 million abortions are induced each year in the United States. They are performed for a variety of medical, financial, and emotional reasons. Medical abortions are performed to protect the health of the mother, when the strain of continuing the pregnancy, or of giving birth, would present a serious threat, or to prevent the birth of a child suspected to have serious physical or mental defects.

Other abortions are motivated by the desire to prevent the birth of a child who would present an unacceptable financial or emotional demand on its family. A small number of abortions are performed to eliminate offspring resulting from sexually violent encounters or incest.

Historically, abortion sometimes was used simply as a form of birth control. With the ready availability of condoms and birth control pills in modern times, this use of abortion became almost obsolete. In a sense, however, it may be about to return, in the form of the so-called abortion pill, RU-486, which has been used widely in France, and which was cleared for experimental use in the United States in 1994.

Legal History

Abortion is an ancient practice, used in classical Greece and Rome. Although it was generally frowned upon as immoral and disreputable, it was also used by some residents of colonial America and the early United States.

Objections to abortion strengthened throughout the western world in the nineteenth century. In 1869, the Catholic Church roundly condemned the practice in all forms and circumstances. In the United States, meanwhile, doctors began pressing state governments to pass laws against it. By the first half of the twentieth century, abortion was illegal throughout the country, except when it was needed medically to save the life of the mother.

Despite the criminal nature of the act, a great many abortions continued to be performed secretly. Some were carried out by doctors, either for profit or out of sympathy with unhappy pregnant patients, some by so-called back-alley abortionists, shady figures who aborted solely for money, often under unsanitary and even brutal conditions, and with little care for the health of the woman. An uncertain number of women died as a result of such operations.

The sexual revolution of the 1960s and the rise of the modern women's movement generated demand for the legalization of abortion. Proponents of legalization argued that, since the woman naturally bore the discomfort, risks, and pain of pregnancy and childbirth—and often the financial and moral responsibility of raising the child as well—the decision whether to give birth or to abort ought to be left to her. Until a child was born, they argued, the fetus was a part of the mother's body, and the woman had the right to do whatever she chose with her own body.

Several state legislatures responded with softened abortion laws, establishing an increasing number of circumstances (rape, incest, etc.) in which abortions could take place legally when performed by a licensed doctor. This led to a situation in which abortions were regarded legally as murder in some states, while they were both legal and easy to obtain in others. Many women traveled to other states to get abortions they could not get at home. Some abortion advocates, who considered abortion a civil right, complained that this situation was unfair because it discriminated against poor women who could not afford to travel to another state to obtain a safe, legal abortion.

In the 1973 *Roe* v. *Wade* case, the U.S. Supreme Court struck down two state antiabortion laws. Although the ruling was complex (and even, some observers felt, tortured), it had the effect of not only making abortion legal in the United States, but protecting it, under certain circumstances, as a constitutional right.

In the years since *Roe* v. *Wade*, the states have passed a multitude of laws regulating abortion, and the Supreme Court has handed down many decisions regarding these laws. In general, the Supreme Court decisions have tended to support in principle the right of women to have abortions. The Court has, however, allowed state legislatures to regulate abortions to some degree. Furthermore, it has not insisted that Medicaid, or other federal or state funds, be made available to pay for them, in cases in which the life of the woman is not threatened.

"Pro-Choice"—"Pro-Life"

Roe v. *Wade* settled the constitutional question, at least temporarily, but it did not end the bitter debate over abortion. If anything, it exacerbated it. Although the decision was recognized as a major victory for those who favored access to abortion, neither side has been satisfied fully with the decision.

Many Americans remain totally opposed to abortion in any form. No matter when it is performed, they consider it the willful murder of a defenseless human being. Others, however, insist that abortion is not merely a legitimate option for a prospective parent, but a woman's absolute right at any time during the nine-month period in which the unborn child is inside her body.

The two sides quarrel over words which reflect their very different concepts of what is at stake in the abortion debate. Those who favor the right to abortion speak of the "fetus": an impersonal, medical term. The opponents speak of the "baby" or "unborn child." The advocates speak of "terminating the pregnancy." The opponents speak of "killing the child." They even quarrel over what they should call themselves. Those who believe that abortion is a woman's right like to be called "pro-choice," while those who do not believe in abortion like to be called "pro-life." Each side, however, objects to the other's preferred term. The pro-choice forces claim that calling the opponents of abortion "pro-life" implies that those who support the right to abortion favor death. Instead, say the pro-choicers, their opponents ought to be called "antiabortion." Pro-lifers, on the other hand, insist that "pro-choice" is misleading because it implies that those on the other side are neutral. In reality, they claim, the so-called pro-choicers are really pro-abortion. (In general, it seems fairest to call each group by whatever title it chooses to call itself.)

In the political arena, the debate is often cast as a conflict of rights: the right of the woman versus the right of the fetus or child. Pro-choice is generally considered a liberal position and pro-life a conservative one. Yet, many libertarian conservatives are pro-choice, and some notable liberals, including the likes of Nat Hentoff, oppose abortion. Politicians often try to have the debate both ways by saying that they personally are opposed to abortion, but that they do not want their opposition passed into law, therefore effectively favoring the right to choose.

When Does Life Begin?

The abortion debate can be an extremely complex and tortured one, but basically, it revolves around a single, fundamental issue: When does individual human life begin? That is, at what point does human tissue become a human being?

The gestation of the fetus is typically a nine-month process, with many developments along the way. It is possible to argue that human life begins at virtually any point along that progression. On one end, the more absolute pro-life advocates believe that human life begins as soon as the sperm and egg join at the instant of conception. From that moment on, they are convinced, the union is not merely a fertilized egg but an individual human being, however undeveloped. The more absolute pro-choice advocates, on the other hand, deny that the fetus is a person, entitled to the rights and protections of a fully developed human being, until it has been born.

Ultimately, the question of when individual human life begins does not lend itself to scientific proof. It is a matter of philosophical or moral belief. This is strongly evidenced by the fact that the Catholic Church and many fundamentalist Christian religions are strongly opposed to abortion.

Social Questions

Aside from the philosophical and moral issues raised by abortion, there are practical questions as well. Pro-choice advocates argue that abortion is preferable to bringing children into the world, when the parents either cannot or will not nurture and provide for them. There are already too many children condemned to a life of poverty or abuse, they say. Many pregnant women and their families are either economically or psychologically unable to care for any more children. For them, abortion is the only humane alternative.

Pro-life advocates insist that this is a false alternative. If children cannot be provided for economically, they say, the answer is to give them help, not to deny them the right to exist. Furthermore, adoption, not abortion, is the solution for parents who feel themselves unable to support, or to protect, their own children.

5

Several pro-life groups attempt to find homes for children whose mothers cannot, or will not, raise them. The Nobel Peace Prize-winning nun, Mother Teresa, pledged that her organization would take all "unwanted" children born in the United States. Pro-choice groups respond that many children already born have not been placed in good homes. They accuse the pro-lifers of hypocrisy, insisting that they could not possibly provide homes for 1.5 million more children each year.

Partly because of the continuing controversy and protest, and partly because of economic changes within the medical industry in general, the availability of abortion services seems to be in a small decline. More than 200 hospitals that once had provided abortions had stopped doing so by 1992. Only about half as many medical residency programs were providing abortion training as compared to some years before. On the other hand, the number of clinics performing abortions actually rose during the same period. Most of the decline has taken place in rural America, while most of the increase has occurred in urban areas.

A Growing Militancy

In recent years, radical activists on the pro-life side have taken to increasingly extreme forms of civil disobedience in order to stop what they consider the killing of unborn children. They have tried several tactics to dissuade women from entering clinics where abortions are performed, ranging from quiet argument to shouting and blocking entranceways. More extreme activists have attempted to intimidate physicians specializing in abortion, harassing them in a variety of ways, both in person and over the telephone. In several highly publicized cases, apparently mentally disturbed pro-lifers actually have murdered physicians.

Such violence has been condemned by most mainstream pro-life groups, including Right to Life and the United States Catholic Conference. Nonetheless, police and prosecutors have become increasingly intolerant of pro-life demonstrators. Scores of demonstrators, most of whom have been peaceful, have been sentenced to jail, and courts have even begun to use antiracketeering statutes against some pro-life groups.

See also *Roe* v. *Wade*; Sex-selection Abortions.
For further reading Luker, Kristen. *Abortion and the Politics of Motherhood*. Berkeley, CA: University of California Press, 1984.

Academic Standards

American educators and public alike have developed serious concerns over the state of American education in the late twentieth century. To some extent, these have derived from complaints made by some business owners that high school graduation certificates no longer guarantee that new employees will have the basic language and math skills needed to function in a modern business setting. Another factor has been a variety of highly publicized reports purporting to show that American students lag behind students in some foreign nations in subjects like math and science. Such concerns have led for a demand that tougher standards be applied in U.S. public elementary and secondary schools.

Polls indicate that an overwhelming majority of the general public feels that public schools need to do a better job of ensuring that students acquire the basic information and skills they need to function in an advanced technological society. There is also general agreement that students and teachers should be held to higher performance standards than in the recent past. At the same time, however, there is disagreement over what those standards should be, and how they should be applied.

Attempts to Set National Goals

In 1989, President George Bush summoned the nation's governors to an Education Summit that produced six national educational goals. These were later expanded and refined into "Goals 2000," a more detailed plan passed by Congress and signed into law by President Bill Clinton in 1992, that called on the U.S. Department of Education to develop a set of performance standards for public elementary and secondary schools. Under this law, states are free to choose whether to adopt the department's standards for their schools. Goals 2000 has proved to be controversial in a way that reflects some of the basic divisions among American parents and educators. Conservatives, who believe that education ought to be strictly a local matter, are suspicious of what they see as a federal attempt to intrude into local classrooms. Others, who view education more as a national concern, feel that the federal plan does not go far enough in ensuring that whatever tougher standards are developed will be effectively applied in all public schools.

In his 1997 State of the Union Address, President Clinton called for the establishment of new national goals for elementary school students.

Differing Standards

The debate over standards is, to some extent, a political as well as educational controversy. On the one side are those conservative-minded parents and politicians who want a return to what they call the "three *R*s: reading, 'riting, and 'rithmetic." They see schools as a vehicle for disseminating a more or less fixed body of facts and principles in disciplines such as history and the sciences, as well as being the place to develop the ability to perform certain clearly definable mathematical computations.

On the other side are those more liberal parents, teachers, and educational organizations that favor a more flexible and student-centered approach to education. They believe that educational standards should emphasize reasoning abilities, as well as the ability to adjust to constantly changing developments, not only in educational disciplines but also in society at large.

The debate often is framed as a controversy between fact-based and concept-based standards. Liberal teachers and parents worry that a concentration on the dissemination of facts, which often involves an emphasis on learning by rote, will dull creativity. They fear that this will condition young people to see complex realities in stark terms of correct and incorrect, right and wrong—and leave them unprepared to make the political and moral judgments that citizenship in a democracy demands. More conservative teachers and parents, on the other hand, believe that concept-based standards are essentially vehicles for the promotion of political correctness and relativism. They view such standards as a watering down of the educational process, replacing the needed focus on rigorous instruction with a morally and intellectually bankrupt emphasis on neutral thought processes.

Another, more radical, position holds that academic standards should be entirely a local matter. Different school boards, principals, and even individual teachers should be free to set their own educational goals, according to the needs of their communities and the potential of their students. In the eyes of those who hold this view, any kind of national standards smack of what the Republican Senate Majority Leader Trent Lott called federal "micromanagement of schools."

Some who favor local control do so for political or religious reasons. They believe that local school boards will set standards closer to the desires of most ordinary Americans than will national education authorities, whom many believe to be too liberal, and hostile to religion. Other proponents of local control believe that academic standards should be set as high as realistically possible. They worry that standards set at the national, or even state, level are likely to be aimed at some median level of achievement and will therefore shortchange those students who are capable of performing at a higher level.

See also Education Summit (1989); Goals 2000 Act; Political Correctness; Self-Esteem Movement in Education.
For further reading Van Scotter, Richard D. *Public Schooling in America*. Boulder, CO: ABC-CLIO, 1991.

AFDC
See Aid to Families with Dependent Children.

Affirmative Action
Government, business, and educational efforts designed to provide women and minorities with jobs or opportunities which have been denied to them in the past are known as affirmative action.

Affirmative action programs and policies necessarily involve giving preference to members of some groups over others. Depending on the specific program, groups whose members qualify for affirm-

ative action might include women, racial and ethnic groups, as well as the physically, mentally, or emotionally disabled. The group most often disadvantaged by affirmative action efforts is that made up of white males, who traditionally have held most of the power and wealth in the United States.

Granting preference on the basis of group identity, rather than individual merit, goes against the traditional American ideal of equal treatment for all, but it is justified as an attempt to overcome the effects of past discrimination. The irony of affirmative action is that it tries to correct these effects by imposing what has become known as reverse discrimination. The defenders of affirmative action acknowledge this paradox, but insist that there is no way to redress the unfair advantage white males have over women and minorities, as a result of past as well as present discrimination, except by granting those groups an advantage in return. That advantage, given in the present, may seem unfair to individual white males who are disadvantaged because of it. But to do nothing, affirmative action supporters argue, would simply reinforce the unfairness that is inherent already in the situation. If no "unfair" advantage were awarded now, today's white males would be unfairly benefiting from the discrimination of the past, even though they personally might have played no part in it.

Although most of the controversy centers on race-based policies, statistics indicate that women as a group may benefit most from affirmative action. Women, who make up a slight majority of the population as a whole, make up slightly less than 25 percent of all lawyers and doctors and less than 10 percent of engineers. However, there is a much higher proportion of their population in high-paid professions than is true of African-Americans.

The debate over affirmative action often is framed in terms of sports metaphors. The underlying assumption, like that of Social Darwinism, is that economic life is a form of competition. The proponents of affirmative action like to speak in terms of a foot race. As things are now, they say, white males get to start the race far ahead of everyone else. Something has to be done, if not to handicap them, at least to move the starting point ahead for other groups.

The opponents of affirmative action prefer to speak in football terms. What is needed, they say, is simply a level playing field, on which everyone is free to compete equally, and no advantage is given to anyone, regardless of gender, color, or disability.

Origins of Affirmative Action

Affirmative action grew out of enforcement of several civil rights acts and presidential executive orders in the 1960s. At that time, schools and public facilities were being racially desegregated by federal laws and court rulings. Schools all over the country that once had been all white were being required to admit African-Americans. The success of these efforts was judged largely in numerical terms, by the percentages of African-American students in given schools.

In the climate of the time, it was only natural to look at employment figures in a similar way. When a company had few or no African-American employees in well-paid jobs, in a town with many able African-American workers, it was assumed that discrimination was the reason.

That discrimination might or might not have been intended by the employers. In many cases, it was the indirect result of discrimination in other areas of society, for example, the poor schools that African-Americans had to attend in segregated communities, which did not give them the educational background needed for well-paying jobs. There also were a whole range of social customs and practices which, by tradition, encouraged whites to apply for certain jobs and discouraged blacks from doing so. Company spokespersons might honestly say that the reason no African-Americans had been picked for good jobs had nothing to do with bias against them. It was just that no qualified African-Americans had applied.

For African-Americans, however, the result was the same. Because of past discrimination of whatever kind, they continued to be drastically underrepresented in desirable jobs. Something, it was felt, had to be done, not only to end direct discrimination in hiring, but to open up at least some of those long-closed jobs to African-Americans.

The presidential administration of Lyndon Johnson, as well as the U.S. Supreme Court, decided that affirmative action would have to be one of the methods used. Although affirmative action was initially intended primarily to benefit African-Americans, it was applied to other groups that could claim to have been victims of discrimination, notably including women and the disabled.

Varieties of Affirmative Action

The most basic form of affirmative action is outreach: Programs designed to introduce women and minorities to possibilities that may never have occurred to them, or which they had assumed were out of their reach. Attempts might be made to encourage women to enter traditionally male fields such as carpentry, truck-driving, or electrical engineering. A special effort might be launched to locate qualified minority applicants for jobs in traditionally white-dominated fields, such as journalism or business administration. Universities might recruit students in inner-city high schools.

In an effort to shatter the glass ceiling that seems to hold women back from the highest levels of American business, several companies have deliberately sought out women for high-level positions. Agencies that find candidates for executive jobs report that a growing number of major companies have asked them especially to look for qualified females. Although this practice may be illegal, some companies have gone so far as to refuse even to consider men for certain posts. Some outreach programs sometimes go beyond the merely informational to provide actual training or scholarship assistance to eligible applicants.

There are a variety of ways in which affirmative action is put into place when it comes to actual hiring, as well as in awarding admission to educational programs or professional disciplines One policy involves giving a preference among equals; that is, choosing the woman or minority applicant out of any field of equally qualified candidates.

Another is to include gender or color itself as one of the criteria for awarding a job, promotion, or position in a school. In this case, being a member of a group previously discriminated against is considered a qualification in itself—a factor which can be used, along with other factors, to offset the advantage of competing candidates who would otherwise be considered more qualified. Attacked as reverse discrimination, this form of affirmative action is defended sometimes as the only effective way to compensate for group disadvantages brought about by discrimination.

A third kind of affirmative action involves rewarding institutions that offer opportunities to disadvantaged minorities. These include grants to educational institutions for programs aimed at minorities, or subsidies to employers for hiring members of disadvantaged groups. Following the Vietnam War, for example, the government attempted to help Southeast Asian refugees to get off federal assistance and into the U.S. workforce by temporarily subsidizing a portion of their salaries. This allowed companies like Boeing, which hired several refugees for its large plants in Everett, Washington, to employ them relatively cheaply.

This program, like virtually all affirmative action programs, however, was extremely controversial. It aroused particular resentment on the part of native-born workers who felt that the subsidies disadvantaged them. Defenders of the subsidies pointed out that, in return for the government assistance, Boeing and other employers undertook the extra trouble and expense of training the newcomers. Ultimately, they argued, society was better off with the Southeast Asians as employed taxpayers, rather than as unemployed wards of the state. State and federal government agencies sometimes award contracts at least partly according to whether or not the contracting business is woman or minority owned. Grants are sometimes handed out on a similar basis.

How much of a role affirmative action actually plays in the awarding of jobs and other opportunities is unclear. There is a widespread belief, especially among white males who have been turned down for such opportunities, that it is a major—even the overriding—factor in most such decisions. Minorities, however, who still find themselves statistically underrepresented in terms of power and wealth in American society, see affirmative action as a much less significant force.

Although the statistics are incomplete, those that are available seem to support the impression of the minorities. Despite the impression of many entering college students and their parents, for example, a mere 1 percent of the scholarships awarded each year are granted solely on the basis of race; and only a small percentage take race into account at all. Altogether, the General Accounting Office of the U.S. Congress reports that race is a factor in approximately 4 percent of the scholarship money handed out each year.

Three Levels of Criticism

Objections to affirmative action arise on at least three levels. The first is personal bias. Although few will say so openly, there are people who do not want to see opportunities for women and minorities expanded. These critics oppose affirmative action out of conscious or unconscious prejudice, whether against those groups, or in favor of those who have traditionally been advantaged.

The second level of criticism is essentially conservative. It is advanced by those who favor the traditional patterns of American society and see no reason to disrupt them. To some degree, these critics see affirmative action as a symptom of the breakdown of a valued social order, resting on the foundation of a large, predominantly white, middle class made up of families in which the husband/father is the primary breadwinner.

A third level of criticism is advanced by those who have a different vision of civil rights than that of affirmative action proponents. These critics favor the advancement of those who have been disadvantaged, but they oppose taking race, and to a lesser extent gender, into account at all. Although such critics will tolerate, and may even favor, some outreach, they insist that hiring and advancement decisions in industry, education and government should be entirely color-blind. "It is antithetical to the American Dream to measure people by the genetic pattern of their great-grandmothers," said Speaker of the House Newt Gingrich, expressing this view.

Still another level of criticism is rooted in economic ideology. Upholding the principles of Social Darwinism, some critics argue that it is up to individuals to compete with each other for economic advantage, and that society ultimately benefits from this struggle. For this reason, neither the government nor private industry should ever give deliberate advantage to any individual or racial, ethnic or gender group. Positions should be awarded solely on the basis of individual qualifications and ability to do a particular job. Although the less competent individuals may suffer, they say, in the long run this will work out best for everyone.

The Courts

In 1971, the U.S. Supreme Court ordered the Duke Power Company to change the educational criteria (among other criteria) it used to hire new employees, on the grounds that they had a "disparate racial impact." That is, they tended to exclude African-Americans, who, as a group were unlikely to meet them, from consideration. The important thing about the *Griggs* v. *Duke Power Company* decision was the fact that the Court did not find that the company was deliberately using the criteria to discriminate. The key was not the discriminatory *intention* of the company, but the discriminatory *effect* of its practices.

"Disparate impact" became the keystone of enforcement of the 1964 Civil Rights Act. Using it as a yardstick, the courts pressured companies and schools to change their policies in ways that would result in more opportunities for African-Americans and, eventually, for other minorities and women as well. Among other things, this meant that institutions had to be allowed to take race into account when admitting, hiring, or promoting.

Opponents of affirmative action challenged race-based affirmative action in the courts, most notably in the famous Bakke case in 1978. Meanwhile, affirmative action was becoming a hot political issue. Republicans, in particular, tended to be in the forefront of the attacks on affirmative action. The Republican presidential administrations of the 1980s attempted to reduce, if not eliminate, government-sponsored affirmative action programs. They argued that it was wrong to make up for past unfairness against African-Americans by being unfair to white Americans in the present. The U.S. Supreme Court, however, continued to uphold the importance of disparate impact and to support affirmative action in principle.

Court support for specific affirmative action programs has been far from consistent, however. The Court has overturned at least two affirmative action programs that attempted to give preference to minority jobholders over white jobholders with more seniority when it came to laying off workers. And, by 1989, the U.S. Supreme Court seemed to be shifting an ever greater burden onto the supporters of affirmative action programs to show that they were needed.

In 1996, California voters passed Proposition 209, calling for an end to all affirmative action programs in the state. Within weeks, supporters of affirmative action had won an injunction temporarily forbidding the state to give effect to the sweeping proposition. It was widely expected that the court decision would be appealed, and that the constitutionality of the proposition eventually would have to be decided by the U.S. Supreme Court.

Public Attitudes

Most Americans agree with the supporters of affirmative action that past injustices should be corrected, where that can be done fairly. Many, however, believe that affirmative action, as it has been practiced by the federal government, either has been misdirected or has gone too far.

When polled, relatively few Americans object to outreach programs, which attempt to encourage women and minorities to enter fields or institutions previously closed to them. Many would even accept some preference being given to women or minority candidates over equally qualified white males. In most circumstances, however, the great majority generally oppose favoring less qualified candidates over those who are demonstrably better trained, able, or experienced. In most circumstances, they also balk at quotas, which reserve a specific number of positions for members of specific gender or ethnic groups.

By the mid-1990s, the political tide had turned strongly against affirmative action. The Republicans, who won control of both Houses of Congress in the elections of 1994, vowed to change or eliminate federal government policies giving preference to groups based on gender or skin color.

The general public remained divided on the issue, as it always had been. The overwhelming majority of Americans continued to favor the goals of affirmative action, and a significant majority felt that affirmative action programs had helped to open up opportunities for those who had been disadvantaged. Less than half, however, felt that there was any more need for such programs.

Although most people also continued to oppose quotas based on color or gender, the majority surveyed in a 1995 Gallup/*USA Today* poll did favor aggressive affirmative action programs, even those including quotas, which were designed to help poor Americans, regardless of sex or color.

See also American Dream; Social Darwinism.
For further reading Blackstone, William T., and Robert Heslep, editors. *Social Justice and Preferential Treatment*. Athens: University of Georgia Press, 1976.
Rosenfeld, Michael. *Affirmative Action and Justice: A Philosophical and Constitutional Inquiry*. New Haven, CT: Yale University Press, 1990.

African-American/Jewish Relations

See Jewish/African-American Relations.

African-Americans in U.S. Society

According to the U.S. Census Bureau, African-Americans make up 12.5 percent of the American population. More than 130 years after slavery was abolished—and despite a national commitment to the ideals of integration and civil rights—African-Americans still are not fully integrated into American society. In many respects, they remain distinct and separate, set apart not only by color but by key economic and social factors. In most cases, these latter distinctions reflect the continuing disadvantage of African-Americans, as a group, compared to Americans as a whole.

Families

The breakdown of the traditional nuclear family, consisting of two parents and children living together in the same home, first became apparent as a major social problem in the black community. Although the rate of single-parent families compared to traditional two-parent families is now rising in most, if not all, sectors of American society, it still is most acute among African-Americans.

Almost two out of every three black families are headed by a single parent, compared with about one in four white families, and approximately three out of ten American families in general. In 1970, when the current generation of young parents was being raised, the comparable figures were about four out of ten black families and one out of ten white families.

Income and Employment

Several of the most significant differences between black and white Americans are economic. African-American incomes are still far below those of their white fellow citizens. The median family income for African-American families in 1991 was $21,548, compared with $37,783 for white families.

Almost exactly one-third of African-Americans were below the poverty line in 1992, compared with only 11.6 percent of white Americans. That was a rise of more than 10 percent in the poverty rate from 1976, when 30.6 percent of African-Americans were poor.

Black poverty is greatest among families headed by women, with no male spouse. In 1993, such families, which contain 54 percent of all African-American children, had an average family income of $11,905. This was an actual drop of $1,500 from the average in 1979. The numbers of African-Americans with above average incomes is also rising, however. In 1990, 14.5 percent of all African-American families had incomes of more than $50,000, compared with only 9.9 percent with equivalent incomes in 1970.

About one in every nine African-American men were unemployed in the fall of 1995. Among those who do work, a higher proportion work in low-paying jobs than do their white counterparts.

Almost 35 percent of black men have an income of less than $10,000 a year, compared with fewer than 20 percent of white men. On the other end of the economic scale, only about 2 percent of black men have incomes of more than $75,000 a year, compared with approximately 7 percent of white men.

African-Americans are heavily underrepresented in most prestigious jobs and professions. Only 14.7 percent of black men have professional specialties, or hold managerial jobs, compared with 27.5 percent of white men. For example, a mere 1.4 percent of practicing American lawyers are black, and only 2.4 percent of the practicing doctors.

Although black women are somewhat better represented at the professional and executive levels, their numbers, too, still lag behind their white counterparts, 20.1 percent to 29.9%. Black women executives, however, are actually better paid, with an average income of $40,494, compared with an average of $36,719 for white females.

With that exception, the disparity of blacks to whites includes not only most relatively high-paying, high-status positions—from surgeons to top executives in large corporations—but other important jobs which serve as role models to young people planning their own futures. Only about 8 percent of elementary school teachers are black, for example.

Education

African-Americans still lag behind white Americans in most educational statistics. Although their position has been improving over time, the advance has been slow. The percentage of African-Americans graduating from high school, for example, rose from 67 percent to 75 percent in the two decades from 1973 to 1993. This climb was accomplished while white graduation rates held steady at around 83 percent.

The percentage of African-American high school graduates entering college is also climbing. Although the approximately 31 percent of black male graduates who went on to college in 1993 was a rise of only 3.5 percent, the percentage of female college entrants soared by 13.33 percent, to almost equal males at 34 percent. Overall, according to the U.S. Department of Commerce, just over 10 percent of the students enrolled in U.S. colleges for the 1992-1993 school year were black. At the graduate level, the percentages are somewhat lower. African-Americans make up some 7 percent of law school students, for example.

Crime

Underrepresented in well-paying jobs and institutions of higher learning, African-Americans are overrepresented as both victims and as perpetrators of crime. According to the FBI, they make up 47 percent of all murder victims.

Murder, in fact, is the most common cause of death of black males in their late teens and early twenties. It has been estimated by doctors in central Harlem that the life expectancy of black males in that heavily black inner-city neighborhood is less than that of black men in the famine-wracked land of Bangladesh.

One out of every four African-American males between the ages of 17 and 35 is either in prison, on probation, or on parole. In 1992, 583,000 black males were in prison, approximately 46,000 more than were enrolled in college. To some extent, this is accounted for by the high percentage of young African-Americans from poor neighborhoods who turn to drugs and street crimes. But it is also true that black criminals tend to receive harsher, and longer, jail sentences than white criminals convicted for similar crimes.

Attitudes

Not surprisingly, considering their position in the American social structure, polls show that African-Americans tend to have very different attitudes toward U.S. society, and their place in it, than other Americans, particularly white Americans.

According to a 1994 survey conducted by the National Conference of Christians and Jews, over three-quarters of all African-Americans believe that white people control the power and wealth of the country and are unwilling to share it with African-Americans and other minorities. Eight out of 10 African-Americans believe that they have fewer opportunities than other Americans, and that they are discriminated against by employers, banks, and other grantors of credit, as well as by the police and the courts. The percentage of middle-class African-Americans who believe this (86 percent) is even higher than the percentage of working-class African-Americans who do (77%). The majority of white Americans, on the other hand, are convinced that their black neighbors have opportunities equal to their own.

Causes of Disparities

Many reasons have been suggested for the disparities between African-Americans and their fellow citizens. The most far-reaching explanation, and the one most often offered by mainstream black leaders, is racism and the long history of economic and educational deprivation that has resulted from it.

The Civil War may have ended slavery, but it clearly failed to provide an equal opportunity for the freed slaves and their descendants. The masses of black people were still kept separate from white society by various forms of segregation, enforced by a combination of terrorism and law in the South, and primarily by common practice in the North.

For a century, African-Americans were ghettoized in poor neighborhoods, with poor schools, and relatively few employment and business opportunities. Even those African-Americans who managed to find jobs in industries controlled by whites were usually the last to be hired in good times and the first to be fired in bad.

The civil rights movement's success in breaking down the legal barriers of segregation in the 1950s and 1960s gave African-Americans a greater chance to escape their economic bounds. Many have succeeded in doing so, but a significant proportion remain severely limited by lack of education and job training, by the prejudice and discrimination that still exists against them in much of white society, and by the resulting despair.

See also Affirmative Action; Afrocentric Education; Black Colleges and Universities; Civil Rights Movement; Crack Cocaine in the Black Community (Alleged CIA Involvement); Ebonics; Jewish/African-American Relations; Kerner Commission Report; King Case; Nation of Islam; Police Corruption; Simpson Case.

For further reading Gwaltney, John Langston, editor. *Drylongso: A Self-Portrait of Black America*. New York: Random House, 1980.
Low, W. Augustus, and Virgil A. Clift. *Encyclopedia of Black America*. New York: McGraw-Hill, 1981.

Afrocentric Education

Afrocentrism is a world view rooted in a belief in the overwhelming importance of African-based culture. In American education, the term is used to describe courses of study which focus primarily on African and/or African-American history and culture and on issues of special importance to African-Americans.

Many of today's university black studies departments, which exist to explore African history, arts and literature, and their influence on American and world culture, date back to the 1960s. They owed their initial existence to the efforts of black students and faculty members, who were inspired by the civil rights movement and campus turmoil over Vietnam to demand that their culture be taken seriously by the American academy.

These students and faculty members complained that traditional American education had ignored African history and culture in favor of the Greek-based culture which had taken hold in Europe and then been transported to the New World. They insisted that a new emphasis on African culture, and African-based culture in the United States and elsewhere, was needed to counteract the overwhelmingly Eurocentric views that always had pervaded American education up to that point.

Afrocentrism in Primary and Secondary Schools

In recent years, Afrocentrism has been making headway in elementary and secondary schools in heavily African-American urban school districts across the country. Educators in these schools believe that Afrocentric education is vital to the empowerment of young African-Americans. In the past, these educators say, African-American children have been taught primarily about the history and accomplishments of white people. This has sent a message to them, however indirectly, that only white people do things worth learning about. Another complaint

is that African-American students traditionally have been taught from educational materials prepared primarily for middle-class white students. Everything, from the language in which they were written to the context of examples and analogies, has been out of context for African-American students, and often irrelevant to their lives. In the opinion of many black educators, it is as if white American students had been taught exclusively using materials designed for black students in Nigeria. According to the educators, young black students learn better from teaching materials which relate to them as African-Americans. Just as importantly, Afrocentric education serves to enrich the students' self-esteem by informing them about the achievements of people of their own skin color and affirming the significance of their culture.

Opposition to Afrocentrism

Some educators, both white and black, are troubled by Afrocentrism, and particularly by the more radical forms of Afrocentrism being taught in some urban schools today. The critics charge that it is not only academically suspect, but gives young African-Americans a distorted view of the world in general, and of modern American society in particular. Radical Afrocentrists are so eager to find examples of black achievement that they frequently overstate, or even invent, such examples. For instance, say the critics, there is no academic basis for the claims made to black students in some schools that Egyptians traveled in gliders 4,000 years ago, or that some ancient Africans may have understood quantum physics. When it comes to cultural affairs, African literature, jazz, and rap are overemphasized; other, arguably more significant, artistic achievements from Shakespeare to

Beethoven are ignored because they are considered "white."

Another objection raised by opponents of Afrocentrism is that it is divisive and often tainted with blatantly antiwhite propaganda. They allege that Afrocentric social studies courses overemphasize the evils of colonialism, slavery, discrimination, and other white deprivations against black people. Some radical Afrocentrists, they say, rival the bigotry of white supremacists with claims that dark skin is directly associated with superior intelligence and physical coordination. Some educators, both white and black, fear that Afrocentric education is a step in the direction of black separatism.

Even most critics of Afrocentric education will acknowledge that the American education system has been extremely Eurocentric. They argue, however, that Afrocentrism is not an appropriate remedy. Instead, they say, American educators should strive to present a balanced and accurate view of world history and culture. Both black and white students need to be made familiar with the wide range of influences—European, African, Asian, Native American, and others—that have helped to shape America and its culture.

In the long run, say the critics, Afrocentric education does a serious disservice to the African-American students it sets out to help. Although it is important for such students to learn about black history and African-based culture, they argue that this should not be accomplished at the expense of learning about the broader history of their own country and its culture. For better or worse, African-American students *are* Americans and will ultimately have to make their way within an American society which is predominantly white and Euro-based. Preparing them to do so is an im-portant part of the duty of those who educate them.

See also Civil Rights Movement.

Aggravating and Mitigating Circumstances

Not everyone convicted of a capital crime (that is, a crime liable to capital punishment) is actually sentenced to death. Under current law, anyone convicted in a capital trial must be given a second trial to determine whether or not they should be put to death. In this second, sentencing phase, the jurors are asked to weigh all the relevant aggravating and mitigating circumstances before making their determination. These circumstances do not apply to the convicted person's guilt or innocence; that has already been decided. Rather, they apply to the nature of the crime and to the criminal's worthiness for the ultimate penalty the state can impose.

An aggravating circumstance is anything that would make the crime, or the criminal, more heinous. A mitigating circumstance is anything that might tend to lessen the heinousness of the crime or to diminish the criminal's responsibility.

In the early 1960s, the American Law Institute proposed a "model penal code" in which it set out a list of potential aggravating and mitigating circumstances for juries to take into account when deciding whether to impose the death penalty on someone found guilty of murder. These are reprinted below. Not all will apply to all cases, nor are they the only factors that might be weighed in a particular case. They do, however, serve as examples of the kinds of circumstances that make the difference between life and death in American courts.

Aggravating Circumstances

(a) The murder was committed by a convict under sentence of imprisonment.

(b) The defendant was previously convicted of another murder or of a felony involving the use or threat of violence to the person.

(c) At the time the murder was committed, the defendant also committed another murder.

(d) The defendant knowingly created a great risk of death to many persons.

(e) The murder was committed while the defendant was engaged or was an accomplice in the commission of, or an attempt to commit, or flight after committing or attempting to commit, robbery, rape, or deviate sexual intercourse by force or threat of force, arson, burglary, or kidnapping.

(f) The murder was committed for the purpose of avoiding or preventing a lawful arrest or effecting an escape from lawful custody.

(g) The murder was committed for pecuniary gain.

(h) The murder was especially heinous, atrocious, or cruel, manifesting exceptional depravity.

Mitigating Circumstances

(a) The defendant has no significant history of prior criminal activity.

(b) The murder was committed while the defendant was under the influence of extreme mental or emotional disturbance.

(c) The victim was a participant in the defendant's homicidal conduct or consented to the homicidal act.

(d) The murder was committed under circumstances which the defendant believed to provide a moral justification or extenuation for his conduct.

(e) The defendant was an accomplice in a murder committed by another person and his participation in the homicidal act was relatively minor.

(f) The defendant acted under duress or under the domination of another person.

(g) At the time of the murder, the capacity of the defendant to appreciate the criminality [wrongfulness] of his conduct or to conform his conduct to the requirements of law was impaired as a result of a mental disease or defect or intoxication.

(h) The youth of the defendant at the time of the crime.

In the 1976 case of *Woodson* v. *North Carolina*, the U.S. Supreme Court ruled that jurors in the sentencing phase must weigh whatever aggravating and mitigating circumstances may exist in that particular case. Generally speaking, it is not enough for the jury merely to find that some aggravating circumstance or circumstances exist in order to sentence a defendant to death. They must also find that those aggravating circumstances outweigh whatever mitigating circumstances may exist.

See also Cruel and Unusual Punishment; Death Penalty; Death Penalty (Major Supreme Court Decisions).

Agribusiness

Farming in the United States is no longer the small family business it once was. Changes in farm economics have squeezed many small farmers out of business, and these changes have resulted in small farms being swallowed by ever bigger agricultural operations.

Together with enormous advances in cultivation and animal husbandry technologies, weather forecasting, and the introduction of computers, the melding of thousands of small farms into larger and better capitalized operations have produced efficiencies and economies of scale heretofore unheard of in American agriculture.

For many years now, the American farm, whether small or large, has been only the foundation, and not the whole, of an industry known as agribusiness. Agribusiness is a vast enterprise that consists not only of farming, but of the whole net of businesses associated with it, including the manufacturers and retailers of farm machines and implements, chemical fertilizers, and pesticides, as well as the manufacturers who transform farm products into the processed foods most consumers rely on today.

Pollution

Much of the great growth in the productivity of the modern farm has been due to the increased use of chemical fertilizers and pesticides, some 150 of which have been classified by the U.S. Environmental Protection Agency as acutely hazardous.

Used carelessly, or without sufficient concern for the protection of people, livestock, and the environment, these toxic chemicals can contaminate produce and meat products alike. In addition, they can permeate the soil and seep down into the ground water, poisoning the rural water supply. They can also be washed from the surface of the land and into streams and rivers by rains, or blown through the air by winds, thereby spreading contamination far beyond the boundaries of the farm on which they were used.

Although agricultural pollution of the ground and of the water supply remains a serious problem in the United States, the amount of active chemical ingredients used to grow major crops in the United States actually declined approximately 20 percent from 1982 to 1993.

Moved by the desire to cut costs, and by concern about the health effects of the heavy use of chemicals on themselves and on the environment, farmers have found ever more efficient ways of applying chemicals to their crops. As a result, pesticide use has grown little, if at all, in recent years, and the use of chemical fertilizers has actually declined. This is welcome news to environmentalists.

For further reading Johnson, Andrew. *Factory Farming*. Williston, VT: Blackwell, 1991.

Agricultural Pollution
See Agribusiness.

Aid to Families with Dependent Children (AFDC)

Aid to Families with Dependent Children (AFDC) is a combined federal and state program that provides cash payments and other benefits to families with children whose parent, or parents, cannot financially support the family themselves. Although AFDC was eliminated as an entitlement in 1996, it continues in effect, although the amount of time a family remains eligible to receive benefits is limited.

About half the money paid in benefits comes from each of the two levels of government. In 1993, AFDC assistance was provided to an average of nearly 5 million families a month, which included nearly 10 million children.

Historically, AFDC is a direct descendant of some of the earliest of all charitable instincts: the desire to provide for widows and orphans. It was initially designed primarily to allow poor mothers the chance to stay home and raise their children, rather than have to abandon them in order to work. It was believed that having a parent home with young children was a benefit not only to the child and the family, but to society as a whole. Over the years, however, that goal lost public favor, and the program was eliminated as an entitlement in the welfare reforms of 1996.

Benefits

The amount of money and other benefits individual AFDC families receive varies widely, depending first on the state in which they live, and then on the number of family members. In Mississippi, which has the stingiest of all the state programs, the average family gets only about $120 a month. Alaska, with a very high cost of living, is the most generous; a typical family gets $760. Nationwide, the average is about $377 a month. Most AFDC recipients also are entitled to benefits from other programs, including food stamps and Medicaid, which provides health care to the eligible poor. Although government expenditures on welfare programs have been rising, the real value of the benefits received by a typical family has actually been dropping. The amount of AFDC-payments-plus-food-stamps received by a typical family, consisting of a single mother and three children, fell by more than 20 percent between 1970 and 1990.

Who Receives AFDC?

The overwhelming majority of AFDC families have been broken apart by divorce, desertion, or the imprisonment of a parent. Although approximately 98 percent of all children receiving AFDC in the mid-1990s had two living parents, nearly nine out of ten of them lived with only one, usually the mother.

Although most of the mothers receiving AFDC in 1994 were teenagers when their first child was born, only about 16 percent of them were still under 20 years old. Just over half were in their twenties, and 32 percent were in their thirties. Approximately half were married.

For years, regulations in many states required that families receiving AFDC have only one parent living in the home. This requirement, based on the notion that at least one parent in a two-parent family ought to work, had an undesired side effect. It encouraged fathers who could not find work to desert their wives and children, knowing that they would be better provided for when they were gone. This situation was improved somewhat with the Family Support Act, requiring states to offer AFDC-UP (unemployed parents) to intact families in which neither of the parents can find a full-time job. In addition, states were required to set up a Job Opportunities and Basic Skills (JOBS) program, to offer unemployed beneficiaries training on how to get and hold a job. By 1995, each state was required to have some 20 percent of its employable AFDC recipients in the JOBS program, while nearly 20 percent of AFDC families already had at least one parent employed either full- or part-time.

Although African-Americans make up a higher percentage of AFDC recipients than of the general population, as with other welfare programs the great majority of AFDC recipients are white.

The Controversy over AFDC

Total AFDC payments were approximately $22.5 billion in 1993. As much as this was, however, the program consumed only about 1 percent of the massive federal budget. Despite its relatively small impact on government expenditures—much less, for example, than the more than $160 billion costs of Medicare—AFDC is at the storm center of the social and political debate over welfare.

No one, it seems, is happy with AFDC and the job it has done providing help for poor families with children. Those on the political left of the debate complain that it is a mean and niggardly program that demeans the people who receive it. Those on the political right complain that AFDC rewards immorality and laziness. Recipients complain that they are made to fill out endless forms at welfare offices, where they are often treated with suspicion and even distaste by government bureaucrats. There is also a social stigma to "being on welfare," and many recipients are abused by people who accuse them of being freeloaders and bums. Virtually everyone insists that it does not do nearly enough to empower poor families—and particularly young single mothers—to pull themselves out of poverty.

At the core of this debate is a reversal in the American public's attitude toward motherhood. In the past, most Americans assumed that a mother's first responsibility was to raise her child. Work outside the home was considered primarily the responsibility of the husband and father. Many of the earliest charities were designed to help widows and orphans.

AFDC was born of this same desire to provide for women and children whose men had died or deserted them. Recipients were not only allowed, but in a sense expected, to stay at home and raise their children. The program initially was intended, in fact, to make it possible for mothers to stay at home and raise their children. But recent social and economic developments have undermined that view of the mother's role in the family.

Socially, the feminist movement has challenged the traditional wife-and-mother role of women as a restrictive stereotype. Economically, even many once securely middle-class families now find it necessary for both spouses to work to maintain their previous standard of living. With feminists fighting for their right to work, and even relatively prosperous women feeling forced to get jobs, there is less sympathy for the idea that poor women should be allowed to stay at home to care for their children.

On the one hand, single motherhood is much more common and socially acceptable than it used to be, and even the deliberate decision to have a baby out of wedlock no longer carries the stigma that it once did. But at the same time, there is an increasing feeling that anyone who has a child ought to be willing to work to support it. Americans have come to believe that able-bodied mothers should not be supported by society, but should be required to work.

The changing attitude toward the role of women in the society is not the only reason for the widespread disenchantment with AFDC, however. Because a high percentage of the mothers who are helped by AFDC have never been married, many people feel that it rewards what they consider the immorality of unmarried sexual activity. Furthermore, much of the public believes, whether rightly or wrongly, that AFDC is abused widely by physically able single parents who would rather receive AFDC benefits than work. Some critics even believe that a large number of single women deliberately add children to their families in order to increase their AFDC payment. In 1994, however, a panel of 76 experts on poverty declared that, although the availability of AFDC may play some role in the rising numbers of illegitimate births, it is not the decisive factor some critics of the program contend. For one thing, the experts point out, the incidence of illegitimacy has been rising despite the drop in the real value of AFDC payments; for another, the increase in payments families receive for new children in most states is less than the actual costs of supporting another child.

Another cause for the hostility toward AFDC, and one shared by many AFDC recipients themselves, arises from the impression that the program is a dead end. Instead of serving as a temporary shelter for parents in financial trouble, AFDC catches the families in a "welfare trap." In order to continue to receive payments, the parents must have little or no outside income. This actually discourages them from trying to get jobs, because when the value of health care for their children and other benefits are figured in, the jobs most recipients could find would bring them even less than the relatively small amounts they are getting on AFDC.

Once trapped in the program, the critics say, many families never escape. Seeing no practical alternative, they remain on AFDC for generation after generation. Children who were raised on welfare drop out of school in their teens to have children of their own, relying on AFDC to support them as parents, just as it supported them as children.

Statistics, however, do not bear this out. According to the U.S. Department of Health and Human Services, only 15 percent of AFDC families receiving AFDC in 1993 had been on the program for more than five years, and less than 7 percent had been on for more than ten. This means that the great majority—78.2 percent—had been receiving AFDC for less than five years. On the other hand, a substantial number of families who manage to get off AFDC do find themselves back on the program for another temporary period at some time in the future.

Demands for Elimination or Reform

Criticism of AFDC decreased public support for the program, leading to stronger and stronger demands for reform on both the state and federal levels. States led the way in the reform effort with programs designed either to help or to force families out of the welfare trap. Wisconsin, for example, initiated Learnfare, requiring the children of AFDC families to attend school regularly as a condition of the family continuing to receive benefits. The same state experimented with a program denying additional benefits to parents who continued to have children while receiving AFDC. New Jersey denied benefits for new children altogether, except for needed medical care. Ohio launched Project Learn, providing an extra payment to a teenage mother who continues in school, or reduces her payment if she does not. Although many of these programs aroused great interest, there was little evidence that such programs helped families get off welfare in a productive way. Instead, states reduced the welfare rolls primarily by changing the requirements in order to remove families.

Conservative Republicans had long called for drastic welfare reform. In the 1990s, they were joined by Democrats, led by President Bill Clinton, who had campaigned in 1992 on a promise to "end welfare as we know it." As president, Clinton signed a major welfare reform bill shortly before the election of 1996. If it did not entirely end welfare as it had been known before, the bill, as written by the Republican-controlled Congress, did change the system seriously. Among its major provisions, it created more stringent requirements to qualify for aid; it required recipients to work; and, in most circumstances, it set a five-year lifetime limit on the time during which a person would be eligible for certain programs. Clinton's signing of the bill upset many of his supporters, who considered it far too draconian.

Many critics still insisted that reform should go much further. Liberals complained that, although the new measures required recipients to go to work, they failed to provide jobs for them, or even to demand that jobs provided by the private sector would pay a living wage. Conservatives hope to go further to "restigmatize" illegitimacy, making it both financially impractical and socially unacceptable for unwed women to have babies. Many people, including the social critic Charles Murray, have called for programs that would make it easier for financially well-off parents to adopt poor children as well as other ways of providing for poor children without also providing for their parents.

AFDC was eliminated as an entitlement in 1996, abandoning the principle that women should be allowed to stay home with young children whatever their incomes. Supporters of the 1996 reforms argued that they would discourage such women from having children they could not support. AFDC itself continued in effect, although the amount of time a family remained eligible to receive benefits was limited.

See also Food Stamps; Single-Parent Families; Unmarried Mothers; Welfare Magnet; Welfare Reform (1996); Welfare State; Welfare System; Welfare Trap.

Altamont

Coming four months after Woodstock, the disastrous 1969 rock concert at Altamont, California, is often seen in dark contrast to that larger and happier event. Whereas Woodstock is regarded as symbol of all that was best in the youth culture of the 1960s, Altamont is seen as a reflection of all that was sinister in it.

Altamont was a free concert performed by the British rock group The Rolling Stones. Unlike many of the performers at Woodstock, who allied themselves with the peace-and-love themes of the era, the Stones gloried in a reputation as the unrepentant "bad boys" of rock music. Such Stones songs as "Sympathy for the Devil" and "Under My Thumb" churned with aggressiveness and a kind of high-spirited hostility.

In keeping with their on-the-edge reputation, the Stones employed members of the notorious motorcycle gang the Hell's Angels to provide security for the concert, perhaps in an attempt to placate the bikers and prevent them from causing trouble themselves. In any event, a scuffle broke out between members of the gang and an apparently berserk member of the audience, in which the audience member was stabbed to death. Three other people are said to have died at Altamont as well, from other causes.

The contrast with Woodstock was inescapable. Coming near the end of what most people thought of as the last year of the 1960s, the violent death at Altamont seemed to mark a symbolic end to the counterculture experiments of that tumultuous decade. For those who were most sympathetic to those experiments, Altamont represented a sad perversion of the ideals that inspired so many young people in those years. For others, it seemed to expose an underlying sickness they suspected had been there all along.

The event was chronicled in a documentary movie entitled *Gimme Shelter* after one of the Stones' big hits.

See also Counterculture; Woodstock.

American Dream

"The American Dream" is a familiar phrase in the American vocabulary. Immigrants are said to come to the United States seeking it. Politicians present legislation they say will provide it to more citizens. And speakers at awards banquets praise the honorees for being outstanding examples of it.

Such usage touches real chords of responsiveness in those who hear them, but the exact meaning of the phrase is unclear. Or, perhaps more accurately, it seems to vary from speaker to speaker.

In one sense of the phrase, the American Dream is seen primarily in economic terms. At its most basic, it implies financial success, at whatever level. For some people, then, this version of the dream implies a steady, if modest, income: enough to provide for a comfortable home, food and clothing for a family, and the education of the children. For others, it requires something more ambitious than simple security: They see the American Dream as real prosperity—a big house in a good neighborhood, for instance, along with a vacation home in another climate and the ability to retire in some luxury.

On another level, the American Dream includes the notion of capitalistic accomplishment. It is embodied in the vision of a person (usually presumed to be a man) from a poor or immigrant background, who works or gambles wisely enough to amass sufficient capital to buy or start a small business. This he builds into a bigger business, until he accumulates great wealth. This version of the American Dream apparently dates from the nineteenth century and is personified by people such as John D. Rockefeller, Andrew Carnegie, and Henry Ford.

Not everyone sees the American Dream in economic terms. For some, the dream implies political as well as economic freedom. Immigrants fleeing political oppression, for example, see the American Dream as the ability to live their lives without the fear that the government will persecute or imprison them for their beliefs or political activities. This vision of the American Dream is perhaps best summed up in the Declaration of Independence, which promises Americans the right "to life, liberty, and the pursuit of happiness."

How one interprets the American Dream, and how close it seems to reality, is heavily influenced by one's ethnic heritage and current position in society. People of color tend to view it in terms of integration and equal opportunity. With this in mind, a 1994 National Conference of Christians and Jews report, *Taking America's Pulse*, concluded that "whites and people of color are poles apart on the American Dream." The majority of people of color, says the report, feel discriminated against and held back by a society dominated by whites. Most whites, on the other hand, feel that minorities already have something close to equal opportunity in most respects.

However it is interpreted, one version or another of the American Dream serves as an inspiration to many Americans of all backgrounds, who see themselves as striving to achieve it.

Anti-Semitism

On its most personal level, anti-Semitism is the hatred, dislike, suspicion, or other form of hostility directed toward Jews. On a broader level, anti-Semitism has sometimes been incorporated in the domestic and foreign policies of nations.

Both forms of prejudice against Jews are frequently accompanied by a belief in conspiracy theories involving alleged secret organizations, or the state of Israel, or both. American anti-Semitism is an outgrowth of European anti-Semitism, which, in turn, has its roots in long-standing religious and historical controversies between Christians and Jews.

Difficulties of Definition

Anti-Semitism is different from other common prejudices, in that to be a "Jew" is a less clear distinction than to have certain skin color, or a specific national origin. "Jewishness" can be variously defined in religious, racial, and ethnic terms. None of these categorizations is entirely satisfactory in terms of identifying the victims of anti-Semitism.

Although Judaism is, of course, a religious faith, many people who are identified as Jews, both by themselves and by others, neither profess nor practice that religion. Many people of Jewish descent are atheists, or agnostics, or followers of another religion altogether, although they still consider themselves Jews in an ethnic and/or cultural sense. At the same time, there are recent converts to Judaism who have no genetic ties to previous generations of Jews at all.

Although anti-Semites tend to see "Jewishness" in racial terms, most scientists would argue that there is no such thing as a Jewish race. Over the thousands of years of Jewish history, there has been an enormous amount of intermarriage and conversion in both directions. Many of those who might be identified as Jews on the basis of ancient heritage have little to do with Jewish traditions, while many modern Jews are descended from other backgrounds. There are Jews of virtually every physical configuration and of every skin color.

It is equally problematic to define "Jewishness" in ethnic terms. Jews come from a wide variety of national and cultural backgrounds. There are Middle Eastern Jews, Eastern European Jews, American Jews, and even Ethiopian Jews, among others. They can hardly be classified as belonging to a single ethnic group, or even a clearly definable range of ethnic groups.

Anti-Semitism and Christianity

Christians have been particularly subject to the prejudice of anti-Semitism because of the religious differences between the two groups, and because of biblical history as some Christians have understood it. This is despite the fact that Christian anti-Semitism seems irrational, on several levels, considering that Christianity is admittedly based on Jewish religious traditions; that Christians and Jews share much of their Scripture in common; and that the central figure of Christianity was a professed Jew, as were his family members, as well as virtually all of his early followers.

Christian anti-Semitism has been fueled not only by ancient religious divisions but by selective interpretations of the biblical account of Christ's betrayal and death, which hold Jews responsible for his crucifixion. For this reason, it was once common for Christians to refer to Jews as "Christ-killers."

During the Middle Ages in Europe, several Christian monarchs used Jews as scapegoats for the social and economic troubles in their kingdoms. The medieval Christian church frequently encouraged anti-Semitism by participating in, or even launching, inquisitions that persecuted Jews for their religious beliefs.

Although the church provided a theological justification for such inquisitions, these persecutions were typically encouraged by monarchs eager to increase their royal treasuries. Jews who would not convert to Christianity would have their property confiscated by the crown. On some occasions, European Jews were expelled from their native countries, or even executed. The most notable expulsion of Jews from Europe occurred when Ferdinand and Isabella expelled the Jews from Spain in 1492, the same year that Columbus, sailing under the Spanish flag, landed in the New World.

Although many Christians still foster anti-Semitic feelings, and justify those feelings by an appeal to their interpretation of the Bible, several mainline Christian churches have attempted to repudiate Christianity's historic anti-Semitism in recent years. The Roman Catholic pontiff Pope John Paul II has formally absolved Jews of responsibility for the death of Jesus Christ on behalf of the Roman Catholic Church; and the Evangelical Lutheran Church in America, the nation's largest Lutheran denomination, formulated a declaration renouncing the anti-Semitic writings of the church's sixteenth-century founder, Martin Luther, in 1992. The Church-wide assembly, which called for the declaration, went on record as being opposed to "the deadly workings of anti-Semitism in church and society."

Old-World Anti-Semitism

European anti-Semitism was particularly strong in Russia and Eastern Europe during the late nineteenth and early twentieth centuries. It was in Russia that the fake document known as "The Protocols of the Elders of Zion" was first circulated. Containing what purported to be Jewish plans for undermining Christianity and taking over the world, the "Protocols" have formed the basis for anti-Semitic conspiracy theories ever since. It was also in Eastern Europe that pogroms—large-scale violent attacks on Jews—broke out late in the nineteenth century.

Anti-Semitism in Europe was refueled by the reaction to the Russian Revolution of 1917, which some frightened Europeans blamed on Jewish intellectuals. The Great Depression of the 1930s was also blamed on the Jews by people who insisted that Jewish financiers somehow controlled the economy of the world, and therefore must have deliberately brought on the economic crisis.

The recognition of the state of Israel by the United Nations in 1948 was the result of international repugnance at the paroxysm of anti-Semitism known as the Holocaust, in which German Nazis had attempted to exterminate all the Jews in Europe. Ironically, however, the birth of Israel itself fueled a new outburst of anti-Semitism, this time centered in the Middle East. Many Arabs and allied Muslims resented what they saw as the unjust confiscation of Arab lands, and the dislocation of the Palestinians who lived on them.

Anti-Semitism in the United States

Although many European refugees brought their anti-Semitism with them to the United States, anti-Jewish feeling has never been as virulent here as it sometimes has been in Europe. What's more, the hostility felt by the refugees has been greatly weakened by being filtered through generations of the American experience. Nonetheless, prejudice against Jews has been a real, and sometimes significant, force in American culture.

The resentment some Americans feel toward Jews has been at least partly a reflection of what they see as the relative economic success that Jews have achieved in America. Jewish immigrants to the United States tended to put a particularly high value on education compared to some of their counterparts in other ethnic groups. As a result, a larger proportion of second- and third-generation American Jews took advantage of the opportunities for higher education available in the New World, and entered relatively high-paying professions. The resulting success and prominence of individual Jews has tended to arouse sympathy and respect for Jews in the culture at large as well as to feed anti-Semitism in that segment of the population that is prone to it.

Jews have also been active and prominent in the high-profile fields of show business and the arts, from literature to the concert hall to Hollywood. The non-Jewish public's attention has been drawn to this by the tendency of some Jewish comedians, writers, and other artists to make aspects of their Jewish identity central to their work. This has fueled the fears of some anti-Semites that Jews conspire to influence American public opinion by taking control of the media.

In the early and mid-twentieth century, American anti-Semitism was primarily reflected in certain forms of social discrimination. Even while well-to-do Jews were accepted as participants in most areas of economic and cultural activities, they found many social doors closed to them. Such forms of discrimination seem to have been particularly notable among the more prosperous elements of society, where even the most prominent Jews were denied admission to a variety of exclusive clubs, schools, and other organizations. At all levels of American society, there was a reluctance to bless intermarriage between Jews and Christians.

Remnants of this kind of discrimination still exist in many parts of the United States. Unthinking and socially accepted anti-Semitism, however, was dealt a severe blow by the Holocaust that occurred in Europe during World War II. Information about the Nazis' nearly successful attempt to wipe out the Jews of Europe shocked many Americans into a reexamination of their own attitudes. The tragedy in Europe not only aroused compassion for the survivors, and for the victims' relatives in the United States, but shame for America's past tolerance of anti-Semitism.

Overt and virulent anti-Semitism (as opposed to residual prejudice) is relatively rare among the general U.S. population today. That which does exists is found primarily among two distinct and opposed elements of American society: white supremacists and certain elements of the black community.

See also Jewish/African-American Relations.
For further reading Belth, Nathan C. *A Promise to Keep: A Narrative of the American Encounter with Anti-Semitism*. New York: Times Books, 1979.

Bakke Case (*Regents of the University of California* v. *Bakke*)

Twice in the early 1970s, a gifted student named Alan P. Bakke applied for entrance to the Medical School at the University of California at Davis. Twice, he was turned down.

Bakke was not alone in his situation. Admission to the Davis Medical School was highly prized, and 265 applicants were turned down for every one who was accepted. But Bakke, who was white, felt that the university's admission program had unfairly discriminated against him because of his race.

In order to improve the racial and ethnic balance in the medical school, Cal-Davis had set up a two-pronged admission program two years before. Under the program, 84 of the 100 positions available were filled through the normal selection process. The other 16 were filled under a separate process for minority applicants, in which such traditional criteria as test scores and previous grades were not given as heavy a weight.

Bakke brought suit against the university. In effect, he maintained, he had been excluded from competing for the 16 positions which were being reserved for minorities, because of his race. Because he was better qualified, under most criteria, than some of those who were admitted to the 16 minority spots, he should have been admitted. That fact that he was not, he argued, was a violation of his constitutional right to equal protection under the law.

Bakke's suit turned out to be the first major test of affirmative action to reach the U.S. Supreme Court. The decision of the Court was a perfect reflection of the confusion and ambiguity Americans felt toward affirmative action programs.

The Decision

The courts in California agreed with Bakke that the University had discriminated against him. The medical school admission program, said the courts, amounted to an unconstitutional quota. Such a quota would only be acceptable to redress past discrimination on the part of the university. But no history of discrimination had been proved. Therefore, the quota was unconstitutional, and Bakke's rights had, in fact, been violated.

The University appealed to the U.S. Supreme Court. It argued that its admissions program had been established for valid important academic and social purposes. The state, and therefore the University, would derive many benefits from assuring a racially diverse student body at the medical school. The admission of more

African-Americans and other minorities would help to correct past injustices, whether those injustices had been committed by the University or not. A richer racial mix would enliven the academic atmosphere at the University and provide the state's minority young people with desirable role models. And, in the long run, producing more minority doctors would result in the provision of better medical care to the minority communities from which they came.

A sharply split Supreme Court came out with what seemed to most observers a schizophrenic ruling. On the one hand, it agreed that Bakke had, as he claimed, been unfairly discriminated against, and therefore the University was ordered to admit him to the medical school. In this respect, the decision was widely seen as a blow to affirmative action programs.

At the same time, however, the *Bakke* decision approved affirmative action in principle. Although there was no single majority opinion in the case, the separate opinions written by the Justices indicated that schools like Cal-Davis would be permitted to take race into account in their admissions policies and procedures.

The various opinions did, however, seem to set several conditions on the use of "race-conscious" criteria. First, the schools must not take race into account in such a way as to produce racial segregation, or to promote racial hatred. Second, they must not consider race on the grounds that any race is inferior to any other. Third, they must have a valid social purpose for taking race into account, such as correcting past discrimination, or promoting racial diversity in the student body. Actual quotas could only be used when there was a legally established history of past discrimination by the institution involved.

See also Quotas.

Betting
See Gambling; Gambling (Legalized); Sports Betting.

Bill of Rights
The first ten amendments to the U.S. Constitution are known collectively as the Bill of Rights. Taken together, they lay out the fundamental political and legal rights guaranteed to the people of the United States and forbid the federal government to infringe upon them. The constitutional guarantee of many, although not all, of these rights has been extended, by the "due process clause" of the Fourteenth Amendment, to include protection against violation by the states as well.

The rights enumerated in the Bill of Rights arose out of the political traditions of the mother country and the British common law. They were generally recognized and supported by the delegates to the Constitutional Convention. They were not omitted from the original Constitution because they were controversial, but because of a dispute over whether it was necessary to spell them out in that document.

Many delegates felt that it was not. The new government, they argued, would have only the powers specifically given to it by the Constitution. Since those powers would not include the authority to violate the basic rights of the people, there was no need to specifically forbid the government from doing so. Other delegates, however, feared that, unless there was a Bill of Rights to prevent it, the new government might eventually take such powers unto itself. The first argument prevailed and the Bill of Rights was not included in the Constitution as signed in 1787.

The question arose again, however, during the fight for ratification of the Constitution in the states. To win the support of those who feared the powers of the new government, the supporters of the Constitution promised to amend the document to include a Bill of Rights. That promise was kept by the Congress, which passed all ten amendments in 1791. All ten were approved by Virginia, the last state needed to ratify them, on 15 December of that year. The amendments are:

Amendment I: Congress shall make no law respecting an establishment of religion, or prohibiting the free exercise thereof; or abridging the freedom of speech or of the press; or the right of the people peaceably to assemble, and to petition the government for a redress of grievances.

Amendment II: A well regulated Militia being necessary to the security of a free State, the right of the people to keep and bear arms shall not be infringed.

Amendment III: No soldier shall, in time of peace, be quartered in any house without the consent of the owner, nor in time of war, but in a manner to be prescribed by law.

Amendment IV: The right of the people to be secure in their persons, houses, papers, and effects, against unreasonable searches and seizures, shall not be violated, and no Warrants shall issue, but upon probable cause, supported by Oath or affirmation, and particularly describing the place to be searched, and the person or things to be seized.

Amendment V: No person shall be held for a capital, or otherwise infamous crime, unless on a presentment or indictment of a Grand jury, except in cases arising in the land or naval forces, or in the Militia, when in actual service in time of War or public danger; nor shall any person be subject for the same offense to be twice put in jeopardy of life or limb, nor shall be compelled in any criminal case to be a witness against himself, nor be deprived of Life, liberty, or property, without due process of law; nor shall private property be taken for public use without just compensation.

Amendment VI: In all criminal prosecutions, the accused shall enjoy the right to a speedy and public trial, by an impartial jury of the State and district wherein the crime shall have been committed; which district shall have been previously ascertained by law, and to be informed of the nature and cause of the accusation; to be confronted with the witnesses against him; to have compulsory process for obtaining witnesses in his favor, and to have the assistance of counsel for his defence [*sic*].

Amendment VII: In suits at common law, where the value in controversy shall exceed twenty dollars, the right of trial by jury shall be preserved, and no fact tried by a jury shall be otherwise re-examined in any Court of the United States, than according to the rules of the common law.

Amendment VIII: Excessive bail shall not be required, nor excessive fines imposed, nor cruel and unusual punishments inflicted.

Amendment IX: The enumeration in the Constitution of certain rights shall not be construed to deny or disparage others retained by the people.

Amendment X: The powers not delegated to the United States by the

Constitution, nor prohibited by it to the States, are reserved to the States respectively, or to the people.

The Bill of Rights is a living document. It continues to be at the vital center of numerous social, political, and legal conflicts to this day. Many implications of the various amendments, and the rights they enumerate, are discussed in other entries.

For further reading Konvitz, Milton R., editor. *Bill of Rights Reader: Leading Constitutional Cases.* Ithaca, NY: Cornell, 1973.
Rutland, Robert Allen. *The Birth of the Bill of Rights.* Boston: Northeastern University Press, 1991.

Black Colleges and Universities

Sixty-six of the 107 predominately black colleges and universities in the United States are public institutions, which served 72 percent of the 277,261 students that attended all the black colleges combined in the 1992 school year. The other 28 percent of the students were enrolled at the 41 private institutions supported by the United Negro College Fund, which is the most successful black fund-raising organization in the country.

The five largest black institutions are Howard University, Southern University and Agricultural and Mechanical College, Hampton University, North Carolina A&T State University, and Jackson State University. These and the other black colleges and universities provide African-American students with an opportunity to obtain a college education in a more welcoming environment than they might find at a predominantly white institution. They recognize and allow for the differences in the cultural and educational background of many of their students when compared to the typical student at a mainstream school.

Some critics consider the black colleges an anachronism in today's society. For the most part, they were products of a time when most institutions of higher education were reluctant to accept African-American students. In today's society, the critics point out, many "white" colleges are actively recruiting minority students.

The complaints of some critics go deeper than a feeling that the need for the black colleges seems to have passed. For them, these schools are symptoms of voluntary return to segregation, if not a move toward black separatism. They fear that the schools encourage young African-Americans to reject mainstream American society, and to feel rejected by it. What's more, say the critics, by deliberately fostering a predominantly black student body, they open themselves up to charges of discrimination.

It is hard for many whites to understand why some publicly supported institutions should be able to label and promote themselves as "black," when similar "white" colleges would not be tolerated.

The supporters of the black colleges reject these criticisms. Their institutions are far from exclusively black, they point out; and a predominantly black school is no more separatist than a predominantly white one. In fact, the black colleges are at least as integrated as other institutions of higher education, if not more so. In fact, as of 1993, approximately 13 percent of the students at these historically black institutions were white, and another 6 percent belonged to some other racial or ethnic minority. That is almost twice the percentage of African-Americans attending predominantly white colleges and universities.

Although the overwhelming majority of the students are African-Americans, defenders of the black colleges insist that they are not deliberately segregated. These schools are predominantly black only because relatively few white students have chosen to enroll, not because they have been excluded. For this reason, they often refer to themselves as the "*historically* black colleges and universities."

So far, U.S. courts have agreed with the black colleges' contention and have not found them to violate the constitutional ban on segregation. Nonetheless, supporters of the black colleges are concerned that, in states like Mississippi and Maryland, efforts to desegregate the state's predominantly white colleges and universities sometimes involve deemphasizing historically black colleges and encouraging more African-American students to attend historically white institutions instead.

The black colleges pride themselves on the role of their scholars in the history of black people in America, and in preserving and promoting African-American culture. Furthermore, they argue that they are valuable, not just to African-Americans, but to all of American society. As a longtime United Negro College Fund slogan put it, "A mind is a terrible thing to waste."

These schools are especially designed to save and develop the minds most likely to be wasted: those of hundreds of thousands of bright young African-Americans who come from the economic underclass. Many of them who choose to attend the historically black colleges and universities might not survive in the predominantly white culture of a mainstream campus.

See also African-Americans in U.S. Society; Afrocentric Education.

Black English
See Ebonics.

Black/Jewish Relations
See Jewish/African-American Relations.

Blacks in American Society
See African-Americans in U.S. Society; Affirmative Action; Afrocentric Education; Black Colleges and Universities; Civil Rights Movement; Crack Cocaine in the Black Community (Alleged CIA Involvement); Ebonics; Jewish/African-American Relations; Kerner Commission Report; King Case; Nation of Islam; Police Brutality; Simpson Case.

Black Power
See Civil Rights Movement.

Black Studies
See Afrocentric Education.

Boxing (Professional)
Professional boxing, or prizefighting, has long had a symbolic as well as athletic significance for Americans. Although boxing is an international sport, it is probably true that Americans identify with the sport, and with the athletes who participate in it, to a greater extent than most other peoples. The spectacle of two men battling each other with their fists fits in especially well with the American mythology of self-reliance and rugged individualism.

Some people look to boxing at its best as a celebration of those values—as well as of the more fundamental values of athletic skill and physical prowess. Others, though, see the sport as a reflection of much that is bad and divisive in American society.

Prizefighting has been associated, both in reality and in the public mind, with corruption. Many, if not most, fighters come from economically deprived backgrounds and have little or no education beyond high school. They are easily exploited by unscrupulous managers and promoters, and there have been several famous examples of fighters who have earned huge fortunes in the ring, and yet have found themselves virtually penniless a few years after their careers have ended. Many boxers—including such prominent examples as the ex-heavyweight champion Mike Tyson—have been convicted of crimes or have highly publicized associations with convicted criminals.

As much or more than any other sport, boxing has been associated with gambling and with dishonesty related to gambling. Scandals, and suspicions of fighters throwing fights or taking dives, have plagued the so-called fight game.

Ethnic and Racial Identification
For all that prizefighting has been associated with criminality, corruption, and exploitation, there is another side to the sport as well. Boxing in America has always been associated with ethnic and racial pride, and with the aspirations of poor young men.

Boxing has a particular importance for those minorities who, at certain stages in their own histories and that of the sport, have identified with prominent boxers of their own ethnic group, whether those fighters were Americans, or came (as the minorities and their ancestors did) from the old country. In the 1930s, for example, German-Americans identified with the prowess of Max Schmelling, the German fighter who would eventually die as a combatant on the German side in World War II. In the 1950s, Italian-Americans identified in a similar way with the achievements of the American heavyweight champion Rocky Marciano, who never was defeated in his long professional career. Swedish-Americans and others of Scandinavian descent took special pride in 1960, when

Ingmar Johannson, a Swede, became the first non-American ever to be named the S. Rae Hickok Pro Athlete of the Year.

Young men of particular immigrant or ethnic groups have traditionally seen the sport as one of the few ways for them to achieve fame and fortune. In this way, boxing is similar to such other sports as basketball, football, and baseball. More than any of these other sports, however, boxing has been specifically associated with racial aspirations and divisions.

No ethnic group has identified with their fighters so strongly, and for so long a time, as African-Americans. Boxing was the first professional sport in which individual black Americans were able to assert athletic superiority over whites. The early world champions in the premiere heavyweight division—from John L. Sullivan in 1882 to Tommy Burns, who won the title in 1906—were all white. However, from the moment that Jack Johnson, a black American, beat Burns to win the heavyweight championship of the world in Sydney, Australia, in December 1908, boxing has had a special place in the minds and hearts of African-Americans.

That fight occurred at a time when the memory of slavery was still vividly alive in the African-American community. Almost every black American had been a slave, or had parents or grandparents who had suffered under slavery. They gloried in Johnson's ability to stand toe-to-toe with the best white fighters in the world, and in effect to beat them to a pulp, without being imprisoned, much less lynched, for doing so.

By the same token, many white Americans were shocked at this black man's ability to defeat all white opponents. White boxing fans and sports promoters began looking for a "great white hope" to win the heavyweight title back. Even after one was found—the white boxer Jess Willard won the title by a knockout in a fight in Havana, Cuba, in 1913—African-Americans continued to look to boxing as an affirmation of their equality, if not superiority, in at least one area of American life.

In fact, African-Americans have dominated professional boxing in the United States for most of the twentieth century. The list of great black heavyweight champions runs from Jack Dempsey through Joe Louis, Sonny Liston, and the man many boxing experts consider the greatest boxer of all time, Muhammad Ali, to modern champions like George Foreman and Mike Tyson. Great black fighters in other divisions include Sugar Ray Robinson and Sugar Ray Leonard. Some of them, most notably Robinson, have become almost equally honored, and even beloved, by white boxing fans as well as black.

The prominence of black fighters in the heavyweight division has added a special racial edge to the sport. Black fight fans, and even many people in the black community who have no particular interest in boxing as a sport, traditionally take pride in the black champions, while white fans and sportswriters speculate on who the next great white hope would be. Whenever a white challenger faces a black champion, or vice versa, a substantial segment of fans can be counted on to root for the representative of their own race.

Should Boxing Be Banned?

Many people, both in the United States and abroad, believe that boxing ought to be banned. Some are actively appalled by it. They consider it a brutal, even bestial, activity that brings out the worst in the participants and spectators alike. Others oppose it on what might be called philosophical grounds. They see it as a glorification of violence and aggression, two qualities they believe that society, in general, ought to discourage. Still others call for an end to the sport on the humanitarian grounds that it is unhealthy for the participants.

Boxers risk short- and long-term damage to their bodies and their minds. Broken noses and bones, cuts, and loss of teeth are relatively common. Kidney damage, ruptures and trauma to other organs, and internal bleeding are also associated with the sport. Potentially the most dangerous boxing injuries, however, come to the head. Fighters frequently suffer concussions, and progressive injury to the brain typically occurs over the course of a fighter's career. Several fighters have died due to blows to the head received in the ring.

"While the head remains a target there will continue to be tragedies like this one," declared a British Medical Association spokesperson following the death of a Scottish fighter in a 1995 title bout, "and there will be chronic brain damage to a majority of boxers." The most famous boxer of the modern era, Muhammad Ali, developed Parkinson's disease, possibly as a result of boxing-related trauma.

For reasons like these, national and international medical associations have appealed for stricter regulation of boxing. Some, including the British Medical Association, have called for its total ban. Short of banning boxing altogether, suggestions for protecting the fighters include more padding in their gloves and the wearing of protective headgear in professional fights, like that worn in sparring practice and during fights at the amateur level.

Although some critics charge that boxing is not a sport at all, boxers and their fans insist that it is most pure and noble of all the sports. They claim that it is the prototypical contest of man against man, facing each other in the most elemental kind of struggle. As to the obvious risks involved, fans point out that there are risks involved in all forms of sport and argue that boxing may not be the most dangerous. Professional football players may suffer as much risk of chronic injury, and automobile racing is far more life-threatening. In any case, supporters say, fighters have as much right as any other athletes to determine for themselves whether the risks of their sport are worth taking.

See also Sports Betting.
For further reading Sammons, Jeffrey. *Beyond the Ring: The Role of Boxing in American Society*. Champagne: University of Illinois Press, 1988.

Burden of Proof

In the American legal system, the burden of proof in any trial rests on those bringing the charge, that is, on the prosecution in a criminal trial or on the plaintiff in a civil lawsuit. The presumption is that the accused is innocent. It is up to those who allege that he or she is not to overcome that presumption with evidence proving the defendant culpable. In a criminal trial, that proof must demonstrate guilt beyond a reasonable doubt. In a civil trial, the standard of proof is lower. The plaintiff needs only to show that it is more likely than not that the defendant is guilty.

Criminal juries are instructed that the requirement for the state to establish guilt beyond a reasonable doubt means that, if the evidence presented at trial is subject to more than one reasonable interpretation, the jury must accept the interpretation that supports the defendant's innocence rather than the one that suggests his or her guilt. In a civil trial they are instructed that guilt must be proven by a preponderance of the evidence.

It is logical that the burden of proof should rest on the state or on the plaintiff because a negative—that the defendant did not do something—can be impossible to prove. Even so, defendants begin any trial under a severe disadvantage. They are accused of wrongdoing. No matter how hard jurors may try—and trial lawyers suspect that some jurors do not try very hard—they cannot look upon a defendant without prejudice. The mere fact that he or she *is* a defendant brings him or her into the courtroom under a cloud of suspicion. There is at least a feeling, however much jurors may attempt to put it aside, that the police would never have arrested the accused—nor the prosecution have brought him or her to trial—without good cause. Placing the burden of proof squarely on the prosecution helps to compensate for that suspicion.

Capital Punishment

See Cruel and Unusual Punishment; Death Penalty; Death Penalty (Controversies); Death Penalty (Major Supreme Court Decisions).

Charity

Charity refers to acts of altruism and benevolence, and particularly to gifts given to benefit people who are not directly related to the giver in any way. The term comes from the Latin word for Christian love, signifying a love of all humankind. The practice of charity is still often associated with religious values, as every major world religion calls upon its believers to give to those in need.

Charity, in the modern sense, typically refers to contributions of money, time, or labor on behalf of any of a wide range of altruistic causes from medical research to civic projects, educational, artistic, and cultural endeavors, as well as to the relief of human suffering due to poverty, disease, or other forms of disadvantage.

A distinction is usually made between charity, which is private and voluntary, and public welfare programs, which use public resources to help those in need. This distinction is less than absolute, since even certain types of private charity are subsidized in part

by the government through tax deductions allowed for charitable giving.

There are two main kinds of charitable giving. The first is personal charity, which is given by an individual to another individual or group of individuals. The second is organized charity, in which money, goods, or services are dispensed by an institution, such as the Community Chest, the Salvation Army, or Catholic Relief Services. Charitable organizations such as these derive funds from a variety of sources, including personal and corporate donations, bequests, and endowments.

Attitudes toward Charity

There are two distinct, and to some extent opposing, attitudes toward charitable giving. The first, which can be called the liberal view, holds that giving is good, in and of itself. In this view, the main necessary precondition for charity is the neediness of the recipient.

The second view, which can be called the authoritarian view, holds that the prime goal of charity ought to be not merely the alleviation of immediate suffering, but the long-term improvement of the recipient or of society. The authoritarian view, which is probably the most prevalent in the United States today, was summed up more than a century ago by Andrew

Carnegie in his famous essay, "Wealth," in which he assailed "indiscriminate charity" as "one of the serious obstacles to the improvement of our race."

According to Carnegie, "It were better for mankind that the millions of the rich were thrown into the sea than so spent as to encourage the slothful, the drunken, the unworthy.... In bestowing charity, the main consideration should be to help those who will help themselves; to provide part of the means by which those who desire to improve may do so; to give those who desire to rise the aids by which they may rise; to assist, but rarely or never to do all."

Carnegie practiced what he preached, giving hundreds of millions of dollars to public libraries, which he hoped would allow poor but enterprising people to acquire the knowledge they would need to pull themselves out of poverty.

The liberal attitude toward charity is summed up by a scene in the movie *Becket*. In the movie, the wealthy young statesman, Thomas Becket, is named Archbishop of Canterbury. Preparing for his new position, he gives away his luxurious belongings to the poor. When an elder churchman chides him for giving a fine blanket to a dissolute beggar, Becket explains that the blanket will keep the beggar warm. The churchman, who holds the more authoritarian view of charity, protests that the beggar will only sell the expensive blanket to buy drink. "Then *that* will keep him warm," responds Becket.

As suggested by the above scene, the liberal charity-giver would be likely to give money to beggars in the street, but an authoritarian would not. The latter would argue that handouts only encourage beggars to continue to beg, rather than to help themselves by finding productive work.

Whether they subscribe to the liberal or authoritarian view, most givers would agree that, whenever possible, charity should be more than a stopgap provision of food, drink, or shelter. Rather, it should be given in such a way that it helps the recipient to better his or her own condition in life.

The Development of Charity in the United States

The roots of modern charity giving are in the religious precepts that call for giving help to the poor, the sick, and other unfortunates. In medieval Europe, the job of tending to such people typically fell to the church. Certain religious orders were dedicated to providing services to the needy.

During the eighteenth century in the United States, most charity was given on a person-to-person basis. People took care of their families or neighbors—or not, as the case may be. Destitute strangers were left to beg. Even most organized charity was local. Church congregations would be expected to care for those members who had no family or neighbors willing or able to take care of them. This system had obvious drawbacks, not the least of which was that poor localities often lacked the means to provide for their poorest inhabitants. Even in the most prosperous communities, such charity tended to leave many desperate people's needs unmet. Under such a system, a person in need of help had to arouse the sympathies of someone able to provide it. Those unfortunates whose behavior, appearance, or personality provoked dislike or disapproval were unlikely to get help, no matter how great their need might be.

This discrepancy between people's needs and the willingness to provide charity was exacerbated by the fact that most people subscribed to the concept of the deserving and the undeserving poor—that is, the belief that some needy people are worthy of help, whereas others are not. Those generally deemed most worthy were respectable widows and orphans. Those considered undeserving usually included apparently able-bodied men, as well as drunkards, prostitutes, and others considered morally weak.

Still another problem with this system of private, discretionary giving was that it relied upon close and lasting social ties within communities. The system was poorly equipped to deal with the large waves of immigrants that poured into the country during the nineteenth century.

The flaws in this system of local charity had become glaringly apparent by the time the twentieth century began. In any case, the old system was already showing signs of breaking down by that time, along with the relatively close-knit community structures on which it had been built. Thousands of new charitable organizations sprang up in the nation's cities around the turn of the century. Each was designed to fill, or at least alleviate, some specific need that was left unmet by the traditional arrangements. Some, such as the Committee for Ameliorating the Condition of Russian Refugees, were designed to help a particular group of immigrants. Others, such as the Erring Women's Refuge, set out to help a particular category of those in need, often those who no traditional charity-giver was willing to help.

Even most of these new organizations were local, although some, like the Salvation Army, which first came to the United States from England in 1880, spread across the country. The first few decades of the twentieth century saw the development of several service clubs and other organizations that made it a part of their reason for being to do good works and promote the development of their community.

The 1920s, in particular, saw a flowering of community development projects and operations in which local governments, businesses, and other organizations joined efforts on behalf of community betterment. Some of these activities were encouraged by the federal government, in the form of the Department of Commerce. In a sense, these organizations were a reflection of the need to find a new approach to civic charity, although only a portion of their activities would be considered charitable in the most traditional sense.

One of the most lasting of these efforts to establish new kinds of charitable institutions was the formation of what came to be called community chests. These organizations, sometimes allied with local chambers of commerce, collected contributions from a variety of sources and then dispersed them among various local charitable organizations, private and public. The community chest idea has continued to flourish under the rubric of the United Way. The national association of these local organizations is known as The United Way of America.

The Great Depression of the 1930s brought on a new demand for public welfare efforts to supplement, if not replace, private charity. Ever since, federal, state, and local government programs have attempted to meet, on a fairer and more consistent basis, many of the functions that were once left entirely to the churches, individuals, and other groups. Even so, private charitable giving has continued to play a vital role in social welfare, particularly since the early 1980s, which marked the beginning of a movement to cut back on the numbers of recipients' eligible for public welfare programs.

In the 12 years following 1980, total philanthropic contributions from all sources grew in the United States from $48.6 billion to $126.2 billion. In 1993, individual

Americans gave $102.6 billion to charity and $8.5 billion more in charitable bequests. Corporations gave an additional $5.9 billion, and charitable foundations gave $9.2 billion. The largest beneficiaries of these contributions were religious organizations, which received almost half of the total. After religion, the most popular recipients of contributions from individuals were human services, health, youth development, and education.

Foundations were most generous to educational institutions, followed by health care, arts and cultural institutions, and human services. The largest portion of corporate donations went to education, followed by health and human services, then arts and culture.

See also Corporate Responsibility; "Wealth"; Welfare System.
For further reading Bremmer, Robert H. *American Philanthropy*. Daniel J. Boor, editor. Chicago: University of Chicago Press, 1988.
Brilliant, Eleanor L. *The United Way: Dilemmas of Organized Charity*. New York: Columbia University Press, 1993.
Payton, Robert, et al. *Philanthropy: Four Views*. New Brunswick, NJ: Transaction Press, 1988.

Charter Schools

The development of charter schools is one result of the call for educational reform in the 1990s by many parents dissatisfied with the education provided to their children by traditional public schools. The term *charter school* is a broad one used to describe virtually any school that, although it receives a charter from the state and is supported by public funds, is not a part of the traditional school system.

Charter schools often have different qualification requirements and work rules for teachers and may pursue somewhat different educational goals than traditional schools. In return for the public support they receive, and the freedom from certain regulatory restrictions, they typically are required to sign performance contracts, assuring that they will continue to operate to a certain standard for a given number of years.

Most current charter schools have been inspired by reform-minded educators and parents, whether to provide education for children with special needs or disabilities, or to experiment with innovative educational strategies. Although much of the impetus for charter schools comes from parents, much also comes from educational innovators, as well as from businesspersons who hope to found a new and profitable industry in privately developed and operated, although not owned, public schools. Political support for charter schools also comes from conservatives, who see charter schools as a step in the direction of a greater privatization of the U.S. educational system.

More than half of the states have passed some sort of charter school legislation. Each state's criteria for chartering schools are different. Some require such schools to meet the same academic standards as traditional public schools, while others allow them to set their own standards. All charter schools do have to meet federal health, safety, and antidiscrimination standards, however.

Although education is primarily a state function, the federal government has embraced the concept of charter schools. President Bill Clinton has called for the establishment of 3,000 charter schools across the country.

So far, the most ambitious charter school experiments have been those launched by a corporation known as Educational Alternatives, Inc. In addition to several schools in several other communities, the company won a contract in 1994 to run the entire school system of Hartford, Connecticut. The Hartford experiment ran into serious problems in its first year, losing millions of dollars and causing the local school board to take back control over the majority of the city's schools.

See also School Choice.

Checks and Balances

The Constitution of the United States was designed by men who distrusted centralized power. In order to prevent the power of the federal government from becoming concentrated in the hands of any one individual or agency, the founders designed a government in which the three main branches would, to some extent, offset each other and be able to restrain each other should any one branch attempt to usurp too much power.

The legislative branch (which is itself divided into the two houses of Congress) enacts laws and oversees the working of the executive branch. The executive branch (made up of the president and the federal agencies) not only carries out the laws passed by the legislative branch, but, through the presidential veto power, has a limited role in making them, as well; in addition, the executive branch, with the consent of the U.S. Senate of the legislative branch, appoints the men and women who serve in the judicial branch. The primary role of the judicial branch (made up of the U.S. Supreme Court and the lesser federal courts) is to interpret federal laws, as well as ensure that neither federal nor state laws violate the provisions of the U.S. Constitution.

In effect, then, no branch of the federal government functions entirely on its own.

Each needs both of the others in order to operate effectively and requires at least the tacit consent and cooperation of the others to function at all. A similar situation exists in the government of each state.

What is more, the power of the federal government as a whole is limited, to some extent, by the rights and prerogatives of the individual states; and the states' power is limited, to an even greater extent, by the federal government.

This system, in which each branch of government checks and balances the others, is regarded as vital to the limitation of governmental power and to the protection of individual rights and freedoms. At the same time, however, the need for the various parts of government to function together can make it difficult for any level of government to get things done in a timely and efficient manner.

See also Democracy; Initiatives and Referenda; Majority Rule.
For further reading Harris, Fred. *America's Democracy; The Ideal and the Reality.* Glenview, IL: Scott, Foresman, 1980.
Kronenwetter, Michael. *How Democratic Is the United States?* New York: Watts, 1994.

Child Abuse

The term *child abuse* refers to the mistreatment of children by older children or adults. It is most commonly used to describe physical or emotional violence committed against children, as well as any sexual activity between a young child and an older person. Neglect, or lack of due care for children by parents or other adults in positions of responsibility for them, is also regarded as abuse. Recently, the term has been expanded by some who use it to include fetal abuse, in which an unborn child is damaged in some way by irresponsible behavior (such as the use of drugs, alcohol, or tobacco) on the part of its mother.

Nearly 2 million cases of alleged child abuse were reported in the United States in 1985. By 1992, the number had risen to 2.94 million, or approximately 8,000 a day. Of these, about one in three were sufficiently verified for police or social service agencies to take action. Nearly one-half of child abuse reports involve neglect. Approximately one-quarter involve beatings or other forms of physical abuse, and another 15 percent involve sexual abuse. The numbers of confirmed child abuse deaths have been going up as well: from less than 700 in 1985 to 1,299 in 1993. Three children a day perish from malnutrition in the United States, some of them through the neglect of their parents.

The extent to which the growing number of child abuse reports reflects an actual rise in the incidence of abuse is not clear. Police and child welfare authorities believe that child abuse has always been seriously underreported.

Reasons for the Underreporting of Child Abuse

Very young victims of child abuse are, of course, unable to report such events themselves. Older children often suffer the abuse in silence, either because they do not recognize that they are being mistreated, because they feel they deserve it, or because they feel embarrassment, fear, or love for the abuser, who is often a parent or other close relative. The perpetrators—and, when the perpetrator is a parent, their spouses—often fail to recognize the nature of their activities and the extent of the damage that is being done. American culture, like that of many other nations, accepts a certain amount of corporal punishment as a normal part of child rear-

ing, and sometimes, perhaps, a necessary one. The same can be said of the kind of harsh criticism or ridicule of children that can, if cruel enough, become emotional abuse.

Even sexual abusers sometimes convince themselves that what they are doing is normal, and that, in any case, it is not really doing any harm. A surprising number of sexually abusive fathers complain that their wife is frigid, or otherwise unavailable for sexual activities, and rationalize that their daughter has a "duty" to take her mother's place.

Many instances of physical abuse result from overly severe corporal punishment or a parent's lost temper. In the first case, the abuser typically believes that he or she is only doing what is necessary to discipline the child; in the second, that the harm caused to the child was an accident that will never happen again—although, according to many child welfare experts, it frequently does recur. Other perpetrators do recognize the damage they do, and feel terrible about it, but fear the consequences of reporting the abuse.

It is likely that at least a portion of the increase in child abuse reports results from the growing national attention that has been focused on the issue recently and from relatively new reporting laws which require teachers, child care workers, psychologists, medical doctors and other health care workers to report all injuries to children which they believe could have resulted from abuse.

Although the above-mentioned laws undoubtedly bring more cases of child abuse to the attention of the legal authorities, some medical professionals object to them. They worry that reporting such injuries can be seen as a violation of doctor-patient confidentiality. What is more, they worry that awareness that often perfectly innocent injuries may be reported to the police makes some parents reluctant to seek proper treatment for injured children.

Responses to Child Abuse

Child welfare agencies respond to reports of child abuse in a variety of ways. The most important consideration is always the welfare of the child, but where the best hope for that welfare lies can be hard to determine. The first imperative obviously is to see to it that the abuse is stopped. Some abusers are criminally charged. Others, particularly when the abuser is a parent, are referred for therapy or other psychological treatment.

In some cases of intrafamily abuse, the whole family is counseled in an effort to mitigate the damage that has been done and to reduce the likelihood of similar harm in the future. Many agencies and courts make every effort to keep families together while assuring that the abuse comes to an end. Some social service agencies, however, increasingly have become inclined to remove children from homes troubled by violence or abuse. Although this seems a logical way to assure the safety of the children, it raises serious concerns involving the rights of both parents and children.

See also Corporal Punishment by Parents; Corporal Punishment in Schools; Domestic Violence. **For further reading** Chase, Naomi Feigelson. *A Child Is Being Beaten: Violence against Children, An American Tragedy*. New York: Holt, 1975.

Child Labor

At one time, the typical young male in the United States was expected to work at what would today seem an early age. Females often were expected to work as well. Chil-

dren were a vital part of the labor force on the family farms that grew the bulk of American agricultural products in the nineteenth and early twentieth centuries. They were considered so vital to the nation's well-being that the American school year was designed around their work schedule, to make sure that they would be free during those times of year when their help was most needed on the farm.

During the Industrial Revolution, young people of both sexes went to work in the factories in their early teens, and some even before. It has been estimated that in the early decades of the nineteenth century, one out of every three American factory workers was between the ages of 7 and 12. These children often worked 10- and 12-hour days, in dangerous and unsanitary conditions.

In the late eighteenth and early nineteenth centuries, child labor was justified not only as necessary to grow the nation's food, and manufacture the nation's products, but as something that was good for the children themselves. It built character and kept the young people out of trouble. Idle hands, it was said, were the devil's playground.

Early Attempts at Regulation

It was not until the 1830s and 1840s that public attitudes began to change sufficiently for some states to enact laws to protect children from the worst forms of exploitation. One of the prime motives behind these laws was the desire to assure that young people received at least some basic education. Massachusetts was the first state to do so, with an 1836 law that forbid employers to hire children under 15, unless they had had at least three months of schooling in the past year. Over the next few decades several other states passed laws regulating the ages, work hours, and some other employment conditions of children.

These early laws were only partly effective, however. They were ignored by many employers and poorly enforced in many states. At best, they served only to regulate child labor, not to prevent it. Despite them, the number of children in the U.S. workforce increased over the rest of the nineteenth century.

By the early twentieth century, the Progressive movement had mobilized public opinion behind the protection of child workers. When it became apparent that state regulation was not enough, the federal government began enacting child labor laws in the 1910s, but they were struck down by the U.S. Supreme Court, as a violation of the employers' freedom. Congress passed a constitutional amendment to allow itself to regulate child labor in 1924, but too few states ratified it for it to become a part of the Constitution.

It was not until the New Deal of the 1930s—a century after a pioneering state law in Massachusetts—that federal legislation protecting child workers finally became effective. And it was not until 1941 that the U.S. Supreme Court formally acknowledged the federal government's power to regulate child labor in the United States in the landmark case of *United States v. Darby Lumber Company* (1941).

Child Workers Today

In the years since 1941, a complex of state and federal laws have been enacted to regulate the hours and conditions of young workers. For the most part, these laws are designed to achieve three goals: To assure all children have enough time away from work to receive an education; to see that they are not overworked; and to make sure that they are not subjected to unreasonable dangers on the job.

Typical laws set minimum ages for employment in certain industries, and forbid the employment of people under the age of 18 in hazardous jobs. They also forbid the employment of student-age young people during school hours and regulate the number of hours a student may be employed during a school day or week. They also set limits on the number of hours young people different ages can be employed, and, in some cases, what hours of the day those can be as well.

One thing they do not do is ensure young people an equal wage with adults. If anything, they are designed to do just the opposite, exempting teen workers from adult wage scales and even minimum wage laws.

Partly because they are a cheap source of labor for those employers who can meet the standards of the child labor laws, young people are a significant part of the modern American workforce. Children continue to be the main home deliverers of newspapers in the United States, as they have always been. Teenagers still do much of the labor on America's family farms. The children of migrant agricultural laborers also make a significant contribution to family income earned picking fruits and vegetables on a seasonal basis from California to Wisconsin. In addition, teenagers provide the bulk of the workers for the fast food industry, as well as for many seasonal businesses such as summer camps and amusement parks.

See also Child Labor Abroad (U.S. Complicity).

Child Labor Abroad (U.S. Complicity)

Over 100 million children work at hard labor in developing countries from South

America to Morocco. Many of them are bound into one form or another of forced servitude.

According to the antislavery organization, Anti-Slavery International, there are 80 million such children in southern Asia alone. Many are as young as six and seven years old.

The children work in a variety of industries, ranging from mining to manufacturing. Among the products they produce are glass, textiles, and fireworks. Most of the countries in which these children work have laws forbidding the employment of children below the ages of 15. These laws, however, routinely are ignored.

Forced child labor elsewhere in the world is a significant issue in the United States because many of the products these child laborers make are exported to the U.S. An example of a major industry using child labor that exports goods to the United States is the carpetmaking industry in the Indian subcontinent.

Some concerned Americans are made uncomfortable by the thought of buying the products of this kind of labor. They believe that purchases of these goods provide profits to the exploiters of the children and encourage the practice of forced child labor to continue. They urge others to be careful about buying goods—particularly textiles and carpets—from countries known to rely heavily on child labor, such as India, Pakistan, China, and Afghanistan. Rugs with a label reading "RUGMARK," however, are certified to have been made without child labor.

See also Child Labor; Slavery.
For further reading Lee-Wright, Peter. *Child Slaves*. London: Earthscan Publications, 1990. U.S. Department of Labor. *By the Sweat and Toil of Children: The Use of Child Labor in American Imports*. Washington, DC: U.S. Department of Labor, 1994.

Child Support

It is a generally accepted principle, both in ethics and in law, that biological parents share responsibility for raising their child. In the family model which is widely accepted as ideal in the Unites States, the two cooperate to provide emotional, financial, and other forms of support for their child. When couples with minor children split up, however—whether the split is caused by divorce, by the desertion of one spouse, or by some other form of separation—this cooperation frequently collapses.

In most, although far from all, family breakups, primary physical custody of the child falls to one parent. Even so, the noncustodial parent usually retains some legal as well as moral rights and responsibilities toward the child, including at least some economic responsibility for him or her. In cases of divorce or other legal separations, the noncustodial parent is typically required to contribute a certain amount of financial support for the child. The amount and method of the contribution may be worked out voluntarily between the parties, or it may be ordered by the court. This child support is intended solely for the upkeep of the children. It is entirely separate from alimony, which is an allowance awarded for the maintenance of an ex-spouse.

Nonpayment

The unfortunate reality is that a large proportion of court-ordered child support does not get paid in the United States. In 1994, noncustodial parents paid some $14 billion in child support. Child rights advocates argue that more effective enforcement of child support orders, together with a more equitable system of child support judgments, would have resulted in a total payment of $9 billion more in payments due in that year alone. If all of the back payments had been collected, the total would have risen to $34 billion.

Reasons for Delinquency

In the United States, the female parent traditionally has been thought of as the primary caretaker, and the male parent the primary financial provider. For this reason—and because it is still true that men are statistically likely to earn more than their spouses—the mother still is most likely to be awarded primary custody of the children, while the father is most likely to be required to pay child support. Not surprisingly, the majority of parents who are delinquent in their child support payments are men, who have come to be decried as deadbeat dads.

There are many reasons why noncustodial parents fail to pay child support. One has to do with their perceptions of the child support requirement. Many see the amount of support that the court has ordered them to pay as unfairly high, either because they feel that they cannot afford to pay it, or because they perceive the custodial parent as being better off financially than they are themselves.

Another range of reasons proceeds from hostility toward the custodial parent. The noncustodial parent may believe that the custodial parent is misusing the money, or using it for their own purposes, rather than to provide for the child. In some cases, the withholding of child support is seen as a way of getting back at the custodial parent for real or imagined injuries. For nonpaying parents eager to get back at their ex-spouses, the effect on the well-being of the children is secondary to their desire for revenge.

A minority of nonpaying parents are virtually indifferent toward the child. Some may be actively hostile, perhaps because (in the case of fathers) they believe, or wish to believe, that the child is not biologically theirs.

It is generally acknowledged, however, that the most common reason for nonpayment is inability to pay. The majority of delinquent parents are poor, and many are unemployed.

Enforcement

Divorce and other family disputes are handled in state courts, and the primary responsibility for enforcing child support agreements traditionally has fallen on state courts and local law enforcement agencies. These authorities are invariably overburdened with other matters, however, and a great many custodial parents have long complained that child support orders are ineffectively enforced, if they are enforced at all.

The federal government responded to these complaints in the 1990s by taking on a greater role in enforcement of child support orders. The 1992 Federal Child Support Recovery Act allowed federal courts and law enforcement agencies to help track down and prosecute delinquent parents. Enforcement of the Act is limited, however, by a number of legal restrictions and requirements. In order for federal officials to take action, the nonpaying parent must be residing in a different state than the children, which is not typically the case.

Even so, the federal government helped to collect $703 million in delinquent payments in 1994 by such means as seizing the federal tax refunds of nonpaying parents and applying them to delinquent child support payments.

In 1996, a federal law endorsed more powers for states to enforce child support payments, including the revocation of driving licenses and professional licenses previously granted nonpaying parents. Some states had already begun using such measures on their own.

Other federal measures included authorization and initial funding for a nationwide computer hookup designed to make it easier to identify and track nonpaying, noncustodial parents. The system, however, has been slow to come into place, and child rights advocates complain that the combination of tough talk and relatively ineffective enforcement has added to the problem nearly as much as it has alleviated it.

Civil Disobedience

In a famous essay entitled *On the Duty of Civil Disobedience*, the nineteenth-century American philosopher Henry David Thoreau argued that men have a moral duty to disobey immoral laws. He believed that if enough citizens would refuse to obey an unjust law, even to the point of willingly going to jail in order to protest that law, then the government would ultimately have to rescind it. This proclaimed duty has since been transformed into a powerful political tactic in which civil disobedience is used as a form of protest against what the protesters regard as unjust laws.

According to many of its advocates, in order for civil disobedience to be both morally justifiable and politically effective, the law must be broken openly, and those who break it must be willing to take the legal consequences for their actions.

The political effectiveness of civil disobedience comes from its ability to draw public as well as official attention to an issue that has gone relatively unnoticed. Although it is relatively easy for the authorities and the citizenry alike to ignore verbal or written complaints about a given law or policy, it is much more difficult to disregard the fact that people are publicly breaking the law. Beyond that, civil disobedience, when combined with nonviolence,

may have a profound effect on the conscience of the community.

Twentieth-Century Protest Movements

Civil disobedience was practiced by the advocates of voting rights for women at least as early as the 1870s. Early in the twentieth century, the Indian activist Mohandas Gandhi adapted Thoreau's ideas—along with the teachings of Jesus Christ, Leo Tolstoy, and his own Hindu religion—to the protest movements he led in South Africa and India. In the process, he refined the notion of civil disobedience, transforming it into a more spiritual imperative and an effective mass political tactic.

Civil disobedience has been a central feature of many American protest movements in the mid- to late twentieth century. Its most notable American practitioner was Martin Luther King Jr., who encouraged its use in the civil rights movement of the 1950s and 1960s. As a minister sensitive to charges that it was wrong for a man of the cloth to break the law, King justified the tactic in a letter to fellow ministers written while he was in jail for civil disobedience in Birmingham, Alabama.

> One may well ask: How can you advocate breaking some laws and obeying others? The answer lies in the fact that there are two types of laws: just and unjust.... One has not only a legal but a moral responsibility to obey just laws. Conversely, one has a moral responsibility to disobey unjust laws, I would agree with Saint Augustine that an unjust law is no law at all.

The most common form of civil disobedience practiced by the civil rights movement was the breaking of the Jim Crow laws that enforced segregation of the races.

The key stage of the civil rights movement began with the breaking of such a law when Rosa Parks, a black woman, refused to obey a law requiring blacks to surrender certain seats on Montgomery, Alabama, buses to white passengers.

Civil disobedience was also widely used in the anti–Vietnam War, free speech, students' rights, and nuclear disarmament movements, among many others. Most recently, it has been a feature of several pro-life and animal rights protests.

See also Nonviolence.
For further reading Bedau, Hugo A. *Civil Disobedience*. New York: Pegasus, 1969.
Dellinger, Dave. *Revolutionary Nonviolence*. Garden City, NY: Anchor Books, 1971.
Murphy, Jeffrie G., editor. *Civil Disobedience and Violence*. Belmont, CA: Wadsworth, 1971.
Thoreau, Henry David. *Walden and Civil Disobedience*. New York: NAL-Dutton, 1943.

Civil Forfeiture

Civil forfeiture is a procedure by which the government legally confiscates the property of individuals on the grounds that it has either been used in the commission of a crime or is itself the fruit of a crime.

In recent years, civil forfeiture has become a major weapon in the so-called war on drugs. Legal authorities routinely confiscate small boats and planes seized in raids on drug smuggling operations, and sometimes even the homes and automobiles of drug dealers, which the government maintains were purchased with the profits from illegal drugs.

Civil forfeiture has been criticized on several grounds. Among them is the charge that it punishes a person twice for the same crime. Having already tried and convicted the defendant of a crime and applied the suitable criminal punishment, the government then proceeds against the criminal

civilly, taking property from them as well. This double jeopardy argument was rejected by the U.S. Supreme Court in 1996, however.

The second major criticism of civil forfeiture is that it is overused. Even some legal observers who have no objection to the procedure being used against major drug smugglers balk when it is used to seize the property of ordinary citizens or property where a connection to an actual crime is tenuous at best. Another complaint is that the value of the property seized in some civil forfeitures has been disproportionate to the nature of the offense.

Such arguments are bolstered by cases such as one, which received a good deal of publicity in the mid-1990s, in which local authorities confiscated an automobile driven by a married man while soliciting a prostitute. The crime involved was a relatively minor one, while the car was a vital asset, not only to the man, but to his wife. Although the seizure of the family car struck many members of the public as grossly unfair, the forfeiture was upheld on appeal.

Civil Rights Movement

Twentieth-century America has seen a number of movements in support of various claims of civil rights, from gay rights to the right of freedom of speech, and from the right-to-life to the right-to-choose, to the right-to-die. However, the term civil rights movement primarily is used to describe the movement against racial segregation, in support of equal treatment for African-Americans, which achieved its greatest successes in the years between the U.S. Supreme Court's decision in the *Brown* v. *Board of Education* school desegregation case in 1954 and the passage of the Voting Rights Act of 1965.

The National Association for the Advancement of Colored People

Although from the time of the Abolition movement before the Civil War some black Americans and their white supporters had campaigned for the rights of African-Americans, the twentieth-century civil rights movement usually dates from the founding of the National Association for the Advancement of Colored People (NAACP) by a group of black and white Americans on Lincoln's birthday (12 February) in 1909.

Even the NAACP was an outgrowth of an earlier organization—the Niagara Movement, founded by W.E.B. DuBois and 28 other young black men in Niagara Falls, New York, in 1905. A brilliant black scholar who had earned a Ph.D. from Harvard University at a time when few African-Americans had college degrees of any kind, DuBois was the NAACP's original chief spokesman. He believed in African-Americans taking a full and equal place in American society—a radical position in a time when the Jim Crow laws enacted by the southern states to prevent African-Americans from achieving that equality had erected a wall of legal segregation confining African-Americans in poverty and repression throughout the South, and when, even in the North, black people were widely thought of, and treated, as inferior to whites.

The Legal Challenge to Segregation

In the 1896 case of *Plessy* v. *Ferguson*, the U.S. Supreme Court had ruled that racial segregation was legal in the United States, so long as separate but equal public facilities were provided to blacks. Separate but equal, however, was always a legal fiction. In most southern communities, African-Americans had few public facilities of any kind, and those that did exist invariably were inferior to those available to whites.

Unwilling to accept the permanence of segregation, the NAACP led a continuing legal challenge against Jim Crow until, in the landmark 1954 case of *Brown* v. *Board of Education*, the U.S. Supreme Court firmly acknowledged that "[i]n the field of public education, the doctrine of 'separate but equal' has no place." It made no difference, the Court declared, whether the physical school facilities provided to blacks were "equal" to those provided to whites. The simple fact that they were segregated made them "inherently unequal."

The NAACP continued to battle segregation in the courts and soon won a series of decisions outlawing segregation in other areas of American life, from public parks to prisons. These legal victories provided the foundation for the civil rights movement, which developed largely in the effort to put them into practice by desegregating the South. Such a movement was necessary because the white power structure in the South refused to enforce the desegregation rulings of the Supreme Court and dismantle Jim Crow. It was immediately clear that, if the South was to be desegregated in fact as well as in law, ordinary people would have to take the matter into their own hands.

The Montgomery Bus Boycott

The first desegregation effort to capture national attention grew out of an incident in December 1955, in which a black woman named Rosa Parks refused to yield her seat on a crowded Montgomery, Alabama, bus to a white man, as required by that city's Jim Crow laws. When she was arrested, the black community of Montgomery launched a boycott of the city bus system as a protest against the ongoing segregation of the buses. The boycott was led by a young black minister named Martin Luther King, Jr.

City officials took legal action to end the boycott, and King was thrown into jail. Some Montgomery whites responded violently to the boycott, intimidating the boycotters and even bombing King's home. Montgomery's black residents remained determined in the face of threats and violence, stubbornly refusing to ride the segregated buses. The U.S. Supreme Court eventually supported the boycotters by issuing a declaratory judgment in the case of *Gayle* v. *Browder* (1956), overturning the statute segregating Montgomery's buses. In the end, the city surrendered; Rev. King was released and the buses were integrated.

The concerted peaceful protest of the black community of Montgomery, together with the leadership of Rev. King, provided an inspiration and model for the antisegregation movement that followed. In the wake of the Montgomery boycott, King and a number of other black ministers founded a new organization, the Southern Christian Leadership Conference (SCLC), which helped to organize the fight against segregation across the South. The SCLC dedicated itself to the tactic of nonviolent civil disobedience, which King adopted from the models of Henry David Thoreau, Mohandas Gandhi, and Jesus Christ.

Resistance

Most of the violent resistance to the civil rights movement—and to desegregation in general—came from racist organizations like the White Citizens Councils and the many variants of the Ku Klux Klan (KKK). Those groups did not act in a vacuum, however. Their actions were merely the most terrible manifestations of a widespread feeling of anger and desperation in the white community in the South. Whites enjoyed a position of relative privilege in southern society, and they were reluctant to give it up. Even the poorest whites had a status higher than their black equivalents. Long indoctrinated with racial prejudice, many whites of all classes were outraged by the idea that Negroes (the polite term for African-Americans in the 1960s) should have the same rights and opportunities as they did.

Another kind of resistance came from politicians, not all of them from the South, who were concerned that states rights were being endangered, and with them the checks and balances of the U.S. political system. Among them were some of the most highly respected political leaders in the Congress.

Tactics

The civil rights movement of the early 1960s experimented with a variety of tactics, from acts of individual defiance to mass marches and demonstrations. Many of the tactics were adaptations of those used by the labor movement. One of the most effective was first put into practice in 1960 by four black college students who held a "sit-in" at a segregated lunch counter in a Woolworth's department stone in Greensboro, North Carolina. They refused to move from their seats unless they were served.

News of the tactic inspired similar sit-ins across the Middle South. There were incidents of violence when whites attacked the demonstrators, but these attacks backfired; instead of abandoning their demonstrations, the participants won growing admiration by refusing either to move or to fight back. As both trouble and sympathy for the courage and self-control of the demonstrators increased, white customers became more reluctant to patronize establishments where sit-ins were taking place. Many southern restaurants were faced with the option of serving black customers or shutting down. Most chose to stay open, and one by one they opened their doors to African-Americans.

The sit-ins had been initiated by college students, a group of activists who were becoming increasingly important in the movement as a whole. Even before the first sit-in, a number of idealistic and impatient young people, led by a charismatic young man named Stokely Carmichael, had founded their own civil rights organization, the Student Nonviolent Coordinating Committee (SNCC), also known as "Snick."

In 1961, a group of black and white "freedom riders" from the Congress of Racial Equality (CORE) set out in two buses to integrate bus stations from Washington, D.C., to New Orleans. In Montgomery, Alabama, they were attacked and had their bus burned by white racists, who proceeded to turn on journalists covering the events as well. When the local police refused to intervene, the U.S. Attorney General Robert Kennedy ordered federal marshals to step in.

Victory in Alabama

In the summer of 1963, the SCLC targeted Birmingham, Alabama, for a major desegregation effort dubbed "Project C"—for Confrontation. As much as any southern state, Alabama was a symbol of southern resistance to desegregation. White state and local officials had taken strong public stands against integration and what they saw as unwarranted federal government interference in the affairs of Alabama. The governor, George Wallace, even had promised to "stand in the schoolhouse door" to keep blacks out of the state's white schools.

The SCLC's appeal for permission to stage a march in Birmingham was turned down. When demonstrators took it upon themselves to march anyway, the police, led by their flamboyant chief, Eugene "Bull" Connor, responded by attacking the protesters with swinging batons, powerful fire hoses, and vicious dogs. Television and newsreel footage of the brutal assault, contrasted with the courage of the nonviolent demonstrators—many of whom were women and children—shocked viewers across the country. The public was even more troubled when four little girls were killed in a racist bombing of a black church in Birmingham.

Project C aroused a great deal of sympathy for the civil rights movement. When Governor Wallace kept his word and stood in the doorway of the University of Alabama that fall, he was forced out of the way by troops of his own National Guard, who had been ordered by President John F. Kennedy to see to it that black students were admitted.

The Freedom Summer

For many decades, Jim Crow laws effectively had kept most African-Americans in the Deep South from voting. Court decisions had now struck down many of those laws, but black residents of the South needed to be informed of their new rights and given support in exercising them. Large numbers of courageous young people from virtually all the major civil rights organizations traveled to Mississippi in the Freedom Summer of 1964 to give them that help. They knew, as did the white racists, that once large numbers of black people began to vote, the whites' hold on political power in the South would be in danger.

The civil rights workers (called outside agitators by local whites) soon found themselves the targets of threats, and sometimes of actual violence, along with ordinary black Mississippians who dared to register to vote. Three young men, one black and the others white, were arrested for a traffic violation by local police while driving together down a rural Mississippi road. After being questioned briefly by police, they were never seen alive again. Their murdered bodies were discovered a few weeks later. The bodies of anonymous black Mississippians turned up frequently that summer in rivers and woods across the state.

High Points and Fragmentation

The high point of the civil rights movement came on 28 August 1963, when Rev. Martin Luther King, Jr. delivered his famous "I Have a Dream" speech to 200,000 people following the massive March on Washington. The political high point came with the passage of the Civil Rights Act of 1964 the following year. That Act—initially inspired by President John F. Kennedy and skillfully pushed through Congress by President Lyndon Johnson in the wake of Kennedy's assassination—outlawed segregated public accommodations and banned racial discrimination in hiring and union membership and in projects receiving federal funds.

Other important civil rights legislation followed. The Voting Rights Act of 1965 banned poll taxes and the other methods traditionally used to prevent African-Americans from voting in the South. Three years later, the Civil Rights Act of 1968—passed in the wake of the assassination of Rev. Martin Luther King, Jr.—banned most forms of discrimination in the sale and rental of housing.

Even as these major legislative goals were being met, the civil rights movement was fragmenting. It had come to rely primarily on the energy of young activists, many of whom began to drift away in the mid-1960s. Some black militants, including Carmichael and other leaders of SNCC, who had become increasingly disenchanted with white participation in the movement, began organizing themselves around the concept of black power. They believed that blacks should fight for their own rights and not rely on whites to help them. Through sheer force of numbers, resources, and history, whites came to dominate any multiracial organization to which they belonged. African-Americans needed to make their own movement, and their future. However sadly, some whites who had long participated in the movement agreed.

Many white activists, meanwhile, were becoming increasingly distracted by their opposition to U.S. participation in the war in Vietnam. Others diverted their energies to women's rights, disarmament, or other causes. Still others abandoned activism altogether as they aged and entered the workforce.

The assassination of Rev. Martin Luther King, Jr. in 1968 dealt a kind of final blow to the civil rights movement, taking away its best known and most widely respected leader. By that time, however, the movement was already running out of steam, having accomplished major legal and political goals—more, in fact, than almost anyone had dreamed possible only a few decades before.

The Effects of the Civil Rights Movement

The ultimate results of the civil rights movement are incalculable. In the process of killing Jim Crow, it transformed American politics and reshaped American society, even while it improved the lives of millions of African-Americans.

Black participation at almost every level of American society soared during the 1960s, at least partly as a result of the civil rights movement. The rate of African-Americans entering college doubled in the 1960s, as did the numbers of African-Americans in the professions and in the nation's police forces. The numbers of African-Americans holding political power—in Congress, in state legislatures, and in local governments—increased even more dramatically.

These figures were a reflection of a massive shift in the racial attitudes of Americans, both white and black—a change in public consciousness that was brought about largely by the civil rights movement's ability to dramatize the racial injustice that had long existed in society.

Before the civil rights movement, racial prejudice not only was endemic in American society, it went largely unrecognized by most white Americans. Most whites simply took for granted the fact that blacks were intellectually and morally inferior to them, while most blacks assumed that their position at the bottom of society was immutable. The civil rights movement radically transformed those perceptions for many, although by no means all, Americans of all races.

Racial bigotry is still a major problem in the United States, but it is no longer respectable among most elements of American society. Discrimination still exists—in the workplace, in housing, and in other aspects of American society—but it is no longer legal. A massive underclass of poor and uneducated African-Americans still exists, but so does a large educated and prosperous black middle class. Racial ghettos still exist, but their boundaries are no longer enforceable by law.

See also Affirmative Action; African-Americans in U.S. Society; Bakke Case; Jewish/African-American Relations; Kerner Commission Report; Nonviolence.

For further reading Garrow, David J. *Bearing the Cross*. New York: William Morrow, 1986. Raines, Howell. *"My Soul Is Rested": The Movement Days in the Deep South Remembered*. New York: G. P. Putnam's Sons, 1977. Sitkoff, Harvard. *The Struggle for Black Equality, 1954–1980*. New York: Hill & Wang, 1981.

Clemency
See Executive Clemency.

Cloning
See Genetic Engineering.

Cocaine
See Crack Cocaine in the Black Community (Alleged CIA Involvement); Drug Abuse; Drug War.

Cohousing
The cohousing movement is a modern effort to form a new kind of neighborhood, or community. It was born in Denmark in the 1970s and transplanted to America in the late 1980s.

Cohousing communities are designed and operated by the people who organize and own them. There is no one model. A community might be formed in an apartment building, a small housing development, or even a trailer park. In some cases, a cohousing group might decide to buy, or even to build, a building or collection of buildings for itself.

Cohousing communities combine elements of both private and communal living arrangements. The specific rights and responsibilities of the members of each community are determined by the communities themselves. Ordinarily, each individual or family has its own living unit, typically owned as a kind of condominium.

At the same time, each is also entitled to share in certain communal areas, which might include a kitchen, laundry, and recreational facilities. Residents are expected to share in such tasks as cleaning and maintaining the common areas. They may or may not also agree to share other responsibilities, such as cooking or childcare. In addition, they are expected to participate in joint decisions about the day-to-day running of the facilities. Every effort is made to promote interaction and cooperation between residents, so that a sense of friendship, and even of family, is inspired.

Cohousing is related, however distantly, to the Utopian community arrangements of the nineteenth and early twentieth centuries as well as to the hippie commune of the 1960s. It differs from them, however, in that participation does not imply a commitment to any philosophical belief or lifestyle.

See also Homeshare.
For further reading McCamant, Kathryn, and Charles Durrett. *Cohousing: A Contemporary Approach to Housing Ourselves*. Berkeley, CA: Ten Speed Press, 1994.

College Athletes (Paying of)

College sports traditionally are regarded as amateur athletic activities. The student athlete—strong of mind and body, and devoting him- or herself both to learning and to performance on the athletic field—is one of the great ideals of American sport.

At many U.S. colleges and universities, however, sports such as football and basketball, which produce significant revenue for their schools, have become big business, and the image of the student athlete has been replaced, to a great extent, by the image of the professional-in-training.

Operating a college athletic program can be extremely costly for an institution of higher learning, but it also can be extremely profitable. Money from the sale of tickets, from endorsements by athletic equipment manufacturers and other advertisers—and, most of all, from television contracts—can add up to millions of dollars for a school that has a successful major sports program.

The more games a team wins, the more money flows to the institution. The income from a successful football or basketball program can pay for many other sports as well. With this incentive, some colleges and universities invest large amounts of resources into developing winning programs in those sports. It is not unusual for a major university to spend millions of dollars on sports facilities and equipment; hundreds of thousands more each year on coaches and support staff; and many thousands more on travel and other miscellaneous expenses required to field successful collegiate sports teams.

Rules for Recruiting Student Athletes

Ultimately, the key factor in the success of any athletic program is the student athlete. For a college to be competitive in any major sport, it must have high-quality athletes. In order to get them, coaches and scouts expend enormous amounts of energy attending high school and junior college games, evaluating players, and recruiting the best of them to come to their school. Coaches typically entice sought-after athletes by emphasizing the opportunities the young man or woman will have at the school, athletically, academically, and socially.

The only significant financial incentive a coach legally is able to offer a prospective student athlete is an athletic scholarship. Such scholarships typically provide for all or part of the student athlete's tuition, as well as a modest stipend to cover dormitory lodging and food. The number of athletic scholarships available to any school's sports program is strictly limited, however, by the National Collegiate Athletic Association (NCAA), to which all major schools belong. As a result, only a comparative handful of student athletes receive them. The only other financial assistance a school legally can offer an athlete is the possibility of a small amount of assistance in the case of a bona fide emergency.

Athletic scholarships can be important inducements to many student athletes, but they are far from lavish, especially when compared to the salaries paid even the least-valued professional football and basketball players. What is more, many scholarship recipients come from economically deprived backgrounds. Even with scholarships to help them, they often find it hard to afford even a rudimentary social life on big school campus.

Faced with this situation, more and more of the best college athletes are driven to leave college early, or to skip going to college at all, in favor of the chance to be paid for playing their sport professionally. This situation, which not only militates against the education of student athletes but hurts the sports programs of the schools they desert, would be alleviated if the schools could pay them for their services. This, however, is strictly forbidden by the NCAA.

NCAA rules forbid colleges to pay athletes for playing, and even to allow them to be paid by others, such as alumni or advertisers, who might be willing to do so. In addition, athletes are forbidden to accept any gifts of value, loans, or other financial assistance from anyone associated with the school. What is more, unlike other students, they are forbidden to work for any outside employer during the school year.

Student-athletes and their supporters argue that the current system is fundamentally unfair. Why, they ask, should athletes, who bring such special benefits to their schools, be treated less fairly than other students, who are free to work at any job they wish while they attend college?

Objections to the Rules

For decades, coaches, administrators—and, most of all, the student athletes themselves—have chaffed at these rules. They particularly object to what they see as the hypocrisy of the schools and of the NCAA itself, both of which reap huge financial benefits from the students' athletic performances while refusing the athletes any share in the financial proceeds. African-American athletes, in particular, have compared the student athlete's position to that of a slave on a plantation: working hard for others' benefit, while receiving no pay for their labors beyond food and shelter.

The critics of the NCAA rules argue that the rules invite corruption. Many cases have come to light of athletes receiving under-the-table payments from alumni or from sports agents who hope to represent them when they leave school, payments that strictly are forbidden by the NCAA. Worst of all, some athletes have taken money from gamblers to shave points or throw games. Critics suspect that the cases which have come to light may be only the tip of a much larger iceberg. Temptations like these, they say, would be much easier to resist if student athletes were paid a reasonable fee for what amounts to their work on the school's behalf.

The critics have suggested a variety of means of remunerating student athletes. Perhaps the simplest would be to treat varsity college sports as a school-related job. Ordinary students are encouraged to work part-time for their schools (in the college cafeteria, for example, or as a tutors or teaching assistants) as an element of their financial aid packages. Why should the hours that student athletes put into their sports not be paid in the same way that these jobs are?

Other proposals include a variety of direct and indirect payments, which could be provided either by the schools, by trust funds established by alumni, or by sponsorship of school teams or athletic events by advertisers. The NCAA and school administrators worry, however, that such payments would compromise the schools. The reputations of student athletes are inextricably entwined with those of the teams and schools they play for. To this argument, the critics of the rules respond that many college sports programs already accept endorsement money. If the schools are free to take the money, why not individual athletes?

Some critics of the hypocrisy they see as inherent in the current system have gone so far as to propose that college athletes need not be students at all. They suggest that the schools could employ athletes to play on what would amount to school-sponsored minor league professional teams, and the competitions would be used as fund-raising events for the schools.

All these suggestions have been rejected by the NCAA and its supporters, who argue that the long and treasured tradition of amateur college athletics must be maintained. They believe that to pay student athletes would destroy that tradition, as would allowing student athletes to accept endorsement money or other payments from outside sources.

Student athletes already receive a great deal for their efforts, the traditionalists say, including not only a college education, but training in their sports, a showcase for their talents, and an improved chance to make the pros someday.

As to corruption, those who wish to keep college athletics amateur argue that the schools would never be able to pay athletes enough to outbid dishonest outside interests. Ultimately, they imply, a student athlete is either honorable or corrupt. The payment of any reasonable sum by a school sports program is not going to have a meaningful effect on the student's character, one way or another.

See also College Sports (Financial Pressures on).

College Preparation

In the 1950s, only about 25 percent of the American school-age population graduated from high school. By the late 1960s, the percentage had risen to over 50 percent, and by 1980 it had reached nearly 66 percent. According to Department of Education statistics, by the early 1990s public high schools in the United States were graduating 71.2 percent of their students. Among the states, the highest graduation rate (91.4 percent in 1994) is in South Dakota, and the lowest (56.7 percent) is in Louisiana.

Despite this statistically impressive progress in graduation rates, the feeling that America's public schools are less than effective has been growing in the latter half of the twentieth century. This belief has been fostered by a variety of reports. Among them have been some highly publicized comparisons of test scores of students around the world. These scores, as presented in the mass media, indicate that American secondary students routinely score lower than secondary school students from several other developed countries on tests that measure mathematical and scientific knowledge.

Other factors leading to the impression of educational failure include publicized complaints from college professors that many of their entering students lack basic writing and mathematical skills and from employers who report difficulty in finding workers with the basic skills needed to do their jobs. These complaints imply that today's high school graduates are less prepared to face educational and vocational challenges than were previous generations of American students.

Defenders of today's secondary education system respond that such evidence of a decline in the preparation of students entering college is misleading. They point out that the challenges faced by modern high school graduates are more varied and technologically complex than those faced by their predecessors and, therefore, that the challenge of preparing them is correspondingly greater, too. To some extent, they say, the apparent decline in the preparation of students entering college may be primarily a reflection of the greater diversity of today's first-year classes compared to those of 20 and 30 years ago. Comparisons of test scores between American and foreign students are essentially unfair, argue the defenders, because American scores reflect the results of tests given to virtually all American secondary students, whereas, in other countries, the tests are administered only to an elite group of students. Too often ignored, they say, is that students from the better American schools score as high, or higher, than those in other countries.

The lower average scores in the United States reflect the great inequalities that exist among local school systems. Although schools in middle-class and wealthy neighborhoods often provide excellent education, those in poor rural areas and the inner cities provide little real education at all. Although

many urban high schools are, in fact, failing their students, this is a reflection not of the inadequacy of modern American pedagogy, but rather of the lack of sufficient resources committed to schools in poor neighborhoods.

As to complaints from employers, these may reflect a growing unwillingness of businesses to undertake apprenticeship and training programs of their own. What is more, the difficulty many employers face in finding employees who are prepared to perform certain jobs may not reflect a shortage of such potential employees so much as business's unwillingness to pay a sufficiently high salary to attract them.

See also Education Summit (1989); Goals 2000 Act; *A Nation at Risk.*

College Sports (Financial Pressures on)

Financial pressures have been growing on many college athletic programs in recent years, threatening their traditional role as amateur sport. Increasingly, athletic programs are being asked to be self-supporting. As a practical matter, this means that a small number of revenue-producing sports—most often, basketball and football—are required to bring in enough money to support the other sports fielded by the school. This, in turn, means that there is more pressure than ever before to produce winning teams in these major sports.

Winning teams draw crowds, as well as lucrative bowl and championship tournament bids and television contracts. They also bring in money from the makers of athletic goods who are eager to have their products identified with high-profile, winning athletic programs. The money brought in by successful sports programs goes not to the athletes but to the schools. Losing teams, on the other hand, bring in little money and may even turn a potential revenue-producing sport into a financial drain.

Other pressures on college sports programs come from alumni who strongly identify with their alma mater's high-profile sports programs. Schools with big-time athletic programs find that the relative success of their football and basketball teams has a significant effect on the level of donations received from alumni.

The financial pressure on major college sports, and especially on football and basketball programs, has so undercut their role as amateur athletics—played for recreation, self-challenge, and competition by student athletes and supported by the schools for the encouragement of school spirit and the development of fair play and character—as to make them into at least quasi-professional sports.

To some extent, these pressures have always existed at certain schools. They have, however, greatly increased in recent decades, spurred by the intensity of the financial pressures on colleges and universities in general. At the same time, the potential rewards for successful programs have escalated, thanks to the rising demand for television sports programming brought about by the popularity of televised sports and the growing numbers of sports television outlets. These pressures and opportunities make it more important than ever for the major sports to produce revenue for their school.

Still another factor has been Title IX and the growing consciousness of the need to provide more opportunities for women to participate in college athletics. Since women's sports rarely produce significant revenues of their own, the addition of more opportunities for women only ex-

pands the financial burden on those sports that do.

See also College Athletes (Paying of).

Concealed Weapons Laws

Concealed weapons have been considered a special problem by people wishing to control gun-related crime by regulating the ownership or use of guns. The ability to carry hidden weapons helps criminals to take their victims by surprise. For this reason, many jurisdictions have passed strict laws limiting the freedom to conceal weapons on one's person.

Handguns and knives are the weapons most commonly concealed. Of the two, handguns are the subject of most concern, because they are potentially so much more destructive and are involved in more deaths.

The regulation of concealed weapons has always been the most common form of gun control in the United States. The very first federal gun control law ruled constitutional was the National Firearms Act of 1934, which regulated and taxed the sale of shotguns with sawed-off barrels. Prohibition-era gangsters favored those weapons because they could easily be hidden beneath their jackets or overcoats.

As of 1995, all but one of the states either forbade or regulated the carrying of concealed handguns. Ten banned them outright, while 19 required those applying to carry a concealed gun to demonstrate a specific need to do so. Twenty other states required a permit to carry a concealed weapon, which would be granted only to those with clean criminal records. Only one, Vermont, allowed state residents to carry concealed handguns without a permit.

Although the national concern over violent crime has led to demands for more gun control laws of all kinds, it has also led to demands for broadening the rights of ordinary citizens to own and carry weapons to defend themselves. As a result, several states have recently liberalized their carrying laws.

In Wisconsin, the proponents of a measure to end the state's ban on concealed weapons have argued that the ability to carry weapons for self-defense is necessary if law-abiding citizens are ever to "take back the streets" from the criminals who seem to infest them.

Those who favor concealed weapons argue that the knowledge that a weapon is at hand with which they can defend their lives or property gives them a unique sense of confidence and security. At the same time, they argue that would-be rapists, muggers, and other street criminals are deterred by the awareness that a potential victim may be carrying a gun.

Proponents of concealed weapons bans, on the other hand, argue that the sense of security derived from carrying such weapons is false. Instead of discouraging criminals, they say, the possibility that potential victims may be armed actually gives criminals a motive to strike preemptively. They will be tempted to kill or otherwise immobilize their victim before he or she will have an opportunity to use whatever weapon they might be carrying. What is more, say the proponents, concealed weapons increase the chance of spontaneous violence in situations which otherwise might pass peacefully and exacerbate the damage that such violence might cause. In the words of one Wisconsin lawmaker, having more weapons on the street could transform "any fender bender into the O.K. Corral."

See also Gun Control.

Confederate Battle Flag

For many white Southerners, the Confederate battle flag remains a proud symbol of the rebel past. The "Stars and Bars" frequently is displayed on flags and banners throughout the South, as well as on countless T-shirts, mock license plates, and bumper stickers. More significantly, it also appears on the state flags of Georgia and Mississippi.

For those whites who treasure it, the familiar design represents such traditional Southern values as honor and devotion to a cause. For many African-Americans, however, it represents a different kind of tradition, a past of slavery and segregation—and not just for black people. The Stars and Bars is a popular emblem of white supremacy, and replicas of the Confederate battle flag are often carried in demonstrations by members of the Ku Klux Klan (KKK) and neo-Nazi groups.

Because of these associations, and because many black people find it offensive, the Confederate flag has become an issue of controversy in many communities. The National Association for the Advancement of Colored People (NAACP) and other black groups are particularly concerned about the use of the symbol by state and local governments and governmental agencies. Bigots, they say, see this as a kind of official endorsement of their racist attitudes, whether or not the state governments mean it that way. There is some objective reason for this claim. The Stars and Bars was added to Georgia's flag in 1956 specifically to express the state's defiance of federal efforts to force the South to integrate.

Tensions over the symbol flared in several places during the early 1990s. Black students on college campuses protested Confederate battle flags being hung from fraternity house windows. State legislators in Montgomery, Alabama, were stopped by the police from tearing down a Confederate flag that had been raised over the state capitol building. And in 1993, Georgia's governor, Zell Miller, asked the state's legislature to remove the Stars and Bars from the state flag. It refused.

Consumer Price Index (CPI)

The most commonly used measure of inflation in the United States is the Consumer Price Index, or CPI. The CPI, calculated by the U.S. Bureau of Labor Statistics, is based on the average current cost of a so-called market basket of goods purchased by typical American consumers. As well as such universal expenditures as food and housing, the contents of the basket include certain more discretionary purchases, such as automobiles and computers. The exact makeup of the basket is redetermined every ten years or so, based on surveys of the spending habits of urban consumers.

The bureau regularly recalculates the CPI and publishes the new figure as a guide to the current state of inflation. Because it is used by government and private institutions alike as the basis for cost-of-living adjustments (COLAs) in wages and other kinds of payments, the CPI is a key factor in the well-being of millions of Americans. Among those whose incomes depend on the index, at least to some extent, are all those who receive Social Security payments, food stamps, or benefits from other federal programs, as well as government employees and unionized workers who have cost-of-living provisions in their labor contracts.

Drawbacks of the CPI

By the mid-1990s, some economists were calling for a revamping of the CPI on the grounds that it tended to overstate current inflation. They argued that it failed to take fully into account the improvement in quality of many of the goods in the basket.

A 1997 automobile might cost more than a 1996 model, but it was also a better car. Only a portion of the increased price was due to inflation; the rest was due to improved features and greater durability. Therefore, the economists reasoned, only that portion actually due to inflation should be counted in the CPI.

Other critics attacked the CPI for understating the effects of inflation on ordinary Americans. They complained that the index was too oriented toward middle-class urban consumers and so failed to reflect the effects of inflation on poor, rural, and suburban households.

Another complaint was that the inclusion in the basket of high-tech and big ticket items, such as personal computers and automobiles, tended to weight the index toward the concerns of the relatively prosperous households which bought such things. What is more, the mostly stable or slow-rising prices of many such goods tended to hold the index down. For less affluent Americans, however, the prices of food, clothing, and shelter, which tend to go up at a faster rate, were much more significant. This was particularly unfortunate, the critics complained, because these less affluent Americans depended most heavily on the CPI to provide them with COLAs.

The process of periodically reconfiguring the basket of goods used to compute the index has been attacked from two very different perspectives. Although some critics complain that the contents of the basket are not redetermined often enough to reflect significant changes in actual spending patterns, others object that readjusting them at all tends to distort the CPI's value as a measure of inflation over extended periods of time.

Defenders of the CPI acknowledge that no single index can accurately reflect the real change in the cost of living for every

American household. The CPI, they say, is not so much a guide to the effects of inflation on particular people as an indication of the current trend in the prices of basic goods. As such, some suggest that another indicator should be found to help determine COLAs.

Contract with America

In the historic election campaign of 1994, Republican candidates for the House of Representatives, led by Representative Newt Gingrich of Georgia, campaigned on what they called their "Contract with America." As much a social manifesto as a political agenda, the contract emphasized conservative social values and concerns. Democrats attacked the document, calling it a "Contract on America." If it were transformed into law, they said, it would gut many government programs vital to the poor and the middle class.

The Contract, as published in an advertisement paid for by the Republican National Committee, read as follows:

We've listened to your concerns, and we hear you loud and clear.
On the first day of Congress, a Republican House will:
Force Congress to live under the same laws as every other American
Cut one out of every three congressional committee staffers
Cut the congressional budget
Then, in the first one hundred days, we will vote on the following 10 bills:
1. Balanced budget amendment and line-item veto: It's time to force the government to live within its means and to restore accountability to the budget in Washington.
2. Stop violent criminals: Let's get tough with an effective, believable and timely death penalty for violent offenders. Let's also reduce crime by building more prisons, making sentences longer and putting more police on the streets.
3. Welfare reform: The government should encourage people to work, *not* to have children out of wedlock.
4. Protect our kids: We must strengthen families by giving parents greater control over education, enforcing child support payments and getting tough on child pornography.
5. Tax cuts for families: Let's make it easier to achieve the American Dream, save money, buy a home and send the kids to college.
6. Strong national defense: We need to ensure a strong national defense by restoring the essential parts of our national security funding.
7. Raise the senior citizens' earning limit: We can put an end to government age discrimination that discourages seniors from working if they choose.
8. Roll back government regulations: Let's slash regulations that strangle small businesses, and let's make it easier for people to invest in order to create jobs and increase wages.
9. Common-sense legal reform: We can finally stop excessive legal claims, frivolous lawsuits, and overzealous lawyers.
10. Congressional term limits: Let's replace career politicians with citizen legislators. After all, politics shouldn't be a lifetime job.

After these 10 bills, we'll tackle issues such as commonsense health care reform, tax rate reductions, and improvements in our children's education.

When the Republicans won the election, taking a majority in both the House and the Senate for the first time in four decades, they claimed a mandate for the "ten commonsense reforms" in the contract, and proceeded to pass several of the provisions, the most important of which were the welfare reforms of 1996, into law. Some provisions, such commonsense legal reform, were beyond the power of Congress. Still others, notably the call for Congressional term limits, were abandoned, at least at the federal level.

Corporal Punishment by Parents

American parents have used the infliction of physical pain to punish children since colonial times. Corporal punishment was not, apparently, a common practice among Native American parents prior to the arrival of Europeans in North America, however. Rather, it seems to have been brought to America as a primary tool of child rearing by the Puritans of New England. The Puritans considered corporal punishment not only a useful way of enforcing parental and community rules, but a moral necessity. They believed that they were literally beating the devil out of rebellious young people.

Physical punishment of almost any kind—including spanking on the buttocks, paddling, pinching, slapping or hitting with an open hand or fist, striking with a stick, switch, or belt—was widely considered the right, if not the duty, of parents and teachers alike, well into the twentieth century.

Although not all parents used corporal punishment, and few used the most extreme forms of it, the decision whether or not to use such methods was considered to be a family matter, and not a matter for social concern. In recent decades, however,

an expanded awareness of the dangers of child abuse has brought about a profound change in public attitudes toward the physical punishment of children. Very few parents today would find it acceptable to hit a child with a closed fist or with a stick. What is more, the notion that individual parents should be left to decide for themselves the amount of physical punishment to inflict on their children has been abandoned. Indeed, when medical practitioners find evidence of actual wounds or bruising on children, such as those inflicted by the more extreme forms of corporal punishment, they are required to report that evidence to legal authorities. This does not mean, however, that corporal punishment, as such, is frowned upon by most Americans.

Spanking has the sanction of tradition behind it. A great many of today's parents (and perhaps most of today's grandparents) were spanked when they were children and grew up thinking of the practice as a standard method of discipline. Along with such variations as paddling and slapping across the cheek with an open hand, spanking remains a common disciplinary tool in American families. Even many parents who use it sparingly on their own children, or decline to use it all, refuse to accept the proposition that they themselves were mistreated or abused when their parents used it on them.

Spanking is, however, significantly less common than it used to be. According to polling data collected by the National Committee to Prevent Child Abuse, 64 percent of parents in 1988 acknowledged using some form of physical discipline. By 1994, that percentage had dropped to 49 percent. It was the first time in the poll's history that fewer parents had used physical punishment than had refrained from it. There are no comparable figures from before the mid-1980s when the poll was initiated, but it is probable that there had been more use of corporal punishment in earlier decades.

Spanking and the Law

At least five nations—Austria, Finland, Sweden, Denmark, and Norway—forbid all physical punishment of children. The United States, however, does not; nor do the governments of most individual states. Although all states ban child abuse, no state forbids parents to use spankings or other presumably moderate forms of physical punishment on their own children. (Most states do forbid foster parents from doing so, however.)

The line between acceptable discipline and abuse is becoming increasingly hard to draw, however. Several parents have suffered the force of the changing attitudes toward corporal punishment. A Florida woman was taken into police custody and had her child temporarily taken away from her for slapping the misbehaving youngster in a supermarket. In Maryland, a father who was a member of the Parent-Teacher Association was formally investigated for child abuse (although eventually cleared) after his son's finger was injured during the boy's attempt to ward off a spanking.

The modern shift in attitude toward corporal punishment has been sparked by the efforts of psychologists, pediatricians, and children's rights advocates, who argue that it is an outmoded, ineffective, and ultimately self-defeating practice. Physical violence, they say, sends exactly the wrong message to children. Rather than teaching them respect for their parents and a positive desire to behave properly, it teaches them only fear, and a desire not to be caught.

Because it is in itself a form of violence, some psychologists consider it a particularly inappropriate means of punishing violent behavior. Children who are punished for hurting other children or animals by adults who strike them are not being taught that it is wrong to bully or abuse. Instead, they are being taught that might makes right: Adults, who are bigger and stronger than they are, are free to do to them what they had been doing to others weaker than themselves.

Researcher Murray Straus, of the Family Research Laboratory at the University of New Hampshire, has collected evidence suggesting that "spare the rod and spoil the child" may be a fallacy. Children who are physically punished, he maintains, have higher rates of juvenile delinquency and drug abuse than those who are not. What's more, they grow up to be more aggressive, both toward members of their own family and toward outsiders, than those who are disciplined in nonviolent ways.

The root of much of the opposition to corporal punishment is a fundamental aversion to the infliction of pain on children. Opponents of the practice find it particularly ironic that it should be acceptable for adults to strike children, when adults are forbidden to strike each other. Prohibitions are particularly strong against adults—such as employers or military officers—who strike those who are under their authority. Prison officials are forbidden to use physical punishment against even their most dangerous and unruly prisoners. How then, the opponents of corporal punishment ask, can society condone administering such punishments on small children?

See also Child Abuse; Corporal Punishment in Schools.
For further reading Dobson, James. *The New Dare to Discipline*. Wheaton, IL: Tyndale House, 1992.
Resenthal, John K. *To Spank or Not to Spank: A*

Parent's Handbook. Kansas City: Andrews & McMeel, 1994.

Straus, Murray. *Beating the Devil Out of Them: Corporal Punishment in American Families and Its Effects on Children*. New York: Free Press, 1994.

Corporal Punishment in Schools

Corporal punishment was once a standard form of discipline in American schools. Spanking, paddling, striking the back of a recalcitrant student's hand with a ruler, and switching across the buttocks with a branch or other object were all common practices, which many teachers considered indispensable to maintaining order in the classroom.

Since the 1960s, the attitudes of parents, teachers, and school administrators alike have turned increasingly against the use of such punishments. This change in attitude was sparked by a variety of factors, including complaints from outraged parents, growing concern over lawsuits, and an increased awareness of the damaging effects on children of physical abuse.

Some opponents of corporal punishment in the classroom believe that any form of physical violence against students, however carefully calibrated or restrained, is morally unacceptable, potentially dangerous, and psychologically damaging. Others have no objection to corporal punishment per se, but insist that the decision of when and how to apply it should be solely a parent's prerogative.

Among the organizations which have taken a stand against corporal punishment in the schools are a number of educational, parental, and medical organizations, including the American Medical Association (AMA) and the National Parent Teacher Association (NPTA). As of 1995, paddling, slapping, and other forms of physical discipline were banned in 29 states. Such practices were legal in 13 other states, as well as in some jurisdictions within the other 11.

In the 1977 case of *Ingraham* v. *Wright*, the U.S. Supreme Court upheld the provisional right of a school to discipline a student physically. The Court noted, however, that if such a punishment were later shown to be unreasonable or excessive, the victim could sue.

For further reading Hyman, Ronald T., and Charles H. Rathbone. *Corporal Punishment in Schools*. Nos. 48 and 48A. Topeka, KS: Nolpe, 1993.
Mercurio, Joseph. *Caning: Educational Rite and Tradition*. Syracuse, NY: Syracuse University Press, 1971.

Corporal Punishment of Criminals

In 1994, a young man from Ohio named Michael Fay was found guilty of vandalism by a court in Singapore and sentenced to receive six lashes. The punishment, which was not remarkable by Singapore's standards, would have been illegal in the United States.

The thought that an American citizen was to be punished in such a way by a foreign government upset U.S. officials, who protested the sentence. The American public, however, was less concerned. In fact, approximately half of those polled on the issue not only agreed with the sentence, but favored the use of similar punishments in the United States.

Following the publicity over the Fay case, bills were introduced in the Tennessee state legislature to mandate the public caning of people convicted of certain misdemeanors. The corporal punishment, which was to be carried out on the steps of local courthouses, was to be in addition to, not in place of, jail sentences and fines.

The Legal Question

From the time of the founding of the United States, federal crimes have been punished by fines or imprisonment, or by some combination of the two, rather than by corporal punishment. Corporal punishment was an available punishment in some states, however, well into the twentieth century. (The last state to actually whip a criminal was Delaware in 1952.)

Forms of corporal punishment have also been used to enforce discipline within some American jails and prisons. In the 1978 case of *Hutto* v. *Finney*, however, the U.S. Supreme Court ruled that authorities must refrain from "the wanton and unnecessary infliction of pain" on prisoners.

The rejection of corporal punishment as a sentencing option, as well as the total prohibition of torture in the United States, are based on the Eighth Amendment's ban on "cruel and unusual punishments." (Torture is also forbidden by several international agreements to which the United States is a party.) Despite this ban, many Americans continue to favor the reintroduction of flogging and other forms of corporal punishment, in hopes that they would be a more effective deterrent to crime than present punishments.

Objections to Corporal Punishment

Opponents of corporal punishment argue that it is wrong for the state deliberately to inflict pain on anyone, whether criminal or not. They contend that the infliction of pain by the government is a tyrannical practice, contrary to the best American moral and legal traditions. What is more, they say, there is no reason to believe that corporal punishment would be any more effective as a deterrent than other punishments.

See also Cruel and Unusual Punishment.
For further reading Newman, Graeme. *Just and*

Painful: A Case for the Corporal Punishment of Criminals. Albany, NY: Harrow & Heston, 1995.

Corporate Responsibility

In capitalist societies like the United States, the relationship between private corporations and society at large is bound to be a complicated and controversial one. Business plays a vital role in the prosperity of any nation, and every government wants the nation's business enterprises, whether they are private or public, to succeed. Most governments, including that of the United States, subsidize business in various ways and promote the sales of internally produced products and services abroad. For their part, private businesses usually supply not only the bulk of the jobs for the nation's citizens, but the bulk of the taxes to the nation's coffers as well, whether they do so directly through corporate taxes or indirectly through the income, sales, and other taxes paid by their employees.

The benefits corporations provide to the general society are essentially inadvertent. They rarely are brought about by a corporation's sense of responsibility toward the nation or toward society. Instead, they come about indirectly, as uncalculated results of the companies' operations. The extent of these benefits—and whether or not a given company will continue to provide them—is subject to business considerations which often have nothing to do with the welfare of society at large.

Certain kinds of corporate responsibility have been legislated by government, however. Federal and state laws regulate a wide variety of practices affecting the health and safety of workers and consumers alike. Antifraud laws limit commercial trickery, while environmental legislation limits the damage businesses can do to the environment they share with the world.

The Personal Responsibility of Business Owners

Conscientious businesspeople have always been concerned about the effects their business decisions may have on employees and the greater community. Beyond that, however, the question remains whether private businesses, and the owners of those businesses, actually owe more to the society in which they operate than obedience to its laws and, if so, what that further responsibility might be. That question has been a subject of serious debate in the United States at least since the 1880s, when the steel magnate Andrew Carnegie wrote his famous essay, "Wealth."

In the nineteenth century, however, the debate centered around the personal responsibility of a small but enormously wealthy group of businessmen who virtually controlled American industry. People such as Cornelius Vanderbilt and John D. Rockefeller became known as "robber barons" because of the almost total lawlessness with which they accumulated their wealth as well as the ostentatiousness with which they spent it. The majority of these men seemed to assume that they had little or no social responsibility. Others, including Carnegie, believed that people of wealth had a duty to serve a greater social end. Carnegie's prescription, however, was not for the companies controlled by these wealthy men to consider the public welfare in their business decisions, but rather that wealthy business leaders should administer the profits they accumulated for the benefit of society as a whole. The best example of the kind of philanthropy prescribed by Carnegie was his own endowment of public libraries in cities across the country.

Carnegie believed that an employer's obligation to his employees was limited to the need "to provide moderately for the legitimate wants of those dependent on him." Other employers, however, did feel a special obligation, not only toward their employees, but toward the communities in which they operated. To some extent, at least, they did attempt to take the employees' and communities' interests into account when making business decisions.

This sense of personal obligation was fairly common among business owners in the early and mid-twentieth century. However, it has gradually been dying out, thanks partly to the dramatic changes that have taken place in business ownership over the past several decades.

Even so, some corporations do retain a desire to be regarded as responsible corporate citizens of the communities in which they operate. At least since the community development movement of the 1920s, many private companies have hoped to be seen as partners with the local political structure in promoting the well-being of the community, and to some extent that is still true today. Business executives routinely join local clubs and civic organizations that work within the community. In most cities it is expected that successful local businesses will help to sponsor civic projects and to promote the communities of which they are a part. Ultimately, this is seen not only as benefiting the community, but the company as well. The goodwill of the community can be an important asset.

The Effects of Changes in Corporate Ownership

At one time, the ownership and control of most businesses, including many very large ones, was in the hands of one or only a few individuals. The owners often lived in the communities in which the main operations of the business were located. This is rarely true today. Few large modern businesses are owned by single individuals, or even by a relatively small number of partners. Instead, most major corporations are owned by thousands of absentee stockholders, the great majority of whom have no stake in the communities in which the company operates and play no part in the day-to-day decisions that govern the company's policies and activities. For these reasons, most stockholders have little sense of personal responsibility for the effects those decisions have, either on the company's employees or on the communities in which it does business.

Management of most corporations is in the hands of corporate officers, even the most senior of whom are, in effect, employees themselves. As management sees it, the primary obligation is neither toward the community at large nor toward the company's employees, but rather toward the employers, the stockholders. This is not merely a perceived obligation, but a legal one. Management can be sued if it behaves in ways that work to the disadvantage of the company's shareholders.

Management's obligation to shareholders is understood almost entirely in economic terms. Modern management has come to believe that its major responsibility, if not its only one, is to maximize the dividends the company pays to the shareholders or, in the case of companies that pay no dividends, to maximize the price of the company's stock so that the shareholders can, if they wish, sell their shares at a profit.

This concentration on short-term profitability has contributed to many trends that have been criticized as demonstrating a decline in the sense of corporate responsibility. These include such practices as moving business operations out of communities that have come to depend upon them, as well as internal company reorganizing that results in the drastic reductions of company workforces and the dismissal of many loyal and competent employees.

The apparent decline in the sense of corporate responsibility has been accepted as inevitable—or even economically necessary—by many American economists and politicians. Others, however, have sought ways to reverse it. One inventive effort, tried by New York state among others, has been an amendment to corporation law, requiring companies incorporated in that state to consider the welfare of the broader community when making key business decisions. In this way, New York has tried to present a countervailing force to the legal pressure on corporate management to concentrate exclusively on maximizing profits for shareholders.

See also Charity; Downsizing; Gospel of Wealth; Social Darwinism; Worker Layoffs in the 1980s and 1990s.

For further reading Castro, Barry. *Business and Society: A Reader in the History, Sociology and Ethics of Business.* New York: Oxford University Press, 1996. Council on Economic Priorities Staff, et al. *Rating America's Corporate Conscience.* Reading, MA: Addison-Wesley, 1987. *New York Times. The Downsizing of America.* New York: Times Books, 1996.

Counterculture

The term *counterculture* came into use in the 1960s to describe some of the most significant social and creative developments of that time.

In its most limited sense, the counterculture was a political movement, made up of radical young leftists who rebelled against what they saw as a traditional culture built on the two evils of materialism and imperialism. The most extreme elements of this movement included groups like the Weathermen, who went into hiding in order to conduct violent guerrilla campaigns against what they referred to as the "power structure," or the "establishment."

In a more general sense, the term counterculture referred to the whole range of lifestyles, fashions, and attitudes of the significant minority of young people who rejected the tastes and values of mainstream America. In addition to left-wing radicals, they included the mostly nonpolitical hippies, as well as other young people with varying interests in political affairs.

Broadly speaking, the counterculture was identified with sexual and political freedom, experimentation with psychedelic drugs, anti-Vietnam activism, the civil rights movement, long hair, and, to lesser extent, artistic avant-gardism.

Counterculture Values

Philosophically, the counterculture drew heavily although very selectively on *Walden* and other works by Henry David Thoreau and on works by Ralph Waldo Emerson, as well as on such contemporary works as *Living the Good Life* and *The Whole Earth Catalog*. The musical anthems of the counterculture came from rock, urban folk, and protest songs. Among the most representative were Bob Dylan's "Blowin' in the Wind" and "The Times They Are a-Changing." The political elements of the counterculture were influenced by the thoughts of the economist Karl Marx and the anticolonialism of the West Indian Frantz Fanon.

As *counter* suggests, however, the counterculture was defined more by what it rejected than by what it embraced. Chief among the values rejected were excessive materialism, jingoism, conformity, and traditional sexual morality. Elements of the counterculture also rejected much of modern technology and expressed a desire to live in harmony with nature and independently from organized society. Theodore Kazinski, the reclusive, antitechnology suspect arrested in the Unabomber case, can be seen as a 1990s descendant of the Weatherman faction of the counterculture.

Counterculture publications ranged from mimeographed instructions for making Molotov cocktails, to the underground newspapers that flourished on or around most college campuses, to the professional quality journalism of the slick magazine *Ramparts*.

The Generational Split

The counterculture personified a real conflict that existed within American society beginning in the 1960s. Its development was seen as largely generational—that is, as the rejection by a significant part of a younger generation of the values of their parents. And in reality, although some exponents of the counterculture were middle-aged or even older, most were young adults in their late teens and twenties.

Many of these young people honestly despised what they saw as the pervasive greed, racism, cultural intolerance, and closed-mindedness of their parents' generation. They also opposed what they saw as the war-loving imperialism of the nation's foreign policy, as exhibited by its involvement in Vietnam, Latin America, and elsewhere in the Third World. Where most other Americans saw the Cold War as a struggle for the survival of the Free World, the counterculture saw it as a profit-making scheme for the military-industrial complex.

Believing that they had been misled by their elders about virtually everything from the true nature of American society to the war in Vietnam, the counterculture distrusted not only the U.S. government but authority of all kinds. A popular saying among the young was "never trust anyone over 30."

For their part, most mainstream Americans looked upon the counterculture with a mixture of bemusement, anger, and disgust. Many identified the movement not with idealism, but with irresponsible hedonism, drugs, sex, and a lack of patriotism.

The hostility some Americans felt toward the counterculture was so intense as to be irrational. This hostility was reflected in a famous scene of a highly regarded counterculture motion picture, *Easy Rider,* which was directed by Dennis Hopper and released in 1969. The film dealt with two bikers riding across country to consummate a major drug deal. In the movie's violent climax, the two hippies are first ridiculed and then shot from their bikes and killed by two bigots in a pickup truck.

Exploration and Experimentation

Although the counterculture included a variety of more or less organized groups, such as the Students for a Democratic Society, the counterculture was in no way an organized movement in itself. It had no formal, or even informal, membership, standards, or coherent philosophy. Instead, participants in the counterculture tended to celebrate individuality and reject most forms of social organization. A popular piece of counterculture advice was to "do your own thing."

Many exponents of the counterculture explored, however superficially, a variety of religious beliefs and experiences. Some were attracted to the more mystical elements of Christianity, while others were drawn to such Eastern religious philosophies as Zen Buddhism. Some of the more adventurous traveled to Asia to study under Eastern masters in hopes of finding "enlightenment." In doing so, they were following the lead of a number of artists, including members of the British rock group the Beatles, who went to India.

The counterculture was heavily identified with the use of psychedelic drugs, most notably marijuana and LSD, the latter of which was legal in the United States until 1966. Although some proponents of the counterculture took such drugs for pleasure, others took them in the belief that such drugs were "mind-expanding," and would lead them to deeper philosophical and artistic insights. The garishly colored psychedelic art that sprang up in hippie neighborhoods during the 1960s was initially the product of visual distortions and hallucinations caused by such drugs. The guru of this kind of drug use was a Harvard professor named Timothy Leary, who called on the young "to turn on, tune in, and drop out."

Drug use was by no means a universal feature of counterculture life, however. Many of the more politically earnest young rebels rejected drugs as escapist distractions from the serious business of forming a new society, while some of the more philosophically idealistic rejected them as incompatible with living in harmony with nature.

Particularly when it came to the heavy use of drugs, the counterculture was a study in contrasts: high ideals set against a grubby, and sometimes tragic, reality.

Communal Rituals

Even while it extolled the value of individuality, the counterculture embraced ideals of community and brotherhood. These ideals were celebrated not only in the communal living arrangements of many young people, but in at least two distinctive counterculture rites: the happening and the outdoor concert.

Happenings were occasions (sometimes, although not always, announced in advance) in which people gathered to witness, and/or to participate in, a creative experience. Such events might take place at a coffee shop, at someone's apartment, or even on the street. Communal paintings, improvised poems, and individual performance art might all be elements of a happening.

The largest and most enduring rite of the counterculture was the outdoor concert. Young fans of rock and/or folk music would gather, not only to listen to their favorite music, but to celebrate their community with others who shared their enthusiasm. Perhaps even more than today, such concerts were a kind of statement for the young who attended them, not only a way for young people to proclaim their personal tastes, but a means of affirming community with others who felt the same way.

For many observers, the best and the worst aspects of the counterculture were symbolized by two rock concerts that took place near the end of the decade of the 1960s. The first was the famous "celebration of peace and love" known as Woodstock. The second, which came to represent the darker side of the counterculture, was the disastrous Rolling Stones concert held a few months later at Altamont, California.

Aftermath

In retrospect, the counterculture can be seen as a manifestation of many of the same social and political forces that have resulted in other Utopian movements, before and since.

Young people of the 1960s gravitated to communal lifestyles and radical left-wing politics partly out of idealism and partly out of a desire for personal gratification. Some were drawn by the desire to make the world a better place, some by a desire to explore their own consciousness, and some by the desire for free love and cheap drugs.

Although a few continued to follow these desires into their mid-lives, most were eventually reintegrated into mainstream American culture and are today indistinguishable from their middle-aged contemporaries.

Many manifestations of the counterculture were eventually embraced by the mainstream and became part of it. Much of the music of the counterculture, from that of Bob Dylan to that of Janis Joplin, has become accepted as classic. The psychedelic art that hippies once used to decorate their vans is a major influence on today's graphic art.

More importantly, the attitudes espoused by the counterculture—personal tolerance, distrust of government and big business, and the willingness to explore new ideas, experiences, and lifestyles—have infused society. Even today, some Americans are grateful to the counterculture for helping to open up American society and to free it from the puritanism, narrowness, and bigotry of the past. Others blame it for what they regard as a decline in American values, a development which they believe was brought about largely by the counterculture's attack on authority, espousal of the sexual revolution, and the widespread use of drugs.

See also Altamont; Woodstock.
For further reading Brown, Joe David, editor. *The Hippies*. New York: Time, 1967.
Wolf, Leonard, editor. *Voices from the Love Generation*. Boston: Little, Brown, 1968.

CPI
See Consumer Price Index.

Crack Cocaine in the Black Community (Alleged CIA Involvement)

Crack is a crystallized form of the drug cocaine that has become especially popular in the black community. Its popularity is due primarily to two factors: First, it gives a similar kick to that of freebased cocaine, without the physical dangers of the freebasing process; and second, it is remarkably cheap compared to other equally potent illegal drugs.

Crack began to appear in African-American neighborhoods in Los Angeles and elsewhere in the early 1980s. It was soon being blamed by some alarmed residents for an acceleration of the breakdown of family life in the black community, along with such problems as rising illegitimacy and juvenile crime. A suspicion arose that crack's sudden appearance in their neighborhoods, and the devastating effects it was having there, was not accidental. It had arrived too quickly and been too cheap and too easily accessible. Some African-Americans came to believe that these things had to be the result of some kind of white plot against them. Adding to their concerns was what seemed to be the low level of crack use in the white community, where powder cocaine continued to be the form of choice of the drug.

Most whites, as well as many African-Americans, dismissed such suspicions as wildly far-fetched. The overwhelming majority of drug dealers in the black neighborhoods were black themselves. Even if the cocaine they sold on the streets had initially been sold to them by whites, there was no good reason to believe that such sales were anything other than business deals between criminals.

In the fall of 1996, however, a story published in the *San Jose* (CA) *Mercury* newspaper gave some credence to the long-held suspicions. In the story, which was published in several parts, journalist Gary Webb described what he claimed were the origins of the crack epidemic in the black neighborhoods of South Central Los Angeles.

According to Webb, the epidemic originated with the civil war in Nicaragua in the 1980s. Following the victory of the left-wing revolution there, a group of right-wing rebels known as the Contras began a guerrilla campaign against the new Sandinista government. The Contras were strongly supported by the U.S. administration of President Ronald Reagan. When the president was forbidden by Congress to supply the Contras with weapons, elements of the government—including the CIA and a separate operation run out of the White House by Marine Lt. Col. Oliver North—looked for ways to do so clandestinely.

Whether acting independently or in concert with the CIA, the Contras began to traffic in cocaine, for which Nicaragua had long been a major transit point. As Webb told it, the Contras' search for a market led to a drug ring in San Francisco, which in turn found its main customers in the Crips and Bloods street gangs of South Central Los Angeles. The cocaine was turned into crack to make it easily affordable to the relatively poor residents of black neighborhoods.

The newspaper series did much to fuel African-American suspicions. If the CIA supported the Contras, was it not reasonable to assume that it also supported their drug dealings, or, at the very least, turned a blind eye to them? And was the choice of a market for the drug simply coincidental? Would the CIA have been willing to look the other way if Contra-supplied drugs had been going into suburban white communities, instead of into the inner cities?

Webb's series created enormous controversy. Other newspapers, including *The Washington Post*, questioned the accuracy of the information it contained. The CIA—which traditionally refuses to comment on any charges made about its operations—rushed to deny any connection with drug trafficking in the black community. The CIA's top official, Director John Deutch, took the unprecedented step of traveling to

South Central Los Angeles to deny the charges in person and to answer the questions of angry South Central residents. Several ex-Contra leaders were called before a U.S. Senate committee, where they, too, denied any connection with cocaine smuggling. Few African-Americans were willing to accept such denials at face value.

Although the *San Jose Mercury*'s editors later acknowledged some problems with aspects of the story, Webb continued to stand by the accuracy of its central points.

Creationism versus Evolution in the Public Schools

Creationism is the belief that the universe and all living things were deliberately created by a Supreme Being. More specifically, the term is used to refer to the belief, held by fundamentalist Christians, that God created the heavens and the earth in seven days, as described in the Book of Genesis.

The literal truth of Genesis was taken for granted by teachers and students alike in many nineteenth- and early twentieth-century American schools. By the mid-nineteenth century, however, scientific developments were throwing doubt on the accuracy of the biblical account. Whereas biblical scholars had determined that creation must have taken place only a few thousand years before, anthropologists claimed that people had lived on earth long before that, while geologists insisted that the planet had existed for millions of years before the advent of human beings.

Most disturbing of all to creationists was the theory of evolution that the naturalist Charles Darwin had espoused in his landmark book *On the Origin of Species* (1859). Darwin suggested that animal species did not remain constant, but evolved over thousands and even millions of years according to the workings of a process called natural selection.

Fundamentalists—who consider Genesis as a simple, straightforward description of historic events—regard evolution as totally inconsistent with the biblical account, which they interpret as meaning that God created all animal species at more or less the same time. The idea that the human species itself had evolved, perhaps from the same stock as apes, was particularly offensive to many nineteenth- and early twentieth-century Christians. In Christian pulpits and in the popular press, Darwin's views were simplified and mocked as claiming that human beings were descended from monkeys.

State Efforts to Prevent the Teaching of Evolution

The dispute between creationism and evolution came to center largely on the public schools. Which of the two bitterly opposed views of the origins of human life and of the universe should young Americans be taught? Although the scientific community favored evolution, much of the American public was made uneasy by a theory which challenged their religious presumptions.

Christian parents worried that their children's faith would be corrupted by such ungodly teachings. They were supported in their distaste for evolution by school and state authorities in heavily fundamentalist areas of the country, particularly in the South.

In 1925, the legislature of Tennessee passed a law making it illegal to teach evolution in schools in that state. In a nationally publicized trial, a schoolteacher named John T. Scopes was found guilty of breaking that law and fined $100. Although the state appellate court later overturned Scopes's conviction on a technicality, the court did rule that the law forbidding the teaching of evolution was constitutional.

In a sense, however, the Tennessee law was already an anachronism. Evolution was winning the debate within educational circles. Only two more states would choose to join Tennessee in outlawing the teaching of evolution.

Reasons for the Triumph of Evolution

Several factors accounted for the decline in the support for creationism in American schools. The most basic of these was the secularization of American society, which had begun in the nineteenth century and which continued throughout most of the twentieth century. Like much else in American society, education, which had once been closely identified with religious instruction, was becoming an increasingly secular activity. A new breed of teachers, educated in secular universities and state teacher's colleges, tended to find Darwin more persuasive than the Book of Genesis, at least when it came to understanding the natural sciences.

Other factors working against creationism included a growing judicial emphasis on the separation of church and state and a decline in the political and cultural power of rural America, much of which was fundamentalist, in relation to urban America, which was not.

Then as now, not all Christians opposed the theory of evolution. Many, in fact, reevaluated their own beliefs in light of the growing body of scientific information. As evolution became widely accepted inside the scientific community and among the public in general, even theologians and clergymen began to modify their teachings to make them compatible with the new scientific evidence. Although they continued to insist upon a conscious creation of the universe, they suggested that the process may have been longer and more complicated than a literal interpretation of the biblical account had led them to believe. Even many progressive clergy continued to stress, however, that Darwin's theories remained theories that had not been proven beyond all doubt.

By the mid-twentieth century, most Americans seemed to have accepted the proposition that creationism was a religious rather than a scientific belief and, therefore, an inappropriate doctrine to be taught in a public school. Evolution, on the other hand, was considered a scientific theory. The U.S. Supreme Court gave indirect support to this distinction when, in the case of *Epperson* v. *Arkansas* in 1968, it overturned an Arkansas law forbidding the teaching of "the theory or doctrine that mankind ascended or descended from a lower order of animals." The Court ruled the Arkansas law unconstitutional because it was designed to support a "particular religion['s]" interpretation of the Bible.

The Continuing Debate

Those Americans who have no stake in orthodox religion, or else no trouble reconciling the teachings of the Bible with the discoveries of science, find the furor over creationism and evolution insignificant. However, for others—including parents and educators on both sides of the argument—the debate goes to the core of their deepest beliefs.

Fundamentalists object to any attempt to deny the account of creation given in the Book of Genesis. They especially protest such attempts by public schools, which they see as efforts to contaminate their children with what they consider to be a pernicious and atheistic doctrine.

Atheists and agnostics, on the other hand, equally object to the teaching of creationism, which they consider to be unscientific and superstitious nonsense. In a sense, parents on both sides of the debate have the same complaint. They object to the state taking advantage of its power to force children to attend school to indoctrinate them in what their parents consider to be false beliefs.

Although many parents continued to chafe at the teaching of evolution, creationism had become all but dormant as a serious educational issue until the 1980s, when the Christian Right began its political resurgence in the United States. Once again, fundamentalists sought ways to legally ensure that the instruction their children received in public schools would be consistent with what they were taught in their homes and churches.

In 1981, the Louisiana legislature passed the Creationism Act, prohibiting the teaching of evolution in Louisiana schools unless creationism was taught along with it. The act attempted to meet the Supreme Court's stated objections to the Arkansas law by treating creationism and evolution in the same way. The U.S. Supreme Court, however, struck down the Creationism Act in the case of *Edwards* v. *Aqillard* (1987), ruling that it violated the Establishment Clause of the First Amendment.

Edwards may have settled the legal question over the teaching of evolution, at least for a time, but it did nothing to quiet the political and cultural debate. Following the decision, there was a dramatic increase in the political power of the religious right in the United States, particularly on the local level. Activist fundamentalists were elected to school boards in several districts around the country. Together with like-minded parents, they pressed educators to downplay or end the teaching of evolution and to include instruction in what they called creation science.

Although evolution continues to be the primary theory taught in science classes around the country, some educators have bowed to the pressure of creationists to the extent of including instruction in creationism as well, while others do their best to avoid discussing the issue at all.

See also Religion in the Schools; Scopes Case.

Crime
See Crimes against Women; Juvenile Crime; Violent Crime; Violent Crime Control and Law Enforcement Act (1994).

Crime, Juvenile
See Juvenile Crime.

Crimes against Women
Approximately 43 percent of all victims of violent crime in the United States are female. The most commonly reported violent crimes against women are assault (including battering), robbery, rape, and murder, in that order.

Of the approximately 4.7 million women who fell victim to violence in a recent year, according to the Bureau of Justice Statistics of the U.S. Justice Department, approximately one-third were attacked by family members or others with whom they were intimate; a little more than one-third were attacked by an acquaintance; while only about three in every ten fell victim to a stranger. In comparison, only about 5 percent of male victims were attacked by intimates; approximately half were attacked by acquaintances, the rest by strangers.

Although women are disproportionately less likely than men to fall victim to violence in relation to their numbers in the population, they are disproportionately more likely to be victimized in relation to their own attitudes and social behaviors. Because men are more likely to engage in violence themselves, one might assume that they would be more likely to be victims of violence as well. However, although women make up only a little more than one out of every ten perpetrators of reported violence, they make up more than four out of every ten victims of it.

Of the more than half-million suspects arrested for violent crimes in 1991, only 58,343 were women. The disparity is considerably less extreme when it comes to murder, however. Although nearly one-fourth of all murder victims are female, women also make up approximately 14 percent of all people convicted of murder in the United States.

The issue of violence against women was brought to the forefront of public attention by the murder of Nicole Brown Simpson in 1994. The subsequent criminal and civil trials of her ex-husband, O. J. Simpson, showed that she had been the victim of beatings by Simpson years before her death. The increased concern over the issue in the mid-1990s led Congress to pass the Violence Against Women Act, which included programs to encourage the arrest of people suspected of domestic violence and to provide training for police, judges, and others in the law enforcement and judicial communities in dealing with victims and perpetrators of such crimes.

See also Domestic Violence; Spouse Abuse.
For further reading Gelles, Richard J., and Denileen Leseke. *Current Controversies on Family Violence*. Thousand Oaks, CA: Sage, 1993. Koss, Mary, et al. *No Safe Haven: Male Violence against Women at Home, at Work, and in the Community*. Washington, DC: American Psychological Association, 1994.

Cruel and Unusual Punishment

The Eighth Amendment to the Constitution of the United States forbids the infliction of "cruel and unusual punishment" —a concept that is central to the legal debate over a variety of penal issues, the most important of which is capital punishment.

Several rulings by the U.S. Supreme Court have established the principle that whether a punishment is cruel and unusual may depend on more than the nature of the punishment itself. Although certain punishments—such as torture or the amputation of limbs—might be cruel and unusual in themselves, the acceptability of others depends on their appropriateness. The punishment must be proportionate to the crime. For example, a five-year prison sentence may be perfectly appropriate for a burglary, but it would be a cruel and unusual penalty for driving without a headlight. Certain extremely harsh punishments—including death—might be cruel and unusual, even for most homicides, but constitutionally acceptable for a particularly heinous murder.

The definition of what constitutes cruel and unusual punishment can change over time. What may be acceptable to one generation may be unacceptable to another. As early as 1910, the U.S. Supreme Court established in the case of *Weems* v. *U.S.* that the definition of "cruel and unusual" had "an expansive and vital character"; that is, it needed to be reinterpreted in the light of changing public and judicial attitudes.

Punishments must also be considered in relation to the circumstances under which they are enforced. In the 1972 case of *Furman* v. *Georgia*, the U.S. Supreme Court struck down all the death penalty laws in the United States. The court found that there was no consistency in the standards under which the death penalty was being imposed, and that, as a result, the death penalty was being applied in a capricious manner. The effect of this was so discriminatory, according to the Court, that the actual infliction of the death penalty amounted to cruel and unusual punishment.

In the wake of the *Furman* decision, several states set out to write new, consistent capital punishment statutes. Four years later, the Supreme Court ruled that death sentences carried out under several of these new laws would not constitute cruel and unusual punishment.

See also Corporal Punishment of Criminals; Death Penalty; Death Penalty (Controversies); Death Penalty (Major Supreme Court Decisions). **For further reading** Meltsner, Michael. *Cruel and Unusual: The Supreme Court and Capital Punishment.* New York: Random House, 1973. Sheleff, Leon Shaskolski. *Ultimate Penalties: Capital Punishment, Life Imprisonment, Physical Torture.* Columbus: Ohio State University Press, 1987.

Curfews

Rising juvenile crime rates in the 1980s and early 1990s led many U.S. cities to introduce curfews for young people. A high proportion of street crimes, both by and against juveniles, are committed at night. By keeping the potential perpetrators and victims off the streets during those high-crime hours, curfews attempt to reduce the opportunities for such crimes to occur.

The specifics of curfews vary from one community to another. Some are imposed only on certain days of the week, or vary according to the time of the year. Exceptions to curfew hours are often made for young people who are accompanied by their parents, those attending certain adult-organized events, and those on their way to or from work. Typically, teens found on the streets after the declared hours are stopped and questioned by police. If they do not meet one of the exceptions they are

arrested and taken to a juvenile facility, where they must be bailed out.

City Curfews

Dallas, Chicago, and Phoenix are among the major U.S. cities that have imposed curfews on young people. One of the most highly publicized cities is New Orleans, which in June 1994 imposed a draconian curfew on teens age 18 years and younger. In New Orleans, young people have to be off the streets by 8 P.M. on school nights, 9 P.M. on summer weeknights, and 11 P.M. on weekends. Those found in violation of the curfew are taken into custody, often in handcuffs, and held at a curfew center until their parents come to pick them up. Parents of frequent curfew violators are subject to fines and may even be sent to jail.

New Orleans officials consider the city's curfew a success. In the first year after it went into effect, incidents of armed robbery, rape, and auto theft all dropped dramatically. Crime continued to decline, although at a slower pace, the following year. Some criminologists are skeptical of the curfew's role in this decline, however. They point out that the curfew was only one element in a much larger anticrime effort launched by New Orleans in 1994. What is more, crime rates have dropped across the nation in the mid-1990s, including in many cities that have no curfew.

Mall Curfews

Municipalities are not the only entities that declare curfews. Curfews have been imposed by some private institutions as well. The most notable example of this has been the 6 P.M. curfew that the gigantic Mall of America in Bloomington, Minnesota, imposed on young people under 16 years old in 1996. The nation's largest shopping complex, and one of the largest anywhere in the world, the Mall of America had become a center for teens to congregate in the evenings and had been the scene of a number of minor fights and disruptions.

Other malls around the country look to the Mall of America experiment to decide whether to impose curfews of their own. Some may be reluctant to do so, in light of the fact that teens are often among a mall's best customers.

Objections to Curfews

Young people complain that curfews deny them the opportunity to participate in traditional social activities that have been enjoyed by previous generations of young Americans. These include dating, shared homework, and spontaneous sports activities such as sandlot baseball games and pickup basketball.

Civil rights advocates also tend to object to curfews. They point out that the curfew is a weapon of police states, as in South Africa at the height of apartheid. What is more, age-based curfews make no distinction between innocent teens and likely troublemakers. Juvenile crime rates are undeniably high, but the great majority of juveniles are not involved in crime, either as perpetrators or victims. It is blatantly unfair to punish all young people for the offenses of a minority of them. In effect, imposing a curfew treats all teens as potential criminals and views all adolescents as belonging to a criminal class.

Young people are entitled to the same constitutional rights as older people, say the civil rights advocates. These include the right of assembly and the right to use public roadways and facilities, regardless of the hour. If curfews need to be enacted for public safety, they should apply to everyone, not just people under a certain age. To enforce special restrictions only on the young is an unconstitutional form of age discrimination.

Proponents of curfews respond that minors have always been treated differently in law than adults have been, because they are less responsible than adults. Curfews protect as well as restrict. Juveniles are themselves the main victims of juvenile crime, and keeping them off the streets during high-crime hours promotes the safety of the innocent as much as it thwarts the misbehavior of troublemakers. What is more, say the proponents, if juvenile crime rates go down following the imposition of a curfew, as they seem to have done in New Orleans and elsewhere, then the curfew is more than justified.

So far, the U.S. Supreme Court has made no definitive ruling on the constitutionality of age-based curfews. The key to the constitutionality of any particular curfew may be whether the restrictions placed on teens are reasonable in light of the actual crime situation in the particular city involved.

See also Juvenile Crime.

Death Penalty

Death is an ancient punishment. Nearly 4,800 years ago, the Babylonian Code of Hammurabi prescribed death for 25 different crimes. In the seventh century B.C., the Draconian Code in Athens made death the punishment for every crime.

The first recorded execution in British North America was that of an ex-official of Virginia charged with plotting to betray the colony to Spain. The so-called Divine, Moral, and Martial Laws of Virginia prescribed death for so many minor crimes (including killing chickens and stealing grapes) that potential colonists were afraid to immigrate to the colony. By the time of the American Revolution, every colony except Rhode Island made death the penalty for at least ten different crimes.

Not everyone in revolutionary America approved of the extensive use of capital punishment, however. Among other prominent Americans, Thomas Jefferson of Virginia and William Bradford, the attorney general of Pennsylvania, argued for the restriction of capital punishment to the crimes of treason and murder. The well-respected physician, Dr. Benjamin Rush, called for the abolition of the death penalty altogether.

In 1845, reformers from several states established the American Society for the Abolition of Capital Punishment. Its first president was George Mifflin Dallas, the vice president of the United States. Several states did, in fact, abolish the death penalty during the nineteenth and twentieth centuries, although some later reinstated it.

The ongoing debate over the death penalty periodically has been intensified by its application in several of the most controversial criminal cases in U.S. history. The executions of the anarchists Sacco and Vanzetti in 1927 and of the accused atomic spies Julius and Ethel Rosenberg in 1953 outraged millions of Americans who were convinced of their innocence.

The death penalty itself was the focus of the case of Caryl Chessman, a thief and accused kidnapper. Chessman became famous from his cell on death row by waging a highly publicized 12-year battle to save his life—a battle which finally was lost in the San Quentin gas chamber in 1960.

In 1972 the U.S. Supreme Court ruled, in the case of *Furman* v. *Georgia,* that capital punishment as then administered in the United States was "cruel and unusual punishment" under the Eighth Amendment to the U.S. Constitution. In effect, the Court overturned all the existing capital punishment statutes in the United States on the grounds that they led to inconsistent, unfair, and arbitrary applications of the death penalty.

State legislatures around the country set to work fashioning new laws which they hoped would satisfy the Court's concerns. In 1976, in a series of rulings beginning with *Gregg* v. *Georgia*, the Supreme Court approved many of these laws, allowing executions to resume in the United States. Beginning in 1982, the Court has embraced a number of procedures for streamlining habeas corpus proceedings, in an effort to cut down what it sees as frivolous or untimely appeals.

Opponents of capital punishment are upset by these trends, insisting that the death penalty continues to be applied in an inconsistent, unfair, and arbitrary manner, even under the laws approved by the Court. They point to statistics that show that disproportionately high percentages of men (compared to females convicted of similar crimes) and of the economically disadvantaged are sentenced to death in the United States. For these reasons, the nation's largest association of lawyers, the American Bar Association, called for a moratorium on executions in 1997.

Because of its inherent violence and finality, death is generally regarded as the most severe punishment society can mete out to criminal wrongdoers. It is also the most controversial. Most western nations have abandoned capital punishment, except in the most exceptional circumstances. Many—including Austria, France, Germany, and Holland, among others—have abolished it altogether.

In the United States, however, the federal government and 37 of the states continue to sentence large numbers of people to death, although only a relatively small percentage of them are currently being executed each year. There were 31 executions in 1994, for example, leaving 2,890 prisoners awaiting execution on death rows across the United States.

Lethal injection is currently the most common method of execution in the United States, being used in 21 states. Electrocution is used in 13 states; lethal gas in 6; hanging in 3; and firing squads in 2 (the numbers add up to more than the 37 states which have the death penalty because some states use more than one method). Federal executions are carried out by whichever method is employed by the state in which the execution is performed.

Public Attitudes

A majority of Americans favor the death penalty for the worst criminals, particularly for murderers who have killed more than once or who have done so in particularly horrible ways. Partly, the public support for the death penalty is based on a view of justice (i.e., a life for a life, or killers deserve to die) and partly on the fear that, if allowed to live, the criminals might commit similar terrible crimes in the future.

Opponents of capital punishment insist that this seemingly overwhelming public support is not as definitive as it may seem. Although a majority approve of the death penalty in principle, they do not necessarily favor it over other severe forms of punishment that might be applied. In fact, a fairly consistent majority in poll after poll think that a true life sentence without the possibility of parole would be an even better punishment.

People are suspicious of life sentences, however. They know that in the past "life" has sometimes meant a maximum term of life, and that many criminals sentenced to life have, in fact, gotten out of prison long before their deaths. In recent years, however, many jurisdictions have passed so-called life-means-life laws that purport to ensure that those who receive life sentences will never get out of prison.

Temporary Abolition

In the 1972 case of *Furman* v. *Georgia*, the U.S. Supreme Court ruled that capital punishment was, in effect, "cruel and unusual punishment" under the Eighth Amendment to the U.S. Constitution. The Court's decision was not based on a blanket objection to the death penalty per se, but rather on the inconsistency and resulting unfairness of the way it was being administered under the various state and federal laws that then existed.

Four years later, starting with the case of *Gregg* v. *Georgia* (1976), the Court approved new laws which had been written to meet the Court's concerns. As a result, executions resumed in several states, although only at the extremely slow pace of one or two a year. In 1982, the Court approved measures to streamline habeas corpus proceedings and cut down on what it regarded as time-wasting appeals, eventually bringing the numbers of actual executions up to their present levels of around 30 a year.

Charges of Inequities

The U.S. Supreme Court temporarily called an end to executions in 1972 because of what it saw as the capricious and inconsistent way in which the death penalty was being applied. The Court's hope in reinstating the penalty four years later was that the new laws written to meet its objections against the previously existing laws would ensure more fair administration of the most final of all punishments. Yet in 1994, Supreme Court Justice Harry Blackmun declared that application of the death penalty still remained "fraught with arbitrariness, caprice, and mistake."

In the eyes of critics like Blackmun, the arbitrariness of the death penalty has been further exacerbated by the recent series of Supreme Court rulings limiting the right of habeas corpus. In February 1997, the American Bar Association (ABA) called for a moratorium on executions. Like the Court's decision in *Furman* v. *Georgia*, the ABA's demand was not based on a fundamental aversion to capital punishment in principle, but rather on what it described as the "haphazard maze of unfair practices" by which the death penalty is administered.

See also Aggravating and Mitigating Circumstances; Cruel and Unusual Punishment; Death Penalty (Controversies); Death Penalty (Major Supreme Court Decisions); Executions (Public); Executive Clemency.

For further reading Bedau, Hugo A. *The Death Penalty in America.* Chicago: Aldine, 1982.
Flanders, Stephen A. *Capital Punishment.* New York: Facts on File, 1991.
Kronenwetter, Michael. *Capital Punishment.* Santa Barbara, CA: ABC-CLIO, 1993.
Laurence, John. *The History of Capital Punishment.* New York: Citadel, 1960.
Masur, Louis P. *Rites of Execution: Capital Punishment and the Transformation of American Culture, 1776–1865.* New York: Oxford University Press, 1989.
Scott, George R. *The History of Capital Punishment: Including an Examination of the Case for and against Capital Punishment.* New York: AMS Press, reprint of 1950 edition.
Szumski, Bonnie, et al., editors. *The Death Penalty.* St. Paul, MN: Greenhaven, 1986.

Death Penalty (Controversies)

Both sides of the capital punishment debate base their arguments to some degree on the value which they place on human life. Their opposing positions, however, reflect that value in different ways.

For supporters of the death penalty, the value of the life taken by a murderer is so great that it demands nothing short of the killer's life in return. "All religions that I'm aware of feel that human life is sacred," declared Professor Ernest van den Haag of New York University, a leading advocate of the death penalty. "[I]ts sacredness must be enforced by depriving of life anyone who deprives another person of life."

Opponents of the death penalty—particularly those who approach the issue from a religious point of view—respond that all human life is sacred: the murderer's as well as the victim's. If it is wrong to kill, then it is wrong for the state to kill, as well as for individuals. In this view, it is absurd to affirm the value of one person's life by taking the life of another.

Although informed by such philosophical and moral positions, the political debate over capital punishment tends to focus on practical issues. These issues relate to the claimed benefits of capital punishment to society, weighing those benefits in relation to the social and economic costs of the death penalty.

Deterrence

The most frequently given reason for having the death penalty is the need to discourage potential criminals. It is widely assumed that the death penalty is not only a significant deterrent to crime, but the best deterrent possible. The fear of death is virtually universal, and common sense seems to dictate that potential criminals will hesitate to commit a crime that may result in their execution. Some experts agree with this assumption. "The threat of death deters more than anything else," insists van den Haag, "because death is the only thing final in this life."

Yet, the belief that capital punishment is an effective deterrent is far from universal among experts in law enforcement and penology. Although the majority of 386 police chiefs and sheriffs from across the nation surveyed in 1995 favored the death penalty, more than eight out of every ten disagreed that most killers took possible punishments, including death, into account before committing their crimes.

Murders, some experts argue, fall into one of two categories. Either they are heat-of-the-moment outbursts, or they are cold-bloodedly planned in advance. In the former case, the criminal acts in anger, passion, or panic, with no thought of the possible punishment; in the latter, the criminal plans to escape capture and therefore to avoid any punishment at all. Neither weigh the legal penalties before deciding whether to commit the crime.

The statistical evidence on the value of capital punishment as a deterrent is not clear. Historically, murder rates have responded differently to the introduction or elimination of the death penalty in different places at different times. The changes have varied widely enough to suggest that the presence or absence of the death penalty may not have been a significant factor.

Proponents of the death penalty point out that the number of murders committed in the United States rose dramatically in the late 1960s, at a time when the number of executions carried out fell even more dramatically. The number of murders per year virtually doubled from 1968 to 1976, when there were no executions in the United States at all, thanks to the U.S. Supreme Court's decision in the case of *Furman* v. *Georgia*, which declared the death penalty as it had previously been applied to be unconstitutional. On the other hand, the opponents of capital punishment point out that the number of murders committed continued to climb after *Gregg* v. *Georgia* reinstated the death penalty in 1976—reaching a high of over 24,000 in 1992, some 16 years after executions had resumed.

Does Capital Punishment Encourage Murder?

Some opponents of capital punishment argue that the death penalty actually encourages murder. They argue that the threat of death raises the stakes of getting caught, making criminals more desperate to avoid capture. This in turn makes them more likely to kill any witnesses to their crimes, as well as to fight it out with police rather to surrender.

A recent trend to make more and more crimes, such as certain kinds of drug dealing, subject to the death penalty has a similar effect say the opponents. If a drug dealer or other criminal is subject to the death penalty already, he or she has little reason to avoid killing in the course of their other criminal activities.

Some psychologists claim that the impulse to commit murder and impulse to commit suicide are closely related. Some suicidal criminals who cannot bring themselves to self-destruction may kill, at least partly in the subconscious hope that they will be caught and executed by the state. This is borne out, to some extent, by cases like that of Gary Gilmore, the first person executed after the *Gregg* decision. Gilmore had killed brutally and with little apparent reason, and, once convicted, was so eager for death that he fought the efforts of death penalty opponents to save him from execution. The case was the subject of *The Executioner's Song*, a best-selling book by Norman Mailer.

Expense

A reason frequently given by Americans for their support of capital punishment is their resentment at the need for honest taxpayers to pay the expenses of keeping vicious criminals in prison. It is a common assumption that it is cheaper to execute a criminal than to maintain him or her in prison for life. However, this is not necessarily true.

When the prosecution elects to ask for the death penalty, it does more than raise the emotional stakes for the defendant; it raises the financial stakes for the prosecution as well. The U.S. Supreme Court insists that the finality of the death penalty requires extra scrutiny to ensure that the trial and sentencing process are fair. This means that capital cases (those that may result in a death penalty) are more expensive than ordinary trials, and, in the case of convictions, lead inevitably to more expensive appeals and clemency hearings.

Once convicted, condemned inmates are considerably more expensive to confine than ordinary prisoners. As explained by Richard McGee, a past administrator in the California prison system, "The actual cost of execution, the cost of operating the super-maximum security condemned unit, the years spent by some inmates in condemned status, and a pro rata share of top-level prison officials' time spent in administering the units add up to a cost substantially greater than the cost to retain them in prison the rest of their lives."

Proponents of the death penalty argue that these costs could be cut substantially by removing the special legal protections given to defendants in capital cases and assuring a quick execution upon conviction. Opponents respond that to do this would mean rewriting the Constitution and abandoning some of the most treasured traditions of U.S. law.

Inequities

Opponents of the death penalty point to a variety of statistical inequities in the administration of the death penalty—inequities they say makes death a cruel and unusual punishment. Only a small proportion of those convicted of murder since the resumption of the death penalty have been sentenced to death; and, of those, only about 8 percent have actually been executed.

Many factors contribute to the inequities. The most obvious factor influencing whether or not a criminal will be executed is geography. Only about three-quarters of the states have capital punishment, and among those that do, some of them sentence people to death relatively frequently, while others apply the punishment rarely, if at all.

Gender is another key factor. Women make up over 51 percent of the population, and 14 percent of those convicted of homicide, but less than 2 percent of those sentenced to death.

Race may be the most important determinant of all. Although African-Americans make up scarcely more than 12 percent of the U.S. population, they make up 40 percent of the residents of death rows across the country, and about 39 percent of those who are actually executed. Statistically, the race of the victim is even more important than the race of the perpetrator. Approximately 80 percent of all capital cases involve white victims, although approximately half of all murder victims in the United States are nonwhite. This means that only about 20 percent of those cases in which the prosecution even asks for the death penalty involve nonwhite victims. The rate of executions drops to almost nothing for those cases involving the killing of a black victim by a white perpetrator. From 1976 until early 1995, only two whites were executed for murdering African-Americans.

Executing the Incompetent

In theory, the death penalty is supposed to be reserved for the worst of criminals: those whom society decides must be held most accountable for their crimes. In order to ensure that this is the case, the U.S. Supreme Court has ruled that mitigating as well as aggravating circumstances must be considered before determining whether someone convicted of a capital crime should be sentenced to death.

Nonetheless, the opponents of capital punishment, as it is administered in the United States today, complain that the death penalty is sometimes applied to the young, the mentally ill, and the retarded—those who are less than competent and far from fully responsible for their actions. Among those who have been executed since the restoration of the death penalty in 1976 were an adult Georgia convict with a mental age of 12 and a Virginia man who was not only mentally retarded, but who had been diagnosed as a paranoid schizophrenic on three separate occasions, by three different state mental institutions.

What is more, the United States is one of the few nations in the world that executes people for crimes committed when they were minors. In fact, scores of criminals in their mid- to late teens have been sentenced to death in recent years. The minimum age for application of the death penalty in Wyoming is 14. Although no one that young has actually been executed since 1976, the U.S. Supreme Court has ruled, in the cases of *Stanford* v. *Kentucky* and *Wilkins* v. *Missouri* (both 1989), that it was constitutionally acceptable to execute two men who were 16 and 17 years old when they committed their crimes.

Opponents of the death penalty argue that, whether constitutional or not, executing minors and the mentally incompetent is barbaric. Supporters of such executions argue that it is society's will that, whenever a crime is heinous enough, the perpetrator should die for it, regardless of age or mental infirmity.

Risk of Mistake

No issue is more troubling to opponents and proponents of capital punishment alike than the possibility that the state might execute an innocent person. This possibility alone is frightening enough to convince some that the death penalty should be abandoned.

Supporters of capital punishment argue, however, that the death penalty saves lives as well as takes them (through deterrence and by preventing killers from killing again), and that some risk to the lives of innocent defendants is worth taking in order to save the lives of innocent potential victims.

The actual extent of the risk that an innocent person will be executed is subject to debate. In 1987, two opponents of the death penalty published a study in which they named 350 people they claimed had been wrongfully convicted in this century of crimes for which they either were, or could have been, sentenced to death. Most of the cases involved prisoners who either had been pardoned or had their convictions overturned because of new evidence. In the years since that study was published, several more people have been released from death rows after being cleared of the crime that sent them there. How many other innocent people have already been executed, or are currently awaiting execution, there is no way to know.

Nonetheless, defenders of capital punishment argue that the possibility that an innocent person, or even a handful of innocent people, may die is not sufficient reason to abandon the death penalty. Taken to extremes, they say, the potential for injustice could be used as an argument against any punishment at all. Although the state must be as careful as possible to ensure that only the guilty are convicted, once that care has been taken, there should be no reluc-tance to mete out death as a punishment.

A related argument sometimes put forward against capital punishment is the concern that the prospect of the death penalty may actually discourage convictions in capital cases. Knowing that a guilty verdict will result in an irrevocable punishment, some juries may choose to let a guilty defendant go free rather than to risk a fatal mistake.

See also Aggravating and Mitigating Circumstances; Cruel and Unusual Punishment; Death Penalty; Death Penalty (Major Supreme Court Decisions); Executions (Public); Executive Clemency.
For further reading Bedau, Hugo A. *The Death Penalty in America*. Chicago: Aldine, 1982. Kronenwetter, Michael. *Capital Punishment*. Santa Barbara, CA: ABC-CLIO, 1993. Stevens, Leonard A. *Death Penalty: The Case of Life and Death in the United States*. New York: Coward, McCann & Geoghegan, 1978. Szumski, Bonnie, et al., editors. *The Death Penalty*. St. Paul, MN: Greenhaven, 1986. van den Haag, Ernest, and John P. Conrad. *The Death Penalty: A Debate*. New York: Plenum, 1983.

Death Penalty (Major Supreme Court Decisions)

The U.S. Supreme Court has never ruled that capital punishment is unconstitutional per se. It has, however, frequently ruled that aspects of the way the death penalty has been administered in one or more of the states have been constitutionally unacceptable.

The following are some key Supreme Court rulings involving the death penalty.

In re Kemmler (1890) In a case involving what would become the first execution by means of electrocution in U.S. history, the Court ruled that "the punishment of death is not 'cruel'" within the meaning of the word as used in the Eighth Amendment to the Constitution's prohibition against "cruel and unusual punishments."

Weems v. ***United States*** **(1910)** The Court vacated the punishment of an American who had been sentenced to 15 years at hard labor for forgery. The sentence had been handed down in the Philippines, which was then under U.S. control. Although the punishment was appropriate under Philippine law, the Court ruled that it was "cruel and unusual" under the Eighth Amendment to the U.S. Constitution. The most significant element of the Court's ruling was its assertion that the meaning of the Eighth Amendment was subject to change over the years, due to "enlightened" public opinion. Although *Weems* itself was not a capital case, the decision would open the way for new interpretations of the term "cruel and unusual" in future death penalty decisions.

United States v. ***Jackson*** **(1968)** The Court ruled that the death penalty cannot be used as a club to force defendants to plead guilty, overturning a law that provided a maximum penalty of life imprisonment for a defendant who pled guilty to a capital crime, but allowed death for one who was found guilty after pleading innocent. The Court ruled that the law was an effort to circumvent an accused person's Fifth Amendment protection against self-incrimination, as well as the Sixth Amendment right to a jury trial.

Maxwell v. ***Bishop*** **(1970)** In the case of an African-American sentenced to death for rape in Arkansas, the Court refused to consider a claim that his death sentence had been influenced by the fact that he was black. The convicted man presented statistical evidence that a black man convicted of raping a white woman was three and one-half times more likely to receive a death sentence in Arkansas than anyone convicted of raping someone of their own race. The Court seemed unwilling to evaluate a purely statistical claim of racial discrimina-

tion in sentencing, although it did vacate the rapist's sentence on other grounds.

Furman v. ***Georgia*** **(1972)** In a 5 to 4 ruling, the Court declared that capital punishment, as it was then administered in the United States, was "cruel and unusual punishment" under the Eighth Amendment. The five justices in the majority gave varying reasons for their decisions. Two argued that capital punishment was cruel and unusual per se; others pointed to evidence that the death sentence was being applied in a discriminatory manner; one, emphasizing how few of those eligible for the death penalty were actually executed, compared the capriciousness of execution to the capriciousness of being hit by lightning. The effect of the *Furman* decision was to put an end to all executions in the United States, at least temporarily.

Gregg v. ***Georgia*** **(1976)** In this and other decisions handed down in July 1976, the Court approved newly written capital punishment laws in Georgia, Texas, and Florida. These laws included sentencing guidelines designed to meet the Court's objections, expressed in the *Furman* decision four years earlier, to the way capital punishment had previously been administered in the United States. The Court's decisions allowed executions to resume in the states involved. Similar laws were soon approved for other jurisdictions, although few executions actually took place until the 1980s.

Woodson v. ***North Carolina*** **(1976)** Striking down a North Carolina law that made the death penalty mandatory for certain crimes, the Court ruled that the aggravating and mitigating circumstances in each specific case had to be weighed before a death sentence could be imposed.

Coker v. ***Georgia*** **(1977)** The Court overturned the death sentence of a man who had been convicted of rape. Even though the rape had been committed while the defendant was an escapee from a Georgia prison, the Court ruled "that a sentence of death is grossly disproportionate for the crime of rape and is therefore forbidden by the Eighth Amendment as cruel and unusual punishment."

Lockett v. *Ohio* **(1978)** In striking down an Ohio law that forbade juries to consider the defendant's character and other factors in deciding whether to sentence him or her to death, the Court ruled that the defense must be allowed to present evidence of virtually any mitigating circumstances they wished during the sentencing phase of a capital trial.

Bullington v. *Missouri* **(1981)** The Court ruled that the prosecution could not ask for a second death sentence in the case of a defendant who had won a new trial after already having been convicted and sentenced to death for the same crime.

Endmund v. *Florida* **(1981)** The death sentence of a man who had been convicted of the robbery and murder of an elderly Florida couple was overturned on the grounds that his participation in the crimes was not sufficient to justify death. Although he had driven the getaway car, the Court found that he had no intention to kill.

McClesky v. *Kemp* **(1987)** The Court turned down the appeal of a black man named Warren McCleskey, who had been sentenced to death in Georgia for the murder of a white person. McCleskey's lawyers had presented a major statistical analysis establishing that Georgia murderers whose victims were white received the death penalty four times as often as those whose victims were black. Although the majority of the Court acknowledged that there was clear evidence of a "discrepancy" in death sentencing related to race, the Court refused to overturn a particular sentence without proof that the jury in that specific case had been influenced by race.

Penry v. *Lynaugh* **(1989)** Although the Court ruled that it was not necessarily unconstitutional to impose the death penalty on a mentally retarded person, it went on to say that jurors must be told that they could consider mental retardation as a mitigating factor in deciding whether or not to do so.

Stanford v. *Kentucky* **and** *Wilkins v. Missouri* **(1989)** The Court refused to overturn the sentences of two young men convicted for murders committed when they were 16 and 17 years old. Writing for the majority, Justice Antonin Scalia noted that most states that have capital punishment permit it to be applied to 16-year-olds, and that doing so, therefore, could not be considered "unusual" under the Eighth Amendment.

McClesky v. *Zant* **and Coleman** v. *Thompson* **(1991)** Turning down another appeal by Warren McClesky (*McClesky* v. *Kemp*) the Court ruled that, in the future, prisoners could no longer file more than one habeas corpus petition unless exceptional circumstances required it. In *Coleman*, the Court further limited death row prisoners' access to habeas corpus by ruling that a failure to submit an appeal in a timely fashion in state court rules out any future consideration of the appeal in a federal court.

Herrera v. *Collins* **(1993)** The Court refused to allow a lower federal court to review the case of Leonel Herrera, who had been convicted of murdering a Texas policeman. Herrera's lawyers argued that new evidence cleared the convicted man while implicating his brother in the crime. In its decision, the majority of the Court ruled that the time had long since passed for Herrera to appeal on the grounds of actual innocence, no matter how convincing the evidence might be. In an unusually strong dissent, three justices charged that: "Execution of a person who can show that he is innocent comes perilously close to simple murder."

See also Aggravating and Mitigating Circumstances; Cruel and Unusual Punishment.

Democracy

The term *democracy* comes from a Greek word meaning "rule by the people." As commonly understood, it refers to a form of government that derives its legitimacy from the consent of the people and rules in their name.

Plato and Aristotle wrote about democracy 2,500 years ago, and democratic governments, of sorts, existed in ancient Greece and Rome, as well as among some Indian tribes in North America. Democracy in the modern sense began to evolve in England and Europe in the seventeenth century, as European monarchies began to invest significant amounts of authority in the hands of elected officials. In the following century, the United States led the way in abandoning monarchy altogether, in favor of an elected, representative form of government. Most other major western nations eventually followed suit, although some retained titular monarchs even while transferring the bulk of real power to elected officials.

Varieties of modern democratic government range from the direct democracy of the Swiss cantons, in which all adult male citizens vote on public issues, to indirect democracies such as those of the United States, England, and Canada.

All modern democracies, however, share certain attributes. These include devotion to the ideal of human liberty; some form of majority rule, usually involving elected representatives; and the protection of the rights of political and other minorities. The great dilemmas of modern democracy involve finding ways to reconcile these principles, which often come into conflict.

In the United States, the devotion to human liberty has best been expressed in the nation's first great founding document, the Declaration of Independence. Majority rule is effected on the federal level largely by means of the elected representatives in the U.S. House and Senate and in the elected chief executive, the president. The state and local governments have similar representative offices. In addition to elections, the will of the people is sometimes expressed more directly through initiatives and referenda. The rights of minorities are protected through the Constitution of the United States, and particularly that portion of it known as the Bill of Rights.

See also Bill of Rights; Checks and Balances; Initiatives and Referenda; Majority Rule.
For further reading Greider, William. *Who Will Tell the People?* New York: Touchstone, 1992. Kronenwetter, Michael. *How Democratic Is the United States?* New York: Watts, 1994.

Desegregation
See Civil Rights Movement.

Diversity

Diversity is a characteristic that is valued and aspired to by many (although by no means all) American institutions, from universities to local police forces. Among the characteristics in which diversity is commonly sought are gender, skin color, ethnic origin, language, rural or urban background, religious affiliation, and economic class.

Diversity can be contrasted with homogeneity. The attitudes of institutions that value diversity can be contrasted with other American institutions (such as the Ku Klux

Klan, the Daughters of the American Revolution, the Nation of Islam, the Knights of Columbus, etc.), which limit their memberships to people who share a common trait or background.

Different institutions value diversity for different reasons. Some regard it as a benefit in itself. For example, many colleges and universities seek to diversify their student populations in the belief that a variety of ethnic, regional, and economic backgrounds makes for a more challenging and well-rounded academic environment.

Other institutions have more pragmatic reasons for pursuing diversity. A police force in a city with large African and Asian minorities might seek out African- and Asian-American officers who might have a better understanding of those communities and be more welcome in their neighborhoods. A newspaper might seek to employ more women and ethnic minorities, in hopes that they will provide special insights into the needs and interests of like readers.

Ideally, one might expect that governmental institutions would be among the most diverse of all in a society as diverse as the United States. In reality, however, such institutions are frequently among the most homogeneous. None are more so than the representative legislative bodies of the federal government. Until recently, the U.S. Senate and House of Representatives were made up almost exclusively of white males. Even now, women and ethnic minorities are drastically underrepresented relative to their numbers in society. The Supreme Court did not get an African-American associate justice until 1967, nor a woman until 1981. President Clinton took steps to bring more diversity to the executive branch in 1992, when he announced that he would make his administration "look more like America."

Domestic Violence

Violence committed by family members against other members of the same family or household is a major problem in the United States today. In addition to the physical harm inflicted on the individual victims, domestic violence has serious implications not only for the entire family, but for law enforcement and the courts.

There are various permutations of domestic violence. One spouse may attack the other; two spouses may fight with each other; parents or other adults in the household may abuse children, either sexually or physically; children may attack each other or their parents; adults may physically abuse elderly family members. Aside from child abuse, the most common form of domestic violence seems to be attack by males (husbands or male lovers) on their female partners.

Although domestic violence is sometimes an isolated occurrence, certain patterns are apparent to psychologists and law enforcement officials familiar with the phenomenon. The most significant is the fact that domestic violence seems to beget more domestic violence. Psychologists and law enforcement officials alike report that a high proportion of abusive parents and spouses were raised in homes where similar forms of abuse took place. Abused children are three times as likely as those who were not abused to manifest chronic aggressive behavior in later life. What is more, several forms of domestic violence often exist in the same family. Parents who abuse their spouse are at risk to abuse their children as well, and abused children are more likely than others to grow up to abuse their elderly parents in turn.

See also Child Abuse; Crimes against Women; Spouse Abuse.

For further reading Deats, S. M., and L. T. Lenker, editors. *The Aching Hearth: Family Violence in Life and Literature*. New York: Plenum, 1991. Gelles, Richard J., and Denileen Leseke. *Current Controversies on Family Violence*. Thousand Oaks, CA: Sage, 1993. Koss, Mary, et al. *No Safe Haven: Male Violence against Women at Home, at Work, and in the Community*. Washington, DC: American Psychological Association, 1994.

"Don't Ask, Don't Tell" Policy

Traditionally, homosexuality has been frowned on by the U.S. military services. In addition to an underlying assumption that sexual activity between members of the same sex was unnatural and immoral, gay and lesbian relationships have been seen as a threat to good order and military discipline. For these reasons, being homosexual was long regarded as an insurmountable bar to entering the military, as well as grounds for dismissal if it was discovered later.

One of Bill Clinton's first acts when he took office as president in 1993 was to announce that he was ending the policy against gays and lesbians in the military. His effort was met with such strong opposition, however—not only from the Joint Chiefs of Staff and from within the ranks of the services, but from the public at large—that he reformed his original intention. Instead of a straightforward end to discrimination, the president instituted a compromise policy which became known by the catch phrase, "don't ask, don't tell."

At the same time as it established the right of gays and lesbians to serve in the military, the new policy forbade them to participate in overtly homosexual activities, to proselytize for the gay lifestyle, and even to acknowledge their own sexual preference.

"Don't ask, don't tell" failed to satisfy either those gays and lesbians in the military who felt unfairly restrained by the policy or those who favored the services' traditional ban on homosexuals. It did, however, serve to quiet the political debate over the issue.

A year after the policy was first established, the Pentagon declared it a success, although the Servicemembers Legal Defense Network, an organization advocating the rights of gays and lesbians within the services, claimed that even homosexuals who attempted to remain discreet continued to be hounded and harassed.

The first major legal challenge to "don't ask, don't tell" was launched by an ex-Navy man named Paul Thomasson, who had been discharged from the service after writing to his superiors to inform them that he was gay. Thomasson sued to be reinstated on the grounds that the Navy's policy unconstitutionally infringed on the free speech rights of military homosexuals by, in effect, forbidding them to talk openly about their homosexuality.

Gay and lesbian organizations were divided over Thomasson's legal challenge. Although they sympathized with his position, some preferred to wait for a constitutional challenge based on the claim that "don't ask, don't tell" unfairly discriminated against homosexuals by denying them the same right to sexual activity granted to other military personnel.

Thomasson's case reached the U.S. Supreme Court in October 1996, but the Court refused to hear it. The immediate effect of this nondecision was to let stand a lower court's decision against Thomasson. This effectively left the "don't ask, don't tell" policy in place, but without actually affirming its constitutionality. By declining to comment on the merits of the case, the Court left open the possibility that it might rule on the constitutional issues raised by the policy in a later case.

See also Homosexuality; Homosexuals (Gays and Lesbians) in the Military.

Downsizing

Downsizing is a strategy adopted by many businesses in the United States and elsewhere, aimed at cutting costs and reducing workforces. It involves eliminating what are seen as unnecessary tasks, services, and jobs—changes that inevitably result in drastic cuts in the number of people employed by a company.

Virtually every large American industry was affected by downsizing to some extent during the 1980s and 1990s, with some companies announcing layoffs numbering in the thousands, and even the tens of thousands. The hardest-hit workforces, however, were in those industries most subject to automation, in which high-tech machines and electronic instruments were able to replace human workers. From the mid-1980s to the mid-1990s, for example, the giant communications firm, AT&T, cut 115,000 people from its workforce.

The firings, or layoffs, that result from downsizing are different from more traditional workforce reductions in two ways. First, a larger proportion than usual of the jobs eliminated tend to be in the low and middle levels of management. Second, the companies cutting employees are often not only profitable, but growing.

Profitable companies that choose to downsize argue that they need to do so not merely to cut labor costs, but to become more efficient, and therefore, more productive; that is, they can produce more goods and services per worker. Typically, they say that they need to do this to succeed in an increasingly competitive world marketplace. U.S. firms, they point out, now have to compete with companies in less-developed countries where wages and benefits are traditionally lower. Therefore, the companies say, U.S. companies need to become "leaner and meaner" in order to produce goods that can be sold at comparable prices.

Downsizing has helped to increase the productivity and profits of many U.S. companies, but critics of the practice wonder whether it is worth the price of so many people losing their jobs. The tensions and resentments produced by downsizing have been major factors in the changing attitudes toward work that have taken place in American society in the 1980s, with profound effects on both the American work ethic and the average employee's job security.

See also Worker Layoffs in the 1980s and 1990s.
For further reading *New York Times. The Downsizing of America*. New York: Times Books, 1996.

Drug Abuse

As many as 72 million Americans have used an illegal drug at least once in their lives. Between 14 and 21 million, including as many as one out of every four 18- to 45-year-olds, use some form of illicit drug in any given year.

The most commonly used illegal substance in the United States is marijuana. Other frequently used illegal drugs include heroin, cocaine (both in the form of powder and in the more concentrated form known as crack), and a range of chemically manufactured substances known as "designer drugs."

The Early History of Drug Use in America

The taking of various substances to alter mood, to induce visions, and either to stimulate or to tranquilize oneself is nothing new in America. Drugs made from native plants were used for these purposes by some Native Americans in pre-Columbian days. Hemp, or marijuana, was well known in colonial times. The practice of opium smoking was brought to the United States by Chinese immigrants in the nineteenth century. Many of the soldiers who were given morphine for the pain of Civil War wounds became addicted and continued to rely on the drug when the war was over.

Heroin and codeine were common ingredients of patent medicines and other products in the late nineteenth and early twentieth centuries and were used heavily by men and women to treat a variety of real and imagined ailments. Alcohol and nicotine, in the form of drinks and tobacco, have been widely used for centuries. These and other drugs have been used excessively by some Americans, and in moderation by others, at virtually every point in the nation's history. It wasn't until the early twentieth century that the government began drawing a firm distinction between licit and illicit drugs, and certain substances were banned outright. The manufacture of heroin, as well as the nonmedical use of cocaine and several other drugs, was banned in the United States in 1924. Other drugs, however, including alcohol and tobacco, remained legal.

Use versus Abuse

Although there have always been people who frowned on the recreational use of drugs, most Americans object only to what is commonly defined as their abuse. However, the distinction between the acceptable use of drugs and the unacceptable abuse of them is not always easy to make.

The term *abuse* typically is used loosely, often to describe any form of drug use of which the speaker disapproves. Generally speaking, however, most Americans would probably agree that the use of such banned substances as crack cocaine and designer drugs constitutes drug abuse. Some go further, considering any use of drugs for their recreational, mind- or mood-altering properties to be an abuse, except when prescribed by a doctor for a legitimate medical purpose. On the other end of the spectrum are those who argue that at least some currently illegal drugs, such as marijuana or LSD, can be used moderately and safely, and that such use should not be regarded as abuse.

The majority of Americans accept the proposition that many legal drugs may be either used or abused, depending on the circumstances and extent of their employment. A variety of legal drugs are staples of the American way of life. Prescription drugs, including some powerful narcotics, stimulants, and depressants, are vital tools of medicine as it is practiced in the United States. Most Americans find the use of such drugs perfectly acceptable, as long as they are used as prescribed. Even the medical use of drugs is sometimes challenged, however, by those who argue that doctors and psychiatrists are too ready to prescribe tranquilizers, stimulants, and painkillers for problems that could be better managed without them.

Over-the-counter drugs, or patent medicines, are big business in the United States; they are used by almost every American at one time or another to soothe a sore throat, open blocked nasal passages or contracted bronchial tubes, or alleviate a headache. Tens of millions of adults and young people alike imbibe caffeine in soft drinks and coffee every day. Millions more consume alcohol, while millions of others maintain varying levels of nicotine in their systems through the use of cigarettes, cigars, pipes, or even nicotine patches.

Arguments can, and sometimes are, made that all unnecessary use of drugs is abusive and should be banned. In the case of those drugs which have remained legal, however, this position has not received sufficient public support to change the law.

Costs of Illegal Drugs

The cost to society of illegal drugs is enormous, even in purely economic terms. Americans spend an estimated $110 billion on illegal drugs annually, more than three times as much as they spend on legal drugs. Much of this money leaves the United States and goes to Colombia, Peru, and the small handful of other nations where cocaine and other popular illicit drugs are produced and processed for sale in the United States.

In addition to the direct costs of drugs, the U.S. Department of Health and Human Services has estimated that illegal drug use costs society another $59 million or more in indirect costs. These include medical and mental health treatment for drug addicts and their victims, as well as losses associated with drug-related crimes and the expenses of incarcerating drug criminals. As much as $33 billion a year may be lost to American industry as a result of defective products, lost productivity, and absenteeism brought about by drug abuse.

Directly and indirectly, illegal drugs account for a huge number of illnesses, injuries and deaths each year, along with the resulting medical and other expenses. The sharing of needles among intravenous drug abusers is the second leading cause of the spread of acquired immune deficiency syndrome (AIDS). In addition, hundreds of thousands of people suffer from drug overdoses or drug-related violence each year. More than a half-million such visits

to hospital emergency rooms were reported in 1994, for example. In 42 metropolitan areas the same year, 8,426 deaths were reported.

Effects on Families

Many of the most serious victims of drug abuse are children. Almost 300,000 drug addicts give birth to babies each year. Many of those babies are born addicted to drugs themselves and have to be painfully weaned off of them in their infancy. Some are seriously damaged by the effects of the drugs on their system before they are born. They include the so-called crack babies as well as other infants damaged in various ways by their mother's use of illegal drugs during pregnancy.

The destructive effects on families caused by one or more family members' abuse of drugs affects children as much or more than anyone else in the household. Families dealing with serious drug abuse are invariably dysfunctional, and children raised in such families are highly susceptible to becoming runaways, delinquents, or drug abusers. Depending on the kind of drug involved, abusers are likely to react irrationally, and even violently, to ordinary family situations; conversely, they may withdraw, becoming inaccessible to children and other family members looking to them for emotional support.

Drugs also are implicated in many instances of domestic abuse, from violence against spouses to child abuse.

Drug-Related Crime

Drug-related crime reached epidemic proportions in the inner cities of many American communities in the 1970s and 1980s and continues to plague them today. It has since increasingly infected small-town and rural America as well, although not yet to the same extent. Drug-related crimes include not only those actually committed by drug abusers (such as drug-induced violence and robberies committed for money to buy drugs), but also all criminal acts committed by drug dealers and smugglers in the course of doing business.

Although cause and effect is difficult to establish when it comes to crimes committed by drug users, statistical evidence suggests a close relationship between drug use and crime. According to surveys reported by the U.S. Bureau of Justice Department Statistics, one-third of all jail prisoners and two-fifths of youthful prisoners in long-term state facilities admit to having used drugs or alcohol when committing the crimes for which they were incarcerated. Even more significantly, 49 percent of adult state prisoners surveyed acknowledged being under the influence during the commission of their crimes; fully 61 percent reported that either they or their victims, or both, had been using drugs or alcohol at the time.

The epidemic of drug-related crime has taken an appalling toll not only on the individual victims involved, but also on the quality of life in late twentieth-century America. Whole neighborhoods in many cities have become war zones in the battles between drug gangs battling over turf; whole housing projects have been, in effect, taken over by drug dealers, subjecting the families living there to constant tension and fear.

The streets in most major cities are not safe at night, at least partly because of marauding drug addicts searching for likely victims who might be mugged for drug money. Even in the daytime, pedestrians in many American cities are continually harassed by drug and alcohol addicts begging for money with which to supply their habits.

Approaches to Fighting Drug Abuse

Three general approaches have been suggested for combating the negative effects of drug abuse on American society. The punitive approach calls for an emphasis on law enforcement, stepping up interdiction and police efforts and increasing the severity of penalties for drug- and drug-related crimes. The second, a demand-side approach, sets out to reduce demand for illegal drugs by discouraging their use among the young and by providing more effective counseling and treatment for those already addicted. The third approach attempts to alleviate the widespread criminal activities associated with illicit drugs by legalizing, or at least decriminalizing, most currently illegal drug use.

Only a handful of countries, such as Denmark, have opted for the legalization approach. Like most other nations, the United States has resisted that option, regarding legalization as morally unacceptable and unlikely to be effective. Instead, the United States has endeavored to combine the first two options, placing its primary emphasis on the punitive approach. Since the early 1970s, the federal government has conducted what U.S. politicians refer to as a "war on drugs," although with inconsistent and, so far, largely disappointing results.

See also Drug War; Drugs (Frequently Abused); Marijuana (Medical Use); Smoking.

Drug Testing

Drugs are a major factor in a variety of social ills ranging from violent crime to accidents, damaged health, and lowered work productivity. Although still extremely controversial, mandatory testing for drug use, including alcohol, is increasingly utilized as a means of combating these problems.

So far, mandatory drug testing programs have been used primarily by employers checking on employees who have been injured on the job or, more generally, in industries such as transportation, in which safety is a prime concern. Under federal regulations, all bus and truck drivers, airline pilots, and others who transport goods and passengers are subject to random breath tests. Testing of workers who transport passengers or use public roadways is generally favored by a public concerned about its safety. Although random tests by the government, and especially by employers, are opposed by many unions, they have been supported by some union leaders.

Drug testing is more controversial when it is applied in other industries. Workers remain suspicious and resentful of employers' attempts to test them for drugs, particularly legal ones. According to a 1994 Lou Harris poll, 93 percent of employees would object to being checked for smoking and 69 percent to being tested for alcohol.

Employers cite a number of concerns that, in their view, justify drug testing of workers. They argue, for example, that employees who use drugs may present risks to themselves, to their fellow workers, and, in some cases, to the public at large. In addition, they point to statistics suggesting that drug-using workers (even smokers) may be more expensive employees than non-drug users, for a variety of reasons, including lower productivity, greater sick time, and higher medical expenses.

Mandatory drug testing raises significant medical, privacy, legal, and other issues. Why should the government or a private employer have the right to require individuals to subject themselves to what are essentially medical tests against their will? This is particularly worrisome in light of the fact that the signs of some drugs remain in the body long after the effects of the drugs have worn off, meaning that tests may detect past, as well as current, drug use—use that in no way affects a person's performance on the job.

Drug testing is also criticized on the grounds of unreliability. Critics point out that all such tests are potentially fallible. Those inexpensive enough to be used on a wide-scale basis by most employers give significantly high percentages of both false positives and false negatives. The ingestion of certain innocent foods, such as sesame seeds, can produce substances in the body that may trigger positive drug test results.

There are also serious concerns about the use that might be made of the information gleaned from drug tests. Although some employers have a policy of offering counseling or other help to employees who test positive for addictive or otherwise dangerous drugs, some use a positive drug test as justification for firing the employee.

What is more, employers are presumably not bound by the code of medical ethics that binds doctors and other health care providers to confidentiality. Nor do many businesses, which receive the results of such tests on their employees, take the same kinds of security measures presumably in force in hospitals and other medical organizations. Among the questions raised is, how likely is it that fellow employees will find out the results of each other's tests? Will insurance companies and other potentially interested parties be given the information? Will law enforcement agencies be informed if illegal drugs are detected?

Many would insist that the latter, at least, would be perfectly appropriate. If someone is performing an illegal act, why should they object to the method by which that act is exposed? Others argue that being forced by an employer to take such a test, which could then be used against the employee in a court of law, is a form of self-incrimination that should be outlawed.

Drug Testing of Teenagers

Drug testing has also become an increasingly serious issue among teenagers. Drug use by the young is a major concern of parents and school officials alike, and many of them have turned to various forms of drug testing in efforts to combat it.

In an effort to eliminate drug use by students, some public junior high and secondary schools have instituted various forms of drug testing. The practice is controversial, with many students, parents, and civil libertarians complaining that it is a violation of privacy—particularly in the case of students who are subjected to tests even though there is no reason to suspect them, as individuals, of using drugs. Despite such complaints, school-related drug-testing initiatives continued to expand throughout the mid-1990s. In 1997, several schools announced plans to require prom-goers to submit to breathalyzer tests.

During the 1996 presidential campaign, President Bill Clinton called on the states to institute drug testing for all teenagers who apply for driving licenses.

For parents concerned about possible drug use by their children, but who are reluctant to take them to a local medical laboratory, where they might be seen and recognized, home tests have been approved by the Food and Drug Administration. These tests allow hair or urine samples, which can be collected at home by concerned parents, to be sent to laboratories that will test the samples and return the results to the sender.

See also Drug Abuse; Drug War.
For further reading Potter, Beverly A., and J. Sebastian Orfali. *Drug Testing at Work*. Berkeley, CA: Ronin, 1990.

Drug War

Drug abuse and the many problems associated with it have devastated American society in the second half of the twentieth century. It has been estimated that the direct and indirect costs of illegal drugs come to upwards of $200 billion a year. This includes more than $100 billion in payment for the drugs themselves, as well as the costs of drug-related crime, the medical and mental health treatment necessitated by drug use, and losses to American industry resulting from defective products, missed work time, lost productivity, etc., due to drug abuse among the American workforce.

A large proportion of the alarmingly high rates of crime in the United States are related to drug abuse. Almost one-half of all adult offenders serving time in state prisons in the United States acknowledge having been under the influence of drugs when they committed the crimes for which they are incarcerated.

The U.S. government has responded to the drug problem with a variety of measures designed to reduce drug abuse and fight the crime associated with it. In recent decades, a succession of American presidents have proclaimed these efforts a "war on drugs." The drug war has consisted primarily of interdiction and other law enforcement efforts, antidrug abuse campaigns, prevention and treatment programs, and increasingly harsh sentences handed out for drug-related crimes.

Early Federal Efforts to Control Drug Abuse

The first federal efforts to control drug abuse were directed against narcotics, a class of addictive drugs used medically as painkillers. In 1914, the Harrison Narcotic Act outlawed the sale to the public of large quantities of opium (the raw material for heroin and morphine) and certain other drugs. Almost all nonmedical uses of narcotics were banned in 1924—some five years after the ratification of the Eighteenth Amendment, which banned most forms of alcohol, and four years after the Volstead Act came into effect to enforce Prohibition. Alcohol continued to be considered a much more serious social problem than drugs for many years to come.

Although marijuana was outlawed in 1937, it was only in the 1960s—when the use of hallucinogenic drugs became so widespread that people began to talk about a growing "drug culture" among the young—that substantial national alarm was aroused on the drug problem. Even then, the enforcement of antidrug laws was still considered primarily a local matter.

Declaring War on Drugs

In 1973, President Richard Nixon announced that he was declaring a "war on drugs." That war was primarily diplomatic, however, and centered on efforts to end the importation of Turkish opium and Mexican marijuana into the United States. The former effort was largely successful, at least for a time, while the latter was a dismal failure. It was not long, however, until even the antiheroin program collapsed, as Turkish opium was replaced with opium from the Golden Triangle in Southeast Asia.

President Ronald Reagan declared a second drug war in the early 1980s, although his administration was reluctant to spend much money on it. The Reagan war was fought on two fronts, by two very different forces. The first offensive was an attempt by federal law enforcement agencies to interdict the flow of illegal drugs into the United States. Led by Vice President George Bush, and made up largely of Drug Enforcement Agency (DEA) agents and the U.S. Coast Guard, the interdiction effort produced a major success in ending Miami, Florida's role as the main port of entry for South American cocaine into the United States.

As they had with heroin in Nixon's war, however, the drug traffickers proceeded to finesse the government's efforts, rerouting the main supply of cocaine through Mexico, whose porous border with the United States made the smuggling of cocaine a relatively easy matter. Nearly two decades later, enormous amounts of cocaine continue to flow across the Mexican border into the United States.

The second front in the Reagan drug war was a highly publicized campaign, conducted largely by first lady Nancy Reagan, to discourage young people from experimenting with drugs. The campaign's slogan, "Just Say No!," was trumpeted across the country by advertisements in a variety of media. Although criticized for being naive, and even somewhat ridiculous, the campaign may have been the most successful element of any of the nation's drug wars to date. For whatever reason, the number of new young drug abusers dropped dramatically as the 1980s came to an end.

Congress passed a major antidrug abuse bill in 1988, providing $1 billion more to the fight against illegal drugs than the Reagan administration requested. In addition to boosting federal spending on the drug war, the bill established a cabinet-level National Office of Drug Control Policy to oversee it, gave the military an increased role in interdiction, and set up new law enforcement and drug treatment programs.

Following Reagan in office, President George Bush vowed to continue the drug war. "Take my word for it," he promised in his inaugural address, "This scourge will stop!" Spending for the war on drugs continued to rise during the Bush administration, although critics complained that it was nowhere near as much as would be needed to really bring an end to the scourge—if that were even possible. Other critics complained that the money was being wasted on a scattergun approach to the drug problem. By trying to fight the war on every front, they complained, the administration was ensuring defeat everywhere.

Prevention and Treatment

Although the bulk of drug war funds continued to go toward law enforcement within the United States and interdiction of drugs from abroad, the drug war took a slightly different tack under President Bush's successor, Bill Clinton. In 1994 and 1995, the Clinton administration increased the relative emphasis on fighting demand for drugs, particularly by stepping up efforts to treat drug abusers and educating young people about the dangers of drugs.

Spending on drug treatment programs had already gone up dramatically since the first declaration of the war on drugs in 1981. In that year, just over half a billion dollars was being spent on treatment. By 1994, the expenditure had climbed to over $2 billion. Even so, only about 30 percent of the federal money (and 20 percent of the state money) spent in the drug war went to fighting demand, that is, to programs designed to prevent people from using drugs or to treat those already addicted.

Critics of the drug war argue that these priorities should be reversed substantially. Judged by the failure of current prevention and drug treatment programs to meet the goal of eliminating, or even seriously curtailing, the demand for drugs, they argue that the resources put into treatment and prevention have been woefully inadequate.

Existing programs do not even provide treatment for those users who present the greatest problems for society. In a typical year, some 200,000 criminals with drug habits get out of prison without receiving any treatment for their addictions at all. Not surprisingly, some 160,000 will eventually return.

Evaluations of the Drug War

Even with all the resources that have been devoted to the fight against drugs, the succession of drug wars has had limited, if any, real success. Although drug use by the young did drop for a time in the late 1980s, it began to rise again almost immediately. What is more, all the problems associated with drug abuse in the 1960s, 1970s, and 1980s continue to plague the country in the 1990s, and among some segments of society, at least, they are worse than ever.

Explanations for the failure of the war on drugs vary. Some critics argue that, despite the political rhetoric, the government has never fully committed itself to combating illegal drugs. Although the money spent on fighting drug abuse has been substantial, they point out that it has been far less than what the nation would spend on a real war against a military enemy. If the drug war is to succeed, they say, it must be an all-out war.

Other critics argue that the trouble has not been a lack of effort or resources, but rather that the drug war has largely been misdirected. These critics tend to fall into two broad camps and to proceed from two quite different views of the problem presented by drug abuse.

The first, and probably the largest, camp regards drug abuse as a more or less straightforward crime problem. These critics believe that the drug war has wasted too many resources on the effort to control the demand for drugs by prevention and treatment programs. They argue that antidrug efforts should concentrate on eliminating the supply of drugs by stepping up law enforcement efforts both along the U.S. border and on the streets of American cities and by making penalties for drug and drug-related crimes even more draconian.

The second camp considers drug abuse to be primarily a social problem and argues that the drug war should concentrate on solving the social, economic, and psychological disorders that lead to the demand for illegal drugs.

Still another group of critics argues that both of the above approaches have been tried, and that neither has worked. They believe that drug abuse, as such, is an unsolvable social problem. They argue that the only effective way to at least limit the damage done to society by drug abuse is to legalize drugs and then regulate their sale and use. Those favoring legalization are a distinct minority. Despite the obvious failure of the drug wars conducted so far, most Americans seem to believe that the solution to the drug problem, if any exists, consists of more of the same. The *idea* of a war on drugs seems to have a visceral appeal to the American public.

See also Drug Abuse; Drugs (Frequently Abused).

Drugs (Frequently Abused)

Four main categories of mind- or mood-altering drugs are frequently abused: narcotics, stimulants, depressants, and hallucinogens.

Narcotics, used medically to reduce pain, are also commonly used recreationally to induce a feeling of well-being or euphoria. Among the most often abused narcotics are the opiates, opium, morphine, codeine, and heroin, all of which are products of the opium poppy. Other narcotics, such as methadone, are manu-

factured directly from chemicals. The narcotics are particularly dangerous because they tend to be addictive and because the feeling of well-being they engender leads some users to increase their use of them until they overdose. Since some of the most popular narcotics, including heroin, are injected with needles, they are also associated with the spread of acquired immune deficiency syndrome (AIDS) and other infectious diseases.

Stimulants, their name suggests, excite the user's central nervous system. Medically, they are used to fight exhaustion and to help activate the sluggish nervous system associated with certain physical and mental conditions. Recreationally, they are used to produce sensations of intense excitement or pleasure, commonly known as "highs" (which accounts for the term "uppers," a common synonym for stimulants). Highs, however, are frequently followed by "lows," which cause users to take more stimulants to counteract them. Cocaine and its modern derivative, crack, are among the mostly frequently abused stimulants. Excessive use of stimulants—whether over the long term or in the form of a single overdose—can cause serious mental stress and paranoia, as well as serious heart or lung damage, and even sudden death.

Depressants, like stimulants, act on the central nervous system. Stimulants excite the system; depressants tend to soothe, or sedate, it. Certain depressants, such as the barbiturate Nembutal, and tranquilizers, including Valium and Librium, are frequently prescribed by doctors and psychiatrists to calm exceedingly excitable or anxious patients. Misuse of depressants can lead to nausea, blurred vision, tiredness, mental confusion and forgetfulness, which in turn can result in unintentional and potentially fatal overdoses. In the long term, overuse of depressants can also lead to serious brain and liver damage.

Hallucinogens, or psychedelics, affect the users' perceptions, distorting the sights they see and the sounds they hear in unpredictable ways. They can also distort thought processes, inducing mental states that produce (or, perhaps, mimic) artistic inspiration on the one hand, or psychotic illness on the other. Marijuana is the most frequently used hallucinogen. Other common hallucinogens include lysergic acid diethylamide (LSD), mescaline, and phencyclidine (PCP).

See also Drug Abuse; Drug War.

Dumps
See Landfills; Superfund.

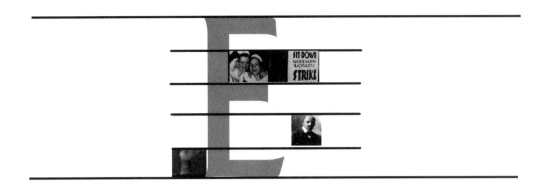

Ebonics

Many African-Americans speak in a more or less distinctive manner, using a syntax and vocabulary quite different in diverse ways from the standard American English regularly spoken by most other Americans, both black and white. The term *Ebonics* was coined for this way of speaking by psychology professor Robert Williams, author of the 1975 book, *Ebonics: The True Language of Black Folks.*

Ebonics is used in rap music, as well as some African-American literature, including works by Toni Morrison and Alice Walker. Although many speakers shift relatively easily between Ebonics and standard English, depending on the circumstances and company in which they find themselves, others—primarily those reared in virtually all-black communities—speak only Ebonics and are unable or unwilling to communicate in standard English.

Educational Controversy

The appropriate definition of Ebonics is a matter of some dispute. Although many think of it as little more than a combination of slang and bad or incorrect grammar, some linguists regard it as sufficiently different to merit designation as a separate language or dialect in itself. Among these are the experts of the American Speech-Language-Hearing Association, who classified Ebonics as a dialect as early as 1982.

The proper designation of Ebonics became a political as well as academic controversy in late 1996, when the Oakland, California, Board of Education resolved to treat Ebonics as a separate language in the district's schools. The board felt that those students who came to school speaking Ebonics faced the same kind of barrier to learning in English as immigrant youngsters who came speaking only a foreign language. Schools in Oakland and elsewhere were having even less success teaching such students standard English than they were in teaching immigrants.

One reason for this difficulty might have been that African-American students identified their way of speaking with their ethnic identity. Many naturally resented, and therefore resisted, teachers' efforts to denigrate their way of speaking—to label it "bad usage" or "incorrect"—and to treat it as an indication of ignorance.

The traditional techniques for teaching such students having failed, the board hoped that applying the special techniques usually used to teach English as a second language would be more successful. The intention was not to teach Ebonics to students, but rather to make sure that teachers were sufficiently familiar with it to communicate with those students who spoke Ebonics already. The ultimate goal was to teach the Ebonics speakers standard English and other academic subjects more effectively. By acknowledging Ebonics as a bona fide language, it was thought, schools might be able to improve the students' self-esteem and lessen their resistance to learning standard English. At the same time, the board hoped that students who were made to feel confident about the language skills they already possessed would be more open to learning new ones.

The decision to treat Ebonics as a language was essentially a pedagogical one. Some educators even suggested that Oakland was only planning to do what educators in several other school districts had been doing for a long time. Nonetheless, the announcement of the board's decision set off a national controversy that was more political than educational. The goal of the board's resolution—to teach standard English more effectively—was lost in a sometimes bitter argument over the social implications of treating Ebonics as a separate language.

Some critics suggested that the Oakland board planned to use the new designation of Ebonics as a way of obtaining federal funds that are provided for teaching English as a second language to foreign-language speaking students. The U.S. Department of Education, however, quickly announced that Oakland was unlikely to receive such funds for teaching Ebonics speakers.

Much of the early criticism of the plan came from those who misunderstood its purpose, interpreting it to mean that Oakland schools would be teaching Ebonics to students. More informed criticism came from language experts who felt that to declare Ebonics a language was to give it a linguistic dignity it did not deserve. Although black English might be fairly described as a dialect, these critics argued, it was not different enough from standard English to be considered a true language.

Probably the most impassioned reaction against treating Ebonics as a language came from some outraged African-Americans who denounced the plan as an insult to African-American students. Among these critics were several prominent African-Americans, including the poet Maya Angelou, who complained that it was wrong-headed and denigrating to treat native-born and raised African-American youngsters as equivalent to foreign-speaking immigrants. Other prominent African-Americans, however, including the civil rights leader Hosea Williams, applauded the recognition of Ebonics as a separate language.

Education Summit (1989)

Having declared his desire to be the "education president," George Bush called a joint White House/National Governors Association meeting in September 1989 to discuss the state of American education. Dubbed the Education Summit, the conference was held at the University of Virginia in Charlottesville.

The summit's objective, as set out in a report issued in 1990, was to make the nation "internationally competitive" through the improvement of the U.S. education system. For that to happen, the report declared, "All of our people, not just a few, must be able to use their minds well, to think for a living, and to understand the world around them.... They will need a deep understanding of a wide range of subjects in order to bring appropriate knowledge and judgments to situations they confront."

In order to accomplish this, the report set out six national performance goals for American education to meet by the year

2000: (1) Preschool programs and nutritional and health care assistance were to be provided to disadvantaged children so that all students would enter school ready to learn; (2) the national high school graduation rate was to be increased to 90%; (3) students were to be required to demonstrate competency in specific curricula by the time they left grades 4, 8, and 12; (4) American students were to lead the world in science and mathematics; (5) all adults were to be literate and to possess the knowledge and abilities needed to be good citizens of the United States and to compete in the global economy; and (6) American schools were be free of drugs and violence.

These goals were later expanded and codified in the Goals 2000: Educate America Act, which passed Congress and was signed into law by President Bill Clinton in 1992.

See also Academic Standards; Goals 2000 Act.

Eisenhower's First Inaugural Speech

Certain presidential speeches reflect the attitudes and aspirations of the American people at a given point in history. Such, for example, was President Franklin D. Roosevelt's 1941 State of the Union Address, which became known as the "Four Freedoms" speech. It reflected the views of many Americans on the eve of America's participation in World War II. President Dwight D. Eisenhower's first inaugural address did the same for Americans in the early years of the Cold War.

The speech was delivered on 20 January 1953, when American troops were still engaged in combat in Korea. The United States was beginning to realize that internationally it had become something new in history—what would be called a super-

power—and the leader of what Americans referred to as the Free World. Domestically, the country was poised to embark on a period of economic prosperity unlike any most Americans then alive had ever known.

At this key point in the nation's history, President Eisenhower set the nation's course for what would turn out to be more than 40 years of Cold War confrontation to come. But he did more than that: he addressed the values that he—and many ordinary Americans—saw as governing the nation as it gathered its will for the struggle to come.

The world and we have passed the midway point of a century of continuing challenge. We sense with all our faculties that forces of good and evil are massed and armed and opposed as rarely before in history....

For our own country, it has been a time of recurring trial. We have grown in power and responsibility. We have passed through the anxiety of depression and war to a summit unmatched in man's history....

In the swift rush of great events, we find ourselves groping to know the full sense and meaning of these times in which we live. In our quest of understanding, we beseech God's guidance. We summon all our knowledge of the past and we scan all signs of the future. We bring all our wit and all our will to meet the question: How far have we come in man's long pilgrimage from darkness toward the light? Are we nearing the light—a day of freedom and peace for all mankind? Or are the shadows of another night closing upon us?

This trial comes at a moment when man's power to achieve good or to inflict evil surpasses the brightest hopes of and the sharpest fears of all ages. We can turn rivers in their courses, level mountains to the plains. Oceans and land and sky are avenues for our colossal commerce. Disease diminishes and life lengthens.

Yet the promise of this life is imperiled by the very genius that has made it possible...

At such a time in history, we who are free must proclaim anew our faith.

This faith is the abiding creed of our fathers. It is our faith in the deathless dignity of man, governed by eternal moral and natural laws.

This faith defines our full view of life. It establishes, beyond debate, those gifts of the Creator that are man's inalienable rights, and that make all men equal in His sight.

In the light of this equality, we know that the virtues most cherished by free people—love of truth, pride of work, devotion to country—all are treasures equally precious in the lives of the most humble and of the most exalted...

This faith rules our whole way of life. It decrees that we, the people, elect leaders not to rule but to serve. It asserts that we have the right to choice of our own work and to the reward of our own toil.

It inspires the initiative that makes our productivity the wonder of the world. And it warns that any man that seeks to deny equality among all his brothers betrays the spirit of the free and invites the mockery of the tyrant...

The enemies of this faith know no god but force, no devotion but its use....

Here, then, is joined no argument between slightly different philosophies. This conflict strikes directly at the faith of our fathers and the lives of our sons. No principle or treasure that we hold, from the spiritual knowledge of our free schools and churches to the creative magic of free labor and capital, nothing lies safely beyond the reach of this struggle. Freedom is pitted against slavery, lightness against the dark...

We must be ready to dare all for our country. For history does not long entrust the care of freedom to the weak or the timid. We must acquire proficiency in defense and display stamina in purpose.

We must be willing, individually and as a nation, to accept whatever sacrifices may be required of us. A people that values its privileges above its principles soon loses both.

These basic precepts are not lofty abstractions, far removed from matters of daily living. They are laws of spiritual strength that generate and define our material strength.

Patriotism means equipped forces and a prepared citizenry. Moral stamina means more energy and more productivity, on the farm and in the factory. Love of liberty means the guarding of every resource that makes freedom possible—from the sanctity of our families and the wealth of our soil to the genius of our scientists.

And so each citizen plays an indispensable role. The productivity of our heads, our hands, and our hearts is the source of all the strength we can command, for both the enrichment of our lives and the winning of the peace.

See also "Four Freedoms" Speech.

Employee–Management Teams

Employee–management teams have become increasingly popular in many industries. Such teams, which come in many forms and are called by many names, are typically composed of workers, supervisors, and management personnel. In theory, team members work together to reorganize such processes as work flow and division of labor, in order to improve the productivity, efficiency, and profitability of the company.

Workers tend to have mixed feelings about employee–management teams. They like the fact that such teams give employees a greater voice in their own work situations. Unions, however, object when employee–management teams make policies that affect such traditional labor-management issues as wages and benefits. Workers also complain that employers take it upon themselves to pick the employees who will serve on such teams, or establish a process for selecting team members that gives the employer effective control of the teams' makeup. This, they argue, is a violation of the right of workers to choose their own representatives.

Employers have certain rights to control the work practices of employees. Employee–management teams, however, have some characteristics of democratic institutions. To the extent that their activities constitute a form of labor-management negotiation, it is vital that the workers be able to pick their own representatives. Courts have agreed that some employers' methods for picking members of such teams violate a provision of the National Labor Relations Act that makes it illegal for an employer to "dominate" a labor organization.

Empowerment

To empower means to enable. The idea of empowering ordinary citizens to have some part in the governing of the country, and of their own lives, has always been fundamental to a democratic society. It is only in the second half of the twentieth century, however, that the term itself has acquired social and political force. In doing so, it has undergone a major transformation.

In the 1960s, empowerment was considered a politically liberal idea. Civil rights workers and demonstrators attempted to empower African-Americans to demand, and ultimately win, the full rights of citizenship. Lyndon Johnson's administration's Office of Economic Opportunity launched Community Action Projects in Appalachia and other economically distressed areas, in which Volunteers in Service to America (VISTA) workers attempted to empower poor people to fight the power structure and to resist economic exploitation by employers, banks, and other economic institutions.

By the 1990s, however, the term empowerment had been enlisted in a very different cause. Commandeered by political conservatives like Speaker of the House Newt Gingrich, it had become a rallying cry for many of the same people and interests that had once been denounced as the power structure. In its new sense, empowerment came to mean freeing people from what conservatives consider the burdensome obligations imposed by the federal government, including what they denounce as excessive taxes and unnecessary health and safety regulations on business. In addition, it implied removing poor Americans from what conservatives saw as an unhealthy reliance on government welfare programs, thereby empowering them to succeed economically on their own.

The modern significance of the idea of empowerment, and its effectiveness as a slogan, was demonstrated by the fact that both political parties have attempted to commandeer it for their own purposes. The Republicans named the television network they established to promote conservative ideas and values National Empowerment Television (NET), while the Democratic Clinton administration referred to their major program to revitalize the depressed cores of many of the nation's inner cities as the creation of "empowerment zones."

See also Empowerment Zones.

Empowerment Zones

The inner cities of virtually every large American urban area, and of many small ones, have been in decline for several decades. "White flight" and a decaying infrastructure of roads, buildings, sewers, and other utilities have made the once prosperous city centers increasingly unattractive, both as sites for businesses to locate and as places for people to live. Jobs and people alike have moved to the suburbs. Factories and other big employers have moved to the outskirts of town, taking most of the area's well-paying jobs with them. Many of the major retail stores that once brought visitors to the downtown areas have followed the best-paid of the city's residents to the suburbs, establishing themselves in suburban malls.

As a result, large areas of the central cities themselves have been left to their poorest residents, who have nowhere else to go, and to the drug dealers and other criminals who prey on them. This is a serious problem, not just for the inner cities, but for the entire community. Most experts believe that a major urban area cannot prosper for long without a healthy core.

One suggestion for revitalizing the inner cities is for the government to encourage investment and development in designated urban areas through grants and tax policies. This idea, which originated in England, was pressed in the United States by Republican Congressman Jack Kemp in the 1980s. It was put into practice, in a small way, under Presidents Reagan and Bush during that decade through the establishment of what they called "free enterprise zones," or simply "enterprise zones."

The Clinton administration adopted the idea somewhat more aggressively than the Republicans had done. In 1994, for example, six cities, including Chicago and Baltimore, received federal grants of approximately $100 million each to be applied to needed social services. At the same time, in order to spur investment—and the jobs expected to result from it—businesses that located within what were now called "empowerment zones" were eligible for special tax breaks. In addition, 64 other cities were awarded smaller "enterprise community" grants to nourish investment there.

See also White Flight.

English As an Official Language

From the time of the founding of the United States, English has been by far the predominant language of the nation. The language that has always been spoken by the great majority of U.S. citizens, it has also been the language used for most private business, as well as the overwhelming majority of business conducted by all levels of federal, state, and local government. The dominance of English has never been seriously challenged at any time in the nation's history. And yet, despite some efforts to do so, it has never been designated as the official language of the United States. To some degree, this has been because there has been no need to do so, given the language's overwhelming popularity. Another reason has had to do with respect for, and acknowledgment of, the large numbers of relatively new immigrants who have traditionally made up significant portions of the nation's population.

The original decision not to enshrine English as the official language was made at the time of the nation's founding, largely in deference to the significant number of German-speaking residents of the new nation. In the two centuries that have followed, wave after wave of new immigrants have come here, speaking a myriad of different tongues, while members of many of the hundreds of Native American tribes in the country have continued to keep their own distinct languages alive. For the most part, each immigrant group has clung to its original language for a generation or so, even while increasingly adopting English as well. Eventually, for most members of the ethnic group, the original language has been lost.

In the meantime, as a practical matter, vital government services traditionally have been made available in languages other than English in parts of the country with large language minorities. This was true, for example, in the late nineteenth century in areas of the East and Midwest with large German-speaking populations. Today, it is true in heavily Hispanic areas, as well as in areas with significant populations of relatively recently arrived Southeast Asian immigrants. Courts have deemed the provision of such services necessary in order to provide non-English-speaking residents with the due process of law guaranteed by the Constitution.

From time to time, however—and most recently in the mid 1990s—constitutional amendments have been proposed that would establish English as the official language of the United States. Recent proponents of such an amendment fear that increasing numbers of Spanish speakers, the United States's largest linguistic minority, are neglecting to learn English. Although this puts them at a disadvantage in many ways, it puts many English speakers at a disadvantage as well, as more and more jobs require bilingual workers able to deal with a growing non-English-speaking population.

Proponents of English as an official language point to certain neighborhoods, and in some cases whole cities, in which Spanish is heard as often as, if not more often than, English. It is not right, they argue, for English-speaking Americans to be surrounded by a "foreign" language in their own country. More positively, the proponents argue that having a single, officially recognized language would create a greater bond for American society. Such a linguistic bond, they say, is particularly necessary for a polyglot country such as the United States.

Opponents of such an amendment point out that the move to make English the sole official language raises serious First and Fourth Amendment issues. What is more, they say, it unfairly singles out Hispanic-Americans and their language for discrimination. Beyond that, the opponents argue that the proponents are acting out of jingoism, irrational fear, and ignorance of American history. They claim that the situation today is not notably different than at many times in the past. The Southwest, for example, has always had a large number of Spanish speakers. What is more, they argue, the English-as-the-official-language movement is fighting a nonexistent problem. According to the U.S. Census Bureau, at least 95 percent of all residents of the United States speak English today.

See also Immigrants and the English Language.

Evolution
See Creationism versus Evolution in the Public Schools; Scopes Case.

Exclusionary Rule
The U.S. legal system is constructed on the rights enshrined in the Bill of Rights of the Constitution of the United States. Criminal defendants have the same constitutional rights as anyone else, including the Fourth Amendment right "to be secure in their persons, houses, papers, and effects, against unreasonable searches and seizures."

All of those involved in the criminal justice process—including the police and prosecutors—are bound to honor those rights. When they do not, the U.S. Supreme Court has ruled, they must not be allowed to benefit from their failure to do so. Specifically, the state must not be allowed to use against the defendant evidence that was obtained by violating that defendant's rights. Nor, by extension, can it use other evidence that was obtained later, as a result of leads provided by the original, illegally obtained evidence. Such evidence is "fruit of the poisoned tree," and therefore, it is regarded as poisoned as well. This legal requirement is known as the exclusionary rule because it excludes evidence obtained in violation of the Fourth Amendment.

The exclusionary rule is most often invoked to exclude evidence collected in illegal searches and seizures. It can also be used to exclude other kinds of evidence, however, including information garnered from an illegal wiretap, confessions given under duress or without a Miranda warning, that is, without informing the suspect of his or her rights, and evidence collected as a result of such confessions.

The exclusionary rule is not absolute, however. Generally speaking, even illegally obtained evidence will not be excluded if it would certainly have been discovered in the normal process of the investigation, if it had not already been obtained through misconduct.

Reasons for the Exclusionary Rule
Two main rationales are advanced for the exclusionary rule. The most basic is the need for the state to obey the law, and to do so most scrupulously when it is in the very process of enforcing it. If the police, who are the agents of the state, ignore this necessity and break the law, the state must pay a price for it. This principle—that the state should not be allowed to benefit from the misbehavior of its agents—is essentially a variation of the legal principle that the criminal should not be allowed to profit from his or her crime.

The second rationale for the exclusionary rule holds that it is needed for its deterrent effect. Only when the police and prosecutors know that their case will be hurt, and might be seriously damaged, by violating the rights of suspects, will they lose the motivation for doing so. Ultimately, then, the rule does not only protect the rights of suspects, it leads to better law enforcement procedures as well.

History of the Exclusionary Rule
The exclusionary rule was first invoked by the U.S. Supreme Court in 1914, when, in the case of *Weeks* v. *United States*, the Court overturned a conviction based on evidence seized in a search for which the police had not obtained a search warrant. The *Weeks* case had come to the Supreme Court from

the federal courts; as a result, the original exclusionary rule was solely a federal principle. Although the courts in some states adopted similar or identical rules for themselves, the Supreme Court did not apply the rule to all state courts until its 1961 ruling in *Mapp* v. *Ohio*.

Starting in the mid-1970s, the Court began to establish exceptions to the rule. The most significant of these, and the one most troubling to supporters of the rule, is known as the "good faith" exception. It holds that evidence collected by police using an illegal warrant may still be used, provided the police had acted in good faith and were unaware that the warrant was invalid.

Controversy

The exclusionary rule is one of the most controversial of modern legal principles. Proponents believe that it is necessary, both for fairness and to restrain police overzealousness. Without it, they say, the police—who tend to see their most important job as apprehending criminals, rather than as safeguarding individual rights— would routinely violate the rights of suspects. The rule's supporters see the rule as vital to assure that the criminal justice system maintains the difficult balance between society's need for protection from criminals and the rights of individuals who are subject to police investigation.

Critics of the rule complain that it frustrates justice. Their concern was summed up by Judge Benjamin Cardozo of the New York Court of Appeals in his ruling in *People* v. *Defore* in 1926: "The criminal goes free," lamented Cardozo, who later became a justice of the U.S. Supreme Court, "because the constable has blundered."

Many critics, inside and outside the judiciary, refuse to accept the notion that the prosecution should be forbidden to use real

and valid evidence—evidence that might make the difference between conviction and acquittal—in order to punish the police. They admit that police misconduct can be a serious problem, and that the "constable" should be discouraged from blundering; still, they insist, the price the exclusionary rule extracts for that misconduct hurts society more than it hurts the police. Some more direct way should be found to punish police misconduct, one that does not result in freeing guilty criminals.

The critics doubt that the rule has much deterrent effect in any case. They argue that it is too indirect: by the time the illegally collected evidence is thrown out at trial, the sanction is perceived to be the prosecutor's problem, not that of the police.

The rule's supporters, on the other hand, insist that police misconduct would be much worse without it. Besides, they say, to revoke the rule now, after it has been in effect for so long, would be seen by zealous police officers as a positive encouragement. It would be like giving them a license to misbehave.

See also Miranda Warnings.

Executions (Public)

In the eighteenth and nineteenth centuries, the carrying out of the death penalty was a public occasion, and executions continued to be carried out in public in some place in the United States until well into the twentieth century. In many communities, they were major civic events. The sight of a brutal thug dangling on a rope was thought to be edifying, a dramatic illustration of the consequences of a misspent life. Scaffolds were erected in town squares or jail yards, where they would be easily accessible to interested spectators. Men, women, and even children were encouraged to attend and to witness malefactors receiving their final punishments.

Over the course of the nineteenth century, American society became increasingly squeamish over the spectacle of state-imposed death. New York gave up conducting public executions fairly early in the nineteenth century, and Pennsylvania became the first state to actually ban them in 1834. As late as 1879, however, the U.S. Supreme Court ruled, in the case of *Wilkerson* v. *Utah*, that public execution did not violate the Eighth Amendment ban on "cruel and unusual punishment." And in some places, executions continued to be attended by large and sometimes festive crowds. An estimated 20,000 people gathered to watch a hanging at Owensburg, Kentucky, as late as 1936. By that time, however, most executions had been moved inside the prisons, away from public view. The last public hanging in the United States took place in a Kentucky jail yard on 13 June 1938. Since then, attendance at executions has been limited to a select company of official witnesses, members of the press, and (sometimes) relatives of the victims.

Although most people probably welcomed the removal of executions from public view, others decried it. Among them were some opponents of the death penalty. Even today, some opponents of capital punishment charge that it is hypocritical and cowardly to conduct executions behind closed doors and out of public sight. They suspect that the real reason for doing so is not concern about the rights of the condemned, or even about the sensibilities of the public, as such; rather, it is the fear that revulsion at the sight of execution would undermine public support for the death penalty. On the one hand, they complain, the state claims that executions are needed to frighten potential criminals; on the other, it shields those same potential criminals—along with the rest of the public—from the very horrors that are intended to frighten them.

Televising Executions

If executions are going to be conducted at all, some opponents of the death penalty argue that they should be carried out where everybody can see them. In today's world, that means on television. The author William Styron sarcastically suggested televising executions in 1962. If society is serious about capital punishment being a deterrent, he wrote, executions ought to be televised so that "the entire population . . . could watch the final agonies of the condemned." Until that is done, "even the suggestion that we inflict the death penalty to deter people from crime is a farcical one."

Public television station KQED in San Francisco took up this idea in all seriousness when it sued for the right to televise a California execution in 1991. Similar requests have also been made—so far unsuccessfully—by other television producers, including the popular TV host, Phil Donahue.

An Ohio judge handing down a death sentence to a man convicted of a particularly brutal double murder in 1994 ordered that the execution be made available to television cameras. He further expressed the hope that film of the horrible crime scene would be televised as well.

Questioned by an interviewer, the judge expressed no opinion about the deterrent value of televising the event. Instead, he declared that people should be able to witness the execution simply because the public should "be aware of right and wrong." By early 1997 that execution had not taken place. If and when it does, it is likely that the prison authorities will appeal the judge's order and attempt to prevent the execution from being televised.

See also Death Penalty; Death Penalty (Major Supreme Court Decisions).

Executive Clemency

The executive branches of state governments have the power to grant clemency to condemned prisoners: either to commute their sentences to life or some lesser term or to pardon them outright and set them free. In most states, this power belongs to the governor. In some, such as Texas, it is vested, at least partly, in a board of pardons or other executive agency. The president of the United States has a similar pardon power on the federal level, granted by Article II, section 2 of the U.S. Constitution.

The availability of executive clemency is considered vital to the just implementation of capital punishment, because it provides the potential for mercy on humanitarian grounds, as well as a last-minute opportunity to correct obvious mistakes that are not correctable by the regular workings of the judicial process. To not hold open such a possibility, the U.S. Supreme Court has said in the case of *Gregg* v. *Georgia* (1976), "would be totally alien to our notions of criminal justice."

The last-minute phone call from the governor that snatches the condemned man from the jaws of death is more than a myth, but it is still an extremely rare occurrence. Governors are political officeholders, and the death penalty is popular among voters. Most governors are reluctant to grant clemency for fear of being considered soft on crime. During the entire decade of the 1980s, in which 2,724 death sentences were handed down, clemency was granted in only 23 cases.

See also Death Penalty.

Family Farms

The United States began as a nation of small farmers. At the time of the American Revolution, nine out of every ten Americans lived and worked on the land. For the first century of the new country's existence, most Americans continued to live and work on farms. The great majority of these were small operations, owned and worked by a single family.

All able-bodied members of the family worked together. They made many of their own tools. They plowed the land, planted the seeds, nurtured them through good times and bad, and harvested the resulting crops. They raised their own food, with enough left over in a good year to sell or trade, enabling them to buy the other goods they needed for survival.

The family farm was not merely a fact of many Americans' lives. It was considered a fundamental part of the nation's identity. What's more, the values of the family farm—closeness to the land, hard work, and family togetherness—were considered fundamental to the American character. The United States continued to see itself as an agricultural country, with firm roots planted in the American soil, well into the twentieth century, but no longer. For many decades, now, the family farm has been disappearing, both as a common form of business and as a way of life.

As late as 1935, there were more farms than ever in the United States, 6.8 million of them; and one out of every five Americans still made his or her living working on them. Today, there are fewer than 2 million farms in the United States, fewer than at any time since 1850, when there were only 31 states in the union. Fewer than two out of 100 American workers are employed on the land. And yet, there is more land devoted to farming than ever.

What has happened? Farm economics have changed so much that is hard for the small farming operations of the past to survive. Modern machines and growing methods have made farming more and more efficient. Modern farms are technologically as advanced as many other businesses. Modern farmers have to be familiar with computers and laser-guided implements, and they make use of sophisticated satellite data and tissue analysis.

As a result of all this, fewer workers can now produce much more food on the same amount of land. There is no longer a need for as many farm workers as there used to be. However, the machinery to accomplish these things is very expensive and often requires a great deal of land in production, and large crops, to recoup the costs. In several kinds of agriculture, only large and efficient operations can make enough of a profit to stay in business.

Periodic crises, from the Great Depression to the farm crisis of the 1970s and 1980s, have driven more and more family farms into bankruptcy. Other kinds of pressures have been building as well, even on those smaller operations that can survive economically. Farm families, like families in other parts of society, have become smaller, and more and more of the young people who would once have taken over the family farm are moving to the cities to make their futures in other careers.

For all these reasons, the majority of the old family farms have been bought up and consolidated. Today, a mere 124,000 people own almost half of all the farmland in the country, and the trend is toward fewer owners taking over more of the land. Although most American farms are still owned by a single family, many of the owners are now absentees: people who do not actually live on, and work, the farms they own. Those who do are getting older. According to the U.S. Census Bureau, the average farmer in 1994 was 53.3 years old.

Even on those farms still owned and operated by a single family, farming has become less a way of life than a business, and the trend seems bound to continue. Although overall farm production is up, profit margins are extremely tight. Increasingly, the other elements of agribusiness—particularly the large food processors—are coming to dominate the interests of the shrinking numbers of small family farmers.

A way of life that once dominated American society and helped to form the American character is dying out.

For further reading Bartlett, Peggy F. *American Dreams, Rural Realities: Family Farms in Crisis*. Durham: University of North Carolina Press, 1993. Goldberg, Jacob. *The Disappearing American Farm*. New York: Watts, 1996.

Family Violence
See Child Abuse; Domestic Violence; Spouse Abuse.

Flag Burning
Flags are symbols, and for Americans, no flag is more powerful in its symbolism than that of the United States. Its familiar nickname, "Old Glory," expresses the awe and the affection in which it is held.

Americans treasure, and even revere, their national flag in a way that it is difficult for foreigners to understand. It is the country's most honored emblem of national unity. Its design reflects the makeup of the nation: the stripes numerically represent the original colonies; the stars, the current states. Traditionally displayed by people of all political parties who want to demonstrate their patriotism, it is especially prominent in times of war or perceived national danger, as well as in times of great national pride.

As a political totem, however, the flag represents not only the nation, but also the government, and, by extension, the policies of the government in power. For this reason, the flag is often at the center of political demonstrations, both for and against government policies. Although those who wish to display their support for such policies fly the flag proudly, those who wish to display their opposition to the same policies sometimes do so by abusing the flag that symbolizes those policies. The symbolic power of the flag gives such abuse a special power of its own. The almost religious devotion with which many Americans regard the flag makes any mistreatment of it deeply offensive to them.

During the 1960s and early 1970s, anti-Vietnam War protesters frequently desecrated U.S. flags, or representations of the flag, in order to show their outrage at

America's role in the war. The most dramatic, and therefore controversial, form of flag desecration was the setting of actual flags on fire.

State Efforts to Ban Flag Burning

The burning of a flag had a peculiar ability to provoke the anger of those who favored America's participation in the war. Many looked to their state governments to protect the national symbol they held so dear. Several state legislatures responded by passing laws making it illegal to desecrate the flag or show contempt for it in any way. The constitutionality of these laws was challenged, and several of them were eventually struck down by the U.S. Supreme Court. The legal arguments were complex, and the Court decided each case on particular grounds. Underpinning the Court's rulings, however, was an interpretation of flag burning as a form of symbolic speech, protected by the First Amendment.

Politically inspired flag desecration became relatively rare after the United States pulled out of Vietnam in the early 1970s, and flag burning ceased to be a significant public issue. It came to the fore again in 1989, however, when a demonstrator burned a flag outside the Republican National Convention in Houston, Texas. Texas had a law that made it illegal to desecrate a U.S. flag in any way that "seriously offend[ed]" other people. Some of the witnesses to the demonstration had been angered by it, and the protester was arrested, tried, fined, and sentenced to a year in prison. The Texas Court of Appeals overturned the conviction, and when the case of *Texas* v. *Johnson* (1989) reached the U.S. Supreme Court, the high court agreed that this flag burning, too, had been a form of protected speech.

A key element in *Texas* v. *Johnson* was the fact that flag burning was not illegal in Texas per se. There, as elsewhere, burning was actually the accepted means of disposing of a worn or damaged U.S. flag. This meant that the law in question was specifically directed against political speech because it only punished the act of flag burning when that was done in order to express a political view.

The Flag Protection Act of 1989

Public opinion remained strongly opposed to flag burning, despite the Court's ruling in *Texas* v. *Johnson*. Responding to that political reality, Congress rushed to pass the Flag Protection Act of 1989, making it a federal crime to "knowingly mutilate, deface, physically defile, [or] burn" an American flag. Supporters of the act believed that this law sidestepped the constitutional issue by making flag abuse illegal in itself, regardless of the political motive of the abuser or the reactions of those who might be offended by it. The law, they insisted, was written to punish conduct— the act of deliberately damaging a flag— rather than speech, symbolic or otherwise.

This argument failed to persuade the U.S. Supreme Court, however, which ruled the Flag Protection Act unconstitutional in the landmark case of *United States* v. *Eichman* (1990). "Although the Flag Protection Act contains no explicit content-based limitation on the scope of prohibited conduct," wrote Justice William Brennan, writing for the Court majority, "it is . . . clear that the Government's . . . interest is 'related to the suppression of free expression.' Punishing desecration of the flag dilutes the very freedom that makes this emblem so revered, and worth revering."

Four justices disagreed with the majority, however. "The flag uniquely symbolizes the ideas of liberty, equality, and tolerance," Justice John Paul Stevens wrote in dissent. Those wishing to express disagreement with government policies had many other means at their disposal, he argued. They did not need the right to desecrate this unique symbol of the nation's "shared ideals."

Later that same year, Congress made an unsuccessful attempt to pass a "flag-burning amendment" to the Constitution that would have given both the federal government and the states the right to ban the abuse of the flag.

After 1990, flag burning largely dropped from public attention, much as it did following the war in Vietnam. However, the issue never entirely went away. In 1995, two Tennessee lawmakers introduced bills calling for the public caning and imprisonment of certain criminals. One of the offenses for which they demanded this physical punishment and public disgrace was flag burning.

Fluoridation of Water

In 1945, an experiment was launched in Grand Rapids, Michigan, to discover whether putting the chemical fluoride in a city's water supply could reduce the number of cavities in children. The fluoride was added, and the children of Grand Rapids were observed to compare their rate of tooth decay to that of similar children elsewhere.

The experiment was planned to take 15 years, but by 1955 the results were already so obvious that the scientists issued their report. According to the report, the teeth of the Grand Rapids children were so much healthier than those of other children that it was clear that fluoride protected growing teeth against cavities. Armed with this evidence, communities across the country began to add fluoride to their water supplies.

Forty years later, approximately half the nation's water supply is fluoridated, including the water in most big cities. Dentists in other areas routinely give fluoride treatments to local children. The chemical has been added to many toothpastes as well. Dentists insist that there is no question that this has resulted in a dramatic increase in the health of America's teeth. Children in the United States today have some 60 percent fewer cavities than the children of 50 years ago, despite a diet that is, if anything, richer in sugar and fats.

Opposition to Fluoridation

From the start, fluoridation was bitterly opposed by people who feared that the addition of this chemical—or, indeed, of *any* chemical—to the nation's water would cause cancer. Many people still fear this, although there has apparently been no proof of any corresponding increase of cancer in areas with fluoridated water.

The most avid opposition to fluoride in the 1950s and early 1960s came from politically extreme groups like the John Birch Society, which feared that fluoridation was a Communist plot to poison the U.S. water supply. Some right-wing groups still oppose fluoridation on the grounds that it is a kind of government-enforced medication. Citizens, they say, should have the right to choose for themselves what their health care will be.

The fluoride controversy has quieted over the years. Nonetheless, opposition remains strong enough to keep many communities from fluoridating their water supplies.

Food Stamps

The food stamp program is the largest federal program designed to help people avoid malnourishment. By 1995, one in every six American families contained someone who received food stamps.

Food stamps are vouchers that the poor and otherwise distressed can use, much like money, to purchase food. Food stamps, which can be used in supermarkets and grocery stores, cannot legally be used for cigarettes or other nonnutritional goods.

Recipients of food stamps are means tested. More than 80 percent of all food stamps go to families with children, and approximately 98 percent go to people below the official poverty line. The rest go to elderly and disabled people with incomes just above that line. People who already receive Supplemental Security Income (SSI) assistance, however, may not be eligible for food stamps if their SSI payment includes a grant for food.

The average food stamp benefit for most recipients amounts to about 95 cents per meal. Despite this relatively low subsidy, the overall program is quite expensive, costing federal taxpayers about $27 billion in 1995.

The food stamp program amounts to a major subsidy to the U.S. food industry. In addition to providing help to the poor, the food stamp program adds over $10 billion in income to the coffers of the American farming, food processing, and food sales industries each year. In order to protect this subsidy, the lobbying power of these industries has been mobilized to protect the program from the political forces that have severely cut, or eliminated, several other federal welfare programs.

Like other welfare programs, food stamps have come under attack for what critics charge is waste and abuse. Periodic disclosures of illegal dealings in food stamps led the Clinton administration to announce a major crackdown on food stamp fraud in 1995. Although food stamps are continued under the Welfare Reform Act of 1996, the ultimate effects of the act on the program remain to be seen.

"Four Freedoms" Speech

Franklin Delano Roosevelt was elected president of the United States four times (in 1932, 1936, 1940, and 1944), serving in that office longer, from 1933 until his death in 1945, than any other president in history. Although born into wealth and privilege, he had the ability to understand and inspire ordinary Americans better than any other politician of his time.

His 1941 State of the Union Address—which would become known as the "Four Freedoms" speech—was given at a time of great international peril. War was already raging in Europe and Asia, and Americans were afraid of being drawn into the conflict, a fear that would be realized later that year when Japanese planes attacked the U.S. naval base at Pearl Harbor. Predictably, the president's speech dealt largely with international affairs. Included within it, however, was a ringing expression of the aspirations and secular faith of the American people in a liberal and hopeful age.

The following excerpts provide succinct explanations of what many Americans hoped for from their "political and economic systems"—as well as the way they saw the world, and their nation's place in it—in the middle of the twentieth century.

The nation takes great satisfaction and much strength from the things which have been done to make its people conscious of their individual stake in the preservation of democratic life in America. Those things have toughened the fiber of our people, have renewed their faith and strengthened their devotion to the institutions we make ready to protect.

Certainly this is no time for any of us to stop thinking about the social and economic problems which are the root cause of the social revolution which is today a supreme factor in the world. For there is nothing mysterious about the foundations of a healthy and strong democracy. The basic things expected by our people of their political and economic systems are simple. They are: Equality of opportunity for youth and for others. Jobs for those who can work.

Security for those who need it. The ending of special privilege for the few. The preservation of civil liberties for all. The enjoyment of the fruits of scientific progress in a wider and constantly rising standard of living. These are the simple and basic things that must never be lost sight of in the turmoil and unbelievable complexity of our modern world. The inner and abiding strength of our economic and political systems is dependent upon the degree to which they fulfill these expectations. Many subjects connected with our social economy call for immediate improvement. As examples: We should bring more citizens under the coverage of old-age pensions and unemployment insurance. We should widen the opportunities for adequate medical care. We should plan a better system by which persons deserving or needing gainful employment may obtain it.

I have called for personal sacrifice. I am assured of the willingness of almost all Americans to respond to that call.

A part of the sacrifice means the payment of more money in taxes. I shall recommend that a greater portion of this great defense program be paid for from taxation than we are paying today. No person should try, or be allowed, to get rich out of this program; and the principle of tax payments in accordance with ability to pay should be constantly before our eyes to guide our legislation. In the future days, which we seek to make secure, we look forward to a world founded upon four essential human freedoms.

The first is freedom of speech and expression everywhere in the world. The second is freedom of every person to worship God in his own way everywhere in the world. The third is freedom from want, which, translated into world terms, means economic understandings which will secure to every nation a healthy peacetime life for its inhabitants everywhere in the world. The fourth is freedom from fear—which, translated into world terms, means a worldwide reduction in armaments to such a point and in such a thorough fashion that no nation will be in a position to commit an act of physical aggression against any neighbor—anywhere in the world. That is no vision of a distant millennium. It is a definite basis for a kind of world attainable in our own time and generation. That kind of world is the very antithesis of the so-called new order of tyranny which the dictators seek to create with the crash of a bomb. To that new order we oppose the greater conception—the moral order. A good society is able to face schemes of world domination and foreign revolutions alike without fear.

Since the beginning of our American history we have been engaged in change—in a perpetual peaceful revolution—a revolution which goes on steadily, quietly adjusting itself to changing conditions—without the concentration camp or the quicklime in the ditch. The world order which we seek is the co-operation of free countries, working together in a friendly, civilized society.

Freedom of Religion
See Bill of Rights; Religion in the Schools; Religious Expression in Public Schools (Federal Guidelines); School Prayer.

Freedom of Speech
See Bill of Rights; Political Correctness; Pornography.

Gambling

The great boom in gambling that swept the United States in the early 1990s resulted primarily from two developments: the introduction of state-run lotteries by more than 20 state governments and the spread of gambling casinos on Indian reservations, which are exempt from many of the state laws that prohibit such institutions elsewhere. In the later 1990s, several state legislatures allowed riverboat gambling in some state waters and gambling in old mining towns that have become tourist attractions.

Casino Gambling

According to a 1994 survey, the popularity of casino gambling, in particular, has been soaring in the United States. Members of 27 percent of all American households went to a gambling casino at least once in 1993—more than attended the games of America's supposed "national pastime," baseball. That compared with members of only 17 percent of U.S. households who visited casinos three years earlier. Those casino-goers spent $13 billion in 1993—more than the value of all the goods and services produced by the entire economies of such nations as Afghanistan, Kenya, and Bolivia.

Despite the recent proliferation of casinos from Atlantic City to the Indian reservations of the rural Midwest, Las Vegas, Nevada, remains the mecca of casino gambling in the United States.

Other Forms of Gambling

Casino gambling accounts for only a fraction of the gaming that goes on in the United States. Individuals make bets with each other all the time, wagering on everything from trivia questions to sporting events. They play cards, dice, and board games for money, in bars, clubs, and in private homes.

Sports gambling, whether legal or illegal, is an enormous business in the United States, although Nevada remains the only state that allows legal betting on team sports such as football, baseball, and basketball. However, many states permit wagering on horse and dog races.

Illegal sports betting goes on in virtually every community in the United States. It has been estimated that as much as $4 billion is wagered on a single Super Bowl football game. Of that, only about $65 million of it is bet in Nevada, where it is legal. The rest is placed with illegal bookmakers, in pools, or in private bets between individuals.

Concerns about Gambling

Although an increasing number of states and communities have opted to legalize gambling of certain kinds, opposition to governments at any level condoning gambling remains strong. Because organized gambling was illegal for so long, organized gambling has come to be associated with organized crime, and many citizens are justifiably concerned that inviting gambling into their communities may mean inviting organized crime as well.

The popularity of gambling is distressing to people who are morally opposed to the practice, as well as to those who worry about its effects on the financial and emotional stability of compulsive gamblers and their families. The opponents of gambling complain that all organized gambling is essentially a fraud. The odds are invariably set so that the house, the bookmaker, or the lottery operator is bound to win in the long run—and the individual bettor is bound to lose.

Some Americans view gambling as an example of much that is wrong with modern social attitudes. They identify the urge to gamble with greed, and condemn it as the desire to get something for nothing and a negation of the Protestant-American work ethic.

Some of the strongest opposition to gambling comes from certain Christian churches that oppose it on moral grounds. Other religious institutions have no moral objection to gambling as such, so long as it is done in moderation by those who can afford it. Some, most notably including many Roman Catholic Church parishes, take advantage of the charitable exception several states make to their bans on gambling to operate fundraising bingo games.

See also Gambling (Legalized).

Gambling (Legalized)

Gambling is frowned upon by many Americans for moral and social reasons. This distaste is enshrined in the laws against various forms of gambling that exist almost everywhere in the United States.

Legal regulation of gambling in the United States traditionally has been considered primarily a state matter, so most of the laws against gambling have been state laws. Each state has been free to ban or legalize those forms of gambling it sees fit. By the late 1990s, the majority of states had chosen to ban almost all forms of gambling within their borders.

Several states made exceptions for raffles and bingo games, when conducted by religious or other charities, and several for pari-mutuel betting at horse and/or dog racetracks. California permitted poker clubs, where players could gather to find an honest game, while a handful of states allowed some kinds of slot machines in certain locations. Aside from such limited exceptions, however, gambling—and particularly high-stakes gambling—was outlawed almost everywhere in the United States.

The Illegal Gambling Business

Despite the legal sanctions against gambling, games of chance and the betting of money on college and professional sports have always been popular activities in the United States. Individuals have always wagered with each other, and illegal card games, and even casinos, could be found in every big town in America, and most small ones as well.

The illegal status of these enterprises led to municipal corruption, with gamblers paying off local police and politicians to allow them to operate. For the most part, this corruption was local, and relatively minor, until the mid-1930s, when organized crime became heavily involved in the gambling business.

The repeal of Prohibition in 1933 deprived of a business the criminal mobs that had made their fortune trading in illegal alcohol. Looking around for a new source of illegal revenue, they hit upon gambling. By the time the 1930s ended, organized crime was running casinos, bookie joints (where people could bet on sporting events), and numbers games all over the country.

The Move toward Legalization

The first state to defect from the universal ban on casinos and other high-stakes gambling was Nevada, which legalized them in 1931. It was not until 1946, however, when the gambler and mob figure Benjamin "Bugsy" Siegel built the Flamingo, an elegant casino (or "carpet joint") in the small town of Las Vegas, that the legal gambling business really took off in Nevada. By the 1950s and 1960s, scores of casinos in Las Vegas and Reno, Nevada, were drawing eager gamblers from all over the country and much of the rest of the world.

Casino gambling was, and still is, an economic boon to Nevada, where taxes on gambling bring in some 40 percent of the state's revenues. Not surprisingly, other states began considering the advantages of legalizing at least some forms of gambling, although they remained reluctant to follow Nevada's lead. The reluctance came from a variety of sources. In addition to a lingering moral distaste for the act of gambling itself, the ties between gambling and organized crime troubled state legislators. Many local governments, meanwhile, worried that the introduction of casinos would change the nature of their communities, as it had changed that of Las Vegas, turning it from a relatively small and quiet desert town to a show business and gambling mecca. On a smaller scale, local

authorities elsewhere feared that the introduction of casinos would distort their economies and exercise an unwholesome influence on the young.

The lure of a major source of tax revenues was strong, however, and in the mid-1970s New Jersey became the first state to join Nevada in legalizing casino gambling. It did so, however, on a limited scale, restricting the licensing of casinos to the once thriving tourist community of Atlantic City, which had fallen into decline. The state hoped that many of the gamblers who flocked to Las Vegas from the eastern United States could be induced to do their gambling closer to home and, in the process, revitalize Atlantic City. Casino gambling has indeed helped the city's economy, although local critics charge that it has also increased organized crime activities in the community, while doing little to improve the lives of the city's large underclass.

State Lotteries

Also by the mid-1970s, New Jersey and several other states had initiated state-run lotteries. Although casinos and lotteries offered new sources of revenue for financially pressed state governments, lotteries had certain advantages. Casinos increased revenues by increasing the tax base, but lotteries offered a chance for states to profit directly from the gambling urge of their citizens. Furthermore, lotteries, not only regulated but operated by the states themselves, would not be an invitation to organized crime and other unsavory elements to come into the state in order to grab a piece of the action.

State lotteries were defended as kind of voluntary tax: No one forced anyone to buy a lottery ticket, but those who did were willingly contributing to the public coffers.

Even so, gambling opponents in many states bitterly resisted the formation of state lotteries. Gambling was gambling, they insisted, no matter who ran the operation. Lotteries, like casinos, would play upon the weaknesses of the people of the state, luring them into throwing away funds needed by themselves and their families in the vain hope of striking it rich. In a way, the fact that the lotteries would be run by the state made it even worse, they claimed. It put the state itself into an immoral business, and made it a kind of a shill, encouraging the unhealthy obsessions of that minority who were addicted to gambling.

In order to sidestep some of the controversy, politicians in many states left the decision up to the voters. Lottery initiatives were turned down in several states, but accepted in several others. Where they were accepted, opposition was typically overcome by earmarking the proceeds for a particular public purpose, such as supplementing funding for education or lowering property taxes.

Those states that did institute lotteries typically included conditions intended to limit the extent of state-run gambling. In some, prize money was limited. In Wisconsin, a law directed that any lottery advertising should be accurate and informational in nature, and not designed to entice people who had no prior desire to gamble. Once lotteries were actually in place, however, such restrictions were often relaxed or ignored in the interest of increasing state revenues.

By the mid-1990s, 29 states and the District of Columbia each had their own lotteries, in addition to two multistate lotteries, Powerball and Northern New England.

The Indian Casinos

Meanwhile, Native American tribes had been asserting a right to operate their own casinos. Because of their special status, rec-ognized in treaties with the U.S. government, they claimed that the state laws against gambling did not apply on tribal lands. Several state governments, which did not want to permit gambling, objected to the tribes' demands. In 1988, Congress passed what amounted to a compromise measure, known as the Indian Gaming Regulatory Act (IGRA). This acknowledged the tribes' right to operate casinos, but required them to operate only those games of chance agreed upon by the state governments. In effect, the IGRA forced tribal and state governments to negotiate terms whereby the tribes could run casinos.

The result was the rapid development of casinos on reservations across the country. The most successful is the Foxwoods Casino, which is run by the Mashantucket Pequots in Ledyard, Connecticut, and which in 1994 was taking in approximately $2 million a day. By 1997, it was predicted, Indian casinos would be operating in at least 28 states.

Non-Indian casinos, operating under special conditions, also have been approved in a few states besides Nevada and New Jersey. In the West, a few have been allowed as part of the historic recreation of old mining towns. Although they still outlaw casinos on state lands, a few states in the Midwest have licensed them on state waters, permitting the operation of casinos on riverboats floating on the Mississippi. As of early 1995, Utah and Hawaii continued to ban all forms of gambling.

Prospects for the Future

For better or worse, legalized gambling is still a growing enterprise in the United States. Gamblers Anonymous, an organization that provides help for people addicted to gambling, was so overwhelmed by clients in 1994 that it nearly doubled the number of its meetings.

Still, there are signs that the boom that had started with the opening of the Indian casinos might be ending. Several states are exploring new measures to exert greater control over gambling within their borders, and Congress seems likely to consider stricter federal regulations in the future.

See also Gambling; Sports Betting.
For further reading Thompson, William N. *Legalized Gambling*. 2d ed. Santa Barbara, CA: ABC-CLIO, 1997.

Gays and Lesbians
See Homosexuality; Homosexuals (Gays and Lesbians) in the Military.

Gender Discrimination
See Glass Ceiling; Women in Sports; Women in the Military; Women in the Workplace.

Gender Gap
The development of sophisticated political polling has revealed that there is often a substantial difference between the ways men and women vote. This difference is popularly referred to as the gender gap. Although the voting pattern of each sex obviously contributes equally to the difference between them, the term is most often used as a synonym for the women's vote. There seems to be an unstated assumption that the way men vote constitutes a norm, from which women occasionally deviate.

The gender gap is more than a statistical curiosity. It can be decisive in particular elections. President Bill Clinton, for example, was reelected in 1996 because women voted more heavily for him than men voted against him. In fact, the federal elections of that year provided the most dramatic evidence yet of the gender gap. In several of that year's Congressional races,

as well as in the presidential elections, the majority of women voted for the Democratic candidates, while the majority of men voted for the Republicans. The dramatic disparity was noted by political strategists of both parties, who acknowledged that women had been the most significant definable voting group in the entire election. Women, as one Dole/Kemp campaign aide put it, "were the swing consumers in the election of 1996." They also constituted the largest voting bloc in the election, outvoting men by 52 to 48.

Political strategists believe that even more significantly than its effect on specific elections, the gender gap is having—and is likely to continue to have—a major role in setting the political agenda for the United States. The data indicate that women tend to vote more on issues that affect the security of the family (health care, child care, education, and issues that affect the balance between family and work, etc.), whereas men tend to vote more on concerns about the budget and national defense. The larger the gender gap becomes, and the more frequent the elections become in which women vote in greater numbers than men, the more the so-called women's issues can be expected to dominate the national political debate.

Genetic Engineering
Genetic engineering is the process of determining the characteristics of a living organism by manipulating genes. Genes are units of a substance called deoxyribonucleic acid (DNA), found in all living organisms, which carry inherited characteristics from one generation to the next. It is the arrangement of specific genes along the chromosomes that determines certain traits, ranging from the color of a human

being's eyes and hair to the growth potential of a plant. Those characteristics can be changed, either by adding genes to the organism or removing genes from it.

Scientists obtain genes to use in genetic engineering in a variety of ways. They can take them from other individuals of the same species, or from a different form of life altogether. They can also chemically manufacture genes identical to those found in nature, a procedure done for the first time in 1976. It is even possible for them to invent new genes, virtually from scratch.

No matter how the genes are obtained, the still-young science of genetic engineering holds great promise for developments in many fields, especially in medicine and agriculture.

Potential Health Benefits

A genetic engineering technique is currently being used to manufacture certain natural substances, such as enzymes and hormones. Genes of the substance, which could once be produced only in the bodies of animals or human beings, are introduced into fast-growing bacteria. As the bacteria grow and reproduce, they generate the desired substance as well, in greater quantities than could ever be obtained before. This process already provides a valuable source of insulin, a hormone needed to control diabetes.

Genes that cause human diseases are put into experimental animals. This provides a predetermined population of subjects that have the disease, making it much easier to test drugs and therapies to combat the disease.

Doctors look forward to the day when they can prevent such inherited conditions as Down's syndrome and Alzheimer's disease from being passed from one generation to another by locating and removing the genes that transmit them. Other diseases may be fought in reverse, by introducing genes that make a person resistant to a particular disease, or to the bacteria or virus that causes the disease.

In time, geneticists may be able to identify scores of genes that render people susceptible to a wide variety of diseases. Eventually, they hope to be able to take a "DNA fingerprint" of newborn babies to determine which diseases they are especially vulnerable to. Knowing this, doctors will then be able to prescribe therapies to protect the newborns. Furthermore, such knowledge will allow people to adjust their behavior accordingly. A woman who knows she has a gene that predisposes her to alcoholism, for example, will be forewarned not to drink. A man who knows he has a gene predisposing him to cancer might be less likely to smoke. The ultimate effects of this kind of knowledge could be enormously beneficial for the health of the population as a whole.

Other Benefits

Although human medicine may ultimately be the greatest beneficiary of genetic engineering, most actual applications so far have involved lower forms of life: bacteria, plants, and animals. In a world where millions of people suffer from malnutrition, much genetic experimentation has been focused on ways to increase the food supply.

Genetic engineering can make food easier to produce, transport and store. In a process called cloning, a cell is induced to spawn genetically identical duplicates of itself. Cloning can be used to reproduce especially hardy or fruitful strains of grains and vegetables.

The disease resistance of food plants can be increased genetically, as can their shelf life. The first genetically engineered food crop was a strain of tomato that went on the market for the first time in 1993. It had been given a gene that counteracted the gene that makes ordinary tomatoes rot soon after they turn red. Although some shoppers and consumer groups were concerned about the ramifications of the fact that the tomatoes were the product of gene manipulation, the potential significance went largely unremarked by consumers more concerned with the durability of the produce than its origin.

Because genetic material can be transferred from one species to another, the pool of genes available to any one species can be enormously expanded. This seems to make it possible for food scientists to produce much stronger varieties of many plants, and to produce them faster, than unassisted nature has done.

The Danger of Accident

Despite its great promise, genetic engineering is extremely controversial. One of the greatest concerns is the possibility of a disastrous accident. There is fear that careless or irresponsible genetic experimentation could render currently nontransferable diseases infectious. Genes that cause a deadly but noninfectious illness like Lou Gehrig's disease could accidentally (or even deliberately) be introduced into an infectious bacterium or virus and cause a terrible epidemic.

The Recombinant DNA Advisory Committee of the National Institutes of Health has the job of overseeing genetic engineering projects to keep such accidents from happening. It does not, however, have either the authority or the ability to police all the labs and scientists conducting genetic experiments.

Concerns about the Products of Genetic Engineering

Many people deeply distrust not only the process of genetic engineering, but the products that result from it. There is tremendous resistance to genetically altered food products among many Americans, ranging from consumer advocates to leading chefs.

Although the U.S. Food and Drug Administration (FDA) has ruled that such genetically engineered products are safe and do not even have to be labeled to inform consumers, large numbers of consumers do not want to use them. This reality was demonstrated by the negative response when the FDA first approved bovine somatotropin (BST) for use by farmers in February 1994. BST is a genetically engineered form of bovine growth hormone (BGH) that increases a cow's milk production by as much as a gallon a day. After investigating the hormone, the FDA ruled that it was not only safe for the cows, but that it had no effect whatsoever on the quality or safety of the milk they produced. Several major consumer groups were unconvinced. They feared that BST was not safe, no matter what the FDA said. They announced that their members did not want to use milk and milk products from animals injected with the substance and asked the FDA to insist that food manufacturers label such products. Insisting that there was no need to do so, the FDA refused.

Even so, many farmers vowed not to use BST, some because they shared the consumers' concerns and some because they worried that the increased milk production from BST would drive dairy prices down. Responding to the public's fears, a number of food manufactures promised not to use milk from cows that had received the hormone, and several large food store chains promised not to sell any products produced with milk from BST-treated cows.

In addition to such concerns, some people worry that developments like DNA "fingerprinting" may tell people more than they ought to know. Suppose a person is found to have a gene that guarantees that he or she will fall victim to some terrible, and incurable, disease early in life. Would it really help someone to know that they are certain to die a horrible death? Would insurance companies or employers use such information against those who might prove to be financial liabilities?

Another danger worrying social scientists is the possibility that DNA fingerprinting in the womb could lead to an upsurge in abortions. It could even pave the way for a rebirth of eugenics—an early twentieth-century movement to improve hereditary qualities in humans—by encouraging prospective parents (or the government) to abort offspring whose "fingerprint" showed them to be less than perfect. Other less comprehensive tests already being done frequently reveal major birth defects that lead some parents to choose abortion. The more sweeping profile that could result from developments in genetic testing could make abortion much more common.

Ultimately, the hostility many people feel toward genetic engineering goes deeper than the fear of any specific danger that may result from it. They are troubled by human beings taking it upon themselves to alter the genetic makeup of life forms. They see this as a fundamentally unnatural attempt to create and manipulate life itself. They see genetic engineers as modern-day Dr. Frankensteins, and they worry that the results of their experiments may turn out to be equally monstrous.

Even some who are not troubled by the process of adding or removing genes, as such, are uneasy about mixing genes from different life forms together, especially genes from human beings and animals. Others are particularly alarmed by the effort to invent new genes, a function they insist should be left to nature or to God

depending on their beliefs. The idea that such genes can be patented, and that scientists and businesses can therefore "own" whole life forms, appalls them. It is fundamental philosophical and/or religious concerns like these that underlie the public debate over genetic engineering.

The Cloning of Mammals

Although the cloning of individual cells and relatively simple organisms such as plants has been going on for many years, until recently the possibility of cloning mammals had remained theoretical. DNA research demonstrated that such a thing was possible, but the idea that it might actually be done remained primarily grist for science fiction until February 1997. At that time, scientists in Scotland announced that they had successfully cloned an adult sheep named Dolly. Shortly afterwards, other scientists reported the cloning of a monkey.

The debate over the wisdom, morality, and potential real-world consequences of the cloning of human beings has now begun in earnest. Until the announcement in Scotland, most scientists and bioethicists had assumed that there would be much time for that debate to mature before society would have to deal with the reality of human cloning. That announcement, however, has given the debate a new urgency.

For some, the possibility of human cloning offers the prospect of ultimately eliminating disease, advancing human life expectancy, and improving the overall genetic pool. For others, such speculation raises the specter of a sophisticated kind of genetic cleansing, analogous to ethnic cleansing, and the Nazi dream of the creation of a super race, presaging at best a grim and homogeneous future for humanity.

Gentrification

The term *gentrification* refers to the transformation of rundown, low-income housing into middle- or even upper-class housing. In recent decades, gentrification has overtaken many of the urban neighborhoods that once provided homes for elderly, poor, and otherwise marginal city residents.

Gentrification was begun largely by adult children of the ex-urbanites who had fled the cities to the suburbs in the 1950s and 1960s. This new generation reversed the process of suburbanization by making their way back into the cities. Purchasing relatively cheap buildings in poor neighborhoods, these young, middle-class professionals rehabilitated the houses, not only making them more livable, but increasing their value as well.

As these individual buildings grew in value, so did the property surrounding them. Neighborhoods that had once been shunned as slums or near-slums by anyone who could afford to live elsewhere now became attractive to ever more prospective residents.

Real estate developers moved in, and, together with the new class of residents, bought up and remodeled an increasing number of low-income apartment buildings and residential hotels, until the character of the neighborhoods was entirely transformed.

Although gentrification has been welcomed by most city governments as an essential element of the city's revitalization after decades of decay, it has created enormous problems for the poor and elderly residents forced out of their homes by rising rents and real estate taxes. In many cases, there has been nowhere else for them to go, and they have joined the ranks of the homeless. This, in turn, has put increasing pressure on the city governments.

Gifted and Talented Programs
See Magnet Schools.

Glass Ceiling

At the beginning of the twentieth century, almost all American women employed outside the home worked at menial jobs. They sewed clothes in sweatshops or cleaned and cooked in other people's houses. A handful worked in shops, while the more aggressive and strong-stomached became nurses. As the century moved on, however, more jobs in factories and other businesses began opening up to women. In the decades after World War II, women began flooding into those jobs in greater numbers, until today they fill almost half of all jobs in the United States.

Even so, until fairly recently, the great majority of the women who managed to find their way into the executive offices of American business came as secretaries, the highest position to which they realistically could aspire. But not anymore. Women are increasingly represented in management positions. In many large businesses, they have been rapidly climbing the corporate ladder of better and better jobs. But, even today, it seems that even the most talented and hard-working of them eventually bump their heads against a "glass ceiling"—a job level above which women cannot rise.

Compared to their proportion in the workforce as a whole, women are drastically underrepresented in the ranks of top level executives at American corporations. Although they make up approximately 45.5 percent of all American workers, and an increasing proportion of middle-management positions, they make up only about 8 percent of the top 20 executives in the typical major U.S. corporation.

Feminists argue that the glass ceiling is the result of a prejudice against women in the workplace that still exists at the highest levels of American business. They say there is a feeling among the males who presently control most corporations that the top positions should be filled by men; that women are somehow unreliable; that they are not to be trusted with the ultimate economic and executive power. No matter how qualified a woman may be or how well she does her job, the feminists insist, it is almost impossible for her to break through that glass ceiling of prejudice.

Many business leaders, however, insist that the feminists are overstating the prejudice that exists against women in the executive suite. They suggest that there are other reasons for the lack of women in high positions. Although women are now almost equal to men in numbers in the U.S. workplace, they are not necessarily equal in terms of training and experience. In most companies, the influx of large numbers of women has been relatively recent. This means that, while there may be as many women as men in a given corporation, the men are likely to have worked for the company longer, and so, to have had more experience in the kind of management positions that would qualify them to fill the very highest positions. This problem, the business leaders suggest, will solve itself in time, as more and more women get executive experience.

Nonetheless, the current disproportion between men and women is so great that it is recognized as a serious problem. In an effort to correct the situation, a growing number of large businesses—including Burger King, Xerox, and Allied Signal—have been actively recruiting women to fill some high-level jobs.

See also Affirmative Action; Prejudice; Women in the Workplace.

Goals 2000 Act

The Goals 2000: Educate America Act passed Congress and was signed into law by President Bill Clinton in 1992. This act set national standards for elementary and secondary schools for the first time and directed American education to achieve the following goals by the year 2000:

1. All children entering school should be ready to learn.
2. Nine out of ten students will complete their high school educations.
3. All students will be able to demonstrate competence in the major subject areas—English, math, science, foreign language, civics, economics, art, history, and geography—upon completion of specific grades.
4. Programs will be made available for all teachers to help them improve their skills.
5. U.S. students will lead the world in math and science.
6. Every adult American will possess the needed skills—including literacy—for them to participate in the global economy.
7. All schools will be safe and free from drugs.
8. All schools will encourage parental involvement in the education of their children.
9. In addition to these ambitious goals and standards, the bill provided hundreds of millions of dollars in federal grants, which the states could compete for, to improve the schools.

Although Goals 2000 passed Congress with support from members of both parties, it was opposed by some who believed that education should be solely a state and local responsibility. They objected to any national standards, which would set curriculum or professional qualifications for local schools or tell the states what kind, or quality, of education they must provide. Because of this opposition, the program was made voluntary, and states were eligible to apply for the grants authorized by the act, whether or not they accepted the performance standards contained in the bill.

The federal government has continued to pursue the matter, however, and in his 1997 State of the Union speech, President Bill Clinton renewed the call for the establishment of national goals for elementary school students.

See also Academic Standards.

Gospel of Wealth

The so-called gospel of wealth was a late nineteenth- and early twentieth-century philosophy that attempted to reconcile social Darwinism with the message of the Christian gospel. One of several nineteenth-century viewpoints on the effects of the Industrial Revolution that still echo in the American psyche today, it can best be viewed in counterpoint to the view summed up in the phrase "the social gospel."

Contradictions in the American Attitude toward Wealth

By the beginning of the twentieth century, the United States was already deeply engaged in the transformation from an agricultural society to an industrial one. That process had produced a small but enormously powerful new class of fabulously wealthy American industrialists. They were, as a group, so ruthlessly acquisitive and competitive that critics referred to them as the "robber barons."

Men like Cornelius Vanderbilt and John D. Rockefeller dominated whole industries. They ruled their business empires with iron fists, relentlessly destroying any potential competitors and working their laborers like slaves. They built enormous mansions for themselves so luxurious that they have been called "America's castles."

In their persons, and in their great success, these men embodied some of the most glaring contradictions in what was becoming recognized as the American character. On the one hand, they were looked up to as quintessentially American heroes. The young country was proud of its industrial success, and these men were both causes and symbols of that success. Their careers seemed to sum up the American virtues of enterprise, ambition, and self-reliance.

On another level, however, the materialism of these men, and the lavishness of their lifestyles, seemed to contradict some of the fundamental Christian values that most Americans of the time espoused. The Christian message, after all, called on believers to turn the other cheek to their enemies and to give all they had to the poor—two forms of behavior that seemed entirely foreign to the captains of American industry.

The gospel of wealth grew out of a desire to reconcile these contradictions. In a sense, it can be seen as an attempt to find a way for Americans to hold onto their material ambitions as well as their faith in Christianity.

The Message

The fundamental message of the gospel of wealth was best summed up by Reverend William Lawrence, an early twentieth-century Protestant clergyman, who declared, "Godliness is in league with riches."

Lawrence and other believers in the gospel of wealth argued that, on the whole, wealth is a good thing, both for those who accumulate it and for society in general. What is more, it is generally achieved through virtuous behavior. The wealthy are not only in a better position to help others, through charity and otherwise, but they are more likely to do so.

The phrase "gospel of wealth" comes from the historic 1889 essay, "Wealth," by the steel tycoon Andrew Carnegie. No one was more troubled by the apparent inconsistencies between great wealth and Christianity than Carnegie, who had come to America as a poor Scottish immigrant and clawed his way up to the top ranks of the robber barons. In his essay, Carnegie argued that an individual's ability to accumulate great wealth was, in effect, proof that he deserved not only to possess it, but to dispense it. Enormous riches were not given to such people as himself to squander on personal pleasures, however. Instead, they were given for the wealthy to administer on behalf of society as a whole.

The key to Carnegie's version of the gospel of wealth was its focus on men who, like himself, had made their own fortunes through their own enterprise. (At the time Carnegie was writing, virtually no consideration was given by anyone to the possibility that a woman might accumulate great wealth, although she might inherit it.) It was not merely the possession of great wealth that proved one's worthiness to possess and administer it, but the ability to accumulate that wealth through one's own efforts. There was no room in Carnegie's gospel for inherited wealth.

Effects on American Thought

Carnegie's essay was undoubtedly self-serving. He was trying to convince not only himself and his fellow robber barons, but also his less prosperous fellow citizens who might be jealous of his affluence, that the concentration of great wealth in a single pair of hands was not as unjust as it might seem. He also wanted to convince them that great wealth imposed a duty on its possessors. Carnegie's essay went beyond the personal to provide what amounts to a philosophical basis for American capitalism. The author argued, in effect, that great personal wealth was not only excused, but justified, but by hardheaded philanthropy.

The gospel of wealth was not overtly American: Lawrence and Carnegie wrote in terms of mankind as a whole. Yet, their beliefs were intrinsically American in spirit, and it is not surprising that they had their greatest and most lasting effects in this country.

Belief in the gospel of wealth was not confined to a few wealthy robber barons. Its principles were disseminated, at least indirectly, by many newspaper editors and politicians in the early twentieth century. These principles, which equated success with virtue, helped to establish certain connections in the way ordinary Americans thought about society and their place in it. In the eyes of many Americans, they legitimized not only the possession of great wealth, but American business as well. If the accumulation of wealth was, at least in some cases, a gift from God, then the method by which that wealth was accumulated must, to some degree, be godly too.

The gospel of wealth has had a significant effect on American social attitudes throughout the twentieth century. It helps to explain, for example, the otherwise surprising lack of resentment that poor and middle-class Americans traditionally have felt toward the possessors of great wealth— a very different attitude than that of their counterparts in other western societies.

Accepted by many early twentieth-century Americans, the values epitomized by the gospel of wealth went out of fashion during the Great Depression of the 1930s. Although few people are aware of the gospel of wealth as such, today its values continue to underlie many Americans' attitudes toward wealth. They are clearly reflected, for example, in the political and economic views of many modern political conservatives, including the believers in the "trickle-down" economic theory that became popular in the 1980s.

See also Charity; Social Darwinism; "Wealth."
For further reading Kennedy, Gail, editor. *Democracy and the Gospel of Wealth.* Boston: D. C. Heath & Company, 1949.

Gun Buy-Backs

Concern over the ready availability of guns, and the growing amount of gun-related violence, led to the institution of gun buy-back programs in the 1980s. With the cooperation, and sometimes the assistance, of local law enforcement agencies, a variety of individuals, police departments, civic organizations, and businesses initiated programs in which money or goods were exchanged for guns turned in by citizens. For the most part, these programs were aimed at collecting specific kinds of weapons—usually either handguns or automatic weapons—in hopes that removing them from the streets and homes would cut down on the numbers of gun-related deaths and injuries.

Some buy-backs offered only a token amount, ranging from $25 to preseason football game tickets. Others offered something more substantial. In New York City, for example, Lucien Picard offered gold watches worth hundreds of dollars in return for automatic weapons.

Some programs were especially imaginative. When a young boy in New York City told his father he'd be willing to give up his Christmas presents to get guns off the street, the father started a program offering gift certificates from Toys 'R' Us stores in return for guns. St. Louis used money confiscated from criminal activities to finance much of its 1991 buy-back that netted 8,500 guns.

For a time, buy-backs became a kind of fad and attracted a great deal of public attention. Although the original impetus slowed fairly quickly, periodic local buy-backs have continued in some localities. In most cases, the payment is worth less than the gun would draw on the open market. But many people take advantage of the programs for other reasons—perhaps because they feel uncomfortable having guns around, they consider them a danger to their children, or simply because they feel it is socially useful to remove a potentially deadly weapon from circulation.

See also Gun Control.

Gun Control

There is no way to know exactly how many privately owned guns currently exist in American homes, vehicles, pockets, and places of business today. The best estimate is some 220 million firearms. In the representative year of 1990, 37,155 people died of injuries inflicted by these weapons. They included the victims of hunting mishaps and other accidental shootings, but approximately two out of every three of the deaths—including 12,847 murders and an even large number of suicides—were deliberate.

Perhaps the most troubling statistics regarding firearm deaths are those involving children. Shooting is now the second leading cause of death for people between 15 and 19 years old in the United States, and the most common cause of death for black males of that age. And the number of gun deaths is rising: 1,468 people under the age of 18 were killed by guns in 1992, more than twice as many as five years earlier.

According to the American Trauma Society, gun injuries are not only more physically devastating than knife or battering wounds, they are also much more expensive to treat. The dollar cost of American gun injuries and deaths is estimated at more than $20 billion annually.

A Need for Controls?

The argument for gun control is rooted in statistics like those quoted above, which implicate guns in a high percentage of killings, maimings, suicides, accidental shootings, robberies, and other crimes. Looking at such figures, many Americans conclude that the ownership and use of the deadly weapons implicated in so many deaths and maimings need to be regulated more tightly. Some argue that certain kinds of firearms—including handguns and automatic weapons—should be outlawed altogether.

Handguns are specially targeted because more than half of all the firearms involved in deaths are handguns. In 1991, for instance, there were 24,000 handgun deaths, of which only 1,400 were accidental. Automatic weapons, which are favored by many survivalists, are singled out because, according to the advocates of gun control, they are essentially military weapons. They have no place in private hands, because, unlike hunting weapons and target pistols, they are designed only to kill people.

Those who favor controls argue that guns encourage crime and violence and make them immeasurably more destructive than they would be without them. No one, they say, is likely to rob a bank with a knife or club. Accidents with guns are almost inevitably more serious than accidents with other weapons. Suicide

attempts carried out with firearms are much more likely to prove fatal than those with other methods. Where firearms are unavailable, argue the advocates of gun control, people who quarrel may come to blows. Where firearms are handy, disputants are apt to shoot each other. "The vector for [the disease of] yellow fever is the mosquito," says a spokesperson for the pro gun control Physicians for Social Responsibility. "The vector for violence in our society is the gun."

The opponents of gun control counter that it is misguided to blame guns for what criminals and careless people do with them. "Guns don't kill people," says a National Rifle Association (NRA) slogan. "People kill people." When handled properly, guns that are used for hunting, or target shooting, are as harmless as knives used for preparing food. The NRA, a massive organization made up of hunters, target shooters, gun collectors, and other firearms owners, has led the legal and political battle against most forms of gun control. Guns, it argues, are not only not responsible for the problem of violence afflicting the United States; they are an important part of the solution. Far from causing crime, they actually help prevent it. In a society as troubled by racial and economic tensions as U.S. society today, says the NRA, many Americans rightly consider a gun a necessity for self-defense. The fear that potential victims might have guns with them discourages many robberies and assaults, they say. And when crimes do occur, guns allow the victims to protect themselves and their property.

Gun control proponents respond that the self-defense argument is overstated. They point to FBI statistics that show that less than 300 of the 24,000 handgun deaths in 1991 were either justifiable homicides or killings committed in self-defense or in the defense of others. Gun control opponents counter that such figures fail to show what they claim to be the many lives saved as a result of the crimes that were thwarted by the mere presence of a gun in the hands of a crime victim, or by the many crimes that never happened because of the threat that a potential victim might be armed.

The proponents of gun control argue that armed self-defense is largely an illusion and that the presence of guns in the hands of fearful people makes mayhem, injury, and death more likely, not less. They point to cases in which nervous citizens have shot and killed innocent people, and even members of their own families, mistaking them for burglars or other potential criminals.

Gun control proponents also deny the claim that guns are somehow more necessary as defensive weapons for Americans than for residents of other countries. There is nothing inherently more immoral, more criminal, or more violent about Americans than there is about residents of other countries. Riots, fights, and other kinds of violence are as common elsewhere as here. Urban crime is approximately as frequent in Paris and London as in comparable American cities, they argue. And yet, street killings are relatively rare, thanks primarily to the scarcity of guns.

Furthermore, gun control proponents claim, many countries where guns are rare or totally unavailable are just as racially and ethnically varied as ours, and yet are less violent. India, for example, is even more diverse than the United States; it has hundreds of ethnic groups, speaking over 1,600 different dialects of some 14 major language groups. Ethnic, class, and religious prejudices are at least as bitter and intense as those in the United States. India is also much poorer than the United States, with a per capita national income of less than $400. And yet, the rate of violent crime—and particularly of murders—is much lower in India. The main reason, argue the proponents of gun control, is the almost complete absence of guns in the hands of ordinary citizens.

The Right to Bear Arms

The NRA and other opponents of gun control argue that virtually any effort to regulate or ban guns is a violation of constitutional rights. This argument is based on the Second Amendment to the Constitution, which states, "A well regulated Militia being necessary to the security of a free State, the right of the people to keep and bear arms shall not be infringed."

In colonial times, free white males were required by law to own firearms and to hold themselves available to bear those arms in service with the colonial militias, the NRA points out. Even at the time the Bill of Rights was passed, the gun advocates point out, virtually all white men were considered members of the state militias. In the centuries since, the distinctions between free white men and other U.S. citizens have been eliminated. Thus, the gun advocates say, the Second Amendment assures all individual Americans an absolute right to possess any kind or amount of guns.

The proponents of gun control interpret the Second Amendment very differently. For them, it protects the rights of states to maintain "a well regulated Militia," not the right of individuals to own private firearms.

The ultimate interpreter of the Constitution, the U.S. Supreme Court, has rarely ruled on provisions of the Second Amendment. When it has, the Court has not read the Amendment as broadly as have the opponents of gun control. As early as 1886, in *Presser* v. *Illinois*, the Court ruled that the amendment applies only to the federal government and does not limit the right of state governments to regulate firearm possession.

The most important decision to date regarding federal regulation of firearms is *United States* v. *Miller,* which was announced in 1939. Inspired by the outbursts of gun violence attendant to Prohibition, the Great Depression, and the rise of organized crime, Congress had passed the National Firearms Act of 1934. The act, which regulated and taxed the sale of sawed-off shotguns and machine guns, aroused Second Amendment concerns in many American gun owners. A unanimous Supreme Court, however, ruled that the federal government could legally require the registration of sawed-off shotguns. The Second Amendment, said the Court, protected only those weapons that would ordinarily be used by a state militia. That category did not include the sawed-off shotgun, which was essentially a criminal's weapon.

Although *Miller* did affirm the government's right to regulate gun ownership, the opponents of regulation can use it to support the right of private ownership of automatic weapons, which are, by the gun control advocates' own admission, essentially military-style weapons.

The Supreme Court has been silent on the issue for several years, while the political debate over gun control has been heating up. Lower federal courts, however, have denied several Second Amendment claims against state and local gun regulation. Until the Supreme Court makes a definitive ruling, however, the Second Amendment question will remain open.

Federal Regulation

Throughout most of America's history, the regulation of firearms has been considered primarily, if not exclusively, a state or local police function. Many communities have banned, or put severe restrictions on, the purchase or ownership of handguns. Even in the Old West, some communities required transients entering town to check their guns with the authorities. The carrying of concealed weapons without a permit has long been banned in many localities. In many other communities, however, particularly those in the South and far West, there are no restrictions on gun ownership at all.

The advocates of gun control complained (and still complain) that the many disparities from city to city, and state to state, undercut the local and state laws that do exist. Residents of communities that make it difficult to purchase firearms can simply travel to neighboring towns or states to buy whatever firearms they want. These complaints led to a growing demand for federal regulation of certain kinds of weapons, especially handguns and automatic weapons.

More than 30 years after the initial federal gun control law, Congress passed the Gun Control Act of 1968. It came in response to the assassinations of President John F. Kennedy and Martin Luther King, Jr., both of which were committed with rifles from ambush, and it forbade the unregulated ordering of certain kinds of weapons, thought of as assassination weapons, by mail. Until then, virtually anyone capable of filling out an order form could send away for guns.

The demand for federal gun control heightened again in the 1980s and early 1990s, largely in reaction to an assassination attempt on President Ronald Reagan in March 1981, combined with the increasing incidence of drive-by street shootings and gun violence in schools. In 1993, Congress responded with the passage of the so-called Brady Law.

The most sweeping federal gun control legislation passed so far, the Brady Bill requires a five-day waiting period for the purchase of handguns. The bill also established a national computer network to facilitate background checks to determine whether potential gun purchasers had records of criminal activity or serious mental instability. The law was named after Reagan's press secretary, James Brady, who was shot and permanently disabled in the assassination attempt on the president. Brady—previously an opponent of gun control—and his wife campaigned hard for passage of the bill.

The success of the Brady Law was controversial. A year after passage, proponents insisted that tens of thousands of gun sales had already been denied to proven criminals, mental incompetents, and other potentially dangerous individuals. Opponents, on the other hand, argued that overall crime rates remained unaffected.

The Democratic Congress passed a major crime bill in 1994, which, over the protests generated by a massive lobbying campaign by the NRA, contained several gun control provisions. These included a ban on 19 specific automatic weapons and a prohibition on the sale or gift of firearms to certain classes of individuals, including adults under restraining orders resulting from domestic violence and juveniles.

The crime bill was the biggest political defeat ever for the powerful NRA, and the tide seemed to be moving decisively in favor of stricter federal regulation. The proponents of gun control had hoped to enact a more sweeping gun control bill, dubbed Brady II by some, which would require federal registration of gun owners, among other things. In the election later that year, however, several of the Democrats who had voted for the automatic weapons ban lost their seats, and a largely conservative Republican majority swept into power in both houses of Congress. The Republicans were unlikely to enact any further gun control measures; if anything, they were inclined to undo some that were already in existence.

See also Concealed Weapons Laws; Gun Buy-Backs.
For further reading *A Clash of Arms: The Great American Gun Debate*. Upland, PA: DIANE, 1994. Kruschke, Earl R. *Gun Control: A Reference Handbook*. Santa Barbara, CA: ABC-CLIO, 1995.

Gun Laws
See Concealed Weapons Laws; Gun Control.

Guns
See Concealed Weapons Laws; Gun Buybacks; Gun Control.

Habeas Corpus

Habeas corpus is the legal term for one of the most fundamental rights in U.S. law. Frequently called "the Great Writ," it refers to the courts' authority to check the government's power to arbitrarily deprive people of their liberties.

In theory, a court order known as a writ of habeas corpus (from the Latin phrase meaning "present the body") calls on the official holding a prisoner to bring him or her to the court. By granting such a writ, the judge takes on the responsibility of determining the legality of the imprisonment. In practice, the writ may be used to inquire into virtually any kind of detention, whether the person is being held in prison, in a police station, in a mental institution, or even under a medical quarantine imposed by an agency of any level of government. Habeas corpus even can be used to review the legality of a detention carried out by a private individual claiming some legal power over another individual, such as a parent over a child.

History

Habeas corpus originated in England. An early form, in which a witness could be forced to testify in court, dates to the Magna Carta in the thirteenth century. Since the late

fifteenth century, the Great Writ has been used to review government actions.

Habeas corpus came to the American colonies as one of the keystones of British common law. Following the American Revolution, the right to habeas corpus was included in the U.S. Constitution, and it has been enshrined in the constitutions of each of the states as well.

Abraham Lincoln suspended habeas corpus for a time during the Civil War. Some legal experts objected that the action was unconstitutional, despite a constitutional provision implying the writ could be suspended "when in Cases of Rebellion or Invasion the Public Safety may require it." Those who objected based their constitutional argument on the principle that only Congress, not the president, has the right to dispense with the writ. Congress did eventually endorse the president's decision, making the objection moot. Habeas corpus has been suspended in some respects at other times in U.S. history, as well. For the most part, however, the courts have jealously protected the Great Writ, and the other branches of government have been respectful of it.

Limits on Habeas Corpus

Although almost no one quarrels with the need for habeas corpus in a free society, critics do argue that it is too often misused, or overused, or both. Much of the criticism of habeas corpus has centered on the willingness of federal courts to review the cases of prisoners held by the states after they have been tried in state courts, under state law. That practice was somewhat limited by *Stone* v. *Powell*, a 1976 U.S. Supreme Court decision that held that once a prisoner's claim that he or she had been wrongfully convicted due to an illegal search and seizure by the police had been rejected by the state courts, the prisoner had no right to appeal on that same basis to the federal courts.

The powers of the writ have expanded over the years as the definition of personal liberty has expanded. That long expansion may be in the process of being reversed, however. Although traditionally there has been no limit on the number of times a prisoner might apply for habeas corpus, in recent years the U.S. Supreme Court has indicated its irritation with receiving repeated applications.

The main critics of habeas corpus are conservatives who feel that the courts are too "soft" on criminals. In particular, they complain that the courts have been too willing to set prisoners free on the basis of what the critics consider mere legal technicalities. Others argue that these technicalities are, in reality, the only protections Americans have against the arbitrary exercise of power by the government and warn that habeas corpus is the only tool available to enforce those protections.

See also Death Penalty (Major Supreme Court Decisions).

Head Start

Head Start, the federal program designed to prepare low-income children for school,

was instituted by the Economic Opportunity Act of 1964, which was the foundation of President Lyndon Johnson's War on Poverty. In the three decades since, some 13 million children have participated in the program. Originally established under the Office of Economic Opportunity (OEO), Head Start was moved to the Department of Health, Education, and Welfare in 1969. It is now run by that department's successor, the Department of Health and Human Services.

The Need for Head Start
Children from low-income families are often less well prepared for school than their classmates. Starting out behind, many of them are never able to catch up. Convinced early on that they are not as "smart" as other students, they give up on education and limit their possibilities in life.

One reason for low-income children's educational disadvantage is that they have had less exposure than other children to such educational building blocks as numbers and the alphabet. Head Start gives them that exposure and allows them to begin their formal school training on a more nearly equal footing with other students their own age.

What the Program Does
Head Start centers around the country serve as combination preschools and day care centers for over 700,000 students each year. Even more children are likely to take advantage of Head Start in the future, when a Summer Head Start program that was canceled in 1982 is brought back into service. Eligible children are able to attend for the entire 12 months preceding their first enrollment in school. Those who attend receive meals and snacks during the day. In addition to the direct training Head Start provides the children, the program helps

mothers and fathers to increase their parenting skills. There is abundant evidence that Head Start children do in fact enter school better prepared than non–Head Start children from similar backgrounds.

Although most of the children served by Head Start are poor, the program is also open to families above the poverty line, who pay a sliding fee for their children to participate.

Reactions to Head Start

Head Start was the most popular of all the War on Poverty programs from the beginning, and it has remained one of the most popular government social welfare programs ever since. It has been supported—and its budget expanded—under both Democratic and Republican presidential administrations.

Even so, the program has come under increasing attack in recent years. Critics charge that benefits of the program are temporary. They cite studies that seem to show that the comparative advantage Head Start children enjoy when they enter school tends to disappear as they move through the school system. By the later grades, there seems to be little if any difference between them and non–Head Start students. Supporters of the program argue that this is not a fault in Head Start, but proof that still more programs are needed to help disadvantaged students later in their school careers.

Even supporters of Head Start charge that not all the local centers are equal in quality and that the program as a whole is underfunded and understaffed. Only a small percentage of the children who could benefit from its services are actually enrolled. It has been estimated that in order to correct these problems, the Head Start budget would need to be more than doubled. In 1994 the Clinton administration recommended doing just that, asking Congress to raise the Head Start budget from its current $3.3 billion to $8 billion over the next three years.

Health Care Reform (1994)

The U.S. health care system is an incredibly complex network of private and public institutions. It includes scores of state and federal government agencies, along with thousands of private and public hospitals and clinics, insurance companies, drug companies, and professional organizations, as well as countless thousands of individual doctors, nurses, technologists, and other health care providers.

Americans have long prided themselves on this health care system, which is considered one of the best—and perhaps the single most technologically advanced—in the world. And yet, the United States has a lower life expectancy and a higher infant mortality rate than several other developed countries.

Most experts agree that the relatively poor showing of the United States in these respects is not due to the care provided by American medical practitioners; rather, it is the result of the way in which that care is distributed among the population. For those in a position to take full advantage of the U.S. health care system, it provides the most complete, up-to-date, and proficient care available anywhere in the world. Many Americans, however, are unable to take full advantage of this excellent health care system—a problem that became increasingly acute in the 1980s and that came to a political head in the early 1990s.

The Perceived Need for Health Care Reform

By the early 1990s, there was a growing feeling among the American populace that the health care system was in crisis. That crisis was made up of a combination of factors, the most important of which was the alarming escalation of health care costs. The dramatic rise in these costs was driven partly by the soaring costs of drugs and partly by the development and increased use of extremely expensive technological advances.

Costs had gotten so high that, except for the very wealthy, Americans could no longer afford to pay out of their own pockets for an extended illness or emergency requiring high-tech care. Even routine medical and dental care was too expensive for millions of Americans to afford. Those who could afford to pay for an occasional visit to the doctor were reluctant to do so, fearful of the unpredictable costs they might incur.

Most Americans were covered by some kind of medical insurance through their (or a family member's) employment, but rising health care costs, together with internal problems at some insurance companies, were driving up private insurance premiums. At the same time, many businesses were cutting back on the medical services for which they would pay or were eliminating medical care as a benefit of employment altogether. At the same time, more people were being pressed to join health maintenance organizations (HMOs) and other forms of managed care, in which the patient's choices of medical care providers and courses of treatment were limited to those approved by the particular plan to which they belonged.

Worse, many Americans were not insured at all. Estimates of those without health insurance at any given time ranged as high as 37 million. Some—perhaps most—of the uninsured had access to medical treatment in an emergency, since most hospitals and many physicians will treat anyone in medical crisis, regardless of their abil-

ity to pay. But they got no preventive care. This meant that minor problems were more likely to develop into more serious and expensive conditions. When a medical crisis drove uninsured people to the emergency room, the high costs of emergency service had to be borne by the public.

If acute medical problems were expensive to deal with, long-term care for the aged or the chronically ill was far too expensive for most people to afford. Medicare and Medicaid provided help to the elderly and the poor, but only after such patients had exhausted most or all of their own economic assets.

Designing a Health Care Proposal

Health care reform was a central issue in the 1992 presidential campaign. The Democratic candidate, Bill Clinton, campaigned strongly on the need for reform, arguing that health care services needed to be made available to all Americans at the same time that costs had to be restrained. Once elected, President Clinton put his wife, Hillary Rodham Clinton, at the head of a panel of hundreds of health care experts, politicians, and others charged with designing a major reform of the U.S. health care system.

The health care panel was the subject of political controversy long before its health care reform plan was announced. In order to reduce the inevitable political pressures on the panel, the group met in private, and the names of the panel members were not released. This led to angry charges of closed-door government, as well as to much suspicion about the panel's makeup and intentions among medical providers and others who were nervous about health care reform.

Hillary Clinton became the center of the political storm over the designing of the heath care reform bill. The president's selection of his wife to lead the health care reform design effort was upsetting to many Americans. Although Bill Clinton had campaigned side-by-side with his wife, and promised that she would be an important element of his administration, traditionalists objected to a first lady being given a formal position of substantial political power.

Although most Americans—along with a majority of senators and representatives—agreed that change was needed, there was little agreement about what form the change should take. The key disputes had to do with the scope of proposed reforms and the method of paying for them.

Some Democrats, including President and Mrs. Clinton, insisted that health care should be universal. They favored a broad-ranging plan that would make available to everyone a more-or-less complete range of care. Most Republicans, along with many conservative Democrats, favored a more limited approach. Some wanted only catastrophic coverage, and some supported government help only for those who could not pay for their own insurance privately.

The most liberal reformers called for a "single-payer" plan, similar to Canada's national health insurance plan, under which the government would provide comprehensive medical insurance for all citizens. Most others favored paying for the plan, however broad it turned out to be, with some combination of private and governmental insurance plans.

The Health Care Reform Bill

The ambitious plan that President Clinton proposed to Congress in September 1993 would have covered all Americans under a vast managed care program of "health alliances." The plan was to be paid for largely by employers as a part of the benefits pack-age paid to their employees. Small businesses and the self-employed would be subsidized for the expense, and the unemployed would be covered by insurance provided by the government. The costs of health care were to be held down by negotiations between the "alliances"—some of which would be established by the states and some by large employers—the insurance companies, and health care providers.

In an apparent attempt to satisfy all the conflicting points of view on health care reform, the Health Care Reform Bill became so complex that it took up 1,342 printed pages. Unfortunately for the plan's legislative future, most of the special-interest groups quickly focused on those elements of the plan to which they objected, rather than those they liked. As a result, the plan was met with heavy criticism from almost every side and received very little political support.

Large employers were upset by a provision that required them to pay 80 percent of the health care insurance premiums of their employees. Doctors were upset by elements of the plan that they felt smacked of "socialized medicine." Insurance companies were upset by further government intrusion in their industry. Roman Catholic authorities and other pro-lifers were upset because the plan covered abortions. Drug companies were upset by provisions to hold down the price of their products. Although these and other interest groups launched public attacks on the plan, only the AFL-CIO launched a counterattack in its favor.

Even those groups that hoped to see health care reform passed concentrated their efforts on changing elements of the plan to which they objected, rather than supporting the plan as a whole. As a result, the public and Congress heard a mounting crescendo of criticism, and the overall impression of the plan was negative.

Defeat in Congress

The congressional debate over the Health Care Reform Bill ultimately involved 11 separate committees, as well as at least 97 lobbying organizations—most of the latter of which were working to oppose the plan.

With the issue in doubt in Congress, the health insurance industry launched a major public relations campaign to alarm voters about the plan. Network television viewers were bombarded with an effective series of television spots featuring actors playing an ordinary middle-aged, middle class couple named Harry and Louise, who were pictured expressing serious concerns about what the bill would mean for "ordinary" Americans like themselves. Would they lose the right to choose their own doctor? Would they end up paying more for health insurance than they were already?

Realizing that the bill's chances of passage were small, House Majority Leader Dick Gephardt and Senate Majority Leader George Mitchell each introduced bills of their own, as did Senate Minority Leader Bob Dole. It soon became obvious, however, that none of these, nor any of the alternatives proposed by other members of Congress, was likely to pass. The final demise of health care reform was assured in political wrangling and compromise over the Omnibus Violent Crime Control and Prevention Act of 1994. In late September 1994, Senator Mitchell announced that health care reform was dead.

Nearly two years later, in August 1996, Congress passed, and President Clinton signed, a pale shadow of health care reform entitled the Health Insurance Portability and Accountability Act, which allows insured workers who lose their jobs to continue their insurance coverage, provided they can continue to pay for it. This resolved one of the significant side issues that had been addressed by the health care reform effort of 1994, but left unsolved the main problems—the escalating costs and limited availability of medical care.

Home Schooling

Parents are the first teachers most children have, and parents continue to have a major impact on their children's education for many years to come. Most parents, however, do not have the time, ability, or inclination to take over the full responsibility for educating their children. Furthermore, children in the United States are required to receive some kind of formal education until they are in their mid-to-late teens.

For almost a century, the main responsibility for meeting this legal requirement has rested on the public schools. Although a significant minority of parents have always opted to send their children to private or parochial schools, only a handful chose to educate their own children at home.

Most of the relative handful of parents who did attempt to educate their children at home usually fell into one of four categories. The first were devout followers of some religious belief that had no parochial school system and who were worried about the effect that public schools would have on their children's faith. The second were those with progressive ideas about education that they wanted to put into effect with their own children. The third were those who felt that their children, whom they believed to be especially gifted, would not be sufficiently nourished by the available state-certified schools. The last were white parents who, in the wake of the racial integration of many previously segregated schools in the 1960s and 1970s, were either fearful or resentful of their children attending school with African-Americans or other minorities.

The numbers of parents educating their children at home were held down by the fact that, in most jurisdictions, home schooling was virtually illegal. Few, if any, parents could meet the strict standards required of teachers by the law. In recent decades, however, an increasing number of states have passed laws making it easier for parents to keep their children at home.

Typically, these laws require parent-teachers to cover a range and depth of material equivalent to what the child would be exposed to in a traditional school. They also require that the child be periodically tested to be sure that he or she is learning at a sufficient rate.

Even now, home schooling is rarely attempted throughout a child's education, as few parents feel qualified to handle a full curriculum from kindergarten through high school. Instead, it is usually limited to one or several primary grades, which many parents feel are particularly formative. By 1994, however, more than 700,000 U.S. children were being educated at home, more than 56 times as many as 20 years before.

Homeshare

The practice of different individuals and families sharing housing with each other for economic or convenience reasons is an old one in the United States. Words like "roommates" and "housemates" were coined to define these relationships. In the early 1990s, however, this practice became formalized in the homeshare movement.

Participants in homeshare want to share accommodations for a variety of reasons. The most common is probably financial: the need for someone to help share living expenses. Others, particularly the elderly or infirm, are looking for help in carrying out routine household tasks. Still others are simply lonely and feel a need for companionship.

Traditionally, most homesharing arrangements have been made either individually, among people who knew each other, or under the auspices of some organization, like a university, with which all parties were allied. Others, who could not find roommates or housemates in such ways, put ads in newspapers or other publications looking for strangers to share rent or mortgage payments. However, this was a daunting process for many people, particularly those who feared that respondents might prove to be financially or emotionally unstable, worries that all too frequently proved to be true. By the early 1990s, homeshare projects began springing up that were specifically designed to help people get together. Individuals or families looking for others to share long-term living accommodations sign up with the project. The project advertises for them, screens them and other applicants to make sure that they have no criminal record and that they are financially dependable, and then helps to match them with other individuals or families with whom they would be compatible.

By the spring of 1994, hundreds of homeshare projects were in operation in cities around the United States, and more are being formed all the time.

See also Cohousing.

Homosexuality

Homosexuality is the primary attraction of an individual for those of his or her own sex. As with other minority concerns, the terminology is controversial. Although males who feel such an attraction have traditionally been referred to as homosexuals, in recent decades most have come to prefer the term "gays," feeling that "homosexual" has taken on a pejorative tone. Females also sometimes refer to themselves as "gay" or "lesbian." The common term for heterosexuals is "straights."

Although homosexuality has existed since the beginning of recorded history, and has been a feature of virtually every known society, its exact nature is still a matter of heated debate. Most psychologists agree that virtually everyone feels some attraction toward members of their own sex at some point in their lives. Homosexual schoolboy and schoolgirl "crushes" are common in youth, although many who experience them deny the sexual aspects of such feelings. Similar attractions may also occur at other stages of life.

For the great majority of people, however, these are passing feelings, soon overwhelmed by a predominant attraction to individuals of the opposite sex. There is no generally accepted explanation of why this is not the case for a significant number of other individuals who remain attracted almost exclusively to their own sex. (Others, of both sexes, are bisexual: that is, strongly attracted to members of both sexes.) Sexual anthropologists claim that homosexuality seems to occurs in approximately the same percentage of people in almost every society. Estimates vary, but average 10 to 11 percent.

Concepts of Homosexuality

Homosexuality has been variously persecuted, tolerated, or accepted by different elements of American society. In general, however, known homosexuals have been subject to wide-ranging discrimination in such areas as hiring, housing, and child custody.

Although there are homosexuals in virtually every walk of life, and of every political persuasion, the ready acceptance of homosexuality as a lifestyle is generally associated with a liberal political point of view, whereas intolerance of it is generally associated with conservatives. To some degree, this may be due to the strong identification of Christian fundamentalists, who are strongly opposed to homosexuality for religious reasons, with conservative politics.

Some people, both homosexual and "straight," regard homosexuality as a natural condition. They point to the fact that same-sex sexual activity is commonplace among many animal species. Others, however, regard homosexuality as a perversion of the natural order—either as a moral failure or a psychosexual disorder that requires treatment. Still others accept homosexuality as a natural human state but regard homosexuals as unfortunates who are trapped by a defect in their nature.

In the past, American popular opinion considered homosexuality to be one of the worst of all vices. It was so shocking that it was referred to in the United States and elsewhere as "the sin that dare not speak its name." Even today, homosexual activity is considered immoral by many straight Americans, and the open homosexual lifestyle is looked on by many with distaste. Among antihomosexual elements of society, several demeaning terms are employed for homosexuals, including "queer" and "fairy" for males and "dyke" for females. Despite the widespread disapprobation of homosexual activity, a significant proportion of straight Americans, including many who regard homosexual behavior with distaste, are tolerant of gays and lesbians who do not openly flaunt their sexuality.

Although some regard homosexuality as a preference—a choosing of one gender over another for sexual gratification—others regard it the way they regard heterosexuality: as a given of one's nature over which one has no choice. Among those who believe that homosexuality is a fundamental part of the individual's makeup, some hold that it is primarily a psychological reality, while others believe it is genetic—that one is biologically preprogrammed to be either gay or straight.

Another widely held view maintains that homosexuality is primarily the result of environment—that it is a learned behavior, which one can fall into through example, peer pressure, or seduction.

Religious Views of Homosexuality

Whether or not they regard attraction toward members of one's own sex as sinful, most traditional religions consider overt homosexual acts to be sins. Orthodox Jews and many Christian sects cite a small number of texts from the Bible to prove their point, notably Leviticus 18:22: "You shall not lie with a man as with a woman; that is an abomination."

Jewish and Christian homosexuals respond that no modern religion regards the proscriptions contained in Leviticus as literal commands from God. They point out, for example, that the same book calls for homosexuals to be put to death, along with adulterers of both sexes and those who "revile" their parents.

Some more liberal Christian sects are tolerant of gays and lesbians, and some individual clergy and congregations within even the mainstream churches are overtly welcoming of them. Although most Christian and Jewish authorities have moderated their teachings on homosexuality in recent decades, the religious condemnations of homosexual behavior, both past and present, have undoubtedly helped to form the negative attitudes that exist toward homosexuals in much of American society.

Employment Issues

It is partly the concept of homosexuality as a sin and partly the fear that it might be taught, whether directly or by example, that lead some Americans to believe that homosexuals should be forbidden to hold jobs that put them into regular contact with young people—particularly those jobs that put them in authority over children or in which they would be regarded as role models by the young. They fear that impressionable young people could be swayed into following homosexual lifestyles in imitation of such role models. A related concern is the widespread prejudice, denied by homosexuals as well as by many psychologists and social scientists, that homosexuals are more likely than straights to sexually abuse children.

Certain segments of American society have long been especially tolerant of homosexuality itself and of individual homosexuals. The creative communities (literature, art, theater, dance, fashion, etc.) have traditionally been especially accepting of homosexuality, which may explain why a relatively high proportion of homosexuals are drawn to the arts.

Although known homosexuals have long been discriminated against in hiring, some businesses have recently made an active effort to open up to gays. In the late 1980s several major American corporations, including the giant IBM corporation, extended spousal benefits rights to the partners of homosexuals. Such measures remain controversial, however. For example, antigay groups launched a boycott against Disney World after the Walt Disney Corporation extended benefits to the partners of its gay employees.

Legal Rights Issues

At one time, homosexual acts were crimes virtually everywhere in the United States.

147

That is no longer the case. Such acts are now legal—or at least not legally prohibited—in approximately half the states. This reflects a significant change in attitude on the part of the American public as well as state legislators. That change is far from complete, however.

Laws against homosexual behavior remain on the books in half of the states. In some states, the acts most commonly associated with homosexuality are outlawed even when performed by members of the opposite sex, whether or not the heterosexual couple is married. Although such laws are rarely enforced against adults pursuing consensual sexual activities in private, their mere existence amounts to a legal condemnation of homosexuality and lends support to those who discriminate against homosexuals in employment, child custody, housing, and in other ways.

Homosexual activists have challenged the constitutionality of these laws, appealing to the courts to protect their rights under the First, Ninth, and Fourteenth amendments. They have claimed their right to sexual freedom under the right to privacy—a right that the courts have supported in regard to a variety of other sexual matters. In the 1986 case of *Bowers* v. *Hardwick*, however, the U.S. Supreme Court explicitly rejected the claim that the right to privacy protected homosexual activities, even if those activities were carried out within the individuals' own homes.

See also "Don't Ask, Don't Tell" Policy; Homosexuals (Gays and Lesbians) in the Military; Same-Sex Marriages.

Homosexuals (Gays and Lesbians) in the Military

For most of the twentieth century, homosexuality was a bar to military service. Known gays and lesbians would not be accepted into any branch of the U.S. military, and homosexuals who entered the military without revealing their sexual preferences were subject to dismissal whenever those preferences became known. The Pentagon held that homosexuality in and of itself was incompatible with military service.

During the days when the military services were more or less strictly segregated by sex, it was felt that sexual attraction between servicemen and servicewomen, both within the same rank and between ranks, was a severe strain on the discipline and order needed in military life. This argument lost some of its power as more women were accepted into all branches of the service and men and women were increasingly thrown together on and off duty.

Serious problems remained, however, in the view of the Pentagon. Prejudice against homosexuals was extremely strong among enlisted men and women as well as among officers of both sexes. Military personnel who were even suspected of homosexuality, whether accurately or not, were routinely subjected to harassment from their peers and superiors alike. Life was made so difficult for many gay and lesbian servicemen and servicewomen that they left the military. Those who remained were subjected to contempt and harassment from their fellow servicemen and servicewomen. This not only had a bad effect on morale, according to the Pentagon, but also made it difficult to enforce needed military discipline.

In November 1993, a federal appeals court struck at the Pentagon's policy of barring homosexuals from military service in the case of a Navy midshipman who had been dismissed from the U.S. Naval Academy at Annapolis, Maryland, shortly before he was due to graduate. The court declared that a "cardinal principle of equal protection of law holds that the government cannot discriminate against a certain class in order to give effect to the prejudices of others."

Sentiment against allowing gays to serve in the military remained strong, however, both inside the services and among the public at large. It was rumored that some of the strongest opposition to gays came from within the Joint Chiefs of Staff itself.

President Bill Clinton, who personally favored allowing gays in the military, attempted to reach a compromise between his own and the court's views on the one hand, and traditional military policy on the other, by instituting the "don't ask, don't tell" policy, which remains in effect.

See also "Don't Ask, Don't Tell" Policy.

Household Makeup

The stereotype of the typical American family—a working father, homemaker mother, and children, all living together—today applies to fewer than one in four U.S. households. Nonetheless, approximately 70 percent of households with children still consist of families composed of two parents and children living together. Although that is still the most common of the many varieties of American households, no form of household can really be described as typical.

Other common varieties include blended families, consisting of previously married spouses, with children from two or more previous households; a single parent, with children from one or more families or relationships; grandparents living with and taking care of grandchildren; single-person households; roommates sharing expenses; unmarried heterosexual couples, with or without children; gay or lesbian couples, with or without children from previous relationships; and single housemates.

There are certain statistical differences between households of different ethnic groups. Hispanic-American and Asian-American households, for example, tend to be larger than those of most other ethnic backgrounds. In 1990, less than 37 percent of black children under the age of 15 were living with both parents, compared with just over 80 percent of white children. Black and white families alike are breaking down at a faster rate than in previous decades. In 1970, when the current generation of young parents was being raised, 41.5 percent of all black children and 10.5 percent of all white children lived with one parent, or with someone other than a parent. By 1993 the comparable figures were 64.4 percent and 22.8 percent, respectively.

Human Rights
See Universal Declaration of Human Rights.

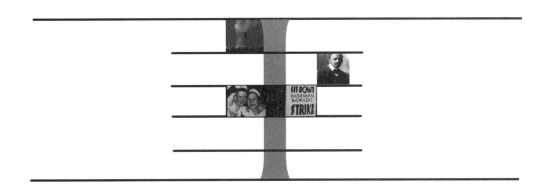

Immigrants and the English Language

According to information collected for the 1990 U.S. census, some 31.8 million Americans spoke some language other than English at home. Spanish was the most common non-English household language, followed in order by French, German, Chinese, and Italian. This did not indicate that all of these foreign-language speakers were unable to speak English, however. Rather, the census found that approximately 95 percent of all U.S. residents were fluent in English.

Many present-day Americans overestimate the numbers of immigrants who do not speak English and resent the tendency of immigrants to retain their language of origin. They feel that it is somehow ungrateful, and even insulting, not to immediately adopt the language most Americans think of as the language of the United States. "If they want to be Americans, they should speak like Americans," is a common attitude. "If they don't want to speak English, they should go back where they came from."

The suggestion that there is something "un-American" about a failure to learn English is particularly ironic in light of the fact that immigrants to the United States have traditionally retained their languages for a generation or two throughout American history.

Patterns of Language Retention

Historically, immigrants who come to the United States from non-English-speaking nations have learned to speak English at their own speed, a speed that has varied according to their circumstances. Members of immigrant groups who arrive in large waves tend to make the transition to English relatively slowly. Clustering together in neighborhoods, such as the Little Italys and Chinatowns, they establish their own social and economic institutions, making it relatively easy for them to conduct their daily lives in their native languages. In recent decades, this has primarily been true in certain Latin American neighborhoods and in neighborhoods with a high concentration of relatively recent Hmong-, Vietnamese-, and Chinese-speaking immigrants.

Individual immigrants and families, who lack the social support of substantial communities who speak their language, tend to adopt English more quickly. Among both groups, however, the transition to English is often generational. Those who come as children master English quickly and easily, while older immigrants are much slower to become comfortable in the language, often learning to speak, read, and write only rudimentarily, if at all.

Immigrants maintain their language of origin for a variety reasons. Many find it difficult to learn another language, particularly after they have reached adulthood. Even for many of those readily able to learn English, their own language is more comfortable for them. Having left so much of their own lives behind to take up the life and customs of a foreign land, their native language may be the one anchor that holds them to their past. Others keep their first language deliberately, and even defiantly, not wishing to abandon their culture.

Immigrant families tend to speak their native language at home long after they have switched to English in their outside lives. This often remains the case until the older generations have died off. This was true in some small rural communities in the Midwest, for example, which remained heavily German- or Polish-speaking well into the twentieth century. Within a few generations, however, most immigrant families will have lost their proficiency in their language of origin altogether.

See also English as an Official Language.

Immigration (Illegal)

In addition to the hundreds of thousands of legal immigrants and refugees who enter the United States each year, hundreds of thousands of other foreigners take up residence in the country illegally. Some enter the country illicitly; others come as tourists, students, or in some other legal manner, but fail to leave when their visas expire.

Mexico is by far the most significant source nation of illegal immigrants to the United States. Of the more than 1.25 million illegal immigrants caught trying to

enter the United States in 1992, more than 90 percent came from Mexico. Although some came with the intention of living permanently in the United States, others came in search of temporary employment with the intention of returning to their native country at some time in the future. Other significant sources of illegal immigrants include Asia (especially China), Latin America, Haiti, and several other poor countries in the Caribbean.

Illegal aliens fill an economic need, working for low wages as domestic servants and migrant farm laborers and in other jobs that few legal American residents are willing to fill. Nonetheless, their presence prompts resentment from many Americans, particularly in states where the illegal population is heavily concentrated.

The Burden on the States

Nine out of ten of all immigrants, legal and illegal, live in California, Florida, Illinois, New Jersey, New York, or Texas. This puts a disproportionate share of the economic costs and social strains associated with high illegal immigrant populations on a relatively small number of states and localities. The nation's two most populous states, California and New York, have gone to court to demand that the federal government take more of the financial burden off of state taxpayers. So far, the courts have refused to intervene.

Such costs can be significant. In the case of *Plyler* v. *Doe* (1982), the U.S. Supreme Court ruled that illegal immigrants are covered by the Equal Protection Clause of the Fourteenth Amendment to the U.S. Constitution, and therefore protected by the same constitutional rights as other persons. *Plyler* involved the refusal by the state of Texas to pay for the education of undocumented immigrant children. The principle established in *Plyler* requires, in effect, that state governments provide the same basic services—including education and emergency health care—to illegal aliens as to other state residents.

In a time of rising medical costs, the expense of emergency medical care for illegal immigrants is a particularly sore point. As a result of pressure from the political establishments in Texas and California, payment for their emergency treatment is paid directly to hospitals, rather than to the immigrants themselves.

On the other hand, illegal immigrants provide significant economic benefits to society as well. It is estimated, for example, that between 30 percent and 50 percent of the seasonal farm workers in California are illegal aliens. Without them, many crops in California and similar states would either go unharvested or be forced up so dramatically in price, due the increased costs of native-born labor, as to put a heavy burden on the nation's food consumers.

Recent Efforts to Control Illegal Immigration

The 1986 Immigration Reform and Control Act, aimed at easing the illegal immigration problem, included penalties for American employers who knowingly hire illegal workers and declared an amnesty for illegal aliens who had been in the country since 1982. Nearly 1.4 million immigrants applied for amnesty by the May 4, 1988 deadline set by the bill.

Another major illegal immigration bill, passed in 1996, doubled the size of the U.S. Border Patrol, facilitated procedures for deporting illegal aliens found within the United States and stiffened penalties for the smuggling of illegal immigrants into the United States.

See also Immigrants and the English Language; Immigration (Legal); Refugees.

Immigration (Legal)

As described in the title of a book by John F. Kennedy, the United States is, and has always been, *A Nation of Immigrants*. Throughout the history of the United States, immigrants have provided continuous infusions of new blood, new energy, entrepreneurial spirit, and economic stimulus to the nation. With the exception of the Native Americans, who came to North America before historic records were kept, most present-day residents can trace their personal ancestry back to one or more foreign lands.

Recent Immigrants

By the end of 1995, approximately 23 million of the more than 260 million U.S. residents claimed another country as their place of birth. This was the largest proportion of foreign-born population since 1940, although much smaller than the proportion of foreign-born residents in the first half of the twentieth century.

Just over 720,400 immigrants were legally admitted to the United States in 1995. This number does not include approximately 152,000 refugees who entered the country in that year. Refugees are considered a special case under U.S. law, which even allows some aliens to stay who have arrived on U.S. soil as tourists, but who would face serious danger or political persecution if they were returned to their own country. The number of refugees accepted into the United States varies annually. In recent years, more refugees have come from Latin America than from any other major region of the world, while the fewest have come from Africa.

By far the largest percentage of nonnative-born residents of the United States (almost 30 percent) came here from Mexico. Another 5 percent came from the Philippines, and smaller numbers came from China (including Taiwan and Hong Kong), Cuba, Canada, El Salvador, Great Britain, Germany, Poland, Jamaica, and the Dominican Republic, in that order.

The average age of all immigrants is 28, and they are divided almost equally between men (51 percent) and women (49 percent). The great majority take up residence in their ports of entry or other large cities, with New York City, Los Angeles, Miami, and Washington, D.C. being the most favored.

Historic Efforts to Regulate Immigration

For most of the first century of the United States's existence, immigration to the United States was essentially open. The nation was expanding and eager for people to settle what had recently been wilderness. Far from worrying about potential overpopulation, Americans were concerned that there might be too few people to fuel the nation's growing economy and to populate its expansive landmass.

Anti-immigrant sentiment has been a recurring phenomenon in American history, however, from the Nativist, or Know-Nothing, movement of the mid-1800s to calls in Congress in 1997 for a total moratorium on immigration. This periodic hostility toward immigration has been sparked by a variety of motives, from simple antialien prejudice to fears of job competition and concerns about real or imagined threats to traditional American culture.

By the mid-nineteenth century, as more second-, third-, and fourth-generation Americans began to feel a strong sense of an increasingly American heritage and national identity, they began to regard immigrants as "foreign" elements who competed with native-born Americans for jobs and corrupted American traditions. Although much of this feeling was directed against Roman Catholics, there was also a strong strain of ethnic and racial prejudice in anti-immigrant sentiment—a feeling that has been reflected in Congressional efforts to restrict immigration, which began in 1862, when Congress forbade U.S. flag vessels from carrying immigrants from China to the United States. This was followed, in 1882, by the Chinese Exclusionary Act, banning Chinese immigrants altogether.

Theodore Roosevelt worked out a so-called gentlemen's agreement with Japan in 1907 in which the Japanese government agreed to restrict the numbers of Japanese agricultural laborers who emigrated from that country to the United States. In return, the United States pledged to combat discrimination against Japanese residents here.

Since 1875 Congress has passed a variety of measures designed to exclude various categories of "undesirable" immigrants, such as convicted criminals, prostitutes and others of questionable sexual morality, and victims of communicable diseases, among others. Also excluded were would-be immigrants who were deemed likely to become wards of the state. Other congressional measures regulated the conditions under which able-bodied workers were allowed into the United States in order to keep them from competing for jobs with native-born Americans.

Twentieth-Century Immigration Policies

A 1917 measure banned emigrants from much of Asia and required those from elsewhere to pass a literacy test. Political subversives were officially banned the following year. The National Origins System, introduced some years later, limited the number of immigrants who would be accepted annually from any country to a small percentage of the American residents of that nationality already living in the United States in 1920.

Quotas based on national origins were, in their own way, as ethnically and racially discriminatory as the Asian exclusions had been. Although by different means, the quotas continued to favor the same white, non-Asian immigrants who had always been preferred. The new quotas allowed for more immigration from western Europe, whose peoples were considered highly desirable, and less from eastern Europe, whose peoples were considered suspect. What is more, some other nationalities continued to be banned altogether. It was not until 1943, for example, that China was finally given a quota.

Although quite strict, the national origins quotas were not entirely rigid. Exceptions were made for some spouses and children of American citizens. The biggest exceptions came following World War II, when some 202,000 European refugees from that conflict were allowed into the United States. A special act of 1953 opened the way for other refugees to come in the future.

U.S. immigration policies were reorganized by the Immigration and Nationality Act of 1952, although quotas continued to limit the number of immigrants who would be accepted from each country. The 1952 act also initiated a system that gave preference to would-be immigrants with professional or other job skills needed in the United States.

Reacting to the apparent racism of the nationality-based quotas, amendments to the Immigration and Nationality Act ended those restrictions in 1965. They were replaced with an overall limitation on the numbers of immigrants who would be accepted from each of the eastern and western hemispheres. Within these broad limitations, permission to enter the United States was awarded on a nondiscriminatory basis.

Even these hemispheric distinctions were abandoned when a single worldwide quota was established in 1977. This new overall limitation, which varies from year to year, was set at 290,000 in its first year, with the proviso that no more than 20,000 immigrants would be accepted from any one country. The quota later ranged from the mid-500,000s to the 600,000s during the 1980s, then rose in the early 1990s to a high of over 1,825,000 in 1992 before dropping precipitously to below its original 1977 level in the mid-1990s.

Refugees and other special categories of immigrants are exempt from the numerical quota. Within it, preference is given to potential immigrants with close relatives in the United States or special skills that are needed here.

Modern Concerns about Immigration

Critics of liberal immigration policies have long been worried about the impact of immigration on the size and makeup of the U.S. population. Immigration, they complain, tends to result in a much greater increase in the overall population than the mere numbers of immigrants themselves would suggest. This is because a high percentage of immigrants come from regions of the world where the fertility rates are much higher than in the United States. For at least the first few generations, immigrant families tend to have substantially more children than long-established American families. As a result, critics of immigration complain, even steady immigration rates tend to skew the U.S. population increasingly toward the foreign-born, the non-English-speaking, the poor and the less educated—all characteristics found more commonly among first-generation American families than among the population as a whole.

The troubling effects of high immigration are felt more strongly in states such as California, Florida, and New York, which have high proportions of recent immigrants, and felt least in states such as Maine and North Dakota, where immigrants are comparatively rare.

Critics in some regions complain that the presence of high levels of immigrants leads to increases in crime. Such complaints are particularly (although not exclusively) common to places like south Florida, which are home to relatively large numbers of immigrants from drug-exporting countries.

Supporters of more liberal immigration policies respond that immigration is not particularly high today. It is, in fact, lower both in absolute numbers and in the immigrants' proportion of the population than it was only a few decades ago. What is more, the proponents of liberal immigration point out that the critics invariably overestimate the negative effects of immigration and underestimate the positive ones. Immigrants, they argue, are vital to American society. In addition to providing an ongoing infusion of creative and entrepreneurial energy, they fill in the gaps in the American workforce, taking jobs that native-born Americans are reluctant to fill.

Proponents of immigration point out that much of what each succeeding generation of Americans thinks of as distinctively "American" was, in fact, contributed by previous generations of immigrants. Citing the individual contributions of immigrants from Andrew Carnegie to Albert Einstein—and ethnic group contributions from the Christmas tree to Tex-Mex, German, and Cajun cooking—the supporters ask what American social, economic, and artistic life would be like without them. Future generations of immigrants, they suggest, have even more to contribute.

See also Immigrants and the English Language; Immigration (Illegal); Refugees.
For further reading Hutchinson, E. P. *Legislative History of American Immigration Policy, 1798–1965*. Philadelphia: University of Pennsylvania Press, 1981.
Kennedy, John F. *A Nation of Immigrants*. New York: Harper, 1964.
McClellan, Grant S. *Immigrants, Refugees, and U.S. Policy*. New York: H. W. Wilson, 1981.

Initiatives and Referenda

An initiative is a petition process that in some jurisdictions allows citizens to bypass a representative legislature in order to introduce a law themselves. It is up to the supporters of the initiative to collect enough valid signatures to bring the measure up for a vote, either in the legislative body or in a referendum. A referendum is an election in which voters are asked to choose between two or more positions on an issue.

There are two kinds of initiatives. An indirect initiative places a measure before a legislature, and a direct initiative places it in a referendum in which it will be voted up or down by the voters. Typically, if the legislature refuses to act on a measure brought before it by a successful indirect initiative, the measure will be put on a ballot for a vote by the people.

Like initiatives, referenda also come in two varieties. A binding referendum enacts the measure directly into law, and an advisory referendum merely requires the legislature to vote on it.

Initiatives and referenda are used to bypass, to force action from, or to override balky legislatures, which might refuse to act on a popular issue for a variety of reasons. Representatives might, for example, think that a proposal is a bad idea (even if the majority of voters favor it), and yet be reluctant to vote openly against it, knowing that such a vote would be unpopular with their constituents. Or a measure might be stalled in the legislative process, whether by infighting among the representatives or through the influence of a special interest.

Many states and localities make the initiative and referendum process available as a remedy for such situations. However, initiatives are not available at the federal level.

History
The initiative process was first recognized by the state constitution of Georgia in 1777. In the early decades of the twentieth century, the process was enacted by Progressives in several states who believed that their state legislatures were controlled by corporate interests and would not work what the Progressives believed to be the people's will.

Probably no state makes more use of the initiative and referendum process than California. The 1978 passage of Proposition 13, by which California voters ordered the state legislature to cut property taxes, not only launched a tax revolt in other states, but awakened a new interest in the initiative process as well. By 1996, the number of initiatives that had been proposed in California had climbed to over 200.

Initiatives and referenda can override state legislatures; they cannot, however, override either state or federal constitutions. At least two important California propositions—Proposition 187, which forbade state agencies to provide medical care and other social services to undocu-mented aliens, and Proposition 209, which outlawed affirmative action by the state—were immediately challenged in the courts over constitutional issues.

Issues and Concerns
The initiative and referendum processes are ideological only in the sense that they imply a value in democracy. Used primarily by liberal Progressives in the early years of the twentieth century, they are employed mostly by conservatives today.

Initiatives and referenda are especially attractive in times like the late twentieth century, when many people feel a deep distrust of their government. In theory, they have the appeal of direct democracy, providing a way of taking matters at least partly out of the hands of politicians, bureaucrats and special interests and putting them squarely into the hands of the people. Some social scientists, however, believe initiatives and referenda are less democratic in their results than they are in theory.

In practice, initiative and referenda allow active minorities to exert an influence far greater than their numbers. Relatively few people tend to vote in initiative and referendum elections, and those who do are usually those who are most passionate about the issue being voted on. This enables a minority with a particular interest in an issue to decide the question for the entire citizenry. Supporters of initiatives and referenda see nothing wrong with this. After all, they say, the voters who are most concerned voters with an issue are usually the ones who are most affected by the issue, and who know the most about it. They are, therefore, the people best qualified to make a decision about it. Those who choose not to vote, on the other hand, are saying, in effect, that they are content to let others decide. It is better to leave policy decisions to a direct vote of the concerned citizenry, than to the wealthy and powerful interests that too often dominate votes in state legislatures.

Some critics of the initiative and referendum process argue that, far from undermining the power of money in politics, they actually increase that power. Although initiatives may be launched by people with deep concerns about an issue, most voters tend to be ignorant of some issues. They are vulnerable to having their opinions formed by whichever side runs the most effective, which usually means the most expensive, advertising campaign. These critics contend that it is often easier for moneyed interests to influence public opinion than it is to influence an entire legislature.

Supporters of initiatives and referenda acknowledge that, like all political processes, they are far from perfect or foolproof. Even so, the supporters insist, they are the most democratic (and therefore the most desirable) way for many issues to be decided. In the end, whether one favors initiatives and referenda over the traditional legislative process depends on which one trusts more: the judgment of elected politicians, or the direct judgment of the electorate.

See also Democracy.

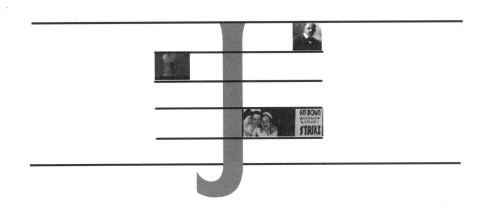

Jewish/African-American Relations

African-Americans and Jews have been among the worst victims of prejudice and bigotry. Black slavery in the western hemisphere and the Nazi effort to exterminate the Jews in Europe are two of the most terrible examples of the horrors these evils can produce.

For much of the twentieth century, this history of suffering led African-Americans and Jews to join together in a common effort to combat prejudice in the United States. This was particularly true in the 1950s and 1960s, when many members of both groups united to pressure the government to pass laws protecting the rights of all Americans. Although the civil rights movement of that time most directly affected African-Americans, many Jews played prominent roles. They were active in groups like the National Association for the Advancement of Colored People (NAACP), took part in the Freedom Rides, and were among the victims of the murders of civil rights workers that took place in the South in those years. On college campuses, Jewish students frequently provided the main white support for demands for black studies programs, while some wealthy Jews even raised funds for black power organizations such as the Black Panthers.

Growing Divisions

Despite these shared struggles, the unity between the two groups was never complete. No one is completely free from prejudice, and there has always been a certain amount of antiblack bigotry among Jews, as well as a certain amount of anti-Semitism among African-Americans. To a great extent, however, these prejudices were overridden by their shared interest in fighting bigotry and discrimination in general. But in recent years, divisions have been growing between the two groups, and the coalition between them has been breaking down.

Although some mainstream black leaders deny it, other black leaders, some of whom are associated with the Nation of Islam, have been inflaming anti-Semitism among certain elements of the African-American community today. At the same time, many American Jews share the antiblack prejudices of some white Americans. Even some Jews who are not overtly prejudiced are becoming increasingly resentful of what they see as unreasonable demands by the black community. Furthermore, they feel that their past efforts to further the black cause have gone unappreciated.

The History of the Split

Conflict between the two communities became obvious in the late 1970s and 1980s, when some prominent African-Americans—most notably U.N. Ambassador Andrew Young and the Reverend Jesse Jackson—attempted to promote progress toward peace in the Middle East by reaching out to the Palestine Liberation Organization (PLO). The PLO was vehemently anti-Israel and had committed many terrorist acts against Jews. American Jewish leaders had always demanded that their friends around the world refuse to deal with the PLO. They considered the contacts by Young and Jackson as a kind of betrayal and a sign of growing anti-Jewish bias among African-American leaders.

The domestic political alliance between the two groups was also showing signs of strain. Black groups were pushing hard for affirmative action programs, designed to help black students and workers overcome generations of past discrimination and catch up with their white counterparts. More and more, Jews began to object to affirmative action programs, opposing them in the courts and elsewhere, fearing they would result in innocent Jews and others being displaced by less qualified African-Americans.

The anger that exploded when a small African-American boy was killed by a car driven by a Jew in the Crown Heights section of New York City in 1991 seemed to show that tensions were even stronger among ordinary members of the two communities than among their leaders. Tension rose again in 1994 when Khalid Abdul Muhammad, a spokesperson for the Black Muslim group, the Nation of Islam, gave a viciously anti-Semitic speech at a black college. The speech was greeted with applause by its young black audience. In order to expose the anti-Semitism it saw in the Nation of Islam, the Anti-Defamation League of the B'nai B'rith printed excerpts from the speech in a full page ad in the *New York Times*. The Nation responded by attacking the B'nai B'rith for spying on the black community.

Many mainstream black leaders, including Jesse Jackson and Representative Kweisi Mfume (Democrat, Maryland), denounced the speech and called on the Nation's leader, Minister Louis Farrakhan, to repudiate it. Farrakhan did repudiate the "manner" of the speech by his subordinate, but proceeded to launch a new verbal attack on the Jews himself. Many Americans of all colors were as appalled by the anti-Semitism of Farrakhan's "apology" as they had been by the original remarks. Nonetheless, several prominent black leaders—including Mfume, the head of the Black Caucus in Congress, and Benjamin Chaves, the executive director of the NAACP—seemed to be satisfied and continued relations with the Nation of Islam.

The reluctance of some black leaders to condemn Farrakhan seemed to be due partly to their own prejudices and partly to fear of jeopardizing their roles as leaders in the black community. The Nation of Islam's anti-Semitism seems to appeal most strongly to angry young inner-city African-Americans who are looking for someone to blame for the poverty and despair that afflicts their neighborhoods. Even many mainstream black leaders, who are used to working hand-in-hand with Jews in the civil rights struggle, are reluctant to alienate these young people.

The apparent willingness of some black leaders to accept anti-Semitism, if not actively encourage it, does not bode well for the future of black/Jewish relations. Nonetheless, people on both sides were encouraged by the willingness of several other black leaders to condemn Farrakhan's remarks. It is clear that the effort by well-meaning people on both sides to heal the breach between them will continue. But it is also clear that there is a great deal of work to do.

See also Anti-Semitism; Civil Rights Movement; Nation of Islam.
For further reading Kaufman, Johnathan. *Broken Alliance.* New York: Macmillan, 1988.

Jury Nullification

Ordinarily, the jury in a criminal case is expected to bring in a verdict of guilty or not guilty depending on whether or not the prosecution has convinced them, beyond a reasonable doubt, that the defendant committed the criminal act charged in the indictment. There are occasions, however, on which juries bring in a verdict of not guilty, even though they are convinced that the defendant did commit the alleged act. They do so because they believe that the law the defendant broke was a foolish, wrong-headed, or unjust one or because they believe the penalty likely to be imposed would be harsher than the offense deserves. This kind of refusal to convict has been dubbed jury nullification, because, by declining to enforce the law, the jurors are in effect nullifying it.

Nullifying juries fulfill what can be regarded as a political function, along with their judicial one. In doing so, they act as one of the checks and balances that limit governmental power. They also act as barometers of public sentiment on controversial government policies. During the latter stages of the war in Vietnam, for example, as more and more of the American public turned against the war, juries became increasingly reluctant to convict young men for violating the draft laws.

History

In American history, jury nullification predates the founding of the United States itself. In the early eighteenth century, the law of seditious libel forbade journalists to print anything that would bring the colonial government, or its leaders, into disrepute. In 1735, the colony of New York charged John Peter Zenger, the publisher of the *New York Weekly Journal*, with seditious libel for attacking the colony's governor, William Cosby, in print.

Zenger had clearly published some vicious attacks on Cosby, but his lawyer, Andrew Hamilton, insisted in court that the attacks were true. Therefore, he argued, they should not be considered libelous, even though colonial law made all such attacks libelous, whether they were true or not. In a decision that would prove to be a watershed in the battle for a free press in America, the jury acquitted Zenger.

Although the Zenger case was a high point in the history of jury nullification, distaste for the practice was aroused in many Americans by the refusal of many nineteenth- and early twentieth-century juries to convict members of mobs for lynching suspected criminals, and by several southern juries that refused to convict clearly guilty white defendants of murdering civil rights workers or African-Americans in the mid-twentieth century.

Is There a Right of Nullification?

Although the fact of jury nullification is undeniable, the concept is extremely controversial. A jury's right to exercise the power of nullification is nowhere spelled out in the U.S. Constitution; rather, it is inherent in two realities of the American jury system. The first is that jury deliberations are private, and jury members are not called upon to account for their verdicts, nor to explain how they reached them. The second is that, once the jury in a criminal case has acquitted a defendant, no judge or higher court is free to overrule the verdict.

Many judges refuse to acknowledge that the power of nullification exists. Because they believe that juries who refuse to convict people they know to have broken the law are thwarting justice and undermining the authority of the judicial system, they will not inform juries of it. Instead, the judges instruct jurors that it is their duty to convict the defendant if they believe he or she has violated the law, no matter what they may think of the law itself.

Jury Unanimity

In most states, in order for a jury to convict a defendant of a crime, its verdict must be unanimous. If the jury cannot agree, either to convict or to acquit, the jury is said to be hung, and either the defendant must be freed or a new trial held.

Although accurate national statistics on hung juries are impossible to obtain, estimates range as high as one hung jury in ten jury trials. (Many accused persons either plead guilty or receive a trial before a judge.) Critics of the current jury system complain that this rate is too high. One solution being proposed is to end the requirement for jury unanimity.

The Requirement for Unanimity

The unanimity requirement is a matter of state, not federal, law. The U.S. Constitution requires that criminal defendants be given due process and the right to a trial by jury. It does not say what size juries need to be, nor does it say that their verdict must be unanimous. That requirement, which is traditional in the United States, has been written into most state constitutions. State constitutions rule in the majority of crimi-

nal cases, because most criminal offenses are violations of state statutes and are tried in state courts.

Reformers in many states are pressing their state legislatures to end this requirement. As of the summer of 1995, two states had made exceptions to it. Louisiana and Oregon allowed verdicts to be rendered, even when as many as two jurors disagreed with them. Reformers in California and elsewhere have pressed for similar amendments to the constitutions in those states. Some critics of unanimity go even further. They would like criminal verdicts to be reached by a simple majority vote.

The Debate

Critics complain that hung juries are not only expensive and a waste of time, but also that they allow some guilty defendants to go free simply because the state cannot afford the expense of trying them again. Defenders of the unanimity requirement respond that the presumption of innocence rests with the defendant. A hung jury, they say, is at least a strong indication that the defendant probably should not be tried again.

Under U.S. law, a reasonable doubt in the jurors' minds requires an acquittal. The jurors are assumed to be reasonable. (If they were not, how could the decision be left to them?) In light of that assumption, a doubt strong enough to make some jurors stand up against the rest is likely to be a reasonable one.

The reformers reject this argument. Civil cases, they point out, do not require unanimity. Why then should criminal cases? In their view, removing the unanimity requirement would have several positive effects. It would eliminate many hung juries. It would encourage guilty defendants with weak cases to plead guilty. And it would prevent unreasonable or corrupt jurors from thwarting justice and wasting weeks of effort by prosecutors, attorneys, judges, and fellow jurors.

By and large, opponents as well as defenders of unanimity assume that such changes would result in a higher percentage of convictions, rather than acquittals. Although this may not always be the case, it is likely to be the most common outcome. For this reason, any proposed changes tend to be opposed by civil rights advocates who believe that jury unanimity is an important safeguard of the rights of criminal defendants.

Such safeguards need to be stronger in criminal cases than in civil ones, they say. The stakes are lower in civil cases, where a defendant risks only property. In criminal cases, the liberty—and in some cases the life—of the defendant is at stake. The law recognizes this important distinction by requiring that criminal prosecutions be judged according to a higher standard of proof. Although civil cases can be decided by a preponderance of the evidence, criminal cases must be proven beyond a reasonable doubt.

Supporters of the unanimity requirement in criminal cases argue that it is a boon to the deliberative process and a spur to the jury's search for truth. Knowing that each member's vote will be necessary to reach a verdict, all jurors are encouraged to take each other's views and perspectives into account. In this way, the unanimity requirement avoids the hasty and ill-considered verdicts that might be rendered if jurors could simply cast a majority vote on entering the jury room, and the winners would never have to listen to the concerns of those voting for the losing side.

Perhaps most important of all, the supporters argue that the unanimity requirement deepens society's confidence in the correctness of jury verdicts. If a jury is divided in a controversial case, it is unlikely that the public will be satisfied that justice has been done. If the jury is unanimous, on the other hand, there will be a greater presumption on the part of the public that its decision was, if not inevitable, at least reasonable and fairly arrived at.

Juvenile Crime

The rates of serious crimes involving juveniles continued to rise, even after the rates for serious crimes committed by adults began to stabilize or fall in the mid-1990s.

According to the landmark 1995 U.S. Justice Department report, *Juvenile Defenders and Victims*, the arrest rates of juveniles for violent crimes increased 100 percent in the decade before 1993. The rate of murders involving people between the ages of 14 and 17 increased more than 1.5 times during the same period. What is more, young people from 12 to 17 years old are more likely than adults to be assaulted, raped, or robbed.

The Role of Handguns

Law enforcement experts believe that an increased availability of firearms, and particularly of handguns, is key to the increased rates of juvenile crime. According to statistics compiled from law enforcement sources by *USA Today*, 83 percent of juvenile inmates questioned in 1993 owned a gun. Handguns are the weapons used in nine out of ten murders committed by juveniles, and even in nonfatal confrontations, the ready availability of firearms tends first to raise the potential for violence in spontaneous conflicts that occur between young people, and then to intensify the violence that does occur.

Prospects for the Future

Social scientists are alarmed about the current high rates of juvenile crime, but they are even more troubled by many signs that point to higher levels of juvenile crime in the future. The Justice Department has estimated that the juvenile arrest rate for violent crimes may double again from 1995 to 2010. They point to several trends, in addition to the proliferation of handguns, that they say makes such an increase likely.

Perhaps the most obvious is what law enforcement officials refer to as the "epidemic" of crack cocaine that has swept through America's cities in the 1990s. Even more fundamental, however, are predicted demographic changes, which include a 20 percent rise in the teen population that will occur over the next 15 years.

The rates of poverty are expected to rise for those who will reach their teen years early in the twenty-first century. Poverty is not only a risk factor for violent crime among teens in itself; it is also related to an increased risk of divorce and teen motherhood. These, in turn, are risk factors for criminal behavior.

See also Unmarried Mothers.

Kerner Commission Report

Even while the civil rights movement was at its peak of activity in the 1960s, riots were almost commonplace in the black neighborhoods—or ghettoes—of America's big cities. More than 50 riots exploded in the first eight years of that decade. There were particularly destructive and bloody outbreaks in Watts (a suburb of Los Angeles) in 1965 and in Chicago and Cleveland in 1966. The worst of all, in which 43 people were killed, took place in Detroit in the summer of 1967.

The rage that was simmering in the black communities was clear, but the reason for it puzzled most white Americans. Racial progress was being made, they believed, so why were African-Americans so angry? In an effort to understand the phenomenon, and in the hopes of finding ways to reduce the violence in the future, President Lyndon Johnson set up the National Advisory Commission on Civil Disorders under the leadership of a white ex-governor of Illinois, Otto Kerner. The so-called Kerner Commission studied the problem and issued its historic report in the spring of 1968.

The Kerner Commission Report debunked the suspicion of many whites that there was some sort of conspiracy among black radicals (and perhaps Communists as well) to disrupt the cities. Instead, the report declared, the common perception that racial and economic divisions were healing in the United States was wrong. In reality, they were getting worse.

"Our nation," the Report concluded, "is moving toward two societies, one black, one white—separate and unequal .... Only a commitment to national action on an unprecedented scale can shape a future compatible with the historic ideals of American society."

The Kerner Commission received a great deal of attention and helped to shape the liberal view of the racial situation in the United States for a generation. Nonetheless, it failed to produce the large scale "commitment to national action" it called for. On the occasion of the twentieth anniversary of the report in 1988, a new commission of scholars pointed to statistics that showed that employment and wage gaps between blacks and whites were actually larger than they had been in 1968.

The urban explosions of the 1960s, concluded the report, had been replaced by the "quiet riots" of broken families and soaring unemployment, which were even "more destructive of human life than the violent riots of 20 years ago."

See also Civil Rights Movement.

King Case

In March 1991, an attempt by a black motorist named Rodney King to escape being stopped by police for a traffic offense led to a high-speed car chase in Los Angeles. Cornered, King got out of his car and, according to several police officers present, moved forward as if to assault them. However, before he could do so (if that was his intention), the police attacked him.

As recorded on a videotape taken by a bystander the police did not know was nearby, the police quickly subdued King. Several white policemen then proceeded to kick and club him while he lay helpless on the ground, watched by several other police officers who had been drawn to the scene by police radio.

The videotape of the incident, which was shown over national television, caused a sensation. Most whites were shocked and appalled by what they saw. Although equally appalled, instead of being shocked at the incident, most African-Americans saw it as proof of the police brutality against them of which they had frequently complained.

Largely as a result of the videotaped evidence, four white officers were charged in California state court for their parts in the beating. The defendants sought and won a change of venue to Simi Valley, an almost entirely white southern California community. As a result of this change, they were tried by a jury that contained no black members, and which acquitted them all.

The verdict angered many Americans of all ethnic backgrounds. The evidence of the videotape, which most people had seen, appeared so clear and indisputable that they could see no other explanation for the verdict but racism. To many African-Americans in Los Angeles, the verdict seemed to be a bitter proof that there was no way for them to ever obtain justice against white police. Riots broke out in black Los Angeles neighborhoods, in which 52 people were killed. Smaller riots broke out in other cities as well. The black mayor of Los Angeles, Tom Bradley, declared a state of emergency in the city, and the governor of California called out National Guard troops to restore order.

President George Bush, who at first had proclaimed that "the jury system has worked," then announced that the Justice Department would look into the King affair. As a result of this investigation, the same four officers were later charged in federal courts with violating Rodney King's civil rights.

The second trial was in some ways as controversial as the first. The defendants' supporters argued that to hold it at all was to violate the officers' constitutional right not to be tried a second time for a crime of which they had already been acquitted. The courts determined, however, that the federal trial did not constitute double jeopardy because, although the second case grew out of the same incident, the defendants were being tried for the violation of an entirely different law.

Two of the four officers were found guilty in the second trial and sentenced to two and one-half years in prison, and Rodney King eventually was awarded almost $4,000,000 in damages from the city of Los Angeles.

For further reading Dietz, Robert. *Willful Injustice: A Post-O. J. Look at Rodney King, American Justice, and Trial by Race.* New York: New Press NY, 1995.
National Association for the Advancement of Colored People Staff, et al. *Beyond the Rodney King Story: An Investigation of Police Conduct in Minority Communities.* Boston: Northeastern University Press, 1994.

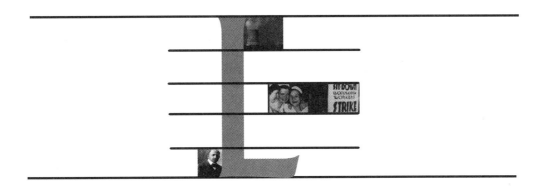

Labor, Child

See Child Labor; Child Labor Abroad (U.S. Complicity).

Landfills

Historically, Americans have regarded the land outside their towns and cities as a vast natural garbage disposal. Needing something to do with the tons of used paper, plastics, batteries, tires, and other waste their residents generated every year, local governments simply carried it outside the town limits and left it there. The surface of the earth itself became an enormous trash bucket, so huge that it seemed it could never be filled up.

However, those governments eventually discovered that the earth's surface is not as limitless as it once seemed to be. The space surrounding their communities was becoming increasingly desirable for housing developments and shopping malls. The mountains of trash were getting so big, smelly, and dangerous, that they were destroying the quality of life of the people living near them. So, instead of simply dumping their waste, communities began to bury it in landfills. This was more expensive, but still relatively cheap and easy. Still, the amount of trash kept growing, and by 1990 the amount of garbage produced annually had grown 80 percent from 1960.

Eventually, many communities were generating so much garbage that even burying it became a problem. It was taking up so much space that they were running out of room even under the ground. Lacking any place other than the earth to dispose of their garbage, however, communities developed ever more sophisticated methods of burying it, known as sanitary landfills.

Sanitary Landfills

A sanitary landfill begins as a large hole in the ground. A layer of garbage is laid down in the hole, a layer of dirt is then piled on top of the garbage, and the two layers are pressed down by heavy machines to compress them as tightly as possible. This allows much more garbage to be put into a smaller space. New layers of garbage and dirt are then alternated, until they reach above the level of the ground around them. Sometimes the layering continues until a hill is formed.

There are some dangers to this method of garbage disposal. The first is the fact that toxic chemicals or biological substances will seep into the earth under and around the landfills. These substances can contaminate the soil or even pollute the groundwater that supplies private and public wells in the area. Another problem is the production of methane and other gases formed by the rotting of food and other organic material in the landfill. The pressure from these gases can build up under the ground. In some cases, it can become so great that the gases will explode.

There are ways to make sanitary landfills secure against these dangers, at least for the foreseeable future. A watertight lining can be used to prevent leakage, and the underground area can be vented to allow gases to escape harmlessly into the air. Securing a landfill is more expensive in the short run, but may turn out to be cheaper in the long run. It costs less to secure a landfill in the first place than to clean up the toxic mess that can result from an unsecured one. Many of today's polluted sites targeted for cleanup by the federal government's Superfund program began as landfills. Another great advantage of a well-constructed secure landfill is that the ground above it can eventually be used for other purposes.

The Future

Environmentalists point out that even the most secure landfill will not remain secure forever. Toxic wastes will continue to exist underground, and there will always be a danger that they may escape, or be uncovered by accident, at some time in the future.

Because of the lack of space and the continuing potential for contamination, no one considers sanitary landfills a satisfactory long-term solution for disposing of solid waste. The earth around cities can only contain so much garbage, no matter how much it is compacted. Even the most efficient sanitary landfills take up valuable space, and garbage keeps accumulating at the rate of about 160 million tons each year.

According to Paul Shrivastava, editor-in-chief of Bucknell University's *Industrial Crisis Quarterly*, most American cities are already running out of landfill space, and

the rest soon will be. For this reason, far-sighted communities are looking toward various forms of waste treatment and recycling for the future.

See also Superfund.

Layoffs

See Downsizing; Worker Layoffs in the 1980s and 1990s.

Leopold and Loeb Case

Certain sensational criminal cases periodically capture the attention of the public and focus it, at least for a time, on one or more issues of social concern. One of the first twentieth-century trials to do so was that of Nathan Leopold and Richard Loeb, two teenagers from wealthy Chicago families, who kidnapped and murdered a 14-year-old boy named Bobby Franks in Chicago in 1924.

The Leopold and Loeb case revealed much that was ugly and unpleasant beneath the surface of American society in the 1920s, from the distorted egos of the two privileged young killers to the anti-Semitism and class resentment the case fostered among much of the American public. In addition, it was the occasion for one of the most persuasive arguments against capital punishment ever made in the United States.

The Crime

The Loebs, Leopolds, and Franks all moved in the same social circles in Chicago. When Bobby Franks disappeared, it was thought that he was being held for ransom until his body was found stuffed in a culvert. Soon after that gruesome discovery, suspicion began to center on the two young men who eventually confessed to the murder.

To most Americans of the time, who were accustomed to acquainting crime with the poor or the obviously deranged, Nathan Leopold and Richard Loeb seemed unlikely killers. They had no need for money, and they were brilliant students who seemed to have great futures ahead of them. They had not, it was eventually revealed, kidnapped the boy for profit. They had, in fact, always intended to kill him, partly to discover what it felt like to commit murder and partly to prove that their superior intelligence would enable them to get away with it.

The case became an instant *cause célèbre* because of the prominence of the families and the cold-blooded nature of the crime, which the press described as a "thrill killing." The public's anger against the killers was further inflamed by the fact that the killers were Jewish and rich and by the widespread suspicion that there was something sexually "unhealthy" in their relationship.

The Trial

The Leopold and Loeb families hired the well-known but controversial Chicago attorney Clarence Darrow to defend the young men. At least partly because of the overwhelming public outrage at the defendants—fueled by rancor at their privileged backgrounds as well as by a strong strain of Midwestern anti-Semitism—the prosecution asked for the death penalty, and Darrow's only job was to keep Leopold and Loeb from being hanged. Knowing how inflamed the public was, Darrow waived the right to a jury trial in favor of pleading for leniency directly from the judge, John R. Caverly.

In a long and impassioned argument, Darrow pleaded not only for the lives of his two clients, but against capital punishment itself. "I am pleading for the future," he told Caverly. "I am pleading for a time when hatred and cruelty will not control the hearts of men, when we can learn by reason and judgment and understanding and faith that all life is worth saving, and that mercy is the highest attribute of man."

Darrow's plea still stands as one of the most powerful arguments against capital punishment. Judge Caverly responded by sentencing both young men to life plus 99 years in prison. Loeb was stabbed to death by a fellow inmate in 1936. Leopold, who underwent a spiritual reformation in prison, was eventually paroled in 1958 and spent what was left of his life working with a religious organization in Puerto Rico.

The Leopold and Loeb case was the precursor of the many infamous murder cases that would become the objects of media frenzies in the twentieth century—from the Lindbergh kidnapping to the O.J. Simpson trial. In particular, it was the first of the series of highly publicized, apparently senseless "thrill killings" committed by American teenagers.

The case was fictionalized by Meyer Leven in a popular novel, *Compulsion*, which was later adapted as a play and a movie.

See also Death Penalty.

Magnet Schools

Most public schools offer a broad curriculum designed to educate students of all interests and abilities. A magnet school, on the other hand, is designed to meet special needs. Magnet schools can be established at any level, from kindergarten through secondary school. The purpose of the magnet school is to attract a mix of students from within a district to a particular institution. The concept has been widely used as a way of promoting voluntary racial and ethnic desegregation.

The magnet may include the whole school or only one or two programs within the school. A typical magnet school might offer advanced courses for so-called gifted and talented students or specialized training in a specific field, such as math, science, or the arts. It might offer a novel educational technique, such as the Montessori method or an open classroom approach.

By the 1980s, over 1,000 magnet schools were operating as parts of the desegregation efforts of cities large and small, from Montclair, New Jersey, to San Diego, California. Within a decade, many of these had become parts of so-called controlled choice programs, which allowed families to choose which schools their children would attend, but only as long as an acceptable racial and ethnic mix was achieved. In most cases, however, magnet schools have been only one element of a more complex desegregation plan.

See also School Choice.

Majority Rule

Democratic political systems, like that of the United States, are based on the consent of the governed. One of the underlying assumptions of a democratic system is that individuals have the right to a voice in the decisions that affect their lives. Another is that no individual has the right to make such decisions for others.

Many political decisions are extremely controversial. People have strong, but opposing, feelings about what the decision ought to be. Although no decision can possibly please everyone, fairness demands that everyone have a say in it. No matter what is done ultimately, some people—all of whom have a stake in the decision—will be unhappy. Yet, some decision has to be made. The democratic answer to this dilemma is some form of majority rule. Each person cannot *make* the decision for the entire society, but each person can have a part in that decision.

In modern democracies, majority rule is usually accomplished by means of a vote.

171

It may be a direct vote of the people, as it is in a referendum, or it may be indirect, in the sense that it is cast not by the citizens themselves, but by their elected representatives.

What governs, then, is not the individual will of each person, but the collective will of the majority of the people, or at least of those participating in the vote. It is a key element of the social contract that underlies democratic political systems that individuals accept the will of the majority—but only within certain bounds and protections.

Limitations on Majority Rule

The great danger of majority rule is that it might turn into mob rule or a tyranny of the majority. History shows many cases of a shared prejudice, or the passions of the moment, leading the majority to trample on the rights of minorities. The Jim Crow laws that codified and enforced racial segregation in the South were an example of this in the United States. So was the Red Scare of the 1950s, which resulted in the jailing or deportation of thousands of alleged Communists or Communist sympathizers because the majority feared their political views.

The founders of the United States recognized this danger and attempted to alleviate it. Thomas Jefferson wrote that although "the will of the majority is in all cases to prevail, that will to be rightful must be reasonable." It was, he said, a "sacred principle" of democracy that "the minority possess their equal rights, which equal law must protect." In order to establish this equal law, the founders added the Bill of Rights to the Constitution, promising the same rights to those in the political minority as to those in the majority.

The need for limitations on majority rule puzzles some Americans. They cannot understand why the will of the majority should not always prevail. This puzzlement can lead to simplistic thinking. The majority of Americans favor the death penalty for murderers, so why should all murderers not be executed? Most citizens favor ending aid to illegal immigrants, so why should illegal immigrants not be denied emergency medical care? Most Americans believe that Socialism is bad, so why can Socialist literature not be banned? Those who ask such questions do not understand that the democratic rights of the majority are based on the rights of individuals and that those in the majority today may be in the minority tomorrow.

The Purpose of Majority Rule

Majority rule is probably not the best way to arrive at the wisest possible decision. If that were the primary aim of the political process, it might well be best to leave decisions solely in the hands of the most informed, intelligent, public-spirited, and fair-minded people in the society or, at the least, to prevent the most ignorant and bigoted citizens from having a voice in the decision-making process.

Indeed, most of the original founders of the United States distrusted the judgment of ordinary citizens. They felt that uneducated and unpropertied citizens would be neither knowledgeable nor responsible enough to decide what was best for society as a whole. Under the Constitution as originally written, only the members of the House of Representatives were to be elected directly by the people, and then only by men of property. The rest of the federal political decision-making process was to be in the hands of the intellectual and propertied elite.

Over the years, however, the American political system has evolved unrelentingly in the direction of majority rule, based on the principle that every person deserves a role in political decisions, however sound or flawed that person's judgment might be.

See also Bill of Rights; Checks and Balances; Democracy; Initiatives and Referenda; Social Contract.

Mandatory Drug Testing
See Drug Testing.

Mandatory Minimum Sentencing

As early as 1790, the federal criminal statutes set death as the minimum, or, more specifically, the only sentence that could be given for certain crimes. This kind of mandatory sentence was a rare exception, however, in either federal or state laws.

For most crimes, a wide range of punishments was possible in the United States, and the specific sentence to be handed down in a particular case was left up to the court in which the case was tried. Judges even were free to suspend sentences, that is, to forgive convicted criminals from having to serve their sentences. In the rare instances in which mandatory minimum sentences were set for specific crimes, they tended to be quite short.

One of the first major modern exceptions to this rule occurred in the Narcotic Control Act of 1956, which set substantial mandatory minimum sentences for certain kinds of drug offenses, including importation of illegal drugs into the United States. It was hoped that drug smugglers and dealers would be deterred by the certainty that they were sure to serve lengthy sentences if convicted. Concluding that the mandatory sentences had not had the desired deterrent effect, however, Congress repealed most of the minimums in 1970.

Three years later, however, the state legislature of New York set its own mandatory minimums for certain state crimes, and within ten years all but one of the other states had followed suit. In 1984 Congress mandated minimum sentences for a number of federal criminal offenses, including drug crimes committed in or near school buildings. The legislative trend toward mandatory minimums has continued into the 1990s, and several thousand defendants have been sentenced each year under such laws.

Reasons for Mandating Sentences
Mandatory minimum sentences are at least partly a political response to public demand for tougher law enforcement. There was a widespread feeling in the 1980s and 1990s that judges were too soft on criminals. In the opinion of many critics, the sentences handed out by judges left to their own devices were too lenient to be effective. For this reason, the mandatory sentences set by legislatures tended to be considerably higher than the typical sentence that had been actually imposed for the offense in the past.

The new mandatory sentences were part of a two-pronged sentencing reform effort, which included the establishment of a commission to formulate sentencing guidelines for the courts to follow in passing sentences for federal crimes. The two prongs of these reforms were, to some extent, at odds with each other. Sentencing guidelines set a range of possible sentences for judges to use, depending on the specific circumstances of the case before them and the nature of the criminal. Mandatory minimums, on the other hand, were designed specifically to remove that kind of discretion from the judges.

Objections to the Mandatory Minimums
Although much of the public applauds mandatory sentences, many judges, defense

attorneys, and human rights advocates have serious reservations about them. Although most critics acknowledge that mandatory sentencing was established to counteract real problems—including discriminatory sentencing, in which African-Americans frequently were given much harsher sentences than whites convicted of similar crimes—they believe that their overall effect is to make the judicial system rigid and unresponsive.

Judges complained that the minimums took away not only their discretion, but their flexibility, preventing them from applying sentences that accord to the circumstances of the particular case and the nature of the particular criminal being sentenced. They objected to this because they believed that different criminals were likely to respond differently to different sentences. Some offenders are good candidates for reform and are likely to respond well to a relatively light sentence, although others are incorrigible and might actually require an even longer time in prison than the mandatory sentences allow. The judges argued that they needed to be able to take such differences into account.

Although mandatory sentencing is intended to ensure that all criminals convicted of similar crimes receive similar sentences, opponents claim that their effect is often the opposite. That is, they ensure that criminals who have committed very different crimes—in very different circumstances—will receive exactly the same sentences. There are a limited number of specified offenses. For example, the same designation could very well cover a career criminal breaking into a bank and a first time offender snatching a $20 bill from an open cash drawer. As long as one crime fits under the same broad classification as another, however, the penalties are required to be the same.

Opponents of mandatory sentencing object to specific minimums that they believe are unreasonable, or even discriminatory. For example, mandatory sentences for offenses involving crack or rock cocaine are set much higher than sentences for otherwise identical offenses involving powder cocaine. Since crack cocaine is more popular in the African-American community than elsewhere, the effect of these guidelines has been that a higher proportion of African-Americans convicted of cocaine offenses routinely receive much longer sentences than whites.

Still another complaint, raised by some politicians as well as judges, is that the longer sentences required, coupled with the inability of the judiciary to reduce those sentences, is contributing to an increasing overcrowding in America's prisons.

Marijuana (Medical Use)

Marijuana is a dried form of the leaf or flower of the cannabis plant. It is most commonly smoked in cigarettes or pipes, but it can also be chewed and swallowed. It is currently classified as an illegal drug by the U.S. Food and Drug Administration (FDA), and its use for any purpose is forbidden by federal law. Although marijuana is used chiefly as a recreational hallucinogen, some advocates of the drug believe that it has valuable medicinal properties and argue that it should be legalized for medical use.

Among the medical claims made for marijuana are that it can counteract the symptoms of glaucoma, prevent the debilitating weight loss associated with acquired immune deficiency syndrome (AIDS) and other chronic illnesses, and ease the pain of cancer and other potentially fatal diseases.

The advocates of medical use of marijuana point to many examples of people who insist that they have been helped by the drug. Those who oppose such use of marijuana respond that the evidence for these claims is almost entirely anecdotal and therefore is neither credible nor statistically reliable. They argue that legalizing marijuana, even if only for medical purposes, would not only increase the market for the drug; it would send the wrong message to young people who might be tempted to use the drug for other purposes.

Before the government even considers making cannabis legal for medical use, the opponents insist, it should wait until the drug has been subjected to the full testing regimen of the FDA. Advocates of legalization reply that this has been impossible legally because anyone attempting to conduct such experiments would be opening themselves up to criminal prosecution. Besides, the supporters of legalization argue, there is no need to wait for a complete regimen of scientific testing. Because of the high levels of illegal use in the United States and elsewhere, society has already had an enormous amount of experience with marijuana. This experience has shown that, even if it is not totally harmless, marijuana is at least arguably less harmful than alcohol and nicotine, two demonstrably dangerous drugs with much less claim to medical benefits. Even if marijuana's medical effectiveness has not been definitively proved, they argue, there is no good reason to prevent those who believe in its efficacy from acquiring it.

Despite the public hostility toward illegal drugs in general, there has been surprisingly widespread sympathy for the effort to allow the medical use of marijuana. In practice, law enforcement officials in many jurisdictions are relatively tolerant of those using marijuana as a form of medical therapy and rarely prosecute either physicians or their patients. When a zealous prosecutor in San Francisco closed down the operations of the Cannabis Buyers Club, a local group of medical-use advocates, and indicted its leaders, a large proportion of the community was outraged.

By late 1996, at least 36 states had passed some kind of resolution asking the federal government to consider legalizing marijuana for medical purposes. In that year's election, California voters passed an initiative making the medicinal use of marijuana legal in that state. As of the end of 1996, such use was legal under the state laws of California and Arizona. The federal government, however, announced that it would continue to classify marijuana as an illegal drug and that doctors prescribing it, even in those states where it was legal under state law, would be subject to prosecution under federal law.

Medicaid

Medicaid is the government insurance program that funds medical services to the poor and to people whose incomes may be slightly above the poverty line but still insufficient to pay for even ordinary health care services.

Like its sister program Medicare, the federal program that provides health insurance for the elderly and disabled, Medicaid was established by the Social Security Amendments of 1965. There are some important differences between the two programs, however. Whereas Medicare is an entirely federal program, Medicaid is jointly funded by the federal and state governments (with the bulk of the money coming from Washington, D.C.) and is administered at the state and local levels. What is more, Medicaid has stringent income restrictions, whereas Medicare does not.

Each state designs its own Medicaid program. Although, under most state programs, anyone eligible for the federal Supplemental

Security Income (SSI) assistance is also eligible for Medicaid, each state is free to set its own eligibility requirements as well as to determine, within certain limits, which services the program will provide clients in the state. In most of the states, the services provided by Medicaid are equal to, or more extensive than, the services provided by Medicare. It is possible for clients who are both poor and either elderly or disabled to be served by both programs at once.

Although few Americans would argue that no medical care should be provided to the poor, Medicaid has come under criticism for costing too much. It has also been attacked for the disparities that exist in the program from state to state. Critics charge that it is unfair for poor people in some states to receive more and better care than those in others.

See also Medicare; Welfare State; Welfare System.

Medicare

Medicare is the federal insurance program that funds health services to some 37 million elderly and disabled Americans. Unlike its sister program Medicaid, Medicare recipients are not means tested to determine whether their incomes are low enough to qualify for aid. Therefore, it is available to everyone who otherwise qualifies, regardless of their income.

Established by the Social Security Amendments of 1965, Medicare is run by the Social Security system. The program consists of two separate but related parts. Part A helps pay for hospital stays and follow-up costs, while Part B helps pay for such other medical expenses as doctors' fees, ambulance rides, and laboratory costs. Like participation in Social Security itself, participation in Part A is mandatory,

whereas people are free to choose whether or not to enroll in Part B. If they do enroll in Part B, however, they have to pay an additional monthly premium.

The most expensive medical financing program in the country, Medicare cost $160 billion in 1994. The Congressional Budget Office predicated that, left unchecked, the program's cost will more than double by the year 2002 as the so-called baby boom generation grows older and becomes eligible for benefits.

Despite its enormous cost, Medicare has never been a completely comprehensive health insurance program. Among the expenses it does not cover are dental care, regular physical exams, dentures, eye exams and eyeglasses, hearing aids, prescription drugs, and routine nursing home expenses. Furthermore, a deductible is charged, requiring recipients to pay a portion of even those bills Medicare does cover before any benefits are paid. Those recipients who can afford it buy supplemental private insurance, which helps them pay for the expenses Medicare does not.

Attacks on Medicare

Along with virtually every other welfare-related federal program, Medicare has come under attack from those who complain that the federal government is too big and too expensive. It is also criticized by many health care providers. Among the complaints: Medicare and other government health programs are hard to deal with; the programs have too many unnecessary and unnecessarily complex regulations; the programs require filling out too many complicated and time-consuming forms, and then refuse to pay if there are mistakes on them; and the programs are often late when they do pay.

The health care providers' most serious complaint, however, is the opposite of the one most often made by Medicare's other critics. Doctors and hospitals protest that Medicare's fees are set unrealistically low and often cause them to lose money on Medicare patients. This, they say, requires them to raise their rates to those patients who pay in other ways.

Some providers refuse to accept Medicare patients. Other doctors and hospitals, however, depend on Medicare for a significant proportion of their incomes, some for virtually all of it. Although Medicare's critics complain that it has contributed to the enormous rise in medical costs in recent decades, its supporters claim that its restrictive fee-setting has actually served as a break on those costs.

See also Medicaid; Welfare State; Welfare System.

Midnight Basketball

Midnight basketball is a youth recreational program that became a key symbol in the 1994 debate over federal government efforts to deal with youth crime. At that time, social agencies in several cities had established late-night basketball leagues to provide inner city youth a place to go at night.

Gyms were kept open for late into the night for city youth, many of whom were statistically at high risk for criminal behavior. The agencies reasoned that by giving young men an opportunity to participate in a wholesome sports activity at a time of night when they had little else to do other than get into trouble, many of them might be steered away from the drug and gang cultures operating on the streets at that time.

Proponents of midnight basketball, including the agencies that ran such programs, claimed that they had a generally positive effect on the young men involved. They recommended that the program be expanded to cities nationwide. Initially,

midnight basketball was considered relatively noncontroversial. However, it became a subject of national political debate when funds to promote it were included in President Bill Clinton's proposed 1994 federal crime bill.

Critics of the bill attacked midnight basketball as symptomatic of a soft and overly liberal approach to the problems of youth crime and drug abuse. They argued that it was wrong-headed to encourage young men, who ought to be getting up early in the morning to go to school or work, to stay up past midnight to participate in any activity, however wholesome. They further complained that providing delinquent youngsters a place to congregate late at night, whatever the purpose, would promote rather than reduce drug use and gang activity. Furthermore, they said, the intense feelings and competitive hostility provoked by hard-fought athletic contests could actually lead to off-court violence.

Despite these attacks, the 1994 Federal Crime Control Act passed with funds included for midnight basketball and other late-night sports leagues. For many conservative Americans, however, midnight basketball remains a symbol of what they see as a wasteful and liberal approach to the problem of youth crime.

Million Man March

In 1995 Louis Farrakhan, the controversial Nation of Islam leader, and Benjamin Chaves, a former head of the National Association for the Advancement of Colored People (NAACP), called on black men to come together in Washington, D.C., in October to participate in what they promised would be a "Million Man March."

More a mass gathering than a march, the event was proclaimed by its organizers as a

177

"day of atonement," at which the men would dedicate themselves to a new spirit of responsibility, pride, and devotion to their families.

It was a goal to which few Americans would object. Many black leaders were reluctant to endorse the march, however, primarily because they feared that to do so would be construed as an endorsement of Farrakhan. Despite great popularity among significant elements of the black community, Farrakhan was extraordinarily controversial. Widely regarded by many Americans of all colors as an anti-Semite, Farrakhan was also suspected by some members of the family of Malcolm X of having been implicated in the renowned Black Muslim leader's assassination.

Despite the lukewarm (or in some cases nonexistent) support from most nationally prominent black leaders, a massive crowd of African-American men did in fact come to Washington, from all over the country and from virtually every economic class. The marchers arrived by almost every mode of transportation available, from ride-share minivans to a television star's rented jet. The event was memorialized by the fictional cross-country journey of a busload of march participants in filmmaker Spike Lee's movie entitled *Get on the Bus*.

The actual size of the crowd that gathered on the Capitol Mall was a matter of dispute, with serious estimates ranging from 400,000 to somewhere close to the 1 million that the organizers had predicted. What was not in serious dispute was that the "march" was the largest gathering of African-Americans ever held and one of the largest assemblies of any kind in American history.

The crowd was addressed by a number of prominent black speakers, including Jesse Jackson, who took the occasion to call for end to all racial bigotry—black as well as white. The bulk of the speakers, however, came from the black separatist tradition, and many—including Farrakhan himself, who was the main speaker of the day—were associated, either directly or indirectly, with the Nation of Islam. For the most part, the message they conveyed was one of self-help for black Americans, and especially of the need for black men to rededicate themselves to the well-being of their families and the betterment of their communities.

Many white Americans were astonished by the sheer number of men the march attracted. Some black commentators, cynical about white America's reaction, commented that what really surprised whites was the fact that so many black men could gather peacefully and soberly in one place. The black community as a whole took heart from the size and spirit of the gathering and from the commitment made by the participants to return to their homes with a new dedication to improving the lot of the black community in the United States.

See also Nation of Islam.

Minimum Sentences
See Mandatory Minimum Sentencing.

Miranda Warnings
The Fifth Amendment to the U.S. Constitution guarantees the right of every person not to be "compelled in any criminal case to be a witness against himself." This means, among other things, that people suspected of crimes cannot be compelled to confess, nor to make statements that might be used against them. Despite this constitutional protection, however, many criminal suspects—innocent as well as guilty—incriminate themselves by making

hasty or ill-considered statements to the police.

In the past, suspects questioned by the police routinely made confessions in ignorance of their constitutional right not to incriminate themselves. Some did so under the impression that they were positively required not only to speak to the police, but to answer their questions. They feared that, if they refused to do so, their very failure to cooperate would be used against them in court. Some spoke to police because they were coerced, intimidated, or persuaded to do so by police trickery; others, because they were so tense, tired, or emotionally exhausted that they were finally willing to say anything to get some respite.

Miranda v. Arizona

In the case of *Miranda* v. *Arizona*, the U.S. Supreme Court set out to mitigate this situation by seeing to it that suspects were informed of their Fifth Amendment rights. The historic ruling came in the 1966 case of a 23-year-old man, Ernesto Miranda, who had been arrested for rape. After being identified from a lineup by the victim, Miranda was questioned for two hours by the police. He made a confession, which he wrote out for the police and which was put into evidence at his trial.

Miranda, who had little education, had not been told that he had the right to talk to a lawyer before deciding whether to speak with the police. In a close (5 to 4) decision, the Court ruled that, even though the police had not been rough or overtly threatening when questioning Miranda, they had effectively compelled him to speak, and therefore violated his Fifth Amendment rights.

The Court ruled that even a person merely subjected to normal interrogation techniques while being "swept from famil-iar surroundings into police custody, [and] surrounded by antagonistic forces . . . cannot be otherwise than under compulsion to speak." No confession made in such a situation can be used in court unless "adequate protective devices are employed to dispel the compulsion."

The Court proceeded to suggest four warnings that would serve as "adequate protective devices" if given to a suspect before interrogation. These devices, which have become known as the Miranda warnings, can be expressed in a variety of ways, but their meaning must remain consistent. The suspect must be informed that (1) he or she has the right to remain silent; (2) anything he or she does say can and will be used against them; (3) he or she has the right to consult a lawyer before talking to the police, and to have the lawyer present when and if the suspect does choose to talk to them; and (4) if he or she cannot afford a lawyer, one will be appointed before questioning.

Reactions to *Miranda*

Police were upset by the *Miranda* decision, as were many ordinary citizens who felt that the Miranda warnings would prove to be a handicap to law enforcement. They feared that suspects would now refuse to talk to police before consulting their lawyers, who would certainly advise them not to talk. Many possible confessions would be lost, making the job of the police much harder and making cases more difficult to prove.

The decision has not proved to be as disruptive to police procedures as its critics feared, however. For one thing, it does not apply to all police questioning. The police remain free to question people not pinpointed as suspects, and even to question suspects without "Mirandizing" them, as long as the suspects are not in police custody or in a similarly restrictive situation.

Most importantly, suspects are free to waive their Miranda rights voluntarily and to speak to the police without consulting a lawyer, and many do so.

Despite the dire predictions of the police, studies have indicated that the Miranda warnings have had no major effect on the efficiency of law enforcement. Even so, many police officers, prosecutors, and members of the public alike continue to resent the Miranda warnings. The *Miranda* decision is frequently mentioned by law enforcement hardliners as the most egregious example of a liberal Supreme Court bending over backward to protect the rights of criminals at the expense of public safety.

Defense attorneys, on the other hand, complain that the Miranda warnings are largely ineffective. The mere *pro forma* reading of a suspect's rights does nothing to change the compulsive nature of intense questioning while in police custody. Since no attorney or neutral person needs to be present when suspects waive their Miranda rights, lawyers believe that the waivers themselves are frequently compelled from unsophisticated and intimidated suspects by the same techniques the Court deplored, and attempted to mitigate, in *Miranda*.

Monkey Trial
See Scopes Case.

Motion Picture Ratings
Most motion pictures released in the United States receive a letter rating (G, PG, PG-13, R, or NC-17) from the Motion Picture Association of America. This rating is prominently displayed in the advertising for the film and is intended to give the moviegoing public a guide to the maturity level of the film. The rating indicates the degree of potentially objectionable content—sex, violence, vulgar language, drug use, etc.—the movie contains. Although the ratings can be used by people of any age as a guide to their own moviegoing, they are particularly intended to assist parents in determining whether a film is likely to be suitable for their children.

Ratings are determined by a board made up of parents who view the film and attempt to apply what they perceive as the community standard among parents in general to the film in question. The judgment they make is not an artistic one, and the rating implies nothing about the quality of the film. Rather, it reflects the content of the film, taking into account not only the amount of potentially objectionable material it may contain, but the way in which that material is presented and whether other parents are likely to find it objectionable.

The current rating system grew up as an alternative to the more stringent Motion Picture Production Code, which had been in use for decades before the powerful producer Jack Warner defied it by releasing his prestigious 1966 film *Who's Afraid of Virginia Woolf?* without the Code seal of approval. Instead of obtaining the seal, Warner advertised the movie as "suggested for mature audiences" and advised theater owners to bar minors who were not accompanied by a parent or guardian.

The film's subsequent financial and critical success led the industry to adopt this approach for movies with especially controversial content or subject matter. Over time, the single "mature audiences" designation has evolved into the five distinct designations of the current ratings system. As described in a 1996 Motion Picture Association of America brochure, those designations represent the following advice:

G. General Audiences—All ages admitted. Signifies that the film rated contains nothing most parents will consider offensive for even their youngest children to see or hear. Nudity, sex scenes, and scenes of drug use are absent; violence is minimal; snippets of dialogue may go beyond polite conversation but do not go beyond common everyday expressions.

PG. Parental Guidance Suggested—Some material may not be suitable for children. Signifies that the film rated may contain some material parents might not like to expose to their young children—material that will clearly need to be examined or inquired about before children are allowed to attend the film. Explicit sex scenes and scenes of drug use are absent; nudity, if present, is seen only briefly; and horror and violence do not exceed moderate levels.

PG-13. Parents Strongly Cautioned—Some material may be inappropriate for children under 13. Signifies that the film rated may be inappropriate for preteens. Parents should be especially careful about letting their younger children attend. Rough or persistent violence is absent; sexually-oriented nudity is generally absent; some scenes of drug use may be seen; some use of one of the harsher sexually-derived words may be heard.

R. Restricted—Under 17 requires accompanying parent or adult guardian (age varies in some jurisdictions). Signifies that the rating board has concluded that the film may contain some adult material. Parents are urged to learn more about the film before taking their children to see it. An R may be assigned due to, among other things, a film's use of language, theme, violence, sex, or its portrayal of drug use.

NC-17. No One 17 and under Admitted—Signifies that the rating board believes that most American parents would feel that the film is patently adult and that children age 17 and under should not be admitted to it. The film may contain explicit sex scenes, an accumulation of sexually oriented language, and/or scenes of excessive violence. The NC-17 designation does not, however, signify that the rated film is obscene or pornographic in terms of sex, language or violence.

The rating system is voluntary, at least in theory. Producers can choose whether or not to submit a film to be rated prior to its theatrical release. A film that is not rated, however, will have difficulty finding theaters willing to show it, as most theater chains and managers will only show films that have received a rating.

Films are frequently made with a particular rating in mind, depending on the audience the producers hope to attract. Producers who plan to market their film to a family audience, for example, will be careful to avoid any content that might keep the film from getting a G. On the other hand, producers who want to attract teenagers often deliberately put in enough nudity, violence, or vulgarity to earn a PG or PG-13 rating. They know that many teens consider themselves too sophisticated to attend G-rated films. By the same token, producers of teen-oriented films take care to avoid an R rating, which might deprive them of a large segment of their intended audience. Even most producers who are eager to attract an adult audience try to avoid the NC-17 rating, however, because many theaters are reluctant to show films with that most restrictive rating.

Producers may appeal a film's rating to a Rating Appeals Board, made up of industry representatives, which has the authority to change it. If this fails, filmmakers are free to reedit their films and bring them back to be rated again.

For the most part, the ratings system is well accepted by the public and the industry alike. Most filmmakers prefer it to the less flexible Production Code, while the main complaint from parents is that they would prefer the ratings to be even more informative.

Some filmmakers do object, however, that the ratings system is not really voluntary, because films that are not submitted to the rating board, or that receive the NC-17 rating, are almost certainly doomed to financial failure. Another objection comes from young moviegoers who resent the fact that they are banned from attending films designated R or NC-17.

Music Festivals
See Altamont; Woodstock.

A Nation at Risk

Early in President Ronald Reagan's administration, Secretary of Education Terrel Bell established the National Commission on Excellence in Education, which reported to him in 1983. The commission's report, entitled *A Nation at Risk: The Imperative for Educational Reform*, accused the American education system of leaving its students unequipped to compete with students in other countries, thereby leaving the nation unprepared to meet the challenges of the modern world. More than any other single event, the publication of *A Nation at Risk* alarmed the American public about the state of education in the United States.

The commission backed up its criticisms of American education with statistical evidence showing that standardized test scores of American students had been declining and, in some respects, were significantly behind those of students in several other countries. Viewed in the context of the Cold War, the report suggested that such evidence put the nation at risk in a military as well as an economic and cultural way. In its most quoted passage, the report asserted,

> If an unfriendly power had attempted to impose on America the mediocre education performance that exists to-

day, we might well have viewed it as an act of war. As it stands, we have allowed this to happen to ourselves. We have even squandered the gains in student achievement made in the wake of the *Sputnik* challenge. Moreover, we have dismantled essential support systems that helped make those gains possible. We have, in effect, been committing an act of unthinking unilateral disarmament.

The commission made five recommendations to improve American education. The most sweeping proposed that all high school students should be taught what the report referred to as the "new basics," defined as at least four years of English, three years each of mathematics, science, and social studies, and a half-year of computer science. The report called on schools throughout the country to reexamine their schedules and to consider such measures as extending the school day or school year in order to meet these new requirements. Teachers were to be better prepared and better paid, and higher standards were to be demanded of students. Finally, the report called on all citizens to support the suggested reforms and to demand that political leaders provide the funding needed to put them into action.

See also College Preparation; Education Summit (1989); Goals 2000 Act.
For further reading National Commission on Excellence in Education. *A Nation at Risk: The Imperative for Educational Reform*. Washington, DC: U.S. Government Printing Office, 1983.

Nation of Islam

The Nation of Islam is perhaps the best-known modern black separatist organization. A branch of the Black Muslim movement, it demands strict adherence to Islamic principles from its followers, forbids them to drink, smoke, or use drugs, and asks them to pray five times a day.

The Nation is particularly active among poor black people in inner-city neighborhoods. It draws many followers from prison inmates, thanks partly to its dynamic efforts at conversion inside the prisons. Although many of its recruits are drawn from outlaw elements of society, it demands extreme self-discipline from converts once they join.

The Nation is notorious among whites for its militance and is highly admired by many African-Americans for the same reason. Preaching black pride, self-reliance, and resistance to white oppression, the Nation promotes black self-help and rejects alliances with white people, no matter how well-meaning. It calls on African-Americans to build their own businesses and cultural institutions, and it operates several farms, businesses, and schools.

History

The Nation of Islam was founded as the Temple of Islam by Wallace D. Fard in Detroit in 1930. It grew out of the black "race pride" and self-improvement movement that had been led by Marcus Garvey, a black separatist, earlier in the century.

Fard, who called himself Wali Farad, was regarded as Allah (or God) by Temple members. The founder vanished in 1934, however, and his organization was taken over by Elijah Muhammad, who was then the head of the Temple's Chicago mosque.

Elijah Muhammad led the group for more than 40 years, but it was one of his disciples who first brought the Nation to national attention. Malcolm Little took the name Malcolm X when he was converted to the group in 1952, shortly after he was released from prison. Black Muslims frequently take the last name X in preference to what they call their "slave names," which they assume were given to their ancestors by the white people who once owned them.

Before long, the charismatic Malcolm X became the Nation's most popular spokesperson, calling on black people to take pride in their African heritage and spurn what he called the "white devils." Although Malcom X brought the Nation many new converts in the black community, he alarmed many white people by his rejection of the nonviolence being preached by Martin Luther King Jr. and other leaders of the civil rights movement.

New converts were also drawn to the group by the conversion of several prominent black athletes. The most notable was the world champion boxer Cassius Clay, who took the Black Muslim name Muhammad Ali in 1964. By that time, a serious conflict had erupted between Malcolm X and Elijah Muhammad, who might have been jealous of Malcolm's growing popularity. The Nation was already splitting into factions around the two men when Malcolm X publicly called the 1963 assassination of President John F. Kennedy a case of white America's "chickens coming home to roost." Elijah Muhammad took this remark, which angered many white people, as an opportunity to "silence" his popular spokesman. No longer able to speak for the Nation, Malcolm X worked out of his own mosque in New York City. In 1964, he made a pilgrimage to the holy cities of the Middle East and underwent a new conversion, this time to orthodox Islam. Although continuing to maintain his fierce devotion to black pride and self-reliance, he repudiated his earlier insistence that African-Americans must reject all whites. Islam showed him that all men could be brothers. In 1965, he was gunned down while speaking in an auditorium in New York, apparently by members of the Nation of Islam loyal to Elijah Muhammad.

The Nation managed to survive the death of Malcolm X and the suspicion the assassination cast on the leadership of Elijah Muhammad. Following Elijah Muhammad's death in 1975, however, a new split developed between Black Muslim factions led by Muhammad's son, Wallace D. Muhammad, and Louis Farrakhan. Farrakhan eventually took over control of the Nation, despite suspicions that he might have been involved, however indirectly, in the death of Malcolm X.

Relations with Other Black Groups

For most of its history, the Nation of Islam has guarded its independence, not only from the white community, but from much of the black civil rights community as well. It has shied away from the more mainstream black organizations, which often attempt to work within the largely white American political system.

In the early 1990s, however, Farrakhan and other black leaders began moving in the direction of unity. The mainstream leaders wanted closer ties with the Nation because they feared they were losing influence among the young black men who were most attracted to Farrakhan. At the same time, Farrakhan apparently hoped to obtain for himself, and the Nation, a greater leadership role within the African-American community as a whole. The Nation's effort to become more mainstream has been hampered, although not destroyed, by its reputation as a virulently anti-Semitic and antiwhite organization.

In 1994, the U.S. Senate unanimously denounced some particularly hateful comments made by Farrakhan's spokesman, Khalid Abdul Muhammad. While assailing whites in general, Khalid attacked Jews and Catholics in particular, calling Jews "bloodsuckers" and the Pope a "cracker." Most mainline black leaders also condemned the remarks, and some called on Farrakhan to distance himself from them. He did repudiate the "manner" of Khalid's words, but at the same time endorsed what he called the "truth" behind Khalid's attack on Jews. Many Americans of all colors were as appalled by the anti-Semitism of Farrakhan's "apology" as they had been by the original remarks. Nonetheless, several prominent black leaders—including Kweisi Mfume (Democrat, Maryland), the head of the Black Caucus in Congress, and Benjamin Chaves, the executive director of the National Association for the Advancement of Colored People (NAACP) —seemed to be satisfied and continued to work toward closer relations with the Nation of Islam.

The Million Man March

In October 1995, Farrakhan and Chaves called on black men to participate in what was proclaimed "The Million Man March." More a gathering than a march, the event was described by its organizers as a "day of atonement" during which the men

185

would dedicate themselves to a new spirit of responsibility, pride, and devotion to their families and to the black community.

A crowd of African-American men, estimated at between 400,000 and 1 million, came to Washington, D.C., and gathered on the Capitol Mall. It was one of the largest demonstrations in Washington history and the largest demonstration by African Americans bar none. Although most national politicians of all races stayed away, the crowd was addressed by a number of prominent black speakers, including Jesse Jackson, who took the occasion to call for end to all racial bigotry, black as well as white. Most of the speakers, however, came from the black separatist tradition, and many—including Farrakhan himself, who was the main speaker of the day— were associated, either directly or indirectly, with the Nation of Islam.

See also Anti-Semitism; Jewish/African-American Relations.

No-Fault Divorce

Divorce was relatively difficult to obtain in the United States until the mid-1970s. Before then, in most states, even when both spouses desired the dissolution of the marriage, one had to sue the other for divorce and prove to a court of law that the defendant had committed some serious breach of the marriage agreement. In some states, the only breaches that could justify divorce were offenses such as extreme cruelty (whether physical or, in some states, mental), adultery, or desertion. This procedure forced the accused spouse into the position of a defendant, having to either acknowledge guilt or to oppose the divorce in a contested legal action.

By contrast, the no-fault divorce laws that now apply across the country allow either party to obtain an uncontested divorce with a minimum of legal fuss. Even contested divorces can usually be obtained on insubstantial grounds such as incompatibility or irreconcilable differences.

The trendsetting no-fault divorce law was passed in California and signed into law by Governor Ronald Reagan in 1969. Within five years, 44 other states had followed California's example. By the early 1990s, all 50 states had some form of no-fault divorce.

Dissatisfaction with Traditional Divorce Laws

There were two main reasons for the traditional legal requirement that one party prove the other guilty of some fault in order to obtain a divorce: to uphold the institution of marriage and to promote the stability of families. Although these were regarded universally as noble goals, the rapidity with which the states rushed to pass no-fault laws in the wake of California's action revealed the depth and breadth of American dissatisfaction with traditional divorce laws. Such laws were felt to be unfair and unnecessary impediments to a reasonable, and even an amicable, dissolution of a marriage. By requiring a formal and adversarial legal proceeding, they compelled both parties to hire lawyers and made the potentially simple act of divorce into an expensive process that many poor couples could not afford.

Beyond that, many dissatisfied couples chaffed under the requirement to assign blame for unhappy family situations in which both parties felt themselves either mutually culpable or equally victimized. Many marriages were unsatisfactory to both spouses, even though neither spouse had committed a serious offense against the other. Even when one spouse was guilty of such an offense, it could be difficult or impossible to prove it legally; and, even when that could be done, the airing of such misbehaviors often led to personal hard feelings and unnecessary public embarrassment, not merely for the guilty spouses, but for children and other family members as well. Why, the backers of no-fault divorce demanded, should the state insist that two people remain bound by marriage when they no longer wanted to stay together? The legal system does not enforce other contracts that all parties agree to void.

The supporters of traditional divorce laws responded that the two spouses were not, in truth, the only parties to a marriage. Children also have rights and interests in the marriage relationship of their parents, and the community at large has a significant stake in the preservation of an institution that has long been considered one of the main foundations of a stable society.

Abuse of the System

One of the most important complaints lodged against the traditional divorce laws was that they encouraged widespread and flagrant abuse of the legal system. Unhappy spouses went to great, and often expensive, lengths to evade the lengthy waiting periods and complex legal proceedings required by many states. Nevada, which had the most relaxed divorce laws in the country before 1969, as well as a short-time requirement to establish legal residency, became a haven for unhappy women from around the country who went there for quick divorces. Others went to Mexico, where divorces were even easier to obtain, although Mexican divorces were notorious for being of dubious legality under the laws of many states.

The need to prove fault encouraged some unhappy spouses to perjure themselves. In some cases, the lies unfairly damaged the reputation of the defendant spouse. In other cases, the lies would be joined in by both parties, seeking as rapid and easy a dissolution of the marriage as possible. Judges sympathetic to couples who wanted to dissolve an unsatisfactory marriage frequently compounded the abuse, overlooking obvious misrepresentations in order to smooth the process as much as possible.

For those too honorable to abuse the law, marriage could amount to an irrevocable commitment. Critics charged that this led to the continuance of many situations in which everyone involved, spouses and children alike, were trapped in unhappy households that they were powerless to escape. The result, the critics alleged, was an excess of depression and other forms of mental illness in society as a whole, as well as of infidelities, emotional abuse of both spouses and children, and incidents of domestic violence.

Some of the strongest support for a no-fault approach, in fact, came from advocates for the victims of domestic violence. Battered and abused spouses welcomed the chance to escape from an abusive marriage without a long, contested legal process that required them to prove their spouse's cruelty in public. Abuse victims feared that such public disclosure, and the resulting humiliation to the abusive spouse, would provoke more violence.

The Situation under No-Fault

The public seems generally satisfied with the no-fault laws. Since the rush of states to pass no-fault divorce laws in the early 1970s, however, there has been an increasing concern with the breakdown of the family and what some see as a growing disrespect for traditional family values in the United States.

This concern has been reflected in rises in the number and the rate of divorces,

187

both of which have soared since the advent of no-fault. In 1968, the year before the passage of California's landmark law, there were some 584,000 divorces in the entire United States, for a rate of approximately 2.9 divorces per 1,000 people. In the 1990s, the yearly number has averaged close to 1,190,000, while the divorce rate has hovered around 4.7 per 1,000. During this same period, the marriage rate has remained fairly steady, between 9 and 10 marriages per 1,000 in the population.

Although the extent to which the no-fault laws should be blamed, or credited, for the rise in divorces is a matter of debate, concerned politicians, members of the clergy, and ordinary citizens place at least some of the responsibility on them. By 1996, movements had grown up in at least 21 states to reform or eliminate their no-fault laws. Defenders of the no-fault laws, however, suggest that the increase in divorces merely indicates that the laws are working as they were intended to work, allowing unhappy spouses the freedom to escape the situation causing their unhappiness.

Nonviolence

Nonviolent resistance to evil is both a philosophic position and a political strategy. Philosophically, it goes back at least as far as the biblical admonition to turn the other cheek. Based on the theory that social change can best be brought about through the use of moral as opposed to physical force, nonviolence is inherent in much pacifist thought.

For some of its advocates, nonviolence is a moral imperative: One should be nonviolent because violence is wrong. For others, it is simply a tactic: Nonviolence is an effective way to overcome an institutionally powerful but morally vulnerable opponent.

As a modern political tactic, nonviolence owes much to the writings of the nineteenth-century American author Henry David Thoreau and his idea of the "peaceable revolution." It is closely related to the tactic of civil disobedience, which also was espoused by Thoreau. Both proved vital to the historic people's movement, led by Mohandas Gandhi, that helped drive the British out of India in the first half of the twentieth century.

In arriving at his own philosophy of nonviolence, Gandhi was influenced not only by Thoreau's ideas, but also by the writings of the Russian pacifist Leo Tolstoy and by the teachings of Jesus Christ and Muhammad, as well as by the traditions of his own Hindu religion.

For Gandhi, nonviolence was much more than a political tactic, or even a strategy. He believed that nonviolence, when employed in a just cause, had a spiritual power that he dubbed *satyagraha*, or "force of truth."

Protests

Gandhi pioneered the use of peaceful mass protest as a political tactic. Combining Gandhi's example with his own interpretation of the Christian message, Dr. Martin Luther King Jr. made nonviolence the guiding principal of his assault on racial segregation in the United States in the 1950s and 1960s.

Like Gandhi, King had a belief in the spiritual power of nonviolence. As a Christian minister, he believed firmly in the redemptive power of suffering and in the moral authority of the integrationist cause. He was convinced that the value of that cause could be proven not only to the world at large, but to the segregationists themselves, by the example of courageous and resolute nonviolent protest against injustice.

Similar methods have been used by other twentieth-century protesters, most notably by anti-Communist movements in Eastern Europe and Asia, by the international nuclear disarmament movement, by anti–Vietnam War protesters in the United States in the 1960s and 1970s, and by antiapartheid activists in South Africa. Nonviolent protest continues to be an important tactic of many movements in the United States today.

In essence, nonviolent protest attempts to combat physical and political force with moral force. It is used typically by minorities faced with the power of government or some other much larger and more powerful force. Nonviolent protesters attempt to demonstrate by example, a contrast between themselves—and, therefore, their cause—and the more powerful forces they oppose. They do this by initiating a situation in which their opponents will be provoked to respond unjustly, either by using actual violence against the nonviolent demonstrators or by arresting and jailing them for inordinate amounts of time.

This implies that the practitioners of nonviolence must be willing to suffer for their cause. By the same token, the opponents must be willing to inflict that suffering. The contrast between the two can have a significant influence in persuading neutral observers of the relative merits of the causes involved. The nonviolent protesters hope that by their suffering of repeated injustices they will sap their opponents' energy, causing them to reexamine and ultimately to abandon their cause in disgust at what it has led them to do.

The effectiveness of nonviolent protest is frequently undercut by violent protests carried out by others supporting the same cause. This blurs the moral distinctions the nonviolent protesters are attempting to demonstrate. This is the case, for instance, with the current right-to-life movement, in which candlelight marches, vigils, and the picketing of abortion clinics express a message of respect for human life, while the killing of doctors who specialize in abortions sends a very different and conflicting one.

For further reading Dellinger, Dave. *Revolutionary Nonviolence*. Garden City, NY: Anchor Books, 1971.
Kronenwetter, Michael. *The Peace Commandos*. New York: New Discovery Books, 1994.
Murphy, Jeffrie G., editor. *Civil Disobedience and Violence*. Belmont, CA: Wadsworth, 1971.

Nullification
See Jury Nullification.

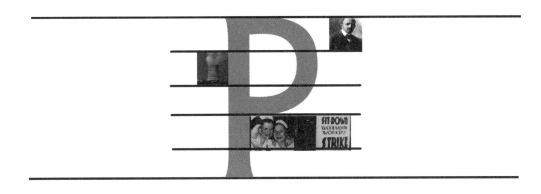

P.C.

See Political Correctness.

Police Corruption

Police corruption is the misuse or abuse of police power, usually (although not always) for personal gain. There are several kinds of police corruption. Some involve money: accepting bribes or taking advantage of the position with the police to steal. The desire to further their careers, or simply to strengthen the case against a suspect they believe to be guilty, leads police to another form of corruption, causing some officers to manufacture or alter evidence, or to perjure themselves in court. Police brutality can be seen as yet another form of corruption, one which disproportionately victimizes African-Americans and members of other minority groups.

The problem of police corruption goes beyond the specific injustices committed by corrupt officers. Corruption contributes to public disrespect for all law enforcement officials and, ultimately, for the law itself. The effects of this disrespect may be greatest, and most destructive, on the young people in those communities where corruption is widespread and well known.

An Old Problem

Police corruption is as long-standing as organized police forces. Because the majority of it goes officially unnoted, there are no reliable statistics as to the amount of corruption, either now or in the past. It is believed widely, however, that corruption is a growing problem in many police forces, although this may be largely the result of greater public attention being paid to it in recent years.

Revelations of police corruption in a number of major cities drew public attention to the issue in the early and mid-1990s.

The most notable revelation of police corruption involved tape recordings of a former Los Angeles police officer named Mark Furhman, which came to light during the O.J. Simpson murder trial in 1995. On the tapes, excerpts of which were played on national television, Fuhrman talked freely about widespread racism, sexism, police brutality, falsification of evidence, and perjury, within the Los Angeles Police Department. Around the same time, scandals involving police in Philadelphia and Atlanta contributed to a growing feeling among the public that police misconduct was becoming pandemic in the United States.

Financial Corruption

For obvious reasons, no accurate statistical records can be kept of police corruption. However, police officials and former officials acknowledge that corruption may be a more serious problem today than at any time since Prohibition.

Although officials insist that the great majority of law officers are honest and competent, they admit that the extent of corruption has almost certainly increased in recent decades due to the enormous trade in illegal drugs.

Because of the drug trade, the opportunities and the illicit rewards of corruption are greater today than at any time since Prohibition. Drug traffickers, who seem to have limitless amounts of money available to them, are the leading payers of protection and bribe money to law officers. In addition, police officers making drug arrests frequently encounter suspects with large quantities of illegal drugs, and/or large amounts of money in cash, with no way to account for any of it. The temptation to take some of these untraceable drugs, or this untraceable money, sometimes proves too strong for officers to resist. Evidence suggests that significant numbers of officers are falling victim to these temptations.

Racial Harassment

Harassment and other forms of mistreatment of minorities constitute another kind of abuse of police power and one that is encountered in many American communities. Racism may be no more common among police officers than among other members of society, but the effects of police officers acting out their racial hostilities can be especially destructive.

African-Americans, in particular, have long complained of brutality and disrespect on the part of the police. They charge that black motorists and pedestrians are fre-quently stopped, questioned, and even searched under circumstances in which no white person would be bothered and claim that black suspects are much more likely than white suspects to be beaten and brutalized. The videotaped beating of Rodney King in Los Angeles in 1991 gave graphic reality to their complaints.

Causes for Increased Corruption

One cause for the apparent rise in police corruption in some cities may be the large-scale new hiring that has taken place in many departments in recent years, as part of the increased national effort to crack down on street crime.

In many cities, the need to find large numbers of new officers in a relatively short time has resulted in a lowering of standards, carelessness in screening applicants, and an inability to provide sufficient training for new officers. The bulk of the new resources that have been devoted to the problem have been applied to putting officers on the streets, rather than to the task of uncovering, investigating, and disciplining official misconduct.

Combating Corruption

Police corruption is difficult to combat for a variety of reasons. It is, by definition, a secret activity, carried out by the very officials ordinarily charged with uncovering such criminal activities. The first line of defense against police corruption is internal. Most police departments of any size have an Internal Affairs Division (IAD), which investigates misconduct within the force. Unfortunately, other police officers tend to view these departments with hostility, leading to an adversarial relationship that undermines the IAD's ability to uncover, and to deal with, corruption. Even otherwise honest police officers are reluctant to testify against their fellow officers.

In some departments, this reluctance hardens into a "code of silence," which is virtually impossible to penetrate.

The inclination of police officers to protect their own is reflected in the attitudes of the powerful police unions. Some ex–law enforcement officials complain that these organizations frequently intimidate even those police chiefs and city officials who attempt to weed out corruption within local departments.

Civilian political officials are often reluctant to admit that a serious problem of corruption exists in their communities, much less to take strong steps to solve it. Several big cities have established civilian review boards, either appointed by city officials or elected by the populace. These boards have had some successes in combating corruption, but, on the whole, they have been ineffective in controlling the problem.

See also King Case.
For further reading Bornstein, Jerry. *Police Brutality: A National Debate*. Springfield, NJ: Enslow, 1995.
Ginsberg, Jerome M. *False Arrest, Malicious Prosecution, and Police Misconduct*. Irvington-on-Hudson, NY: Transnational Press, 1992.
National Association for the Advancement of Colored People Staff, et al. *Beyond the Rodney King Story: An Investigation of Police Conduct in Minority Communities*. Boston: Northeastern University Press, 1994.

Police Misconduct
See Police Corruption.

Police Residency Requirements
The laws of some cities require that police, and sometimes other municipal employees as well, live within the boundaries of the community they serve. To some degree, this requirement is a codification of what used to be the norm in the United States. In the early twentieth century, before the development of suburbs and the building of extensive systems of commuter trains, beltways, and feeder roads, most law officers naturally lived where they worked, as did most other workers. The local sheriff was usually a long-term resident of the community, while local constables often lived not just in the same city, but in the same neighborhood they patrolled.

Today, residency requirements are imposed for a combination of reasons. Among them is a desire to help the local economy by keeping municipal payroll money within the community. More important, however, is a belief that is shared by many civic leaders and law enforcement experts alike, that law officers who live within a community are better able to serve that community's needs.

Advocates of residency requirements argue that local residents will be more knowledgeable about what goes on in their communities. They will find it easier to establish lines of communication with the public and to develop networks of informants. They will also be better accepted by the other citizens who live in the community. This last point is particularly important in some minority or disadvantaged communities and neighborhoods, whose residents view law enforcement officials who live in more affluent communities almost as an occupying force.

Police organizations tend to oppose residency requirements for their members. They argue that it is not fair to limit the freedom of police officers to live where they choose. Law enforcement officials should be as free as other citizens to choose the kinds of neighborhoods their children will be raised in and the schools they will attend.

Beyond that, they argue that residing in the community can actually have negative effects, making it harder for law enforcement officers to do their jobs fairly and impartially. Police who live in the communities they serve are more likely to be personally acquainted with suspects and victims alike. They are more likely to react on an emotional level to criminal activities and to let their personal feelings cloud their judgment. Furthermore, they are more likely to be biased either for or against particular suspects, based on personal like or dislike. This may make them too eager to make an arrest in some cases and more reluctant to do so in others. Living in the community may also make officers more vulnerable to intimidation. Police in several cities have been attacked, and even had their homes fire-bombed, by neighbors angry about some aspect of their police work.

Some civic leaders also oppose residency requirements on the grounds that they make it more difficult for communities to hire well-qualified officers. The best candidates—those who would be most sought after by more than one police force—are not likely to choose an employer who restricts their right to live where they wish.

As of the spring of 1996, 17 states had done away with residency requirements for public service workers, including police. Three states had removed them in part, the rest in total.

Political Correctness

Political correctness (commonly called "PC") is a derogatory term, coined by conservatives, to describe what they claim to be the limits on free thought and expression enforced by liberal academics on American college campuses.

In the conservatives' view, liberal professors and administrators (regarded by the conservatives as leftovers from the 1960s) largely control American academic life. In an effort to maintain that control, and promote their liberal values, the conservatives maintain, the liberals have succeeded in placing oppressive restrictions on what can be discussed on many college campuses, and even the language that can be used to discuss them.

To make their case, the conservatives cite several professors and lesser faculty members whose careers have been damaged for teaching, or even discussing, ideas such as the possible genetic inferiority (or superiority) of a particular race. Furthermore, they charge, outside speakers with academically unpopular ideas about race, economics, or politics are routinely banned from speaking on certain campuses.

The critics of political correctness also point to the codes, which exist on many campuses, that forbid students and faculty to refer to women, or to any ethnic or other minority group, in terms members of that group might find offensive. However well-intentioned such codes may be, say the critics, their effects are pernicious. At one prominent eastern university, for example, a male white student was disciplined for yelling out a window at a group of female students who were disturbing his studies that they sounded like a "herd of water buffalo." The women, who were black, took the remark as a slur on their African heritage, although the offending student insisted that he meant only that they were making a lot of noise. Such cases, conservatives complain, have a chilling effect on free discourse, as well as on academic freedom.

Defenses of PC Policies

University administrators who have come under attack for their policies object to the term *politically correct*. They insist that they are not trying to enforce any specific ideology or way of thought, political or otherwise. They are merely attempting to ensure a proper academic climate within their universities. While rejecting the designation PC, however, they are willing to defend many of the policies to which it refers. Campus speech and behavior codes are defended by university administrators on the ground that they promote civility. Far from being designed to stifle free speech and debate, say the defenders, they are intended to provide an atmosphere in which real intellectual controversy can flourish. To ensure that discussion will be carried out in the polite and mutually respectful manner suitable to an academic setting—a setting in which one side or another will not be shouted down or driven into silence with insults and epithets.

As for the disciplining of faculty members, some conservative academics, as well as many liberals, argue that school and department administrations have the responsibility to exercise some oversight on the content of courses, to make sure that scholarly standards are being maintained. Academic freedom must be upheld, but it should not be used as an excuse for intellectually sloppy work, nor for dishonest demagoguery, nor racist dogma disguised as free inquiry.

The idea of banning certain controversial speakers from campuses makes even many liberals, who otherwise defend PC policies, uncomfortable. Administrators defend it, however, on the ground that the speakers banned are likely to utter what the U.S. Supreme Court has called "fighting words"; that is, words that are likely to prompt an immediate violent reaction from those who hear them. "Fighting words," the Court ruled in the case of *Chaplinsky* v. *New Hampshire,* are not protected by the U.S. Constitution. Therefore, some administrators feel justified in preventing them from being spoken on their campuses in order to protect their students from the potentially violent consequences.

Beyond specific defenses of particular policies, some academics of all political stripes justify what others denounce as political correctness on the grounds of taste and good sense. It is the job of the university, they argue, to draw some sort of line between what is legitimate intellectual discussion and what is errant nonsense. If it does not—if it allows any kind of foolishness, whether well-intentioned or hateful, to be passed off as academically valid—it is abdicating its responsibility.

Others, however, including some liberals, feel that it is a mistake to try to ban the voices of ignorance and bigotry from the campus. Ultimately, says Albert Simone of the Rochester Institute of Technology, "PC is self-defeating." By stopping people from expressing their hateful opinions directly, says Simone, you only force them to disguise their beliefs as something more acceptable. This prevents reasonable people from bringing those views out into the open and exposing them for what they are.

For further reading D'Souza, Dinesh. *Illiberal Education: Political Correctness and the College Experience.* Ashland, OH: Ashbrook Center of Political Affairs, 1992.
Williams, Jefferey, editor. *Political Correctness and the Academy.* London: Routledge, 1994.

Political Refugees
See Immigration (Legal).

Pornography
Considered harmless entertainment by some and a corrupting social evil by others, pornography is one of the most controversial forms of expression. Pornography is notoriously hard to define. In its most general sense, pornography is any writing, painting, drawing, performance, or other

form of expression that deals with sex in a way that is considered offensive. But what is offensive? And to whom?

The difficulty comes from trying to make a distinction between pornography and other depictions of erotic or sexual subjects. That judgment tends to come down to a subjective reaction: Do I find this pleasant, or disturbing? Different people have different levels of interest in, and reaction to, sexually related materials. Furthermore, they have very different attitudes about such materials. Some people find any portrayal of erotic activity, from a kiss to actual intercourse, to be repulsive. Some, on the other hand, find some such materials innocent, and even pleasurable, but are disgusted by others. Still other people remain totally unmoved, either way, by even the most explicit depictions of the most extreme sexual acts.

Pornography (also referred to as "porno" or "porn") is divided into two categories: soft-core and hard-core. The distinctions between these are as difficult to draw as pornography is to define. Hardcore pornography is the kind of thing sold in "adult" book stores. It includes the most graphic depictions of sexual acts, focusing particularly on aroused genitals or on what are commonly regarded as the most perverse or violent sexual acts. Soft-core pornography is less explicit than hard-core, and therefore is relatively inoffensive to more people than hard-core pornography. Examples of soft-core pornography might be *Playboy* magazine and certain "adult" movies shown on cable television movie channels. Soft-core pornography is considered acceptable by many who feel that hard-core pornography should be banned.

The most famous definition of hardcore pornography was given by U.S. Supreme Court Justice Potter Stewart—who admitted that although he could not ex-plain what pornography was exactly, "I know it when I see it"—which is really no definition at all.

Pornography and the Law

Pornography is only illegal if it is held to be obscene. This is another word that is hard to define. In the case of *Roth* v. *United States*, the U.S. Supreme Court defined obscenity as any work whose dominant theme would, "to the average person, applying contemporary community standards... [appeal] to prurient interest." Prurient interest was defined as either "lustful thoughts" or a "shameful or morbid interest in sex." The Court later modified this definition by ruling that prurience did not include "normal healthy sexual desires."

Among other things, *Roth* seemed to imply that works that appealed to prurient interest only slightly, or incidentally, were not obscene. This excluded artistic works that might be pornographic in some respects, but that taken as a whole had at least some "redeeming social importance." Overall, however, *Roth* narrowed the distinction between obscene and nonobscene materials without really clarifying it.

The Court made its definition of obscenity more specific in *Miller* v. *California* in 1973. Restating its requirement that obscenity appeal to prurient interest, the Court expanded its earlier limitation that obscenity be totally without redeeming social importance to require that it lack "serious literary, artistic, political, or scientific value" as well.

Perhaps the most important element in the *Miller* ruling was a restriction that, in order to be considered obscene, a work must describe, in a "patently offensive" manner, specific sexual conduct spelled out in an antiobscenity law. In other words, communities and states had to spell out exactly which sexual acts had to be depicted in order for a work to be considered obscene. This had the ironic effect of introducing words and descriptions into antiobscenity statutes that, in the eyes of those citizens who object to such words, make the statutes themselves obscene. Even so, because of the "patently offensive" manner requirement, the mere portrayal of such sexual acts (except perhaps for what have been called "ultimate acts") is not sufficient for a work to be legally declared obscene.

Most antipornography laws are local. This strikes those who are most affected by such laws as unfair, since it has the effect of making the same work that is legal in one jurisdiction illegal in another. Artists, writers, and performers complain that they cannot possibly tell whether the works they produce will be held to be obscene, since that determination may be different in every community. Nonetheless, this principle has been not only acknowledged but approved by the Supreme Court's reliance on "contemporary community standards" to help determine what is obscene and what is not.

Reliance on community standards does not mean that a local jurisdiction is free to declare anything at all obscene. The First Amendment protects not only the right of free speech, but the right to other forms of expression as well—including artistic works with graphic sexual content—so long as they have "redeeming social value." And in practice, the higher courts have been reluctant to uphold local efforts to declare soft-core pornography obscene. Nonetheless, the U.S. Supreme Court has ruled that a community may use zoning laws to restrict the exhibition of pornography, even when it has not been ruled obscene. In addition, it allows the banning of deliberate distribution of nonobscene pornographic materials to minors.

Objections to Pornography

Despite the difficulty of defining pornography, most people would probably agree with Justice Stewart: They know it when they see it. Furthermore, they find whatever it is that they themselves consider pornographic to be distasteful, whether or not they want to see it legally banned.

The fundamental objection most people have to pornography is moral. For many, this comes from religious conviction. Many religions, including the majority of Christian denominations and Islam, forbid sexual activities outside marriage. Therefore, many people object to the depiction of such activities in a way that might arouse a desire for such activity in the audience.

Much of the concern about pornography centers around the effects of such materials on children. This is particularly true when it comes to child pornography, which involves the portrayal of sexual activity involving children. Parents and child psychologists point out that in today's society it is increasingly difficult to protect children from sexual materials of all kinds. Soft-core pornography, at least, is everywhere. Broadcast television now carries movies that children were forbidden to see in theaters a few years ago. Cable television regularly runs R-rated movies featuring what is called "strong sexual content." Many communities have stores that rent or sell X-rated videos, and some have few scruples about making them available to young people.

Even elementary school children are being exposed to depictions of activities that many adults were unaware existed only a generation or two ago. What, concerned parents ask, is the effect of such early exposure on young people whose attitudes toward sex and the opposite gender are in the process of being formed? Some observers even blame pornography, at least in part, for the rise in early sexual activity among teenagers and the growing incidence of teen pregnancy.

Another major concern is the frequent association of pornography with violence. A great deal of pornography, though by no means all, deals with violence as well as sex. Portrayals of rapes and near-rapes are staples of certain kinds of pornographic materials. Sadism is another frequent subject. A whole genre of pornography depicts sadomasochistic activities, in which the infliction of pain is portrayed as providing sexual pleasure to both the victim and the person doing the inflicting.

Opponents of pornography believe that exposure to such materials does not merely appeal to unhealthy or morbid interests, it may actually provoke such interests. Worse, it may lead people to act out the kinds of unhealthy fantasies portrayed in the materials. Some sex offenders and other criminals have claimed that they were stimulated to commit their crimes by pornography. Perhaps the most infamous of these was Ted Bundy, the Florida serial killer.

Feminism and Pornography

Mainstream feminists tend to object to pornography on the grounds that it is degrading to women and reinforces male prejudices about them. The typical pornographic work, they say, implies male dominance and female submissiveness and suggests that even protesting women are not only willing, but eager, to be ravished by almost any man.

Some feminists go so far as to define pornography as the sexually explicit subordination of women. Seen in that light, they argue that it is an act of oppression against women and should be considered an exception to the First Amendment protection of free speech and expression.

Defending Pornography

The defenders of pornography, and opponents of laws designed to outlaw it, fall into two main camps. The first is made up of artists, critics, civil rights advocates, and others who defend the rights of artists, whether or not their works are pornographic, on the grounds of freedom of expression. They uphold the right of writers, visual artists, and performers to portray sexual activities—including violent and sadomasochistic sex acts—in any way they see fit.

The artist's job, they say, is to explore and interpret human experience. Sex is a significant part of human experience, and only the individual artist can decide how she or he will explore it. This process of exploration is bound to result in some work that other observers might regard as pornographic, or even obscene. That, however, is a risk that society must be willing to take in order to derive the benefits of artistic expression.

Some defenders of pornography make no distinction between pornography and other works. They consider any depiction of human experience, including sexual activities, equally worthy of protection. Others, however, are repulsed by commercial pornography and recognize that much of it has no real artistic or social value. In theory, they would like to see all such material disappear. They believe, however, that there is no practical way to eliminate it without exerting a dangerous chill on serious artists. Even many artists who would never cross the boundaries of good taste set by "community standards" themselves insist that their fellows must be free to do so. They would rather see the most offensive obscenity protected than serious artists hobbled in their effort to explore an important area of human experience.

The second camp is made up of those who not only defend pornography but actively approve of it. Not everyone sees pornography as unhealthy or as a significant threat to public morality. Many consumers of pornography argue that, for them, what others call smut is a form of entertainment, and they see no reason for it to be denied to them. There are psychologists who support their claim. Some go further, arguing that pornography is not only harmless for healthy people, but it may even be helpful for certain disturbed individuals. Far from prompting antisocial or criminal behavior, they suggest that pornography may actually prevent it. By providing potentially dangerous people with a harmless outlet for their unhealthy obsessions, it may relieve their tensions to the point where they will not be tempted to act out their fantasies.

These experts, like some law enforcement officials, are suspicious of the motives of criminals like Bundy who try to lay the blame for their actions on pornographic books and videos. Such claims, they say, are self-serving and may be offered in a fraudulent attempt to arouse sympathy for themselves and lessen their punishment.

For further reading *The Report of the Commission on Obscenity and Pornography*. Washington, DC: U.S. Government Printing Office, 1970.
Simmons, G. L. *Pornography without Prejudice*. London: Abelard-Schuman, 1972.

Port Huron Statement

In 1962, a group of young radicals gathered at Port Huron, Michigan, and adopted the Port Huron Statement, an "agenda for a generation," written by Tom Hayden, a young activist. Hayden later would be tried as a member of the Chicago Eight for helping to foment the protests outside the Democratic National Convention in Chi-

cago in 1968. The agenda stimulated the imaginations and fired the political energies of a large segment of the college-age generation of the 1960s. Branches of Students for a Democratic Society (SDS) soon sprang up on university and college campuses around the country. The Port Huron statement declared:

We are people of this generation, bred in at least modest comfort, housed now in universities, looking uncomfortably to the world we inherit. When we were kids the United States was the wealthiest and strongest country in the world; the only one with the atom bomb, the least scarred by modern war, an initiator of the United Nations that we thought would distribute Western influence throughout the world. Freedom and equality for each individual, government of, by, and for the people— these American values we found good, principles by which we could live as men. Many of us began maturing in complacency.

As we grew, however, our comfort was penetrated by events too troubling to dismiss. First, the permeating and victimizing fact of human degradation, symbolized by the Southern struggle against racial bigotry, compelled most of us from silence to activism. Second, the enclosing fact of the Cold War, symbolized by the presence of the Bomb, brought awareness that we ourselves, and our friends, and millions of abstract "others" we knew more directly because of our common peril, might die at any time. We might deliberately ignore, or avoid, or fail to feel all other human problems, but not these two, for these were too immediate and crushing in their impact, too challenging in the demand that we, as individuals take the responsibility for encounter and resolution.

Although these and other problems either directly oppressed us or rankled our consciences and became our own, subjective concerns, we began to see complicated and disturbing paradoxes in our surrounding America. The declaration "all men are created equal…" rang hollow before the facts of Negro life in the South and the big cities of the North. The proclaimed peaceful intentions of the United States contradicted its economic and military investment in the Cold War status quo.

We witnessed, and continue to witness, other paradoxes. With nuclear energy whole cities can easily be powered, yet the dominant nation-states seem more likely to unleash destruction greater than that incurred in all wars of human history. Although our own technology is destroying old and creating new forms of social organization, men still tolerate meaningless work and idleness.

Although two-thirds of mankind suffers malnourishment, our own upper classes revel amidst superfluous abundance. Although world population is expected to double in 40 years, the nations still tolerate anarchy as a major principle of international conduct and uncontrolled exploitation governs the sapping of the earth's physical resources. Although mankind desperately needs revolutionary leadership, America rests in national stalemate, its goals ambiguous and tradition-bound instead of informed and clear, its democratic system apathetic and manipulated, rather than "of, by, and for the people."

Not only did tarnish appear on our image of American virtue, not only did disillusion occur when the hypocrisy of American ideals was discovered, but we began to sense that what we had originally seen as the American Golden Age was actually the decline of an era. The worldwide outbreak of revolution against colonialism and imperialism, the entrenchment of totalitarian states, the menace of war, overpopulation, international disorder, supertechnology—these trends were testing the tenacity of our own commitment to democracy and freedom and our abilities to visualize their application to a world in upheaval.

Our work is guided by the sense that we may be the last generation in the experiment with living. But we are a minority—the vast majority of our people regard the temporary equilibriums of our society and world as eternally-functional parts. In this is perhaps the outstanding paradox: we ourselves are imbued with urgency, yet the message of our society is that there is no viable alternative to the present. Beneath the reassuring tones of the politicians, beneath the common opinion that America will "muddle through," beneath the stagnation of those who have closed their minds to the future, is the prevailing feeling that there simply are no alternatives, that our times have witnessed the exhaustion not only of Utopias, but of any new departures as well.

Feeling the press of complexity upon the emptiness of life, people are fearful of the thought that at any moment things might thrust out of control. They fear change itself, since change might smash whatever invisible framework seems to hold back chaos for them now. For most Americans, all crusades are suspect, threatening.

The fact that each individual sees apathy in his fellows perpetuates the common reluctance to organize for change. The dominant institutions are complex enough to blunt the minds of their potential critics, and entrenched enough to swiftly dissipate or entirely repel the energies of protest and reform, thus limiting human expectancies. Then, too, we are a materially improved society, and by our own improvements we seem to have weakened the case for further change.

Some would have us believe that Americans feel contentment amidst prosperity—but might it not better be called a glaze above deeply-felt anxieties about their role in the new world? And if these anxieties produce a developed indifference to human affairs, do they not as well produce a yearning to believe there *is* an alternative to the present, that something *can* be done to change circumstances in the school, the workplaces, the bureaucracies, the government? It is to this latter yearning, at once the spark and engine of change, that we direct our present appeal. The search for truly democratic alternatives to the present, and a commitment to social experimentation with them, is a worthy and fulfilling human enterprise, one which moves us and, we hope, others today. On such a basis do we offer this document of our convic-

tions and analysis: as an effort in understanding and changing the conditions of humanity in the late twentieth century, an effort rooted in the ancient, still unfulfilled conception of man attaining determining influence over his circumstances of life.

For those who were stimulated by it, the Port Huron Statement was not merely an expression of their disillusionment with the society in which they had been raised; it was a manifesto, a call to action. It helped to swell support for a wide range of social movements that became identified with the 1960s: movements in favor of the rights of African-Americans, the poor, students, and women; movements opposed to segregation, poverty, the extremes of capitalism, the military-industrial complex, and, of course, the Vietnam War.

Some of the effects of SDS and its agenda were immediate and dramatic; others were more subtle and far reaching. Some continue to echo through American culture today. In his 1996 book, *Slouching toward Gomorrah*, judge Robert Bork pinpointed the meeting at Port Huron as the seminal cultural and political event of the 1960s. For conservatives like Bork, it was a calamitous event, the opening salvo in a youth rebellion that would shake the traditional foundations of American society and undermine many of the values conservatives held most dear.

Prayer in School
See Religion in the Schools; Religious Expression in the Public Schools (Federal Guidelines); School Prayer.

Prejudice
See Race and Prejudice.

Presumption of Innocence

The tenet that people accused of crimes are innocent until—and unless—proven guilty is a fundamental principle of U.S. criminal law. Originating in the British common law, the presumption of innocence has been an elementary feature of the American legal system since colonial days. Although it is not mentioned specifically in the Constitution of the United States, the U.S. Supreme Court has ruled in the case of *Bell* v. *Woolfish* (1979) that the presumption of innocence is encompassed in the "due process" clause of the Fifth Amendment.

The presumption of innocence reflects the fact that the founders of the U.S. had an intrinsic distrust of the power of the state. It is considered a vital element of a fair trial because its absence would make a criminal charge too nearly tantamount to a conviction. This would allow the state not only to persecute innocent defendants, but also to silence its critics by bringing them to trial on the flimsiest of grounds and demanding that they prove their innocence.

The presumption of innocence dictates that it is the prosecution, and not the defendant, that bears the burden of proof in a criminal trial. Despite that, the state has the power to detain the defendant prior to and during trial in certain circumstances.

Working against the presumption of innocence in the minds of jurors, as well as in the court of public opinion, is the prejudicial effect of a criminal charge. It is this effect that causes many lawyers to refer to the presumption as a legal fiction, at least as far as juries are concerned. Jurors rarely are able look upon a defendant without prejudice. They know that he or she has already been investigated, arrested, and charged with the crime. It is hard for them not to assume that this must mean that there is good reason to believe in the defendant's guilt. Knowing that it is their duty to try, however, probably helps make jurors more fair and open-minded in considering the evidence than they would be otherwise.

The presumption of innocence is further sabotaged, in the minds of the public, by the extensive publicity surrounding certain notorious criminal trials, such as that of O.J. Simpson. The widespread public airing of the prosecution case in the newspapers, and particularly on television, together with a lurid concentration on the details of the crime, tends to convince many people of the defendant's guilt. If the defendant is then acquitted, those same people are led to question the wisdom of the presumption of innocence, believing that it helped a person they believe to be guilty to escape conviction.

The presumption of innocence is a legal principle. The state, the courts, and jurors are bound to honor it. Members of the public at large, on the other hand, are free to presume whatever they wish about a defendant's guilt or innocence. Nonetheless, a general loss of respect for the presumption of innocence on the part of the public would be worrisome to judges and other legal authorities. Such a loss could ultimately destroy one of the basic protections of Americans' civil rights.

See also Burden of Proof; Simpson Case.

Privacy

Americans place a high value on privacy. It is generally accepted that a certain core of one's individual and family affairs should be protected against interference, or even investigation, by outside forces—including not only private individuals and institutions, but the government as well.

The notion of privacy is closely related to several other highly valued ideals, including individual liberty, religious and intellectual freedom, and the whole panoply of values traditionally associated with marriage and the family. Despite the widespread acknowledgment of privacy as a fundamental personal and social value, however, privacy is "a broad, abstract, and ambiguous" concept, as U.S. Supreme Court Justice Hugo Black has pointed out.

Even while recognizing that a certain realm of privacy exists and must be respected, the boundaries of that realm can be hard to determine. Among the aspects of one's life that are widely held to contain a significant zone of privacy are one's religious, sexual, political, and financial affairs. Yet few Americans regard any of these areas as completely private. Even while resenting it, most Americans would recognize the government's claim to a legitimate interest in their financial affairs, for example—at least to the extent of verifying their tax liabilities. Few Americans would consider adult sexual activity with a small child to be a purely private matter.

Privacy as a Constitutional Right

The right of privacy is not referred to directly in the Constitution of the United States. Certain elements of the right to privacy can be reasonably inferred, however, from the language of the Bill of Rights. The First Amendment upholds the right to a free exercise of religion, as well as to freedom of speech (which can be said also to imply the right to maintain one's silence about one's private thoughts) and the right to assemble with others. The Third Amendment recognizes at least a limited right of homeowners. The Fifth Amendment protects an accused person's right not to share certain information

about him- or herself, even when that information may be helpful in accomplishing the public purpose of uncovering a crime. Most telling of all is the language of the Fourth Amendment, which refers to "the right of the people to be secure in their persons, houses, papers, and effects."

As early as 1928, U.S. Supreme Court Justice Louis Brandeis asserted, in his dissent in the case of *Olmstead* v. *United States*, that the Fourth and Fifth Amendments granted individuals a Constitutional right to personal privacy that went beyond the security of physical possessions. The majority of the Court, however, disagreed at that time. It was not until 1965 that the Court specifically recognized a Constitutional right to privacy, ruling, in the case of *Griswold* v. *Connecticut*, that a Connecticut law forbidding the recommendation and use of contraceptives violated that right. Other Supreme Court cases dealing with the privacy of sexual and reproductive matters followed *Griswold*. The most important was the 1973 case of *Roe* v. *Wade*, in which the Court ruled that the right of privacy included the right of a woman to have an abortion, at least in the early and middle stages of her pregnancy.

Like other Constitutional rights, however, the right to privacy has been limited by the Court, even in sexual matters. In the 1986 case of *Bowers* v. *Hardwick*, for example, the Court upheld a Georgia law prohibiting sodomy.

See also "Don't Ask, Don't Tell" Policy; Drug Testing; Homosexuality; Homosexuals (Gays and Lesbians) in the Military; *Roe* v. *Wade*; Technology and Privacy.

For further reading Brill, Alida. *Nobody's Business: The Paradoxes of Privacy*. Reading, MA: Addison-Wesley, 1990.
Sands, Trent. *Privacy Power: Protecting Your Personal Privacy in the Digital Age*. San Diego: Xndex Publishing Group, 1996.

Prizefighting
See Boxing (Professional).

Public Executions
See Executions (Public).

Punishment, Capital
See Death Penalty.

Punishment, Corporal
See Corporal Punishment by Parents; Corporal Punishment in Schools; Corporal Punishment of Criminals.

Quotas

Much of the criticism that surrounds affirmative action arises from an objection to quotas and set-asides—measures that reserve a specific number or percentage of positions, contracts, or other advantages for women or minorities. These are usually established as a means of correcting past discrimination against people belonging to these groups.

A typical quota, for example, might require that by a certain date the percentage of African-Americans employed in a particular business should equal their percentage in the local population. A specific percentage of government work contracts might be set aside for businesses owned largely by women or by members of racial or ethnic minorities. Some quotas are established by government agencies or by courts. Others are set by the individual schools or businesses themselves as an internal means of ensuring that they are meeting their responsibility to diversify.

Proponents of quotas argue that they are a useful tool: first, to force reluctant institutions to be aggressive in correcting past discrimination; and second, to measure how successful they have been in doing so.

Critics, however, charge that quotas and set-asides are grossly unfair to those who do not belong to the groups that benefit from the preference granted by them.

Whenever a specified number of positions is held for members of one class of applicants, the critics point out, that same number is specifically denied to everyone else. This, they say, is an unacceptable form of discrimination based on race or gender. Furthermore, say the opponents, the use of quotas to determine the success of antidiscrimination measures shows a misunderstanding of what those programs ought to do. The purpose of affirmative action, in their view, should be to create a level playing field, not to give members of one team an unfair advantage. Using another sports metaphor, they insist that the object of such programs should be to see that everyone gets a fair start, whatever their gender or color; the effect of quotas, however, is to make sure that everyone crosses the finish line together.

The U.S. Supreme Court has accepted some quota plans and rejected others. In the landmark *Regents of the University of California* v. *Bakke* case (1978), the Court suggested that strict quotas were only permissible to redress past wrongs and when legally established by a government agency. In general, the Court has allowed the federal government more leeway in establishing quotas and set-asides than it has allowed the states.

See also Affirmative Action; Bakke Case.

Race and Prejudice

Although most Americans use the terms *prejudice* and *racism* more or less interchangeably, a useful distinction can be made that has to do largely with effects. Prejudice is an individual, psychological phenomenon, whereas racism is a social, political, and economic phenomenon. Simply put, it has been said that prejudice turns into racism when it begins to have significant consequences outside the minds and feelings of specific individuals, that is, when it leads to significant discrimination, or oppression, of one or more racial or ethnic groups.

Racial prejudice can show itself in myriad ways, both significant and petty. Within a year of losing his bid for reelection as mayor of New York City, David Dinkins, a middle-aged black man, reported having twice been bypassed while trying to hail a cab on New York streets in favor of white customers farther down the block. Dinkins's experience is apparently a commonplace one for black men trying to get a cab in America's big cities.

Escalated into racism, the individual prejudices of a sufficient proportion of the members of the dominant group in a society leads to widespread discrimination in employment, education, housing, law enforcement, and other aspects of society. In severe cases, it can even lead to racial seg-regation, whether legally imposed (as in the southern states in the first half of the twentieth century) or de facto (as in many American cities today).

Racial prejudice and racism are dependent upon the concept of race, that is, the notion that people are born into different biological groups, each of which is more or less distinct, and whose members share certain intellectual and moral, as well as physical, characteristics. These races are identified primarily, but not exclusively, by the color of their skins.

Racial Differences

To most modern-day Americans, the fact of race seems obvious and unarguable. People look at each other and see clear physical differences between groups. They perceive apparent behavioral and other differences as well and assume that the existence of these differences are directly connected in some way. Intellectual differences are often assumed as well, based largely on the apparent differences in educational and other attainments between the groups. These differences are then interpreted as genetic and racial, whereas the varied social, cultural, and economic backgrounds of the groups, which might better account for the perceived differences, are either ignored or downplayed.

Scientifically, however, the notion of race is extremely questionable. Although physical differences clearly exist between people of different genetic backgrounds, their significance is debatable. Even skin color tends to vary widely within racial groups. The presence of any intellectual, emotional, or other genetic proclivities corresponding to these physical differences is scientifically unproved.

Can Minorities Be Racist?

It is primarily the relationship between racism and economics that leads some people to assert that African-Americans, or members of other minorities, cannot be racist. Such assertions tend to confuse or anger white Americans, who feel that it gives a kind of permission to minorities that is not given to them.

Those who assert that minorities cannot be racist do not argue that minority individuals cannot be prejudiced, or even that it is morally acceptable for them to be prejudiced. Rather, they assert that the prejudices of minorities cannot rise to the level of racism because minorities lack the power to oppress or repress the white majority. White prejudice, on the other hand, is racist because whites hold most of the economic and political power in the United States. White prejudices tend to be translated into economic discrimination, often enforced by the political and police authorities.

See also Affirmative Action; African-Americans in U.S. Society.
For further reading Allport, Gordon W. *The Nature of Prejudice*. Reading, MA: Addison-Wesley, 1954.
Kronenwetter, Michael. *Prejudice in America*. New York: Watts, 1993 .

Racism
See Race and Prejudice.

Ratings
See Motion Picture Ratings; V-Chip; Video Game Ratings.

References

Employers traditionally have asked for references from a prospective employee's past employers. Employers have relied on reference for an evaluation of the job experience, performance, and character of the prospective employee. Valuable as references have been, however, they are becoming less common in American business today.

The "To Whom It May Concern" letter, which departing employees take with them to show to prospective employers, used to be the most common form of reference. It is the one most preferred by workers because it allows them to see what the past employers have said. Today, however, it is probably the least common form of reference.

Most employers prefer to respond to phoned or written requests for references from prospective employers of their past workers because it allows them to tailor the information they give out to the questioner's particular needs. They feel freer to speak candidly, knowing that their comments will not be directly seen or heard by the ex-employee.

Workers tend to have different attitudes toward references in general, depending on their relationship with their previous employers. Workers who felt appreciated by management in their previous jobs feel that it is only fair that they should derive some benefit from past good performance. On the other hand, workers who have had problems with previous employers feel that it is wrong for those problems to haunt them in their efforts to find a new job.

A Growing Reluctance

In the past, most employers gave references, whether good or bad, as a routine part of doing business. As a result, prospective employers looked upon a good reference as a virtual prerequisite for employment. If job seekers could not provide such references, it was assumed to be because they had not done a satisfactory job in their previous employment. That assumption has broken down, however, as more and more businesses have become reluctant to provide references for past employees.

The main reason for the change in business policy is a growing fear of legal liability. The legal departments of many large firms advised their clients that a bad reference may cause more problems for the employer than for the ex-employee. This has been demonstrated by a variety of lawsuits, in many jurisdictions, in which ex-employees have sued their old employers for what they claimed were inaccurate or unfair negative references.

Faced with this threat, some employers adopted a policy of giving out only the most glowing references, while simply refusing to give out any information for those ex-employees about whom they had any reservations at all. However, even this policy can lead to legal problems. If a company is only willing to provide references for ex-employees it is willing to praise, then a refusal to provide a reference for anyone else actually amounts to a negative recommendation. Even a positive recommendation can result in legal problems. There has been at least one case of a company being sued for "negligent referral" by a new employer unhappy with a worker it believed had been given too positive a reference.

Such concerns have led an increasing number of employers to refuse any references at all, either positive or negative, beyond confirming the dates of employment. This development seems to be an unfortunate one, as it redounds to the disadvantage of employers and job-seekers alike. The

employer loses a valuable source of information about a prospective employee, while the prospective employee loses the benefit he or she might have derived from a good recommendation. Still another effect of this trend is to diminish the importance of the quality of a worker's past performance on his or her ability to find future employment.

Referenda

See Initiatives and Referenda.

Refugees

A refugee is a person who has been forced to leave his or her homeland for any of a variety of reasons. Chief among them are war, natural disaster, and political, religious, or ethnic persecution. The United Nations' Universal Declaration of Human Rights affirms the refugee's "right to seek and to enjoy in other countries asylum from persecution." This right, however, "may not be invoked in the case of persecution arising from non-political crimes...."

Refugees are treated as an exception under U.S. immigration law, and therefore are not subject to the same restrictions as other foreign nationals desiring to come to the United States. This exception is made partly from humanitarian motives, and partly from ideological ones.

Ordinarily, would-be refugees apply to come to the United States while they are still in their homelands or in other nations where they have found temporary refuge. For many, however, this is impractical. They may be fugitives in their homeland or unable to find even temporary refuge in some other country from which to wait out the application process. For this reason, among others, thousands of would-be refugees enter the United States each year—whether legally, as ordinary visitors, or illegally—and apply for asylum after they are here, claiming fear of persecution back home. If that fear is determined to be well-founded, they are permitted to stay. Some 152,000 such refugees entered the United States in 1995, the largest number from Cuba.

History

Following World War II, some 400,000 refugees from the war were admitted into the United States. Three years later, the Refugee Relief Act of 1953 provided for the ongoing entry of victims of war and natural disasters.

During the Cold War (1945–1989), refugee status was used primarily to permit the immigration of people fleeing from oppressive Communist regimes. Since the end of the Cold War, hundreds of thousands of emigrants from countries as varied as Haiti and Pakistan have continued to find refuge status in the United States.

The end of the Vietnam War brought about an influx of Southeast Asian refugees, primarily Vietnamese and Hmong, who had sided with the United States in the war, and who had been left in jeopardy by the pullout of U.S. troops. The 1980s saw the arrival of many refugees from Haiti, as well as from tyrannical governments in Latin America

Proposals for Reform

Although the United States prides itself on hospitality to refugees, the door is not open to everyone. No single country could possibly provide refuge for the many millions of refugees who find themselves stateless around the world. Although the numerical quota that applies to ordinary immigrants does not apply to refugees, not everyone who seeks asylum is granted it. Political asylum is almost never given, for example, to citizens of countries whose governments are supported by the government of

the United States. To do so would be considered insulting to an ally, and contrary to U.S. interests. In the 1980s, for example, leftist emigrants from El Salvador and elsewhere in Central America, fleeing what they regarded as dictatorial governments in their homelands, were frequently refused refugee status in the United States.

Some law enforcement officials believe that the exception granted to those seeking asylum and other refugees is a major defect in U.S. immigration laws that should be tightened. These officials charge that many, if not most, of those who claim asylum are not really fleeing persecution at all. Rather, they are economic emigrants from their homelands, attempting to escape poverty by coming to the more prosperous United States. The United States, the reformers say, cannot provide shelter for the all the world's poor people. Yet, once aliens who are already in the country claim political asylum, it is very difficult to deport them, no matter how frivolous their claims may be. If an immigrant insists that he or she has a legitimate fear of persecution, a long legal process ensues, which can take as many as ten years to be resolved.

As a leader in the Congressional effort to toughen the immigration laws in the early 1990s, Senator Alan Simpson (Republican, Wyoming) proposed giving U.S. immigration officials the ability to "immediately exclude any alien" who comes to the U.S. without papers, and who cannot make a "credible claim"—on the spot—to refugee status.

Refugees and their supporters argue that this would be an inadequate and unjust policy. They point out that people fleeing political persecution, often in the midst of the confusion of war, can hardly be expected to gather together proper documentation. What may be credible to one border official might be incredible to another. The legal protections of the U.S. court system must be available to would-be refugees, their supporters insist, in order to ensure fair handling of their claims.

See also Immigration (Illegal); Immigration (Legal). **For further reading** McClellan, Grant S. *Immigrants, Refugees, and U.S. Policy*. New York: H. W. Wilson, 1981.

Regents of the University of California v. *Bakke*
See Bakke Case.

Religion in the Schools
Religion, and particularly Protestant Christianity, has been associated with education in the United States since colonial times. Many, if not most, of the colonial schools that existed when the nation was founded were run by religious organizations. The declared purpose of many of them was to instill the doctrines of religion in the students, as much as to teach them to read, write, and do figures.

Even after the present system of public schools was established in the nineteenth century, religion continued to have a significant place in the schools, although more indirectly than in colonial times. Although religious instruction, as such, was either eliminated or made indirect, religious beliefs and principles were implied in the values taught. Teacher-led prayers were commonplace, and Christian religious holidays were celebrated.

The main reason that the Roman Catholics eventually set up their own system of parochial schools in the middle of the nineteenth century was not a desire to keep their children from receiving nonreligious instruction in academic subjects. Rather, they objected to the public schools

being, in effect, Protestant institutions. Similar complaints that the schools were teaching Protestant religious beliefs and practices came from Jews, members of other non-Protestant religions, atheists, and agnostics.

The Constitutional Question
The First Amendment to the Constitution of the United States commands that "Congress shall make no law respecting an establishment of religion, or prohibiting the free exercise thereof...." This provision was intended to protect freedom of religion by ensuring that there would be no state religion in the United States, which might then use the power of the government to further itself at the expense of those with different beliefs.

Where the public schools are concerned, the Supreme Court has taken this so-called Establishment Clause to mean that they must not endorse or encourage the practice of any religion. If they should, the schools would be, in effect, discriminating against students and staff who belong to other religions, as well as atheists who believe in no religion at all. Furthermore, it would dangerously implicate the government, which pays for and runs the public schools, in religion.

Not only must the public schools refrain from doing anything that would promote a particular religion, they must refrain from anything that would promote religion in general. Some religious leaders would even argue that there is no such thing as religion in general. Any kind of religious observance, they say, implies some particular belief—if only a belief in a supreme being—however vague and undefined that belief may be.

Many Americans object to the Supreme Court's interpretation of the Establishment Clause. They argue that the

Court has it exactly backwards. The First Amendment, they say, was designed to assure freedom *of* religion, not freedom *from* it as the Court believes.

They argue that the free exercise of religion, which the Constitution protects, includes the right of students and teachers to practice their religions in school as well as elsewhere. They see no reason why school facilities should not be used for religious activities, nor why Christianity should not be taught as the majority religion of their community. Students in the religious minority, they say, can leave the room, or simply decline to take part, when religious observances are taking place.

Those who object to any connection between religion and the public schools argue that allowing religious practices would put an unnecessary, and unacceptable, pressure on the minority students. They would either have to participate in practices they do not agree with or openly declare themselves different from their fellow students. This requires a violation of their privacy that the school has no right to demand.

Forbidden Activities

In recent years, the public controversy over religion in the public schools has tended to focus on school prayer, school choice, and the teaching of creationism or evolution in the public schools, but it shows up in a variety of other ways as well.

Practices that are forbidden either by the Constitution or by the federal guidelines for religious expression in the public schools include direct religious instruction, school-sponsored prayers, religious celebrations, and all other religious activities, services, or meetings conducted by school personnel.

In some cases, even decorations put up for Christmas or Easter have been banned on the grounds that these are Christian religious holidays. For the most part, however, primarily secular symbols, like Santa Claus or the Easter Bunny, have been permitted, while anything suggestive of Christ has not.

The fact that public schools are forbidden to organize, conduct, or endorse any religious gathering does not mean that public school facilities can never be used by religious groups. Student and outside religious groups alike have sometimes been given the right to use school facilities for meetings or services, but only when the same facilities are available to other groups, whether religious or nonreligious, under the same restrictions and conditions.

State Aid to Religious Schools

The ban on religious activities in the public schools does not, of course, extend to privately funded religious schools, whether parochial or nondenominational. They are free to teach their religious beliefs and conduct whatever religious practices they choose. Not content with this, however, some religious schools have sought, and sometimes gained, state aid. When it has been given, this aid has come in forms that the courts held to benefit all citizens, whatever their religion. On the elementary and high school levels, for instance, assistance has sometimes been provided in paying the costs of school buses. On the university level, it has come in the form of research and construction grants available, at least on a competitive basis, to all institutions.

The lower courts as well as the U.S. Supreme Court have been inconsistent on the question of how much help the government may give to religious schools, and what kind. They allow the lending of secular-subject textbooks to religious schools, for instance, but not of tape recorders or other instructional equipment. They allow states to reimburse parents for students' daily busing expenses to and from religious schools, but not for field trips.

See also Religious Expression in Public Schools (Federal Guidelines); School Prayer.
For further reading Jurinski, James J. *Religion in the Schools*. Santa Barbara, CA: ABC-CLIO, 1997. McMillan, Richard C. *Religion in the Public Schools: An Introduction*. Macon, GA: Mercer University Press, 1984. Rose, David. *Home, School, and Faith: Towards an Understanding of Religious Diversity*. Bristol, PA: Taylor & Francis, 1992.

Religious Expression in Public Schools (Federal Guidelines)

Confronted by parents and school authorities pressing for greater opportunities for the expression of religious faith in public schools on the one hand, and court decisions limiting such use on the other, the U.S. Education Department has issued federal guidelines for religious expression in schools. The following excerpts are from key provisions of those guidelines.

Student prayer and religious discussion: The Establishment Clause of the First Amendment does not prohibit purely private religious speech by students.

Students therefore have the same right to engage in individual or group prayer and religious discussion during the school day as they do to engage in other comparable activity….

Local school authorities substantial discretion to impose rules of order…but they may not structure or administer such rules to discriminate against religious activity or speech.

Generally, students may pray in a nondisruptive manner when not engaged in school activities or instruction, and subject to the rules that normally pertain…. Students may

also speak to, and attempt to persuade, their peers about religious topics just as they do with regard to political topics. School officials, however, should intercede to stop student speech that constitutes harassment aimed at a student or a group of students…. The right to engage in [religious expression] does not include the right to have a captive audience listen, or to compel other students to participate. Teachers and school administrators should ensure that no student is in any way coerced to participate in religious activity.

Graduation prayer and baccalaureates: Under current Supreme Court decisions, school officials may not mandate or organize prayer at graduation, nor organize religious baccalaureate ceremonies. If a school generally opens its facilities to private groups, it must make its facilities available on the same terms to organizers of privately sponsored religious baccalaureate services….

Official neutrality regarding religious activity: Teachers and school administrators, when acting in these capacities, are representatives of the state and are prohibited by the establishment clause from soliciting or encouraging religious activity, and from participation in such activity with students. Teachers and administrators are also prohibited from discouraging activity because of its religious content, and from soliciting or encouraging antireligious activity.

Teaching about religion: Public schools may not provide religious instruction, but they may teach about religion… the history of religion, comparative religion, the Bible (or other scripture) as literature, and the role of religion in the history of the United States and other countries are all permissible public school subjects... [however] schools may not observe holidays as religious events or promote such observance by students.

Student assignments: Students may express their beliefs about religion in the form of homework...and other... assignments free of discrimination based on the religious content of their submissions....

Religious literature: Students have a right to distribute religious literature to their schoolmates on the same terms as they are permitted to distribute other literature that is unrelated to school curriculum or activities. Schools may impose the same reasonable time, place and manner or other constitutional restrictions on distribution of religious literature as they do on non-school literature generally, but they may not single out religious literature for special regulation.

Religious excusals: Subject to applicable State laws, schools enjoy substantial discretion to excuse individual students from lessons that are objectionable to the student or the student's parents on religious or other conscientious grounds.

See also Religion in the Schools; School Prayer.

Religious Freedom

See Religion in the Schools; Religious Expression in Public Schools (Federal Guidelines); School Prayer; Separation of Church and State.

Resignation of Richard Nixon

Under the U.S. Constitution, it is up to the House of Representatives to impeach (that is, to formally charge with high crimes or misdemeanors) a president. Once the president is impeached, it is up to the Senate to hold a trial to determine whether he or she should be removed from office.

The only twentieth-century president to be forced to resign under threat of impeachment was Richard M. Nixon, who suffered that indignity as a result of his role in the Watergate scandal. On 29 and 30 July 1974, the Committee on the Judiciary of the House of Representatives voted three Articles of Impeachment against him. Despite the claims of the Republican president that the charges against him were politically motivated on the part of the Democrats who controlled Congress, the articles, which were returned by a 27 to 11 vote of the committee, alleged serious misconduct in office.

Article I charged that "In his conduct of the office of President of the United States, Richard M. Nixon, in violation of his constitutional oath faithfully to execute the office of the President of the United States and, to the best of his ability, preserve, protect and defend the Constitution of the United States, and in violation of his constitutional duty to take care that the laws be faithfully executed, has prevented, obstructed, and impeded the administration of justice...."

Article II accused the president of "repeatedly engag[ing] in conduct violating the rights of citizens, impairing the due and proper administration of justice and the conduct of lawful inquiries, or contravening the laws governing agencies of the executive branch and the purpose of those agencies...."

Article III declared that the president had "failed without lawful cause or excuse to produce papers and things as directed by duly authorized subpoenas as issued by the Committee...."

"In all of this," the document summarized, "Richard M. Nixon has acted in a manner contrary to his trust as President and subversive of constitutional government, to the great prejudice of the cause of law and justice, and to the manifest injury of the people of the United States."

"Wherefore, Richard M. Nixon, by such conduct, warrants impeachment and trial, and removal from office."

It was clear to President Nixon that, if a trial were to be held by the Senate, he risked being found guilty and removed from office. The president avoided that possibility by resigning on 9 August 1974. He was subsequently pardoned by his successor, President Gerald Ford.

The impeachment drive, and subsequent resignation, embittered many Republicans who felt that Nixon had been mistreated by a hostile press and Congress. The pardon embittered many Democrats, who felt that Nixon should have been criminally prosecuted for what he and his administration had done.

See also Watergate Scandal.
For further reading Archer, Jules. *Watergate: America in Crisis*. New York: Thomas Y. Crowell, 1975.
Jaworski, Leon. *The Right and the Power: The Prosecution of Watergate*. Houston: Gulf, 1976.

Restructuring
See Downsizing.

Right to Bear Arms
See Bill of Rights; Gun Control.

Rights
See Bill of Rights; Universal Declaration of Human Rights.

Rock Festivals
See Altamont; Woodstock.

Roe v. Wade
By the early 1970s, abortion had become one of the most vexing and divisive issues in the United States. Most states had strict laws banning the practice, and it is probably fair to say that the majority of Americans opposed abortion as a moral evil. Nonetheless a growing number of feminists, as well as ordinarily nonpolitical men and women, had come to view the antiabortion laws as outmoded and overly restrictive.

Some people insisted that abortion was a right. The most extreme of them insisted that a woman had an absolute right to control her own body, and that this included the right to control, or abort her fetus, as long as it remained inside of, and therefore a part of, her. Others who opposed the strict antiabortion laws would not go that far, but argued that no woman should be required to give birth to a baby in circumstances that would work terrible hardship on her or on the child: for example, when a long pregnancy or childbirth would endanger the mother's health, if the fetus was genetically deformed, or when conception had been the result of rape or incest.

Those who favored the existing laws, on the other hand, argued that the rights that needed protecting were those of the fetus. Both sides in the growing debate accused the other of being cruel, if not barbaric.

In 1971, the U.S. Supreme Court, which had so far avoided the issue of abortion, decided that it was time to rule on the question directly. It chose to do so in a case known as *Roe* v. *Wade*, which was to become the landmark case on abortion and one of the most controversial cases in the history of the Court.

Lawyers acting on behalf of Norma McCorvey (who did not want her real name used, and was called Jane Doe for the purposes of the case) asked the Court to strike down two restrictive state abortion laws. In 1973, by a vote of 7 to 2, the Court did just that. Its ruling in the case established the principle that abortion, in the early months at least, was not only legal, but was protected under a right of privacy implied by the U.S. Constitution.

The majority decision, written by Justice Harry Blackmun, made some key distinctions, based largely on medical arguments about viability—the ability of a child to survive outside the womb. During the first trimester of pregnancy, Blackmun concluded, the woman had a virtually unrestricted right to abort. During the second trimester, the state could regulate proposed abortions in order to protect the woman's health. During the third trimester, at which time the child, if born, would be likely to survive, the state had a strong and legitimate interest in protecting the life of the child. Even in the third trimester, however, states had to allow abortions that were medically necessary to save the woman's life.

The *Roe* v. *Wade* decision failed to satisfy either side in the great political and moral debate that was—and still is—raging in the country over abortion. Those who opposed abortion under any circumstances considered it a crushing defeat. But, although the general public saw the ruling as a great victory for the pro-choice side, those who favored a woman's unrestricted right to abortion, at any time and for any purpose, complained that it was a halfway measure at best. Disappointed with the U.S. Supreme Court, both sides have continued to press their cases in the court of public opinion.

See also Abortion; Sex-Selection Abortions.

Sacco and Vanzetti Case

In 1920, two Italian immigrants named Nicola Sacco and Bartolomeo Vanzetti were arrested for an armed robbery in which two men had been killed in Braintree, Massachusetts. Both men, who had been active in the anarchist political movement, denied any guilt in the affair. Their case would became an international *cause célèbre* and bring the fairness and objectivity of the American justice system into serious question.

The early twentieth century was a time of conflict between a heavily immigrant industrial working class and the wealthy industrialists who employed them in America's manufactories, mines, and other major industries. Workers, many of whom lived in poverty, had few rights and no real power in their dealings with their employers. Fiery labor organizers, many of whom had had experience with anarchist or Communist labor movements in Europe before coming to the United States, were encouraging unhappy workers to unionize and strike. For their part, business owners and conservative politicians were alarmed at the specter of European-style labor unrest in the United States, or even a revolution like the one that had occurred in Russia only a few years before. The first great "Red Scare" of the twentieth century was underway, and the Palmer raids (in which some 3,000 allegedly "subversive" aliens were jailed and hundreds deported) had begun only a few months before.

The sympathies of the American public were torn. On the one hand, there was empathy for the poor workers, who were clearly at a disadvantage when it came to their dealings with their employers. On the other hand, there was a strong strain of conservatism in the public, which opposed the kind of disorder inherent in strikes and other forms of labor unrest and which feared the "foreign" influences that seemed to be invading American labor.

Sacco and Vanzetti quickly became symbols for both sides in the growing class struggle. In the eyes of immigrant union members, left-wing radicals, and rebels of all kinds, they were innocent men who were being railroaded for their political beliefs. Members of the established power structure saw them as dangerous foreigners out to subvert the American way of life.

In what many observers—including some who believed that the defendants were guilty—felt was an unfair trial, both men were convicted of murder and sentenced to death. Protests and demonstrations were held in support of Sacco and Vanzetti, and appeals to spare their lives came from all over the world.

The two men faced their fate with calm and fortitude. Sympathy for them grew as their executions neared, and letters written by them to Sacco's son Dante were made public. Although their English was shaky, their words seemed strangely eloquent. "One day, you will understand....," Vanzetti wrote in an effort to comfort the 13-year-old boy whose father was the subject of so much prejudice and hate. "That day you will be proud of your father; and if you come brave enough, you will take his place in the struggle between tyranny and liberty, and you will vindicate his names [*sic*] and our blood."

Both men were executed in the electric chair of the prison at Charleston, Massachusetts, on 22 August 1927. Many Americans breathed a sigh of relief at the news of their deaths. In their eyes, the murderous subversives were dead, and the turmoil that had surrounded their case could now die too. Others, however, mourned the deaths and agreed with a protest sign carried by the poet, Edna St. Vincent Millay: "American honor dies with Sacco and Vanzetti." The question of the two men's guilt or innocence is still a matter of historical controversy.

For further reading Russell, Francis. *Tragedy in Dedham*. New York: McGraw-Hill, 1971.

Same-Sex Marriages

Marriage is regarded one of the most important foundations of modern American society. As the basis of the nuclear family, it is vital to many of the arrangements and accommodations by which our society functions; and it is a key element of the mores and laws surrounding everything from child rearing to taxation.

Until now, the legal institution of marriage has been reserved for couples of opposite sex. In recent decades, however, more and more couples of the same sex have also sought the right to marry. Many such couples have gone so far as to participate in various forms of marriage ceremonies, usually performed by gay or lesbian members of the clergy, and therefore to consider themselves married. Such unions, however, have never been accepted as legally binding in any of the states, although some cities have recognized them for the purposes of local laws and ordinances.

Gay and lesbian couples desire to get married for many of the same emotional and psychological reasons that heterosexual couples do. They wish to formalize and to reinforce publicly their commitment to each other. They wish to bind themselves to each other legally, as well as emotionally, partly as a pledge of their mutual commitment and partly as an assurance of it. They also hope to win for the gay and lesbian relationship the same legal and social rights and protections enjoyed by heterosexual couples, and ultimately, something approaching the same respectability as well. They hold that marriage is a basic human right, not dependent on the sex of the partners, but on their mutual love and commitment to each other. They point out that many gay and lesbian couples have a better record of commitment and faithfulness than many heterosexual couples do; and they argue that committed couples of the same sex should have the same rights to cohabit, share property, inherit, and so forth, that couples of opposite sexes have.

Social conservatives, including some homosexuals, oppose legalizing same-sex marriages because they believe that doing so would undermine the already threatened legal protections of the traditional nuclear American family, and thereby contribute to further dislocations in society. Religious conservatives who believe that marriage is a sacrament, and homosexuality a serious sin, are appalled by the idea of same-sex marriages. In their view, legalizing such unions would amount to the sanctioning of immorality. They further fear that it would create what they believe to be a false moral equivalence between same-sex marriage and the traditional marriages that they hold sacred.

The movement for legalizing same-sex marriages gained momentum in the 1990s, thanks largely to historic rulings by the State Supreme Court of Hawaii. In 1993, the court ruled, in effect, that same-sex marriages *might* be protected by the provision of the state constitution that bans sex discrimination. Hawaii, like other states, had refused to recognize the right of same-sex couples to marry. In the 1993 preliminary ruling, the court said that the state would have to show a compelling interest in preventing such unions before it could deny them the same right to marry as other couples. Although the court did not actually overturn the state's ban on same-sex marriages at that time, it raised the possibility that it might do so in the future.

One result of this tentative ruling was a political movement on the part of Hawaiian gays, lesbians, and their supporters to have same-sex marriages legalized in the state. This movement was supported by gays and lesbians from all over the United States, as well as by some practical-minded Hawaiians, who cared little about the moral or sexual issue one way or the other. The latter hoped that making such marriages legal would increase tourism in the state by making Hawaii a marriage-and-honeymoon mecca for gays and lesbians from all over the country.

At the same time, the situation in Hawaii caused deep concern among social and moral traditionalists on the mainland. If Hawaii, or any state, did choose to legalize same-sex marriages, it would create a legal dilemma for states who did not wish to do so. Constitutional legal precedent has so far required all states of the Union to recognize the legality of marriages performed in any other state. Although each state has the right to set its own requirements for couples wishing to be married within that state, they do not have the right to disregard the legitimacy of marriages performed under the laws of another state.

It was not clear what position the federal government would take if Hawaii made same-sex marriages legal. During the early stages of the Hawaii case, the U.S. Immigration and Naturalization Service (INS) remained noncommittal as to whether or not same-sex marriage relationships would qualify for the marriage preferences given spouses of American citizens applying for immigration to the United States. Under the U.S. federal system, however, the central government was required to recognize legal marriages performed in any state. This would mean that same-sex couples legally wed in Hawaii would have to be regarded as legally wed for such purposes as computing federal taxes and awarding Social Security payments as well.

The traditionalists pressed Congress to act to prevent what they saw as a serious threat to the sanctity of marriage and the stability of American society. In the election year of 1996, and before the Hawaii court's ruling came down, the Republican-controlled Congress passed, and the Democratic President Bill Clinton signed, a bill which amounted to a preemptive strike against the Hawaii court. The bill freed the federal government, as well as other state governments, from the obligation to recognize same-sex marriages that might be performed under any state's laws in the future. Although popular among the public, this federal law raised important states rights issues, as well as civil liberties concerns, and its constitutionality was considered questionable.

On 3 December 1996, the Hawaiian Supreme Court made a final ruling recognizing the legality of same-sex marriages. According to the court, the state had failed to show a compelling interest in making such marriages illegal. Like the constitutionality of the federal law, the Hawaii court's ruling was likely to face an eventual challenge before the U.S. Supreme Court.

See also Homosexuality.

School Choice

The majority of American children attend the public grade and high schools in their neighborhoods, schools supported by a combination of local and state taxes. Only a minority of parents have chosen to send their children elsewhere. For the most part, these have been the comparatively wealthy, who could afford an expensive private school, or those with strong religious convictions, who were willing to sacrifice to provide their children with a sectarian education not available in the public schools.

Since taxpayers have been forced to pay taxes to support the public schools, whether they have children attending them or not, parents who send their children to private schools currently pay for two school systems at once. This is doubly unfair, they say, because they are already contributing to the public system by reducing the enrollment in overcrowded public schools.

In recent years, parents and others who consider this unfair have been demanding reforms that would give all parents a choice of which schools their children might attend.

The demand for reform has also been sparked by a widespread sense that the public schools are failing the students: that they provide an inadequate education and, in many cases, do so in a dangerous and unhealthy environment.

Ethnic, color, and economic prejudice also plays a part in the decision for those parents who want their children to attend school with people who are more like themselves than those in the nearest public school.

Ultimately, the reformers argue, it is in the interest of every American that all the nation's children be educated. Whether they get that education in public, private, or religious schools should be irrelevant. The government should see to it that children receive the best education possible, wherever they choose to get it.

Choice Programs

Commonly suggested school choice proposals fall into two groups. One would give some form of tax deduction, or exemption from school taxes, to families who are already paying for the private education of their children. The other would give the families vouchers that they could use to send their children to schools of their own choice.

Most of the proposals provide a limited choice, at best. Those programs already enacted in various communities involve only one or a small number of public schools. These are often alternative schools of some kind, such as magnet schools, which appeal to particular kinds of students. Some such might offer advanced programs for the so-called gifted and talented for example; others specialize in specific fields—such as mathematics, the arts, or the sciences—which specifically attract students interested in those fields. The freedom to choose to attend these schools is frequently limited to students likely to benefit from such specialized training.

Other programs and proposals offer students who live in a certain area the choice of attending any public school within that area. Depending on the program, choice is restricted to a particular neighborhood or school district, to a single community, or, in at least one major proposal, to an entire state. In other cases, choice is available only between certain schools or at certain grade levels. A smaller percentage of choice proposals offer educational vouchers or credits that can be applied to either public or nonreligious private schools.

In 1995, Wisconsin's Republican governor Tommy Thompson went even further. He proposed that the state provide over 3,000 vouchers that families could use to send their children to private religious schools, as well as to secular schools, in the 1996–1997 school year.

The Opposition to School Choice

Vouchers and other plans that encourage school choice are strongly opposed by several teacher's unions, as well as other educators who consider the public school system the foundation of American education. They fear that vouchers—which will encourage more parents to send their children to private schools of all kinds—will inevitably drain students and resources away from the public schools. Eventually, they warn, the public schools may be left with only the students the private schools do not want or cannot deal with. These include the students with health and behavior problems and those with special needs that make them especially expensive and difficult to educate.

The reformers respond that what is most important is the education of the children, not the well-being of the public schools. If private schools can provide bet-

ter education to the majority of American students, they should be encouraged to do so. Besides, they argue, it is not necessarily the best students who leave their neighborhood schools under choice programs. The typical transfer student in Milwaukee, Wisconsin's choice program, for example, had "significantly worse" scores on basic math and reading tests before the move to a new school than did the average Milwaukee student .

Ultimately, the reformers insist, increased competition from private and religious schools might actually be good for the public schools in the long run. Pointing to the effect of competition in the retail marketplace, they suggest that the need to compete with private and religious schools will force the public schools to improve the quality of education they offer the nation's children. And, if they cannot, they argue, the public schools do not deserve to survive.

Opponents of expanded choice respond that this would be a tragedy. They insist that the public schools are a vital resource that the nation cannot afford to lose. The public schools bring the disparate elements of our society together, providing the great majority of American children with a unifying common experience and helping to shape our unique American culture. Even more important, they train the nation's children in the rights and responsibilities of American citizenship. These are services that a variety of private and religious schools, each with its own educational and cultural agenda, cannot perform nearly as well.

As a practical matter, many opponents fear that choice will result in an even sharper division between quality schools and poor schools than exists today. They worry that even the most limited proposals, in which the choice is restricted to a small number of public schools, will encourage the best parents, as well as the best students, to flee some schools in favor of others.

At present, when the most active and concerned parents become aware of problems in their children's schools, they fight to have those problems solved. When choice is available, however, those activist parents will simply move their children elsewhere. This will leave the remaining children stuck in the troubled, substandard schools, with no one able and willing to fight to make those schools better. Albert Shanker, the late president of the American Federation of Teachers, argued that this had been the case in the United Kingdom, where parents have long been free to move their children into empty seats in any nearby public school.

Still another level of opposition to school choice comes from groups like Americans United for the Separation of Church and States and the American Civil Liberties Union. They worry that, one way or another, federal money will be used to support religious schools, and therefore religious education. This, they say, would violate the U.S. Constitution's "Establishment Clause," which calls for the separation of church and state. Just as it has long been a constitutional principle that religion should be kept out of the public schools, they say, public tax money should not be used to finance religious schools.

The high court has not yet ruled on whether vouchers that can be applied to religious as well as nonreligious schools are constitutional, but some observers believe it has been signaling that it will approve them, as long as they go to families, and not directly to church schools themselves. If Governor Thompson's program, or some other universal voucher proposal, ever is approved by the Court, it is likely that many other jurisdictions will adopt similar measures.

See also Religion in the Schools; Religious Expression in Public Schools (Federal Guidelines). **For further reading** Cookson, Peter W., Jr. *School Choice: The Struggle for the Soul of American Education.* New Haven, CT: Yale University Press, 1994. Fuller, Bruce, et al., editors. *Who Chooses? Who Loses? Culture, Institutions, and the Unequal Effects of School Choice.* New York: Teachers College Press, 1996. Henderson, David L. *The Case for School Choice.* Stanford, CA: Hoover Institution Press, 1993.

School Prayer

In recent decades, some of the fiercest battles over religion in the schools have been fought over the issue of formal prayer in the public schools, particularly Christian prayer. Such prayer has been banned as unconstitutional by the U.S. Supreme Court, but many Americans object to the Court's position. Prayer, they say, was allowed for over a century, and they would like to see it return.

Opponents of public school prayer object on the grounds that for school officials to introduce a prayer to their students is to imply the school's support for that particular religion. Children who do not share that religious belief, they say, ought not be forced to observe the forms of someone else's religion in the guise of education.

The U.S. Supreme Court and the Establishment Clause

No one objects to prayer in parochial or other religious schools, or even in private schools that have no religious affiliation. The reason for the controversy over prayer in the public schools is the fact that the public schools are agents of the government. Allowing prayer in these government-sponsored institutions, the opponents of school prayer argue, is a violation of the First Amendment's command that "Congress shall make no law respecting an establishment of religion, or prohibiting the free exercise thereof...."

Because children are required by law to attend school, offering prayers there amounts to requiring the young people to participate in a religious observance. Even if students are allowed to excuse themselves from the prayer, they are, in effect, being forced to take a religious stand as part of their required attendance at school.

Attempting to meet these objections, New York officials introduced what they called a nonsectarian prayer into the state schools there. "Almighty God," read the prayer, "we acknowledge our dependence upon Thee, and we beg Thy blessings upon us, our parents, our teachers and our Country." They hoped that this form would allow students and teachers to pray without implying or expressing belief in any particular religion.

In 1962, however, the U.S. Supreme Court ruled, in the case of *Engel* v. *Vitale*, that even such a nondenominational prayer violated the Establishment Clause. The state had no business writing prayers, sectarian or otherwise. It was not the state's role—and, therefore, not the role of the public schools—to encourage, or sponsor, prayer of any kind. The next year, the Court reinforced its ruling in *Abington School District* v. *Schempp*, which forbids public schools to open their day with either a prayer or a Bible reading. Both of these practices had been commonplace in some areas of the country.

In the decades since *Abington*, the Court has upheld its ban on any kind of school-sponsored prayer. It consistently has forbidden any practice whose intention has been to promote or endorse religious activity in the public schools.

In the 1990 *Board of Education* v. *Mergens* decision, however, the Court also accepted a provision of the federal Equal Access Act of 1984 requiring those secondary schools that permit their facilities to be used more or less indiscriminately to other legitimate student groups to open them up to student groups who want to use them for religious expression, including prayer and Bible study, as well. The Court found this acceptable because by providing equal access to both religious and nonreligious "noncurriculum" student groups, schools would neither be endorsing religion nor spurning it.

There has long been a great deal of support in Congress for a constitutional amendment to overrule the Court's decisions and allow school prayer. Proposed school prayer amendments tend to have three main provisions: 1) No law should bar voluntary prayer in the public schools; 2) no student or teacher should be forced to pray; 3) whatever prayer, or prayers, are used should not be composed by the government. These provisions are intended to open the way for school prayer without prejudicing the rights of those who do not wish to participate in it.

The Continuing Debate

Despite what has so far been the Supreme Court's interpretation of the Establishment Clause, the idea of permitting, and even encouraging, school prayer is very popular among politicians and the public alike. Bills favoring school prayer have passed several state legislatures. It is a particularly effective issue for conservative legislators at the federal and state levels, many of whose constituents are fundamentalist Christians with a deep belief in the value of prayer.

The United States, the fundamentalists argue, has always been an overwhelmingly

Christian country. The use of Christian prayer helped schools instill proper moral values in generations of American students and should be allowed to do so again. Polls show that support for prayer in public schools is not confined to born-again Christians. Many people of different faiths, and even of no faith at all, simply cannot understand why the practice should be banned.

As long as no student is forced to participate, they argue, school prayer would only be allowed, not imposed on anyone. What is wrong, they ask, with allowing those students who want to recognize their Creator and ask for God's help an opportunity to do so? The true purpose of the so-called Establishment Clause of the Constitution, they say, is to protect religious activities, not to outlaw them. To ban prayer in the public schools is, in effect, to prohibit the free exercise of religion—precisely the thing the Establishment Clause was intended to encourage.

The opponents of school prayer also include a broad spectrum of Americans. Even many religious Americans worry that the schools, and the government itself, would become too closely allied with specific religious beliefs and attitudes. Many Jews fear that school prayers, in such a predominantly Christian country, will inevitably reflect Christian beliefs. Many Catholics fear that they will have a distinctly Protestant tinge. Atheists, meanwhile, object to the endorsement of any kind of religious practice.

Perhaps surprisingly, a number of Protestant organizations—including most of the mainline Protestant denominations—also object to school prayer, even to school prayer that reflects their own religious beliefs. They fear that the state endorsement of religion implied by school prayer will inevitably lead to state interference with religion. It is not the state's business, they

argue, to write prayers, or to pick which prayers school children will be allowed to say. They prefer that the government stay away from religious matters altogether, particularly when it comes to the instruction of the nation's children, than for the government to have a hand in designing religious practices like prayer.

Despite protests from their fellow religionists, the issue has become symbolic for many Christian proponents of school prayer. They consider the Supreme Court's prohibition to be a glaring indication of a growing godlessness in American society, and a major contributor to what they see as a broad decline in the nation's moral values.

The opponents of school prayer respond that freedom *of* religion means freedom *from* religion as well. Any prayer with real content implies some kind of specific religious beliefs. Given the makeup of American society, those beliefs would almost certainly be Christian. Any prayer without real content, on the other hand, would be a mockery of religion itself. Even if a totally nondenominational prayer could be written, the opponents argue, it would still *be* a prayer, and therefore, an unacceptable state endorsement of religion.

Besides, however voluntary a school prayer might be, the opponents say, there is an implied coercion of students in any officially school-sponsored act. In order to avoid participating, children would have to, in effect, announce their own beliefs. Or *dis*belief. This is an unfair, as well as unconstitutional, demand to put upon children in a public school. The state has no business inquiring, even indirectly, into students' religious beliefs.

The Moment of Silence
One compromise, which already has been adopted by several state legislatures, is for

schools to provide a brief time during which students who want to may pray. This would be done in the form of a moment of silence, which students would be free to use for whatever mental purpose they wish. Although some would undoubtedly pray, others could choose to spend the same time in some form of meditation, or mentally planning their social activities for the coming weekend. It would be up to them.

This idea of a moment of silence is widely approved of, even by such strong opponents of public school prayer as the National Council of Churches—so long as it is not presented to the students specifically as a moment of silent prayer.

The Supreme Court ruled an Alabama moment of silence law unconstitutional in *Wallace* v. *Jaffree* (1985), but only on the grounds that the particular statute specified that the time be made available for voluntary prayer. This was, in the Court's eyes, an endorsement of prayer and therefore gave the law an unacceptable religious purpose. The Court did, however, indicate that it would probably accept a similar law, as long as it spoke only of silent meditation or reflection.

Some opponents of public school prayer, however, feel that even this limited a law would be going too far. Prayer may not be the stated purpose of a moment of silence, they argue, but students will still correctly assume that prayer is its real intention. In effect, they say, a moment of silence amounts to a moment of prayer and is therefore unconstitutional.

See also Religion in the Schools; Religious Expression in Public Schools (Federal Guidelines).
For further reading Jurinski, James J. *Religion in the Schools*. Santa Barbara, CA: ABC-CLIO, 1997. McMillan, Richard C. *Religion in the Public Schools: An Introduction*. Macon, GA: Mercer University Press, 1984.

Rose, David. *Home, School, and Faith: Towards an Understanding of Religious Diversity*. Bristol, PA: Taylor & Francis, 1992.

School Uniforms

Uniforms are nothing new in American schools. They are traditional in military academies, as well as in some prep boarding schools, and even ordinary parochial schools in some communities.

For much of this century, even many public schools used to require a kind of semi-uniform, demanding that boys wear slacks, white shirts, and ties and girls wear skirts or dresses. Such rules had already gone out of favor in most public schools by the 1960s, however. They fell victim to the spirit of informality of the time and a growing respect for the individuality and self-expression of students.

As a result, most modern-day students, and their parents, have grown up wearing casual clothes to school. Even today, although the majority of elementary and high schools do have dress codes, those codes tend to be relatively loose. What's more, they are primarily negative. That is, they ban certain dress and hair styles, rather than require others. In the past few years, however, a growing number of schools have started requiring their students to wear uniforms.

Reasons for Requiring Uniforms

In the past, uniforms were identified primarily with schools that wanted to set themselves apart in some way. A school uniform proclaimed the wearer as someone special, a student from a school distinguished by academic excellence, religion, or special social or economic requirements for attendance. Because of this, they were considered embarrassments by some of the young people who had to wear them and snobbish by many outsiders. Others, including school officials and many parents, as well as many students, regarded them as proud and honorable symbols.

The current reinstatement of uniforms in some schools stems from very different concerns. It is prompted more by serious problems that plague the schools than by any pride in the schools' achievements. This is particularly true in the urban schools that have turned to uniforms primarily as a way of cutting down on violence among the students.

Clothes are extremely important to many young people for reasons of personal vanity and as means of proclaiming their self-identification. This importance has grown to have increasingly negative consequences. Thefts of clothing have become commonplace in many schools, as have fights prompted by the wearing of certain cloths. In recent years, there have been reports of teenagers being murdered for their shoes.

Part of this violence stems from envy and greed. People who cannot afford the high priced items of clothing they covet take them from others. But much of the violence is gang-related. In many areas of the country, members of juvenile gangs proclaim their membership by wearing their "colors." Certain garments, ranging from headbands to professional sport team jackets, have become a kind of uniform in themselves. They indicate membership in a specific gang. The mere wearing of gang colors is often enough to prompt violent, and even deadly, confrontations between rival gangs. Some young people with no gang affiliation at all have been attacked, or even killed, for wearing clothing they had no idea were used as colors by a gang.

School administrators in areas where violence and tensions are high are looking more and more seriously at uniforms as at least a partial solution. Some public school districts already require them for students in some schools or at certain grade levels. Long Beach, California, for example, requires uniforms in all 70 of its elementary schools.

Student and Parent Reactions

Some students resent having to wear uniforms. Some parents also resent having to buy them, where this is required. Other parents are grateful, however. In the long run, they find, uniforms cut down their children's clothing costs, since new school clothes do not have to be bought continually to accommodate quickly changing fashions.

Officials in some schools where uniforms have been in use for some time have found another positive side effect as well. They say that overall grades have improved since uniforms were introduced and attribute that fact partly to the effect uniforms have had in persuading wearers to take their role as students more seriously.

Scopes Case

In 1925, a schoolteacher named John T. Scopes was charged with violating Tennessee's recently passed Butler Act, which forbade "any teacher in any of the universities, normals and other public schools of the state… to teach any theory that denies the story of creation of man as taught in the Bible, and to teach instead that man is descended from a lower order of animals."

The Issues at Stake

Scopes's trial was intended by all sides to be a test case of the new law. Scopes admitted teaching Darwin's theory of evolution to his students in a Tennessee high school, which was a direct violation of the Butler Act. The legal question to be decided was whether the state had the right, for religious reasons, to forbid educators to impart what they determined to be scientific information to their students.

The trial, held in the small town of Dayton, Tennessee, before Judge John T. Raulston of the Circuit Court of Rhea County, was recognized as a major testing ground, not just for the Butler Act, but for a number of pivotal social and intellectual forces. It was widely seen as a battle between science and fundamentalist religion, between modernism and tradition, and between the values of rural and urban America.

In the eyes of Scopes's defenders, the question to be decided was one of intellectual freedom. In the eyes of his prosecutors, it was a question of religious truth. In the minds of the most extreme fundamentalists, it was, more deeply than any of that, a battle between the forces of godliness and evil.

Because fundamentalists interpreted Darwin's theory as an argument that humans were descended from monkeys, H. L. Mencken, the well-known journalist who covered the case for the Baltimore *Sun*, dubbed the event the "monkey trial." The mocking nickname caught on with the press and public alike.

The trial was ensured national (and even international) attention when two famous advocates announced that they would represent the opposing sides in the case. William Jennings Bryan—who had been secretary of state under President Woodrow Wilson and a three-time Democratic nominee for president himself—agreed to help prosecute Scopes. On the other side, Clarence Darrow, the nation's most famous criminal lawyer, was employed by the American Civil Liberties Union to defend Scopes's right to teach what he believed to be true. Both Darrow and Bryan were known as fierce champions of the "little man." Darrow was probably the nation's leading legal defender of civil liberties and the rights of workers, while Bryan was the leading political advocate of the nation's farmers and the values of rural America.

As befit a struggle between giants, the trial became the first to be broadcast, at least in part, to listeners around the country over the new medium of radio. The dramatic high point of the trial came when, in an unprecedented move, defense attorney Darrow called the prosecutor Bryan to the stand as an expert witness on the Bible. Bryan, a devout fundamentalist, willingly defended the literal truth of Genesis, while Darrow ridiculed his beliefs with questions that pointed out apparent logical impossibilities in the biblical account.

The verdict was anticlimactic. As everyone had expected from the beginning, the Tennessee jury found John Scopes guilty. He was fined $100 ($400 less than the maximum possible penalty). In a sad historical postscript, William Jennings Bryan died in his sleep only five days after the trial.

The Aftermath

The Scopes trial was a watershed in twentieth-century American cultural history. For the fundamentalists, it proved to be a hollow victory. The Tennessee appeals court eventually overturned Scopes's conviction on a technicality. Although the court's ruling left the Butler Act intact (and it would remain in effect until 1967), it would rarely, if ever, be enforced. Only two other states would pass laws similar to Tennessee's, and evolution would soon become the standard explanation of the origin of the human species taught in most American schools.

The ultimate importance of the so-called monkey trial was not in its legal outcome, but in its social impact. Most observers felt that Darrow had won the epic confrontation with Bryan; as a result, Tennessee and its creationist law became symbols of ignorance and backwardness to those Americans who considered themselves scientifically and culturally advanced.

The playwrights Jerome Lawrence and Robert E. Lee fictionalized the trial in their 1955 Broadway hit play *Inherit the Wind*, which has become one of the most popular and frequently performed dramas in the history of the American theater.

See also Creationism versus Evolution in the Public Schools.
For further reading Ginger, Ray. *Six Days or Forever? Tennessee vs. John Thomas Scopes*. New York: Oxford, 1974.

Secondhand Smoke

According to government and other health agencies, it is not only smokers who suffer from the deleterious health effects of tobacco smoke. Although not as dangerous as firsthand smoke, secondhand (or passive) smoke also has serious damaging and potentially fatal effects of its own.

According to the U.S. Department of Health and Human Services, tests show that the blood and other bodily fluids of nonsmokers who spend time around smokers contain significant levels of several toxic substances—including nicotine and carbon monoxide—from tobacco smoke.

The Centers for Disease Control and Prevention estimates that 3,000 Americans die each year from lung cancers resulting from exposure to secondhand smoke. That is many times the number brought about by the effects of all the regulated air pollutants taken together. Other conditions commonly associated with tobacco smoke also show up disproportionately in people exposed to secondhand smoke compared to those who are not.

The very young seem to be especially susceptible to secondhand smoke. The fe-tus may be the most vulnerable of all. A particular problem arises when pregnant women continue to smoke, despite evidence that their habit has bad effects on the children they are carrying. Once born, millions of children live in homes with parents who smoke and are forced to inhale secondary smoke on a regular basis.

The desire to protect nonsmokers from secondhand smoke is one of the main reasons for the smoking restrictions that have been enacted by many businesses and governmental agencies.

See also Smokers' Rights; Smoking; Smoking Restrictions.

Self-Esteem Movement in Education

The 1970s and 1980s saw a new awareness of the importance of self-esteem in the lives of individuals of all ages. A feeling of low self-worth, it came to be recognized, led people to undervalue themselves. This, in turn, led them to lower their expectations, not only for their own aspirations in life, but for the treatment they expected from other people as well.

Psychologists say that people who suffer from poor self-esteem tend to do less well than others in school and in work situations; that they take more part in criminal and other antisocial behavior; that they fall victim to drug and alcohol addictions in greater numbers; and that they tend to become involved in more abusive, or otherwise unhealthy, personal relationships.

Although low self-esteem has been found to be a problem for individuals in all classes and categories of society, it seems to be disproportionately associated with women and minorities. Psychologists and sociologists typically explain this by the fact that these groups are frequently undervalued and discriminated against by the wider society. Individual women and members of minority groups are, in effect, taught to think of themselves as less valuable than other people.

The growing perception that damage to self-esteem begins in childhood has led many late twentieth century educators to re-evaluate the American educational system in light of the effect it may be having on the self-esteem of the children in its charge. Their conclusion was that the nature of American education with its emphasis on placement, grades, and awards was effectively lowering the self-esteem of many children.

The Alleged Damage Done by the Traditional Educational System

Much of the traditional American educational system has been built on a competitive model. Students are rewarded for doing better than their peers. They are routinely placed in higher or lower grades, or more or less advanced classes within grades, depending on their abilities relative to other students. Those who receive As are, in their own perceptions as well as that of their teachers, considered to be better in that subject area than those who receive Bs; those with Bs are considered to be better than those with Cs, etc.

In most competitions, educational as well as otherwise, there tends to be one or a small number of winners and a much larger number of losers. To the extent that the competition for grades, whether direct (grading on a curve) or implied, promotes self-esteem in those who receive higher grades, it presumably also diminishes the self-esteem of those getting lower grades. Since only a minority of students in any class receive the highest grade in most schools, the majority of students suffer at least a potential blow to their self-esteem.

Educators who reevaluated American education in light of the damage that this competition might be doing to students' self-esteem began to call for certain changes in American education, particularly on the elementary level. A key event in this reevaluation was a 1990 California educational task force report entitled "Toward a State of Esteem." The task force called on the state's school districts to make raising its students' self-esteem a primary goal. California is the nation's largest and most influential school system, and the report had an effect far beyond the state's borders.

The report—and the self-esteem movement in education that it helped inspire—accelerated a lessening of the stress on objective achievement, as measured by standardized tests and grades, which had already been taking place in some school systems. Among other things, teachers were encouraged to praise children for whatever they accomplished, even if those accomplishments failed to match either traditional standards or the accomplishments of their peers.

In some schools, grading standards have been lowered in order to ensure that students receive grades that encourage rather than discourage them. In others, grades have been abandoned altogether, to be replaced by a simple pass-fail standard or by an essentially positive written evaluation of all students.

Concerns

The intention of the self-esteem movement is to make children feel good about themselves, in the belief that this will foster a less anxious environment in which children will be freer to learn. In the long run, it is hoped that this will contribute to healthier, as well as more educated, generations of Americans.

More traditional educators protest that, far from fostering individual accomplishment, this focus on self-esteem simply contributes to what they call a "dumbing down" of educational standards and results in less knowledgeable and less competent young people.

Although all educators agree that children should be appreciated for their own sakes, whatever their intelligence or academic achievements, traditionalists insist that the first job of education is to teach, that is, to provide children with the knowledge and skills they will need to make their way in later life. This cannot be accomplished, they insist, by lowering educational standards in the name of raising self-esteem. True self-esteem, say the critics, comes from meeting reasonable standards, not from avoiding them.

Supporters of the self-esteem movement respond that its ultimate purpose is not to lower educational standards, but to achieve them in other ways. However, some standards need to be changed, not because they are too high, but only because they are either outmoded or unnecessarily fussy.

The nature of this element of the debate can be illustrated by a major controversy that erupted over spelling. Although spelling has traditionally been a basic requirement of American education, it has recently been deemphasized in many classrooms and school districts, at least partly in response to the self-esteem movement. According to some advocates of the self-esteem movement, strict insistence on accurate spelling acts as an barrier to children learning to love and appreciate words for their own sake. This, they claim, is an unnecessary obstacle in an age of computer spell-checkers. As long as the child can recognize the sound and meaning of a word when it is read, and can approximate that sound in his or her spelling of the word, it is counterproductive to reprimand the child for small mistakes. To do so, the advocates say, is to emphasize small failures at the expense of significant achievement.

The traditionalists respond that, far from being an obstacle to the appreciation of words, spelling should be understood as a key element of that appreciation. It may be more important to understand a word than to spell it, but it is also necessary to be able to reproduce words accurately in order to communicate with others. As to the importance of spelling in the computer age, they point out that computers are absolutely unforgiving of spelling errors when it comes to entering commands or file requests.

For further reading Beane, James A., and Richard P. Lipka. *Self-Concept, Self-Esteem, and the Curriculum*. New York: Teachers College Press, 1986.

Separation of Church and State

The First Amendment to the Constitution of the United States begins, "Congress shall make no law respecting an establishment of religion, or prohibiting the free exercise thereof...." This has become known as the Establishment Clause, the primary constitutional guarantee of religious freedom in the United States. It is also the most fundamental guideline for U.S. governmental policies affecting religion.

The Supreme Court uses a three-pronged test to determine whether a governmental action complies with the Establishment Clause. First, according to the Court's test, in order for a government action to be constitutional, the government must be acting for a secular (nonreligious) reason, that is, one that is not designed either to encourage or to inhibit any religious purpose. Second, the effect of the government's action must neither further nor inhibit religion. Third, the action must not involve the government and any religion in each other's affairs in any significant way.

The Establishment Clause was inspired by the founders' distaste for the situation that prevailed in England at the time of the American Revolution, wherein politics and religion were intimately entangled. The Church of England was the official state religion, and the British monarch was, at once, the head of state and the head of the church. It was, in fact, the religious persecutions and civil disorders that resulted from this intermingling of church and state that drove many from England to America in search of the freedom to exercise their own faiths. By means of the Establishment Clause, the founders hoped to protect their right to such exercise while, at the same time, avoiding the kinds of religious conflicts that periodically rocked the mother country.

In the twentieth century, however, the U.S. Supreme Court has cited the Establishment Clause in several decisions that some Americans see as restricting, rather than protecting, religious freedom. These complaints come mostly from Christians who argue that the United States is a fundamentally Christian country with a Christian tradition that ought to be governmentally recognized and accepted, if not positively encouraged.

In *Everson* v. *Board of Education* (1947), however, the U.S. Supreme Court reinforced the proposition, first expressed by Thomas Jefferson, that the Establishment Clause was "intended to erect a wall of separation between Church and State"—a position that has put the clause at the center of several legal controversies over public issues involving religion, particularly those affecting prayer in the public schools.

See also Religion in the Schools; Religious Expression in the Public Schools (Federal Guidelines); School Prayer.
For further reading Kelly, Dean M., and Richard D. Lambert, editors. *The Uneasy Boundary: Church and State*. Philadelphia: American Academy of Political Science, 1979.

Sex Crimes
See Child Abuse; Sexual Abuse and the Roman Catholic Clergy; Sexual Harassment; Sexual Predator Laws.

Sex-Selection Abortions
Some potential parents have a definite preference for the sex of their child. Perhaps they have several children of one sex already and hope for the opposite sex this time. Perhaps they want a boy to pass on the family name to future generations in the traditional way. Whatever their reasons, these parents want to know as soon as possible whether they will get their wish. When they find out, some of those who are disappointed choose to have an abortion instead of giving birth to a child of the "wrong" sex.

In the past, expectant parents have had to wait until their baby was born to know the sex of the child. Today, however, they can determine it well in advance. Various medical procedures can be used to determine the sex of a fetus, ranging from ultrasound tests, which provide a kind of picture of the baby in the womb, to genetic tests like amniocentesis, which are even more reliable. Hundreds of thousands of women each year ask their doctors to determine the sex of the baby they are carrying. Others find out incidentally, as a result of tests conducted for other purposes. Most parents who want to know are just curious and impatient. They want to look forward specifically to a new son or daughter, to know what kind of name to pick, what color baby clothes to buy.

No one knows how many sex-selection abortions take place each year. No statistics are kept, but estimates range into the thousands. What evidence there is suggests that most of those aborted are females and that the practice is most common among certain ethnic groups, such as some Native Americans and Asian-Americans, who put a high value on sons.

Some doctors see nothing wrong with carrying out tests solely to determine the sex of an expected baby, nor with carrying out sex-selection abortions. They consider the decision of whether to abort or carry the baby to term to be the woman's alone, and they consider it their duty to carry out the wishes of their patient (the pregnant woman), no matter what her reason for that decision. For others, abortion on the grounds of sex raises serious questions, not only of medical ethics, but of sex discrimination. Along with many religious and social experts, they find the idea of aborting a fetus because of its sex distasteful and morally unacceptable.

Even some doctors who perform abortions for other reasons are unwilling to do so for this reason, or for this reason alone. And, except for a handful of absolutists who insist that a woman should be able to have an abortion for any reason (or no reason at all), even actively pro-choice organizations sometimes object to sex as a grounds for abortion. In Canada, a Royal Commission that oversees new developments in reproductive technologies has called on the Canadian government to ban sex-selection abortions.

See also Abortion; Roe v. Wade.

Sexual Abuse and the Roman Catholic Clergy

The sexual abuse of young people by members of the clergy is particularly damaging because of the unique position of trust the clergy occupy in the lives of religious people. When abuse occurs, the effect is likely to be even more devastating to the victim than it might be in other circumstances. What is more, it affects the larger religious community as well, causing a crisis of faith in many believers.

Although abuse is committed by a minority of the clergy in many churches, abuse within the Roman Catholic Church has received the most public attention in the media. Partly, this is due to the fact that Catholicism is the largest single sect in the United States. Partly, too, it is due to what some observers charge has been the slowness and inadequacy of the church hierarchy's response to the problem.

Estimates of the number of priests who may have been involved in sexual abuse range as high as five out of every 100. Several American priests have actually been found guilty of child abuse and sentenced to long terms in prison. It is estimated that the Catholic Church has spent some $500 million over the past ten years settling claims against its priests. The greatest single problem apparently existed in the Santa Fe Diocese in New Mexico, which in 1994 faced 41 suits asking a total of $50 million in damages.

Abuse victims accuse the Roman Catholic hierarchy, in the United States and in the Vatican, of being reluctant to recognize the problem and often unwilling to deal with it once it has been exposed. Even after church officials have been convinced that a priest has violated his trust, the officials are often more concerned with protecting him—and the reputation of the church—than with helping the victim. Victims also charge that church officials are more determined to protect the church's finances from the claims of victims who sue for damages than they are with discovering the truth of the charges and making appropriate reparations.

Some critics within the church believe that much of the problem rests with the fundamental mindset of the Roman Catholic authorities in Rome. Their concern, the critics charge, is not child abuse, but rather the offending priest's violation of his vow of celibacy.

This is a particularly difficult attitude for most modern Americans to understand, in light of the increased concentration on the problem of child abuse that has developed in the United States in recent years.

Church officials in the United States deny that they are either unaware or unwilling to deal with the problem. Rather, they say, they are attempting to deal with it in a responsible way. The church, they point out, believes in forgiveness and redemption. It cannot simply turn its back on priests who have sinned, any more than on ordinary parishioners who have done so. When church authorities discover that a priest has been guilty of abuse, their first concern is to remove him from any position in which he would come in contact with children and to seek treatment for him, preferably at one of the two treatment centers the church has established in the United States for that purpose.

At least some of the dissatisfaction outsiders feel with the church's response, church officials argue, stems from the traditional caution and deliberation with which the institution acts. The church cannot be blamed for refusing to accept every claim that is made against a priest as being true. In fact, some child abuse allegations made against priests have been proved to be unfounded.

The most notorious case of unfounded charges involved Cardinal Bernardin of Chicago, perhaps the most highly regarded prelate in the United States. Soon after charges against him were made public, and Bernardin's previously saintly reputation had been perhaps irreparably damaged, the emotionally disturbed accuser admitted that his apparent memories of abuse, which had been brought out under hypnosis, were probably imaginary.

Catholic officials further explain that it would be financially irresponsible of them simply to open up the church's coffers to those who may have been harmed by degenerate priests. The church has many financial duties, and church officials have fiduciary obligations that must be fulfilled.

See also Child Abuse.
For further reading Rossetti, Stephen J. *Slayer of the Soul: Child Sexual Abuse and the Catholic Church.* Mystic, CT: Twenty-Third, 1990.

Sexual Harassment

Sexual harassment may be broadly defined as unacceptable sexually related behavior by a member, or members, of one sex toward a member, or members, of the opposite sex. More narrowly, it may be restricted to such behavior in which the harasser is in a position of authority or influence over the victim, as in the employer-employee, landlord-tenant, and teacher-student relationships.

Most often, the harasser is male and the victim female, a circumstance that flows naturally from the imbalances in the social and economic relationships between men and women in American society. Religious, business, and cultural traditions all tend to put men in positions of power and authority over women. This has made it possible, and perhaps inevitable, that men would sometimes abuse that power. Physical abuse of male power, in the forms of rape and battery, have been understood to be problematic for centuries. It is only in the mid to late twentieth century, however, that the less obvious abuses of male power have come to be understood as also, if not equally, damaging.

Sexual harassment has been recognized by the federal courts as a legally unacceptable form of sexual discrimination since 1975. Most litigated sexual harassment is job-related, that is, it is an abuse of the employer-employee as well as the male-female relationship. In a landmark 1980 survey of 23,000 federal employees, 42 percent reported being the victims of sexual harassment. Although the typical sexual harassment case involves a female victim and a male perpetrator, men can also be sexually harassed by female employers or coworkers, and sometimes are.

In extreme cases, employers, forepersons, or others in position of authority (usually male) take advantage of their dominant economic position over employees of the opposite sex by asking for—or even demanding—sexual favors. This may be done with a stated or implied threat that, if the employee does not cooperate, she will be fired or penalized in some other way. Even when no overt threat is present, however, the employee may be naturally reluctant to challenge or refuse the person in authority for fear that some kind of job-related retaliation would be taken or that the work relationship between them will be damaged.

In less extreme cases, employers may fondle, hug, kiss, or pinch female employees, make lewd remarks to them, or tell them off-color jokes. Even when there is no threat, or even any overt sexual advance attached to such behavior, it can be extremely unwelcome and embarrassing and cause the employee serious discomfort and stress.

Coworker Harassment

Another form of work-related sexual harassment, one that does not directly relate to boss-underling relationship, involves coworkers of opposite sexes, even though they may be of relatively equal job status. The sexual harassment of coworkers may be carried out by individuals or by groups. In the latter case, the fact that one sex significantly outnumbers the other sex on the job sometimes substitutes for job-related authority in establishing a power relationship between them.

In such circumstances, employees of the majority sex may create what is known as a hostile work environment for employees of the opposite sex. This may be done by the kinds of advances and behaviors described above or by members of the majority making common cause with other employees of the same sex to shut those of the opposite sex out of work-related activities.

Members of either sex might embarrass those of the opposite sex by acting in a grossly gender-related manner. Men might display sexually explicit posters or photos in the workplace, for example, or routinely belch or pass wind in front of female coworkers. Women might make a practice of discussing gynecological problems in front of male employees.

The perpetrators of the lesser forms of sexual harassment may not intend any serious offense by what they do, or even understand that they are doing anything wrong. To them, such behavior may seem only natural, or even friendly. For the victim, however, it can make the workplace not only an unpleasant and stressful place to be, but a seriously intimidating one.

Sexual Harassment and the Schools

Although most of the public attention on sexual harassment has focused on the workplace, it has become a serious concern for many other institutions as well. Schools, in particular, have frequently found themselves embroiled in the sexual harassment issue. Willingly or not, elementary and secondary schools have been assigned responsibility for teaching the current generation of young people about a problem that previous generations hardly recognized existed. This has made them extremely sensitive to the issue inside their own walls. Many schools around the country have initiated "no tolerance" policies when it comes to sexual harassment incidents, whether they involve staff members or students.

Most accusations of sexual harassment that surface in school settings involve charges of male students harassing female students, or teachers harassing students. These are not always the circumstances, however.

In an unusual reversal of the usual power relationship involved in sexual harassment cases, a male high school student in Schofield, Wisconsin, was accused of sexually harassing a female teacher by writing in the school newspaper about a momentary fantasy that the teacher might be sexually interested in him. The fact that the comments appeared in a humor column, and were clearly labeled as fantasy, did not prevent school authorities from publicly declaring the student guilty of sexual harassment. Despite complaints from freedom-of-the press advocates, the school not only disciplined the student, but censored the award-winning student newspaper The Jet in which the column had appeared, and removed the paper's long-time faculty advisor from his post.

If nothing else, the incident showed the tremendous sensitivity that exists in society today to the issue of sexual harassment. If anything, many Americans are beginning to believe that society has become oversensitive about it.

Has There Been an Overreaction?

Although few would argue that sexual harassment is not a real concern, there have been signs of a backlash of sorts to what some people see as an overreaction to the issue. Many were appalled, for instance, when a first grade boy was suspended from a New York school in 1996 for kissing a female classmate on the cheek—a kiss the classmate apparently welcomed.

Although many corporations have instituted strict policies to eliminate sexual harassment in their organizations, labor and feminist groups insist that sexual harassment continues to be a serious problem. Some employees, however, feel that anti-harassment efforts have gone too far. Male employees, they complain, have become frightened of making normal conversation with female employees or coworkers, or even attempting any kind of friendly, open work relationship with them, for fear that their friendliness will be misunderstood. The result, they say, is that the American workplace is becoming more uncomfortable and intimidating for those who work there, rather than less.

Management personnel and others in positions of authority are made wary by their vulnerability to charges that they have sexually harassed an employee.

A false charge of sexual harassment can be a handy weapon for an employee who is angry at a superior for whatever reason, as well as for coworkers who hope to advance their positions within a company at a rival's expense. The popular novel and movie *Disclosure* was based on this premise. Such false charges, critics allege, are relatively easy to bring and difficult to disprove.

As a result, the fear of being accused of harassment has made male employers wary of dealing with female employees beyond the strict demands of their respective jobs.

One unanticipated consequence of the drive to end sexual harassment, then, may be to isolate female employees more than ever. This, in turn, may make it harder, rather than easier, for women to form the kind of personal and professional relationships with their superiors that can be vital to advancement within a corporate structure. In addition, the nervousness produced by concerns about sexual harassment has eliminated much of the on-the-job and after-work socializing that many workers have previously regarded as important side benefits of employment.

One of the most important difficulties in the notion of sexual harassment is that its existence depends to an important extent on the subjective feelings and/or reactions of the victim. Different people may interpret the same behaviors very differently. What one employee may regard as intolerable behavior another may see as harmless sociability. The same sexual advances that may insult and intimidate one employee may be regarded as not only acceptable but positively welcome by another.

Whether sexual advances are desired or not, however, those who are most concerned about sexual harassment argue that such behaviors are and ought to be unacceptable in any work relationship—particularly those relationships involving the authority of one party over the other. They point out that the potential for intimidation is inherent in the superior-underling relationship, whether or not either party is influenced by it, or even conscious of it, in a particular case.

See also Women in the Military.
For further reading Aggarwal, Arjun P. *Sexual Harassment: A Guide for Understanding and Prevention*. Charlottesville, VA: MICHIE, 1992.

Herbert, Carrie M. *Talking of Silence: The Sexual Harassment of Schoolgirls*. Bristol, PA: Taylor & Francis, 1989.

Sexual Predator Laws

Sexual predator is a term politicians use to describe a criminal offender, usually male, who has a history of molesting, raping, or otherwise assaulting women or children. Several states have passed laws establishing special criminal punishments for such repeat offenders.

These so-called sexual predator laws fall into two main categories. First are measures that deny parole for sex offenders or repeat sex offenders or that call for them to be kept in confinement longer than other prisoners who have received the same sentences. Second are laws requiring law enforcement authorities to keep track of sexual offenders after they are released: to find out where they live and inform their new communities, and sometimes their immediate neighbors, both of their presence and of their past sexual offenses.

Sexual predator laws stem from a variety of social concerns. Fundamental is a feeling that, because of their vulnerability, children need special protections from those who would prey on them. Beyond that, several highly publicized cases of children being abused, or even murdered, by criminals who have previously been convicted for sexual attacks on children have aroused anger and fear on the part of parents across the country. Often, the criminals were men living in the victim's own neighborhood, whose residents had no knowledge of their past.

Responding to these public concerns, over 30 states enacted laws requiring released sex offenders to register their addresses and/or calling for the communities or neighbors to be notified of their presence. In 1996, Congress passed a law of its own requiring states to enact such legislation. The constitutionality of this law has been seriously questioned, however, and the issue will almost certainly come before the Supreme Court.

Such laws are frequently referred to as Megan's Laws, referring to a seven-year-old New Jersey girl who was raped and murdered after being lured into a neighbor's house. Although neither Megan's parents nor other residents of the affluent neighborhood had known about it, the offender had a history of violent sex crimes. Similar repeat crimes, committed by criminals with similar records, have occurred in many of the other states that have passed such laws.

At least 13 states also have laws that allow the authorities to keep those defined as sexual predators in confinement, usually in some form of mental institution, after their criminal sentences have expired. This, too, is constitutionally controversial.

Both kinds of sexual predator laws have proven difficult to enforce. Many judges believe that they violate the offenders' rights by, in effect, punishing them twice for the same crime. In New Jersey, a judge ruled part of the original Megan's Law unconstitutional; and Wisconsin judges have refused to enforce a state sexual predator law intended to delay the release of sexual offenders due for parole.

Simpson Case

On 17 June 1994, O.J. Simpson, a former football star, was charged with the murders of his ex-wife, Nicole Brown Simpson, and a young man named Ronald Goldman. The Simpson case would not only seize national attention in a way that few criminal cases ever have, but reveal some stark realities about racial divisions in the United States.

In time, Simpson would face two trials resulting from the murders, one criminal and one civil. Both would be covered more intensely by the media, over a longer period of time, than any other trial in history. Virtually the entire criminal trial was cablecast live over three different cable networks (Court TV, E!, and CNN), and portions of it were broadcast by the major over-the-air networks as well. The judge in the civil case banned television and radio from the courtroom, but the trial was reported in detail daily. One cable network actually reenacted portions of the day's testimony each evening, with actors reciting the words of the lawyers and witnesses.

In addition, both trials were thoroughly discussed on virtually all the public affairs and talk shows on TV and radio. At least two cable talk shows, one hosted by Geraldo Rivera and the other by Charles Grodin, devoted the majority of their air time to the Simpson case throughout the months of the trials.

There were several reasons why the Simpson case attracted so much attention. First was the sensational nature of the murders themselves. The victims' bodies were found, brutally and repeatedly stabbed, just outside Nicole Brown Simpson's home in a residential section of Los Angeles. Then there was the impressive battery of prominent attorneys, both white and black—dubbed "the dream team" by the press—who defended Simpson. By far the most important reason for the prominence of the case, however, was the person of O.J. Simpson himself.

Simpson was probably the most famous American ever to be charged with murder. (The only celebrity who came close was the movie comedian Roscoe "Fatty" Arbuckle, who was acquitted of murder in 1922.) One of the greatest running backs in the history of professional football, Simpson had remained in the public eye as a commentator on television's popular *Monday Night Football*, movie actor, and celebrity spokesman for major corporations like Hertz Rent-A-Car.

The "Race Card"

Although the lawyers on both sides began by insisting that they would keep race out of the case, the issue clearly hung over the trial from the beginning. Simpson was a black man, whereas his alleged victims were white.

The prosecution was able to produce a great amount of physical evidence against Simpson. If believed, it would clearly demonstrate his guilt. The defense, however, insisted that this apparently damning evidence was not believable for two reasons. First, they contended that the investigating officers and Los Angeles lab personnel had mishandled and contaminated much of the evidence. Second, they suggested that white police officers planted key evidence (including blood stains and a bloody glove allegedly worn by the murderer) on Simpson's property.

The second claim was given credence in the eyes of many viewers when the defense was able to discredit Mark Fuhrman, a white police officer who was a key police witness. Despite Fuhrman's denials of hostility toward African-Americans, the defense produced an audio tape proving that Fuhrman had frequently used racial slurs and had even bragged that Los Angeles police officers frequently planted evidence on black defendants. Along with expert testimony suggesting widespread contamination of the forensic evidence, the Fuhrman revelations helped convince some members of the public that the prosecution's case was suspect. African-Americans were especially willing to believe allegations of misconduct against the

L.A. police department, because the department had a bad relationship with the black community. Most white observers, however, remained convinced that the case against Simpson was incontrovertible.

Many of these same white observers were outraged when Johnnie Cochran, one of Simpson's black attorneys, asked the mostly African-American jury in his closing argument to "send a message" to the L.A. police department. Cochran was widely accused of "playing the race card" (that is, of being racially divisive). His remarks were criticized by those who interpreted them as either asking for jury nullification or deliberately encouraging the heavily black jury to acquit Simpson simply because he, too, was black.

The same whites were even more outraged when the jury took only a few hours to find Simpson not guilty of the murders. Many white television commentators and print journalists angrily criticized the black jurors, calling them ignorant, biased, and irresponsible. The testimony had gone on for months, the journalists complained. How could the jurors have possibly considered the evidence fully in a few hours? (Jury members, interviewed by the press, pointed out that they had been considering the evidence all along.)

The African-American public reacted very differently. Deeply suspicious of the Los Angeles police, and of any prosecution of a black man for killing a white woman, the majority of African-Americans were more ready to believe the defense's claims that much evidence against Simpson had been planted. To an extent that surprised white observers, a large segment of the African-American community was cheered by the verdict. Many felt, perhaps, that the Simpson acquittal was a step in the direction of balancing the scales for the many innocent black defendants they believed had been unjustly convicted of murdering white people throughout American history.

Following the criminal trial, relatives of the victims sued Simpson in civil court. In this second—civil—trial, an overwhelmingly white jury found Simpson responsible for the death of Ron Goldman and the battery of Nicole Brown. (Out of consideration for the Simpson children, the families did not formally accuse the children's father of their mother's murder.)

When the verdict of the civil trial was announced on the night of President Clinton's State of the Union Address in February 1997, some cable television stations abandoned coverage of the president's speech in order to cover the verdict.

Reactions

The Simpson case mesmerized America for two and one-half years. It affected the public's attitudes on a variety of major issues, including domestic violence, victims' rights, police misconduct, the television coverage of trials, and the U.S. judicial system in general. For many, it brought into question such traditionally fundamental tenets of U.S. law as the presumption of innocence, the adversarial trial, and the right to trial by jury. Most significantly of all, it influenced attitudes on race.

Reactions to the trial seemed to depend largely on race. White Americans were astounded by the black reaction to the trials and the verdict. They could not understand how so many African-Americans could look at what seemed such overwhelming evidence and still conclude that Simpson was innocent. Many black Americans, on the other hand, were convinced that the evidence only seemed overwhelming to whites because the defendant was black.

African-Americans were particularly offended by white criticisms of the black jurors in the criminal trial. Public opinion polls showed that a very high proportion of African-Americans approved of the verdict in that trial, while a high proportion of whites objected to it. Similarly, whites were strongly in favor of the verdict in the second trial, while blacks were more dubious of it.

The depth and intensity of the disagreement between whites and blacks, particularly in regard to the first verdict, were widely interpreted as evidence of disturbing differences between the way black and white Americans view not only the criminal justice system, but life in the United States.

The two groups even reacted differently to the differences between them. Although whites were surprised at the depth of these differences, blacks were not.

Some social commentators lamented the Simpson case as adding to the racial polarization of American society. Others welcomed it as providing a needed dose of reality to the ongoing racial dialogue between blacks and whites.

See also Jury Nullification; Police Corruption.

Single-Parent Families

The most typical American family still consists of the traditional two parents and one or more children. Nonetheless, more than one-third of all modern families with children have only one parent in the home. There were some 9 million single-parent families in the United States in 1994, approximately twice as many as there had been in 1970. Nearly 90 percent of all single-parent families were headed by women, and one half of those were poor.

The majority of single-parent families result from divorce. Other causes include abandonment by one parent (usually the father) of spouse and children; the death of a parent; the forced separation of the parents, such as those necessitated by the incarceration of one of them or by extended military service; and births to unwed mothers when the father remains detached from the household or (more rarely) is unknown.

Psychologists generally agree that psychological pressures can weigh heavily on the parents and children alike in such families. Parents in single-parent families are faced with a greater individual burden of responsibility for their children than other parents. Lacking a partner with whom to share emotional, financial, educational, and other parental duties, they have less time for other concerns in their lives. As a result, they frequently feel a loss of autonomy and a blurring of their sense of personal identity, as their own needs are engulfed by the needs of their children.

The child in a single-parent family may feel abandoned, unwanted, or unloved by the absent parent. When the custodial parent is of the opposite sex, the child typically lacks a role model. When the absent parent is of the opposite sex, the child frequently lacks the opportunity to form the kind of early close bond with an adult of the opposite sex that some psychologists believe is helpful in forming inter-gender relationships later in life. In both cases, the child grows up without a constant model of the traditional husband-wife relationship.

The situation is neither entirely nor invariably bleak, however. Although the single-parent family may be less desirable than a stable family with both parents present, it is generally considered preferable to a seriously unstable two-parent family torn by violence or other forms of abuse. What is more, the single-parent state is often temporary. Even when it is not—and despite all the many difficulties and potential dangers—single parents are often successful in juggling their many responsibilities, retaining their sense of self, and maintaining a satisfying life for themselves and their children. By the same token, many children raised in single-parent families suffer few or no apparent ill effects from the experience.

See also Unmarried Mothers.

Slave Labor Abroad (U.S. Complicity)

The two main causes of the continued widespread existence of slave labor in the world today are both economic. The desire for profit drives manufacturers to use slave or slave-like labor, while poverty forces tens of millions of people to allow themselves to be enslaved, and even to sell their own children into slavery.

There are four primary forms of slave labor in the world today: forced prison labor, forced prostitution, child labor, and debt bondage. The majority of all the people held in slavery or slave-like conditions in the world today are children. Parents in some poor societies sell their children, or at least their children's labor, in order for the families to survive. Anti-Slavery International, the world's leading antislavery organization estimates that some 80 million children in South Asia alone are caught in slavery or in working conditions that amount to slavery.

Debt Bondage

Child labor often is combined with debt bondage, an arrangement the United Nations defines as "a pledge by a debtor of his personal services or those of a person under his control as a security for a debt, if the value of those services is not applied towards the liquidation of the debt or the length and nature of those services are not respectively limited and defined." In many cases, debtor parents pledge the services of their children in payment on their own debt.

Debt bondage is the most common slave-like practice in the world today. Although it is most common in certain Asian and Near Eastern countries, it occurs in many other places as well, including some areas of the United States. Such arrangements are popular among unscrupulous employers because they provide extremely low-cost labor, which, in turn, allows manufacturers to provide relatively low-cost products to consumers around the world.

American Involvement

According to antislavery activists, American industry and American consumers are complicit in foreign slave labor practices, such as those described above. American-owned corporations, as well as multinational corporations with heavy American participation, exploit such practices in their foreign operations or deal closely with foreign contractors who do.

Inside the United States, reputable clothing and sports stores, electronics outlets, and food stores, including large national chains, routinely traffic in products produced by slave and debt-bonded labor—practices that continue despite the fact that every member of the United Nations has signed the Universal Declaration of Human Rights, which prohibits them.

Among the many products pinpointed by antislavery activists as frequently produced by slaves or slave-like labor are certain fruits and vegetables, grown by slave or debt-bonded labor in Latin America and processed by certain American companies; clothing and electronic products, wines, teas, and industrial machinery manufactured by forced prison labor in China; sugar grown in the Dominican Republic and harvested by forced laborers from Haiti; and some "Persian" carpets woven by young children in the world's leading rug-making nations of India, Pakistan, and Nepal.

American consumers and retailers are often unaware that the goods they buy and sell are produced under these conditions, and it can be argued that they should not be held responsible in any way for practices of which they had no knowledge. To the extent that consumers and businesses willingly trade in these products, however, they can be considered implicated in them.

Measures to Combat Foreign Slavery

The Fair Labor Standards Act of 1938 empowers the U.S. government to bar the importation of any products produced abroad by slave labor or under sweatshop conditions. This power has rarely been used, however. The practical difficulties of uncovering and verifying such practices, much less tracking the goods produced by them, are daunting. It is hard enough for U.S. investigators to uncover such practices within the United States, much less in foreign nations.

The U.S. Labor Department has recently made some efforts to enlist the help of major retailers in fighting slavery and slave-like conditions by encouraging them to audit their domestic suppliers to determine whether those suppliers comply with U.S. labor laws. It is probably unrealistic, however, to expect retailers to effectively monitor, much less to scrupulously investigate, scores, if not hundreds, of individual suppliers.

Publicity and consumer pressure can sometimes be more effective than government action. Thanks largely to such pressure, some gains have occasionally been made. Near Eastern rug manufacturers are now labeling rugs not produced by child labor, signaling to consumers that they can buy them without encouraging the practice. In 1996, Nike and Reebok announced that they would attempt to find a way to ensure that soccer balls produced in Pakistan and sold under their brand names would no longer be produced by slave labor.

See also Slavery.
For further reading *Anti-Slavery Reporter*. London: Anti-Slavery International, yearly editions. Elkins, Stanley M. *Slavery*. Chicago: University of Chicago Press, 1975.

Slavery

Slavery is an economic relationship in which one person is effectively under the total control of another person or institution with no opportunity to free themselves. That control can be enforced, either by law, in societies that permit the legal ownership of one individual by another, or by means of economic or physical intimidation, in societies in which slavery is illegal.

Slavery lasted longer as a legal institution in the United States than in other western nations, and illegal forms of slaverylike practices continue to exist in the United States today.

History

Slavery is an ancient institution that existed in some corners of the world as long as 5,000 to 6,000 years ago, if not before, and has continued to exist in many places ever since. Slaves were part of ancient Greek, Roman, and Chinese societies, among others. A form of semislavery called serfdom formed the basis of Europe's agricultural economy during the Middle Ages.

Slavery was also common in Africa in medieval times, although the conditions of bondage there were often less harsh than in some other lands. Slaves in the Ashanti tribe, for instance, had the right to marry, to own property, and even to possess slaves of their own.

Slavery was accepted, if not always actually approved of, by most ancient religions. The major religions did, however, attempt to put restrictions on the institution by limiting the ways in which it could be practiced, and who could and could not be permissibly enslaved. The Christian and Muslim religions, for example, both pleaded for the merciful treatment of slaves, although neither religion condemned the practice outright.

African Slaves in the United States

In the New World, as in many other places, slavery was most often associated with readily apparent racial or ethnic differences. This suggests that it is somehow considered preferable to enslave people who are noticeably different from the enslavers in some obvious way, whether that difference is in skin color or culture.

Slavery existed among some Native American peoples long before Europeans came to the Western Hemisphere. The Spanish and Portuguese began importing African slaves into the Americas to work their gold mines soon after their arrival in the New World. Estimates of the number of African slaves imported into the Americas range widely. The best estimates range between 9 million and 10 million, approximately 427,000 of whom came to what became the United States. Although Africans made up the only large group of permanent slaves in English America, there were also many bonded laborers from

England and elsewhere who were, in effect, temporary slaves.

At one time or another, slaves could be found in all of England's American colonies, with the possible exception of Vermont. The South, however, was the only region of the United States in which slaves would play a truly major role in the economy. Following the invention of the cotton gin, African slaves and their descendants provided the primary labor pool for the cotton plantations of the southern states.

Despite the slaves' importance to the South, the United States was never really comfortable with the institution of slavery. Thomas Jefferson, a slaveholder himself, summed up many thoughtful American's uneasiness with slavery when he wrote a friend, "I tremble for my country when I think that God is just, and that his justice cannot sleep forever!"

There was a serious attempt to include a ban on slavery among the original provisions of the Constitution, but this effort was defeated by representatives from the southern states, whose cotton industry relied on slave labor. A compromise was reached that kept slavery constitutional but banned any further importation of slaves after 1807.

Even without the addition of new slaves from abroad, the high birth rate among slaves tripled the slave population between 1807 and 1860. It stood at about 4.5 million by the time slavery was abolished by the Emancipation Proclamation.

Some of today's most intractable social problems are the heritage of African slavery. As the only large ethnic group brought to the United States against their will, African-Americans have been at a disadvantage when it comes to fully assimilating in American society. The negative psychological legacies of slavery—among them,

self-doubt on the part of African-Americans, prejudice, hatred and fear on the part of whites—are incalculable.

The enforced breakdown of family relationships that occurred under slavery left many African-Americans lacking the family traditions that most other immigrant ethnic groups took for granted. The legal and social barriers erected in the post–Civil War South (in particular) forcibly prevented the descendants of slaves from integrating for decades, and their aftereffects continue to haunt both blacks and whites today. Although the legal barriers to full integration have been broken down to a great extent, social and economic barriers remain. As a result of these and other factors, African-Americans remain at least a century behind where they would otherwise be in the assimilation process.

Slaverylike Practices in the United States Today

Although slavery, in the historic sense, has ceased to exist in the United States, there are practices that come close to it in several respects. It has been argued, for example, that child pornography and prostitution are forms of modern slavery. That is because minors—particularly preadolescent minors—are not truly independent agents. Although some may participate willingly in such activities, they are not mature enough to judge the morality of their actions or the potential consequences of their participation.

Debt bondage is probably the most common slaverylike practice in the United States today, as it is in the world at large. The United Nations defines debt bondage as "a pledge by a debtor of his personal services or those of a person under his control as a security for a debt, if the value of those services is not applied towards the liquidation of the debt or the length and nature of those services are not respectively limited and defined."

Such bondage was commonplace in the mining towns of Appalachia until just a few decades ago. Miners who worked in certain mines lived in company towns, in which virtually everything was owned by the large coal companies that employed them. Instead of being paid for their labor in money that could be spent anywhere, they were given chits that could be redeemed only at the company store. By controlling the price of food and supplies sold at the store, as well as the rent charged for the company-owned housing in which the miners were required to live, the miners were effectively kept in debt to the company and ensured of continued employment on the company's terms.

Most companies had abandoned these practices by the 1970s, either because they had been forced to do so by legal reforms or because the practices had ceased to be economically profitable. Most debt bondage arrangements that have come to light in the United States since then have involved workers from foreign countries. This may be because foreigners are, in general, more vulnerable to exploitation, being less familiar with American civil rights protections and American legal procedures than native-born citizens.

Most cases of debt bondage that have come to light have involved the agricultural and garment industries. In the early 1990s, for example, a Somis, California, flower grower was convicted of virtually enslaving migrant workers from south of the border. Although his conviction on the most serious counts were later overturned, he was required to spend three years under various degrees of house arrest and to pay $1.5 million to the illegal immigrants he exploited. In the summer of 1995, a migrant worker rescued in a raid on a Minne-sota farm claimed that he and other workers had been shackled and threatened with being shot if they attempted to leave.

Migrant workers are sometimes forced to live in camps near the fields they harvest and subjected to woefully inadequate working, sanitary, and living conditions. While there, the workers are dependent for food and other necessities on the employer, who subtracts their costs from wages that are frequently well below the minimum wage. Such laborers sometimes work from daybreak to sundown for days, only to end up owing their employer money rather than the other way around.

It is not uncommon for whole families of migrants to work the fields together, in a desperate attempt to earn enough to keep them all alive. Child labor is a particularly troubling feature of this kind of slave like labor.

Illegal Immigrants

Illegal immigrants are the most susceptible of all workers to slavery like practices, because they are afraid to approach the authorities to win their freedom. Undocumented immigrants from Asia are particularly vulnerable. In June 1993, a decrepit freighter named the *Golden Venture* that ran aground off the coast of Queens, New York, was found to contain a cargo of almost 300 illegal Chinese immigrants. Many had paid approximately $20,000 apiece to be smuggled into the United States; others, who could not afford the passage, had put themselves into heavy debt to the Chinese gang that owned and operated the ship. Ill-treated and abused on their long voyage, they had been forced to live in stinking holds below decks and to share a single toilet. Some of the women had been raped on the journey. According to U.S. authorities, if the passengers of the *Golden Venture* had not been discovered by the U.S. Coast Guard, they would have been held in debt bondage to the gang that had transported them.

Uncounted thousands of Asian immigrants are being held in such bondage today. Some work in sweatshops; others are forced into prostitution; still others are enlisted into drug-dealing and other criminal activities to pay off their debts. Some 70 undocumented workers from Thailand were discovered being held as virtual captives in an El Monte, California, garment factory in August 1995.

U.S. authorities estimate that approximately 100,000 illegal immigrants from China alone are smuggled into the country each year. No one knows how many of them—and how many other undocumented Asians, Mexicans, and other illegal immigrants—are held in virtual slavery by their smugglers or by others to whom they have been "sold."

Government investigators and labor activists believe that the cases that occasionally come to light are only the tip of a much larger iceberg. There are literally thousands of small farms and cut-and-sew garment factories around the country. Many of the former get away with exploiting migrant labor because they are subject to little or no effective regulation, while many of the latter are fly-by-night operations that frequently change their locations, and even their names. Government enforcement agents admit that keeping track of the myriad of potential abusers is an impossibility, particularly with the limited resources that the government is willing to devote to the issue.

See also Child Labor; Slave Labor Abroad (U.S. Complicity); Sweatshops.
For further reading *Anti-Slavery Reporter*. London: Anti-Slavery International, yearly editions. Elkins, Stanley M. *Slavery*. Chicago: University of Chicago Press, 1975.

Smokers' Rights

Since the publication of the U.S. surgeon general's historic 1964 report on the dangers of cigarette smoking, the federal government has attempted to discourage the use of cigarettes and other tobacco products. Government agencies have been joined in this effort by a growing number of private businesses and institutions that have enacted antismoking measures of their own. Among these measures, public and private, are increasingly higher sales taxes on tobacco products, as well as bans on smoking in a variety of public places and places of business.

Such measures—along with the possibility that smoking may someday be outlawed altogether—have led smokers to feel increasingly besieged and to protest that their rights are being infringed. They argue that it is unfair for the government, or even for private businesses, to single them out for disapprobation and to enact measures designed to make their pastime prohibitively difficult or expensive.

Smoking, they say, is a traditional American pleasure, one that dates to precolonial days. Present-day Americans should be free to enjoy such pleasures, even if it is not medically good for them, as the opponents of tobacco claim. The mere fact that tobacco, or any other product, may present some kind of health risk does not mean that it should be banned, or even severely restricted. Adults have the right to decide for themselves what the risks are, and whether or not they choose to take them. Many other substances, including such staples of the American diet as meat and sugar, have also been linked to disease when used to excess. Should they be restricted too?

Tobacco companies object to what they see as the punitive measures directed against their industry. Although they acknowledge that there may be some relationship between smoking and certain diseases, they insist that the evidence for a causal connection is not as strong as tobacco's opponents claim. Tobacco, they point out, is a legal commodity in the United States, the growing of which as a cash crop has long been subsidized by the U.S. government. As long as tobacco remains legal, the tobacco industry insists that its products should be treated like any other legal products.

Smokers' rights advocates reject the argument that the costs associated with smoking are not borne by smokers alone. They question studies that indicate serious health effects of secondhand (or passive) smoke and insist that there is no overriding social need to compel them to curtail their smoking.

So far, the arguments of tobacco advocates have had little success, either in the courts or in the political arena, beyond ensuring that tobacco remains legal in the United States. However, at least one state, New Hampshire, has passed a smokers' rights law that makes it illegal to refuse to hire someone solely because he or she is a smoker. Even in New Hampshire, however, employers have a right to forbid workers to smoke in the workplace.

See also Secondhand Smoke; Smoking; Smoking Restrictions.

Smoking

Tobacco smoking originated in the western hemisphere, most probably in central America. It had already spread to North America by the time the first Europeans arrived there. Christopher Columbus noted Caribbean Indians smoking tobacco on his first voyage to the New World in 1492. The Indians drew the smoke through tubes, or pipes, and this was the practice adopted by early European explorers and colonials, who undertook to cultivate tobacco as a crop and then to export it to their homelands in Spain, France, and England. Tobacco was so popular that it was, at one time, used as the primary currency in at least one American colony. Cigarettes and cigars began to become popular as delivery systems for tobacco smoke in the nineteenth century. Cigarette smoking soared in favor after a machine to manufacture cigarettes was invented in 1881.

Until the twentieth century, smoking was primarily, although not exclusively, a male activity. During the "flapper era" that followed World War I, an increasing number of daring young women began to smoke in defiance of traditional female stereotypes. The percentage of women who smoked rose even more dramatically during World War II, when women were forced to take on many traditionally male roles on the home front.

Smoking's popularity climbed throughout the first half of the twentieth century, until—spurred on by the surge in female smokers—it peaked in 1963, at which time approximately half the population of the United States smoked. By then, smoking had come to be regarded as a badge of masculinity for men and a badge of sophistication for women. This symbolism was reinforced by the movies of the era, in which smoking was a pervasive feature.

The Effects
of the Surgeon General's Report

In 1964, the U.S. surgeon general issued a landmark report authoritatively linking cigarette smoking to cancer and other major diseases. Opponents of smoking had insisted for years that such links existed, but the surgeon general's report gave their claims a credibility they had not had before.

Following up on the health warnings given in the report, the surgeon general's office required further notices to appear on all cigarette packages, notifying purchasers that smoking was dangerous to the health. Over the years since, these warnings have become progressively stronger and more explicit.

After more than six decades of growth, the consumption of cigarettes in the United States began a decline in the wake of the surgeon general's report. By the early 1980s, the percentage of smokers had dropped to around 33 percent; by 1990, to about 26 percent. At that point, the percentage of smokers began to climb again, reaching approximately 29 percent by 1996.

Much of the reversal of the decline was due to the fact that, as the percentage of males who smoked declined, the percentage of women smokers rose. Particularly alarming to health authorities was the fact that a great deal of this increase occurred among teenage girls.

The reason for smoking's popularity among young women in the 1990s seemed to be related to the reasons for earlier surges in female smoking. At least since the 1920s, young women had seen smoking as a symbol of female liberation. This sense was appealed to by cigarette advertising directed specifically at young women, the least subtle of which was a famous Virginia Slims campaign that encouraged women to smoke with the slogan, "You've come a long way, baby."

Despite the overall decline in smokers in the second half of the twentieth century, smoking remains an economically significant activity in the United States. Americans spend more than $37 billion on tobacco products each year. The diseases caused by smoking require billions of dollars of medical treatment, much of it paid by Medicare, Medicaid, and other tax-supported programs.

Health Risks

At one time, cigarette advertisements actually claimed that smoking was good for the health and had a beneficial effect on the lungs. Although they no longer dare to make such claims, tobacco spokespeople refuse to acknowledge either that nicotine is truly addictive or that a true causal relation between smoking and major diseases has been conclusively proved.

The Centers for Disease Control and Prevention (CDC), however, are convinced that the connection between smoking and many deadly diseases is indisputable. The CDC implicates smoking in the deaths of 420,000 Americans annually, as well as in a variety of serious medical problems, including heart disease and other circulatory problems. Smoking has been implicated in high blood pressure, rapid heart beat, and coronary artery disease (potentially deadly blockages, which build up in arteries and can lead to serious circulatory problems, including heart attacks). The strongest and longest-established links between smoking and disease involve diseases of the lungs. People who smoke are five times as likely as nonsmokers to die of such lung diseases as chronic bronchitis and emphysema.

At least 43 separate substances found in tobacco smoke have been implicated in the development of cancers, either in human beings or animals. Smoking has been blamed for over 2 million lung cancer deaths in the United States since 1964. In 1982, a report by the surgeon general of the United States blamed smoking for 93,500 of the 110,000 lung cancer deaths in that year, as well as for 35,500 deaths from other cancers, including cancers of the mouth, larynx, esophagus, bladder, kidney, and pancreas.

In addition to the disease risks of smoking, the habit discourages the development of bones in the young and promotes loss of bone in aging women. At least two studies have indicated that smokers' bones take longer to heal when broken than those of nonsmokers. Another study that reported that nonsmokers scored higher on IQ tests than those who smoked ten cigarettes a day suggested that smoking may have a deleterious effect on intelligence.

A major 1994 report, funded by an international group of health organizations, estimated that smoking has caused 60 million deaths since 1950 in the developed countries alone. And, whereas the smoking habit has declined statistically in the United States over the past several decades, it is on the upswing worldwide. As a result of rising smoking patterns in developing countries, the World Health Organization warns of an approaching "tidal wave of mortality" in the Third World. If it strikes, much of its force will be generated by the 112 billion cigarettes annually exported from the United States.

As depressing as the medical studies on the effects of smoking may be, studies on the effects of quitting smoking are encouraging. They indicate that even long-term smokers who give up the practice can greatly increase their current health as well as their future life expectancy.

The Question of Addiction

Smoking is unquestionably a habit. The extent to which that habit is essentially psychological or physical, however, is a matter of some dispute. Most health authorities insist that the scientific evidence that the nicotine in tobacco is a physically addictive substance is overwhelming. If the makers of cigarettes and cigars were to bring their products to the market today, these authorities believe, tobacco would be banned as an addictive drug. It is only because smoking is such a well-established practice in the United States—and, perhaps, such an economically important one—that it is legal at all.

A controversy erupted in 1994 over the tobacco industry's practice of controlling the amount of nicotine in their products and producing certain brands with unusually high concentrations of the substance. Critics charged that these products were deliberately designed to be more highly addictive, in order to "hook" people on cigarettes.

Tobacco companies admitted regulating the doses of nicotine in particular brands, but denied that they did so to produce addiction. Instead, they claimed that it was done in an effort to assure uniform quality and to produce brands that appealed to a variety of consumer tastes. If anything, they insisted, the reality was the reverse of what tobacco critics charged. The nicotine in some brands were especially regulated to contain low levels of nicotine in order to attract customers who were worried about the health effects of high levels of the substance.

Smoking and Children

An ongoing controversy focuses on the use of the cartoon figure Joe Camel and other advertising techniques that critics charge are aimed at attracting children to cigarettes. According to the American Heart Association (AHA), some 3,000 American children smoke their first cigarette each day. Counting teenagers, 2,000,000 young Americans begin smoking each year.

The AHA particularly decries these facts, not only because smoking is a major contributing factor to childhood asthma, but also because it may spur the early onset of many other diseases that are most often thought of as adult infirmities. Coronary artery disease, for example, often begins in childhood, although symptoms rarely appear until much later in life.

Discouraging Smoking

The AHA and other opponents of smoking have urged the government to take steps to further discourage the practice in the United States. Among the measures they call for:

An increase in taxes on cigarettes and other tobacco products, making them more expensive to buy.

An end to all agricultural subsidies that the federal government pays to help support U.S. tobacco farmers. These subsidies help to maintain tobacco as a profitable crop and keep the prices farmers charge for it lower than would otherwise be the case. This, in turn, artificially holds down the price of cigarettes and cigars to smokers, and encourages people to buy more of them. The government could go even further by offering help to current tobacco growers in switching to other crops that cause less harm to society.

A ban on smoking in all public places.

An extension of the current ban on tobacco advertising over broadcast television and radio to include other forms of advertising as well. Antismoking advocates are particularly concerned with cigarette sponsorship of sporting events, such as auto races and tennis tournaments, as well as with ad campaigns that seem likely to appeal to children.

Antismoking activists have also asked government and private health agencies to step up their current antismoking advertising campaigns in order to get the message about the dangers of smoking out to the public.

See also Secondhand Smoke; Smokers' Rights.

Smoking Restrictions

In 1963, approximately half of all Americans smoked. At that time, and for some time thereafter, smoking was not only allowed, but accepted, almost everywhere—from private homes to offices and college classrooms. Even some enclosed public places, including movie theaters and sports auditoriums, welcomed smokers. For the most part, smoking was forbidden only in such places as grade and high schools, where people were considered too young to smoke, or in workplaces such as chemical plants and paper warehouses, where large amounts of flammable materials made smoking a serious fire danger.

In recent years, however, the widespread social acceptance of smoking has been withdrawn. Smoking is now discouraged in most public places and many private ones. Many communities have laws regulating where smoking can be carried out in public spaces. Some, such as Davis, California, ban smoking in all offices and public eating places. The state of Maryland outlaws the practice in most workplaces, except for specially designated rooms that have to be closed off and separately ventilated. Even in communities that have no antismoking laws, many restaurants, stores, and other businesses that serve the public have banned smoking on their premises so as not to alienate or offend nonsmoking customers.

Other businesses, including many that do not deal directly with the public, ban smoking out of concern for their nonsmoking employees. Some companies forbid employees to smoke while actually on the job, but permit them to do so outside the building or in special areas set aside for that purpose during work breaks. Smoking bans have even begun to reach into the prisons, where a cigarette has long been considered one of the few pleasures available to inmates. Officials in Texas, where approximately one-third of all prisoners were smokers on the outside, banned the practice in state prisons as of 1 March 1995.

The primary reason for most smoking restrictions is concern about secondhand (or passive) smoke. In the case of businesses, other key motivations include statistical evidence that absenteeism is significantly higher for smokers and that employing smokers may raise a company's medical costs and lower productivity.

See also Secondhand Smoke; Smokers' Rights; Smoking.

Social Contract

The theory that a form of agreement, or contract, exists between the government and the governed is a keystone of modern political philosophy, both conservative and liberal. Historically, this idea of a social contract replaced the old notion of the divine right of kings as the underlying principle of government.

Ancient in its origins, the concept was notably formulated by the seventeenth-century English philosopher Thomas Hobbes, who is regarded as one of the precursors of modern conservative thought. Hobbes argued that it is only by submitting to the will of an absolute monarch that mankind could restrain the selfish and brutish impulses of individuals.

As expounded by another English philosopher, John Locke, the social contract became a vital element in the liberal thought of the Enlightenment. Locke argued that the monarch, or state, was required, as part of its implied bargain with the people, to protect the basic rights of the individual citizens. In essence, Locke believed that the social contract was conditional: The people could rescind it if the government broke its side of the bargain by failing to protect their rights.

The most famous eighteenth-century exposition of the social contract was Jean-Jacques Rousseau's *The Social Contract, or Principles of Political Right* (1762). Rousseau talked about the need for all individuals of every social class to willingly transfer their rights to the community. In doing so, each person becomes an "indivisible" part of the whole, and society operates according to the "general will" of its members. Rousseau's work informed not only the American and French revolutions, but the whole notion of modern democracy.

Influenced by Rousseau's egalitarianism, the founders of the United States believed that every individual had "certain unalienable rights" which not only other individuals but the government itself was bound to respect. Yet, individuals could not be left wholly to themselves to determine the boundaries between their rights and the rights of others. In order for a society in which individuals had rights to function smoothly and fairly, some authority—or government—was needed to define those boundaries and to see that they were respected.

Ultimately, the governmental authority did not derive either from the force of arms or from divine right, but from the "consent of the governed"—that is, from a social contract in which individuals agreed to accept not only their own rights and the rights of others, but also, to some extent, the authority of the government to enforce those rights.

A contract implies the exchange of things of value between the parties. In a modern democracy most political questions tend to revolve around what the government is to give to the people in exchange for the surrender of certain freedoms by them.

Among the most widely recognized responsibilities of a modern government are the protection of rights, the maintenance of public order, protection from attack by outside forces, and the establishment of a currency. In addition, in a welfare state, the government is expected to ensure at least a minimal standard of material well-being for all the citizens, including food, shelter, and some form of medical care.

See also Welfare State.
For further reading Bawden, Lee, editor. *The Social Contract Revisited: Aims and Outcomes of President Reagan's Welfare Policy*. Washington, DC: Urban Institute, 1984.
Boucher, David, and Paul Kelly, editors. *The Social Contract from Hobbes to Rawls*. London: Routledge, 1994.
Davey, Joseph D. *The New Social Contract: America's Journey from a Welfare State to a Police State*. Westport, CT: Greenwood Press, 1995.
DeJasay, Anthony. *Social Contract, Free Ride: A Study of the Public Goods Problem*. New York: Oxford University Press, 1991.

Social Darwinism

The social and economic effects of the Industrial Revolution in the United States were every bit as significant as its effects on the production of goods. Before it had run its course, the United States had been transformed from a predominantly agricultural society (and economy), to an industrial one.

The same period saw the rise of capitalism, an economic system in which a relatively small number of private individuals managed to accumulate great wealth through the ownership of businesses operated for profit, while the majority of people worked for wages.

These great changes in the way people lived and worked required a new understanding of economic relationships, and even of the notion of labor itself. Social Darwinism was an attempt to comprehend—and, ultimately, to justify—these unsettling new economic realities. It attempted to come to terms with economic developments by applying the biological theories of the British naturalist Charles Darwin to economic affairs.

In his 1859 work, *On the Origin of Species*, Darwin had argued that the young members of any animal species must compete for the limited food available. Those who survived this struggle, according to Darwin, were usually the individuals who possessed the vital characteristics of strength, hardiness, and energy that enabled them to win the competition. When these individuals reproduced, they passed on their characteristics to their offspring. Meanwhile, the losers in the competition for resources, who were by definition the feebler members of the species, died out before they could pass on their weaknesses to future generations. Through this process—referred to as "survival of the fittest," or "natural selection"—the species gradually evolved, becoming ever stronger over time.

The Social Darwinists believed that the economic competition for wealth among human beings was similar to the biological competition for food among animals. Just as the struggle for food made a species stronger, they argued, the struggle for wealth made an economy stronger. Those individuals who were best able to compete would naturally accumulate the greatest wealth. Those who were less able to compete would work for wages. Those who were completely unable to compete would fall into poverty.

Although this might seem unfortunate for the losers in the economic competition, the Social Darwinists argued that it was ultimately beneficial for the American economy—and therefore, for American society as a whole. That was because the competition for wealth, as cruel as it could be to the losers, resulted in increased economic efficiency, the production of better goods, and the establishment of the cheapest possible prices for consumers.

"The price which society pays for the law of competition... is great," wrote the fabulously wealthy steel magnate Andrew Carnegie, "but the advantages of the law are greater still." In Carnegie's view, it was "to this law that we owe our wonderful material development... and while the law may be sometimes hard on the individual, it is best for the [human race], because it ensures the survival of the fittest in every department."

Attitudes toward Charity

At the upper end of the economic scale, people like Carnegie believed that wealth would inevitably accumulate in the hands of those best able to deal with it. It followed that the wealthy would make the best caretakers of the vast wealth they accumulated, and that they were uniquely qualified to decide how that wealth should be expended. At the bottom of the economic scale, the competition for wealth was a fierce struggle to avoid poverty—as much a real struggle for survival as that carried out by jungle animals fighting over scarce food resources.

Some Social Darwinists believed that a degree of charity should be provided to those unfortunates who lost out in that struggle. Others, however, disagreed. They viewed charity as a false kindness and believed that any effort to cushion the terrible effects of poverty would only weaken poor people's will to claw their way out of it. In a sense, the more terrible the conditions in which the poor were forced to live—or even to die—the better it would be, not only for the survivors, but for society as a whole.

Political Implications

Social Darwinism had important political consequences, as well as economic ones. If the wealthy were uniquely qualified to spend the wealth they had accumulated, it followed that wealthy citizens deserved the most significant voice in how society's resources were to be spent. Therefore, Social Darwinists assumed, the less taxation the better, particularly on the rich; and the less public spending the better, particularly on the poor.

In its details, Social Darwinism has long been considered an outmoded philosophy. It remains important, however, because its basic principles continue to underlie much popular economic thought. They are particularly reflected in the thinking of some conservative economists and politicians.

See also Gospel of Wealth.
For further reading Bannister, Robert C. *Social Darwinism: Science and Myth.* Philadelphia: Temple University Press, 1988.
Hofstader, Richard. *Social Darwinism in American Thought.* Boston: Beacon Press, 1992.
Kennedy, Gail, editor. *Democracy and the Gospel of Wealth.* Boston: D. C. Heath and Company, 1949.

Spanking

See Corporal Punishment by Parents; Corporal Punishment in Schools.

Sports Betting

Gambling on sports is an old tradition in the United States, as it is in many other countries. It is often cited as one of the main reasons why certain sports—particularly football, basketball, baseball, and boxing—are so popular.

People bet on sports in many different ways. Most make wagers with friends or coworkers. Others bet with strangers by going to bookmakers (bookies) who act as clearinghouses, putting people who want to wager on one side of a proposition (bet) together with those who want to bet the other. The bookie, of course, keeps a percentage of each wager, known as the vigorish, for making the deal. Bookmaking is legal only in Nevada, but illegal bookmakers exist in every state as well as virtually every city of any size.

Bets are not usually made on which team will win a game, but by how much. This is because the winner of many games is not in great doubt. When everybody expects Team A to beat Team B, very few people will bet on Team B to win. In order to make for more betting action, a different form of bet has to be manufactured.

Bookmakers do this by establishing a line, a score difference at which as much money will be bet on one side of the proposition as on the other. A typical line in a football game might be three and one-half points. This means that anyone who bets on Team A will collect if it wins by four points. But they will lose, even if Team A wins, if it wins by a margin of three or less. Bets are also made on side propositions, such as which team will score first, what the halftime score will be, or the total number of points that will be made by both teams.

Sports betting, whether legal or illegal, is big business. Legal betting on a major U.S. sporting event—such as a championship boxing match, the Rose Bowl, or the final game of the World Series—runs into the tens of millions. Illegal betting on the same event climbs into the hundreds of millions. Illegal betting on the Super Bowl, which inspires the most betting "action" of all, has been estimated to be as high as $4 billion.

As with other forms of gambling, most people participate in sports betting as a form of recreation. A small proportion of sports gamblers, however, do become obsessed with it. Local authorities typically consider private betting a fairly harmless activity and make no serious effort to put an end to it.

Bookmaking is another matter, since organized crime is often involved. The local, small time bookmaker who takes the average gambler's bet does not handle enough business to match every bet. He or she typically "lays off" many bets with larger bookmaking operations, often in distant cities. These are frequently tied in with the Mafia or other large-scale criminal operations. Gamblers who deal with bookmakers should be aware that they may be participating, at least indirectly, in organized crime. They should also be aware that they may be encouraging police corruption, since illegal gambling has long been a major source of police corruption in many cities.

Sports betting can lead to another form of corruption as well. Some big bettors, or bookmakers, attempt to bribe athletes to throw a contest. The most infamous example of this was exposed in 1920, when it was revealed that gamblers had convinced several players for the Chicago White Sox baseball team to throw the 1919 World Series against Cincinnati.

See also Gambling; Gambling (Legalized).

Spouse Abuse

Violence between spouses—and particularly violence by men against their wives—

has always existed in the United States, as it has elsewhere in the world. Throughout most of American history, and in some places even well into the twentieth century, wives were regarded almost at chattels of their husbands, who had the right to do with them pretty much as they wished. Although the actual murder of a wife by a husband was regarded as criminal, lesser physical violence was accepted by most people, including many wives, as a part of the natural order of things. Wives who were brutally beaten were often regarded with sympathy by many, and their husbands with disapproval, but the abuse was not considered a matter for the law to interfere with.

New social attitudes in the late nineteenth and early twentieth centuries brought about a gradual change in the perception of this kind of family violence. It gradually became socially less and less acceptable at most levels of society. Until fairly recently, however, it was still largely ignored as a social concern. Instead, it was considered primarily a private matter, to be handled within the family.

The change in attitudes toward what was once called "wife beating" was accelerated by the efforts of the women's movement in the 1970s and 1980s. Then, in 1994, the problem of spousal abuse was thrust to the very center of national attention when the former football star, O. J. Simpson, was accused of murdering his ex-wife and her male friend. The torrent of publicity that followed established spouse abuse as a major social issue in the United States.

The Incidence of Abuse

The newly intense focus on the problem has sparked an upsurge in reported incidents of spouse abuse. This has led to a widespread impression that domestic violence, and particularly the battering of women by their mates, is on the rise. Many experts, however, believe that this may not be the case. For nearly 200 years, they point out, such physical abuse of women by their husbands was a drastically underreported crime.

As many as seven little-known studies that were reported in the 1970s concluded that at that time some form of spouse abuse occurred in between 50 percent and 65 percent of American families. What seems to be an increase in abuse may simply be the effect of more publicity and a growing willingness of abused women to come forward.

A 1994 U.S. Justice Department study found that 2.5 million women over the age of 11 become victims of assault, rape, or murder each year. Approximately two-thirds of them—and fully half of those who are murdered—are attacked by a relative or by someone else close to them. As many as 4,000 a year are murdered by their husbands or boyfriends.

The Justice Department figure of 2.5 million assaults is controversial. Women's groups that deal with the victims of these assaults point out that most of the women who eventually report such abuse, and who therefore enter into the department's statistics, have put up with assaults for years before coming forward. These groups claim that the actual number of serious but unreported attacks are probably much higher than the Justice Department suggests. They say that there may be as many 18 million domestic assaults against women in the United States each year. Others, however, insist that the data used to arrive at such figures exaggerate the real problem, since they count any kind of unwelcome physical contact—even a minor shove or push—as an incidence of domestic violence. Because past and present statistics are so unreliable, it is possible that the real incidence of assaults may decreasing even while the reported numbers are increasing.

Husband Battering

Not all victims of spouse abuse are female. There are battered husbands as well as battered wives. The statistics on husbands, however, are even less reliable than those on women. That is partly because the men are even more reluctant to come forward and implicate their spouses. Many consider it unmanly to admit that they have been battered by a women.

A government study concluded that about 2 million husbands are attacked by their wives each year. Social scientists who have investigated the issue emphasize, however, that this does not mean that the two cases are the same. It is likely that a higher percentage of marital violence is initiated by the men, and that women strike back out of self-defense.

Furthermore, husbands tend to inflict much more severe injuries on their spouses than wives do. Nonetheless, Richard Gelles, director of the Family Violence Research Program at the University of Rhode Island and one of the most respected experts in the field, estimates that some 100,000 men are seriously battered by their wives each year. This, in itself, constitutes a serious problem, he points out, and one that gets much less attention than wife battering. Although many agencies offer help and emotional support to female victims, very few resources are available to their male counterparts.

Patterns of Violence

Men who physically abuse their wives tend to fall into certain specific categories. Some are simply bullies, who use their physical power deliberately and consciously in order to force their spouse to do their will.

Still others engage in an essentially sadistic campaign of domestic terrorism, getting pleasure out of the fear and pain they inflict on their spouse. However, many do not set out consciously to harm their spouses, but rather find it difficult to control themselves, and break into violence when they are angered or hurt. These are often the ones who inflict the most damage and suffer the most remorse afterwards. Unless they are helped, however, the remorse is frequently followed by other outbursts of violence in the future.

Researchers who study physical violence between spouses say that, although there may be a single incident or two of relatively minor violence in approximately half of all marriages, battering is almost always a recurring behavior. Episodes of violence tend to be repeated over and over within the relationship, or sometimes in a succession of relationships. An abusive spouse who divorces and remarries is likely to be abusive to the new spouse as well.

Even beyond that, spouse abuse, like other forms of domestic violence, tends to recur from generation to generation. Evidence suggests that the majority of men who abuse their mates were raised in families where either physical or sexual abuse occurred, whether committed by one parent against another or against the children. Women who become victims of domestic violence frequently grew up in similar homes. Thus, it seems that such behavior may be, at least partly, learned.

Spouse abuse is often linked to the use of drugs and alcohol. Stress of all kinds, and particularly money- and work-related problems, also tend to intensify the severity of the violence. Psychologists say abuse basically has to do with power and control within the relationship. Men and women who abuse their spouses feel a need to dominate their partners, often because they feel inadequate themselves. When disagreements and conflicts arise, they try to assert control by using physical force. Often, the violence is completely unprovoked, but in some unhealthy relationships the victimized partner tries to exert her or his dominance over the spouse in other ways: for example, by exerting dictatorial control of the family finances, by browbeating, or by deliberately arousing the other's jealousy. Instead of attempting to compromise and work out their difficulties, both parties may compete to exert control over the other, since neither knows how to resolve problems in mutually satisfactory ways.

In any case, the level of violence within a relationship often becomes more intense and brutal over time. Far too often, when nothing is done to break the cycle of violence, it escalates to murder. As many as one-third of all homicides are committed by one family member against another, and the majority of these are killings of a spouse.

Police Response

Victims of spouse abuse, whether female or male, sometimes complain that police, most of whom are male, too often take abuse less seriously than other crimes. Too many police, they say, see their job as pacifying a tense situation rather than investigating a crime and arresting a criminal. They often do nothing beyond talking to the people involved and perhaps issuing a verbal warning to the abusive spouse. At times, some outraged female victims complain, male police officers have even seemed to sympathize with the attacker. They will ask the woman what she did to anger the man, seeming to agree that, in some respects, she might have deserved what happened to her.

Police respond to these criticisms by pointing out that domestic violence calls put police officers in a delicate position. Judgment and discretion are both difficult and vital. What has actually taken place is not always clear. Lacking physical evidence, or outside witnesses, it sometimes comes down to one person's word against another's. At times, not even the victim will admit what occurred.

In some cases, the attacker is repentant by the time the police arrive, and the victim is either inclined to forgive or too frightened to describe what has taken place. Many victims do not want their spouses punished, however brutal they have been. There are many reasons for this. Some feel sorry for them or fear that punishment will only make them more angry and violent in the future. Others are afraid that getting the authorities more deeply involved will destroy their marriage. However violent the relationship may be, they still cannot bear the thought of facing the future alone. Whatever the reason, some battered spouses protest bitterly when the police attempt to take the abuser away. It is not even unusual for police officers attempting to subdue men who have been beating their wives to be attacked themselves by the battered women coming to their husband's defense.

In most states, the police complain, there is little they can do if the victim refuses to admit what has obviously happened. Some states, however, have laws requiring police to arrest suspected batterers, even if their victims refuse to implicate them.

Breaking the Cycle of Violence

Spouse abuse is endemic in the United States. Although it is somewhat more common in lower economic groups, it exists to a significant extent in every social and economic class and every ethnic group. Because of its pervasiveness, it is clearly a serious concern for the whole society. For the victims caught up in it, however, it is primarily an intensely personal problem. Women's groups and psychologists who council battered spouses advise anyone involved in a physically abusive relationship to leave it, at least temporarily. Children, they say, should be removed from such a home as well. At the same time, they caution that leaving may be a dangerous thing to do. The worst violence in many abusive relationships is often sparked by the abuser's fear of being left by a spouse. Abusers who feel themselves deserted sometimes become even more violent, either in revenge or as an effort to force the spouse to return. A high proportion of the murders of one spouse by another are triggered by the attempt of the victim to leave. Because of this, counselors say, help and protection should be sought from friends, other family members, or from one of the thousands of shelters set up in many communities specifically to offer safety to the victims of battering.

Help is also available for the batterers themselves, provided that they are willing to seek it. Local agencies can be found in most communities that offer counseling or therapy to abusive spouses who want to stop their violent behavior. Such services can be helpful, although some psychologists caution that counseling is likely to succeed in less than 50 percent of cases.

Some of the more successful forms of therapy are those that involve groups of abusive spouses helping each other to recognize the cruelty and destructiveness of their behavior. Another possibility is couples therapy, in which both spouses participate, attempting to learn how to deal more healthily with the inevitable conflicts that take place in every relationship. None of these measures is likely to succeed, however, unless all the parties truly want to change their own behaviors.

However, more than case-by-case action will be required if spouse abuse is going to be seriously curtailed nationwide. Victims' advocates call on the clergy and other community leaders to focus more attention on the problem. Among other suggestions are: more battered women's shelters and community counseling services; increased training of police, prosecutors and health officials for responding to incidents of domestic violence; and the inclusion of nonviolent conflict resolution courses in the school curriculum.

Most advocacy groups also favor stronger laws against abusers and more vigorous enforcement of those that already exist. Several communities seem to have successfully combined stricter law enforcement with therapy. Duluth, Minnesota, and San Diego, for instance, have managed to reduce the numbers of domestic violence and homicide cases by mandating automatic arrest of spouse batterers followed by months of counseling sessions. Abusers who fail to attend are jailed.

See also Domestic Violence.
For further reading Deats, S. M., and L. T. Lenker, editors. *The Aching Hearth: Family Violence in Life and Literature*. New York: Plenum, 1991. Gelles, Richard J., and Denileen Leseke. *Current Controversies on Family Violence*. Thousand Oaks, CA: Sage, 1993. Koss, Mary, et al. *No Safe Haven: Male Violence against Women at Home, at Work, and in the Community*. Washington, DC: American Psychological Association, 1994.

Student Loans
The costs of a college education have gone up steadily in recent decades, and paying the fees has become increasingly problematical for many families. The increased costs, together with a declining savings rate among parents, has discouraged the traditional financing method of parents saving up to pay their children's tuition. Today,

the typical student combines parental contributions with the proceeds of his or her own labor, as well as a mixture of private and government grants and loans.

Because the government has been cutting back on the funds it provides in interest-free grants, the proportion of financing that comes from loans has been increasing. For every $100 borrowed in 1980, the typical student received a grant of $50; by 1994, this ratio had changed to only $25 in grants for every $100 in loans. Political developments suggest that the ratio may become even more dramatic in the future.

Among the effects of these changes is a great increase in the amount of debt carried by college graduates starting their careers. This higher debt, in turn, has increased the length of time that the typical graduate can expect to carry it. The traditional repayment schedule of a student loan used to be ten years, and many graduates expected to pay it off even sooner. Today, however, student loans can be taken out for 30 years, and many students do just that.

Although the bulk of student loans are still given at relatively favorable interest rates compared to consumer loans, the increasing reliance on debt means that a large proportion of recent college graduates can expect to be paying on their college loans well into the 2020s. This prospect is not just alarming for students and their parents, it is disturbing to economists and social scientists as well. In a society already laden with heavy short-term consumer debt, they fear that the burden of increased long-term debt on a whole generation of young workers will act as a drag on spending and savings for decades to come.

Suburbanization

Before World War II, the most significant migration pattern within the United States was from the farms and small towns into the cities. Following the war, the main movement was out of the cities and into the newly established suburbs. That movement has only recently shown signs of partially reversing.

Like the earlier rural-to-urban migration, the suburbanization of the country has had profound effects on the lives of generations of Americans and helped to transform American culture in countless ways, from the invention of the shopping mall to the popularity of "drive time" radio.

Reasons for the Outmigration

Several factors contributed to the outmigration from the big cities that occurred in the 1940s, 1950s, and 1960s. These included the desire of many city dwellers to live in what they saw as a more tranquil and pastoral setting and to escape the problems of overcrowding, crime, and grime that were endemic to city life. Related to these desires was the "white flight" that occurred in the wake of legal desegregation, as African-Americans began moving into previously all-white urban communities and whites responded by fleeing to more distant neighborhoods.

The pull of lower taxes also worked to draw residents to the suburbs. Suburban governments could offer lower tax rates than city governments for a variety of reasons. Unlike the aging cities, most suburbs had no crumbling infrastructures to maintain and no expensive mass transportation or crime problems to deal with. The rapid growth of their populations amounted to a tax-base windfall for suburban governments, while much of the expense brought about by that growth—new streets, gas and water provision, garbage collection, etc.—were often subsidized, to some extent, by private real estate developers.

Suburbanization made commuting a way of life for millions of Americans. Continuing to work in the central cities, they were forced to rise early and make their way into the city each workday morning and then back out to their homes every evening. The extent of the outmigration, then, was only made possible by the automobile and by major new road systems and commuter railway lines built between the suburbs and the inner cities.

From Bedroom Communities to Cities

Some of the mushrooming suburbs grew up in and around previously established outlying towns and villages, once sleepy and stagnant, but suddenly expanding more rapidly than anyone had ever imagined. Others, however, were brand new. Many of these began as little more than housing developments, the products of a post–World War II development boom fueled by partly by low-interest housing loans provided to returning military personnel the G.I. Bill and partly by Federal Housing Administration loans intended to spur new housing and to encourage home ownership.

A typical suburban neighborhood consisted of rows and rows of quickly constructed and often identical houses. They may have been, as a mocking song described them, "all made out of ticky-tacky," but to a generation of city-raised Americans—hungry for a clean new home resting on a green lawn, with space between it and its neighbor, and a tree in the front yard—the suburbs seemed like a fresh new version of the American Dream.

As more and more people moved out of the inner cities, so did many of the manufacturing companies that provided them jobs. The factories outmigrated for some of the same reasons that their employees did, one of the most important being lower taxes. Stores and other retail businesses

followed their customers, often into a new form of retail plaza called the shopping center, which eventually evolved into the modern, large-scale shopping mall.

In time, many of the suburbs, which had begun as nothing more than "bedroom communities" where people who worked in the city by day went to sleep at night, became small cities in themselves. Nor did the suburbs remain the virtually all-white bastions most of them started out, however inadvertently, to be. According to a study done by experts at the University of Michigan, minorities made up 17.6 percent of the residents of American suburbs by 1990.

Effects on the Cities

Although large numbers of mostly white and relatively prosperous people were moving out of the big cities, others—many of whom were black or Hispanic, and relatively less prosperous—were moving in. This shift in population brought about a shift in the tax bases of the cities at the same time as it increased the need for some kinds of city services. This put serious financial pressure on city governments, a pressure that has had visible effects in the decaying infrastructures and the declining quality of life that has plagued the cities for decades. For the most part, however, and despite all their troubles, the cities have remained the most important centers of America's financial, artistic, and cultural activities.

See also Gentrification; White Flight.

Superfund

Superfund is the massive Environmental Protection Agency (EPA) program assigned the job of seeing that the major toxic waste sites in the United States are cleaned up. Superfund gets its name from the $1.6 billion trust fund that was established for that purpose in 1981. Although considered a huge sum at the time, the original Superfund was soon found to be much too small to do the job. In recent years, Superfund has spent almost as much each year as it was once expected to cost altogether.

How Superfund Operates

EPA officials investigate reports of possible toxic sites. They identify the site and determine the extent of the threat it presents to public health and the environment. Those sites that are considered especially dangerous are put on Superfund's national priorities list. A high priority is given to sites that present a serious danger to people living or working nearby (and particularly to children), as well as to sites where poisonous chemicals may be contaminating a water supply.

After a site has been placed on the list, the EPA conducts a remedial study to determine the best way to clean it up. Superfund was designed to provide the entire costs of the cleanups, and the EPA is not intended to do the actual cleanups itself. Instead, it attempts to force the businesses that created the hazard to repair the damage themselves. This is not always possible, however. Often, the EPA is not able to identify who made the mess in the first place, or the polluter may be financially unable to repair the damage, or out of business altogether. Even when the responsibility for the hazard is clear, polluters are often reluctant to act, and the EPA must take them to court.

Sometimes a settlement is worked out in which the polluter pays part of the expenses and the government pays the rest. When the EPA is unable, for whatever reason, to get the polluter to act at all, the federal government must pay all the expenses itself. So far, Superfund has had to pay for about 40 percent of the total cleanups to date, with the polluters paying for the other 60 percent.

Problems with Superfund

The early years of Superfund were rocked with scandal. Anne Gorsuch, the head of the EPA, was cited for contempt of Congress when she refused to turn over Superfund-related documents in 1982, and Rita Lavell, the first head of Superfund, was sent to jail for lying to Congress about events at the agency. The program has been controversial ever since.

Critics attack Superfund from almost every direction. Environmental groups charge that the EPA's cleanup standards are not high enough to fully protect the public, while businesses charge that the standards are too high—and far too expensive—to be practical. Public interest groups protest that Superfund costs too much and that the taxpayer ends up paying for too much of the bill. Virtually everyone agrees that the years of litigation that result from a typical Superfund action are incredibly wasteful.

The EPA insists that it strikes the best balance it can between the public interest and the capacity of the polluting businesses to pay. To the charge that too much taxpayer money is spent on cleanups, the EPA responds that over 80 percent of the money in Superfund comes from taxes on those industries that do most of the polluting. As for the length of the court battles, the EPA points out that it is not responsible for the delaying tactics of the polluters' lawyers. Even when things go well, however, it takes five and one-half years to clean up a typical Superfund site, and new sites are being added to the national priorities list at the rate of about 100 each year. Of the nearly 1,300 sites recognized by the agency as of January 1994, only 220 had been rendered safe.

See also Landfills.

Sweatshops

On 25 March 1911, fire broke out in the ten-story Triangle Shirtwaist Factory in Greenwich Village, New York City, and 148 people died. Most of the victims were young women who worked in the factory. Some died while trapped in the burning building; others leapt from windows to escape the smoke and flames. The death toll was so high because the employers had locked the doors to the workrooms in order to keep the workers from sneaking out for breaks, a common precaution in such factories.

The tragedy drew national attention to the appalling working conditions in many factories and resulted in the passage of new state laws, in New York and elsewhere, to protect workers from the hazards of employment in sweatshops like the Triangle Shirtwaist Factory. These laws, and the many national employee health and safety regulations that have been enacted since, have done a lot to improve working conditions for most workers. Despite these laws, however, sweatshops continue to exist and continue to ignore the health and safety of their workers.

Modern Sweatshops

A sweatshop can be defined as any place of employment that is marked by unusually low pay, excessively long work hours, and unhealthy or dangerous working conditions. The term is often, although far from exclusively, associated with cut-and-sew shops, like the Triangle Shirtwaist Factory, which service the women's garment industry. That industry traditionally employs poor female workers, a category of worker that has been traditionally among the most vulnerable of to exploitation of all workers. Because of this, the International Ladies' Garment Workers Union has been a leading force in the movement to reform sweatshop practices.

Not all sweatshops involve the garment industry, however. A similar tragedy recently took place in a southern chicken processing plant. There, too, the doors had been locked to discourage employees from leaving before their workday was done.

In recent times, illegal immigrants have been the employees of choice for sweatshop employers. Most of the workers in a typical modern-day sweatshop are women from Asia or from Mexico or other Latin American countries. For that reason, sweatshops are most numerous in such urban centers as New York, Miami, and Los Angeles, which serve as magnets for illegal immigrants.

Desperate for money to feed their children, undocumented immigrants are often willing, and even eager, to work long hours at backbreaking labor for whatever the employer is willing to pay. Because they are illegal, they are unwilling to protest to the authorities over even the most onerous working conditions. By the same token, they fear that if they dare to protest to their employers, they may be turned in to the immigration service and deported to their native country.

As recently as August 1995, 70 immigrants from Thailand were discovered being held in virtual captivity in an El Monte, California, garment factory. The immigrants, who had come to the United States with dreams of economic advancement, were allegedly forced to work for up to 20 hours a day, for periods as long as seven years, in order to pay off their passage to America. They lived crowded into small rooms in the same building in which they worked, and the conditions they reported were as bad as those of many nineteenth-century slaves.

Because many sweatshops are small, fly-by-night organizations, operating on the fringes of industry, it is impossible to discover how many sweatshops actually exist in the United States today. It is possible, however, that they number in the many thousands. In New York City alone there are approximately 6,000 garment factories, and city officials estimate that as many as 2,000 of them function illegally.

Attempts to Regulate Sweatshops

Policing so many unscrupulous organizations is a daunting task, and few states or cities devote sufficient funds to the effort to be effective. The task is made even harder by the fact that employers and employees alike are desperate to keep the details of the sweatshops' operations secret.

Reformers have suggested two main approaches for combating sweatshops. The first concentrates on reducing or removing the bulk of the available workforce. This approach seeks to stem the flow of illegal immigrants that provides so many of the victims of the sweatshop system, and to crack down on the employers who exploit them. An attempt to do the latter was made in the Immigration Control Act of 1986, which provides for penalties against employers who deliberately hire undocumented workers; but so far, the act has been largely ineffective.

Union activists argue that the best way to attack sweatshops is to concentrate on alleviating the working conditions that make them undesirable and dangerous, not on the immigration status of the employees. They demand more government investigation, inspection, and regulation of factories. In addition, they call on the reputable elements of the garment industry and other affected industries to refuse to trade in the products of sweatshop labor.

See also Immigration (Illegal); Slavery.

Talk Radio

For decades following the 1950s—the last years during which comedy and drama made up a major part of the commercial radio schedule—AM radio, like FM, was dominated by music formats, first by what was known as "pop," and later, by the various forms of rock. In the 1990s, music solidified its hold on FM radio, and talk— once only a minor element in the programming of a few stations—boomed in popularity on AM. By the mid-1990s, talk had become not only the fastest-growing, but the dominant form of AM radio in most markets. By 1993, approximately one in every ten radio stations in the country specialized in the talk format.

Although news and public affairs programs, certain forms of religious and cultural programming, and other formats also consist largely of talk, the term "talk radio" is reserved primarily for call-in programs; that is, programs in which the talk is two-way, allowing listeners to call in, express their views, and ask questions of the host or guests.

Many talk radio shows are "advice" programs, featuring psychologists, medical doctors, car repair experts, pet trainers, financial advisors, and other specialists who undertake to help callers with their problems. More controversial, and frequently more popular, are those programs that concentrate on political matters.

Political Talk Radio

The boom in talk radio was led, and perhaps largely caused, by the enormous success of Rush Limbaugh, a conservative humorist and commentator, in the 1980s. Limbaugh, who was at that time the most popular and influential of the talk radio hosts, used his program to bash "liberals"—a term he wielded less as an ideological description than as a crushing insult. Using a combination of freewheeling political analysis and satiric humor, Limbaugh attacked the federal government and the Democrats who then controlled Congress.

Like Limbaugh's program, many of the other successful talk radio programs of the mid- to late 1990s feature conservative hosts and, for the most part, conservative callers as well. Whereas Limbaugh came from a radio background, however, many of the other conservative hosts attained fame, or notoriety, in other fields before turning to talk radio. Among those whose programs have been syndicated with varying degrees of success are Oliver North, the Marine officer who was at the center of the Iran-Contra affair, and G. Gordon Liddy, who served time in prison for his part in the Watergate scandal.

In the late 1980s and early 1990s, Limbaugh and other conservative talk hosts provided a welcome outlet for the political anger and frustration that polltakers had noted in the American public. The hosts seemed to speak for millions of ordinary citizens as they lambasted political leaders, called for lower taxes and welfare reform, and criticized what many Americans saw as pervasive corruption in the federal government. Many also spoke out strongly on behalf of a litany of values—financial self-reliance, Christianity, traditional sexual mores, and strict standards of public morality—that many Americans felt were being threatened by current social trends.

By the early 1990s Limbaugh, who described himself ingenuously as "a harmless little fuzzball," was claiming an audience of more than 20 million "dittoheads," as he called his listeners (and as many of them referred to themselves). Overtly partisan, Limbaugh did his best to support conservative Republican candidates and causes. Some political observers gave him significant credit for the conservative surge at the polls in the 1992 congressional elections, and consequently for the Republican takeover of the House and the Senate. Following the election, he was an honored guest at a major Republican gathering celebrating the victory.

Liberals were unable to find an equally popular host who could balance the political debate on talk radio. Among those who volunteered to try were Mario Cuomo, the former Democratic governor of New York, and Jim Hightower, the colorful former railroad commissioner of Texas. However, they had considerably less success than their conservative counterparts and were soon off the air. With the exception of a few voices on public radio, the few liberal hosts who survived in the late 1990s tended to air in limited markets. Larry King, for many years one of the most successful of all practitioners of talk radio, was often cited as the major exception to the relative failure of liberal talk radio. Although King is, in fact, a moderate liberal, his programs were frequently only marginally political, if at all.

Media critics and politicians differ as to the extent of the long-term ability of political talk radio, whether conservative or liberal, to affect public opinion. For the most part, some insist, talk-show hosts sing to the choir. Members of the audience listen to such shows either to confirm already existing opinions or to be entertainingly outraged by opinions with which they violently disagree. In either case, they are unlikely to be converted to a new point of view.

There is no question, however, that talk radio can occasionally muster public opinion behind a particular cause or issue. With some reason, talk-radio hosts have claimed credit for fomenting a variety of scandals, including check-kiting, in which members of the House of Representatives wrote checks and cashed them despite the temporary absence of funds. The outcry was so great that it forced the closing of the so-called House bank and a curtailing of several other prerogatives of House members.

Shock Radio

Even more controversial than political talk radio is the genre sometimes known as shock radio, the leading practitioner of which is Howard Stern. Rarely, if ever, dealing in political ideas, shock hosts like Stern discuss subjects ranging from sex to current events with an irreverent, iconoclastic edge. They seek to entertain and titillate listeners, with little or no effort to enlighten them. The term *shock* is applied to this genre because the hosts frequently use vulgar words and express deliberately outrageous attitudes that are considered unacceptable on other forms of radio.

Teams, Employee–Management
See Employee–Management Teams.

Technology and Privacy

Most Americans are only slightly aware of how much information about them is already available to government agencies, private businesses, and even individuals. Anyone who really wants to know can find out fairly easily how old others are; who their parents and other close relatives are; how tall they are, how much they weight, and the color of their hair and eyes; where they live, where they shop, and what they like to buy; what their income is, and how much they owe; and much other information that most Americans traditionally have considered to be private.

This information is available from a variety of public and private sources. The ownership of land and other real property is a matter of public record. So are voter lists. Approximately two-thirds of the states sell the information obtained when residents apply for driver's licenses. Credit companies make information about people's financial backgrounds, as well as how much money they currently owe, available to many private parties. Many businesses routinely sell lists of their customers, along with information about what they buy and how much they spend. Even library records, detailing what books a user has checked out, are available to law enforcement agencies.

Modern technology presents several new threats to privacy. Electronic mail (E-mail), the system that allows people to send messages to each other through personal computers, makes print communication much faster and easier than hand-delivered memos or letters. But the privacy of written memos can be preserved by destroying them. E-mail, on the other hand, is frequently preserved, either intentionally or inadvertently, and often without the knowledge of either sender or receiver. E-mail sent or received at work, for example, may be preserved in the company's computer system and can later be read by other people, including the employer.

Some people worry that the real threat presented by modern technology is not so much the destruction of privacy rights as their expansion. They fear that the growing availability of so much personal information will spark a backlash and lead to new laws protecting virtually all personal information from scrutiny. This, they fear, could lead to a closing down of the public record that makes it possible for law enforcement agencies, the press, and other watchdogs working in the public interest to do their jobs.

See also Privacy.

Television
See V-Chip; Violence on Television.

Title IX
See Women in Sports.

Torture
See Corporal Punishment of Criminals; Cruel and Unusual Punishment.

Toxic Waste Cleanups
See Superfund.

Tuskegee Experiment

In 1932, the U.S. Health Service launched a medical experiment in which it observed the effects of syphilis on several rural African-Americans in Tuskegee, Alabama. At that time, there was no known cure for the disease, which affected many people of all races and walks of life and proved fatal to large numbers of them.

The subjects of the experiment were observed over a period of several decades. Although penicillin was found to be an effective cure for syphilis in the 1940s, the subjects were not given the drug in order that observation of the course of the disease, and its effects on them, could be continued.

The methodology of the Tuskegee experiment was not unique, but when word of what the government had done (or not done) became public, the knowledge that the subjects had been willfully left to the mercies of the devastating disease had a profound effect on the African-American community.

To this day, many African-Americans remain distrustful of the medical establishment in general, and of white health care providers and all forms of medical experimentation in particular. Even now, scientists find it extraordinarily difficult to entice black subjects to participate in tests involving new drug and other therapies.

The mistrust of what some African-Americans regard as "white" medicine is hard to quantify, but it is very likely a factor in the relatively poor health statistics of African-Americans compared to other Americans. Although there are several other reasons for this mistrust—including the long history of white-black relations in the United States and suspicion of the government in general—the Tuskegee experiment is perhaps the most dramatic.

On 16 May 1997, President Bill Clinton issued a public apology, on the behalf of the U.S. government, for the Tuskegee experiment.

Universal Declaration of Human Rights

The Universal Declaration of Human Rights, proclaimed by the General Assembly of the United Nations (U.N.) on 10 December 1948, was based on the American Declaration of Independence, the Bill of Rights, and the French Declaration of the Rights of Man, among other sources. Although it does not have the force of law, all members of the U.N., including the United States, have signed it. As the following excerpts demonstrate, it is perhaps the most comprehensive definition available of human rights as they are generally understood around the world.

Article 1. All human beings are born free and equal in dignity and rights. They are endowed with reason and conscience and should act towards one another in a spirit of brotherhood.

Article 2. Everyone is entitled to all the rights and freedoms set forth in this Declaration, without distinction of any kind, such as race, colour, sex, language, religion, political or other opinion, national or social origin, property, birth, or other status....

Article 3. Everyone has the right to life, liberty, and the security of the person.

Article 4. No one shall be held in slavery or servitude....

Article 5. No one shall be subjected to torture or to cruel, inhuman or degrading treatment or punishment.

Article 6. Everyone has the right to recognition everywhere as a person before the law.

Article 7. All are equal before the law and are entitled without any discrimination to equal protection of the law....

Article 8. Everyone has the right to an effective remedy...for acts violating the fundamental rights granted him by the constitution or by law.

Article 9. No one shall be subjected to arbitrary arrest, detention or exile.

Article 10. Everyone is entitled...to a fair and public hearing by an independent and impartial tribunal, in the determination of his rights and obligations and of any criminal charge against him

Article 11. 1. Every one charged with a penal offense has the right to be presumed innocent until proved guilty.... 2. No one shall be held guilty of any penal offense...which did not

267

constitute a penal offense...at the time when it was committed.... Nor shall a heavier penalty be imposed than....applicable at the time the penal offense was committed.

Article 12. No one shall be subjected to arbitrary interference with his privacy, family, home or correspondence, nor to attacks on his honour and reputation....

Article 13. 1. Everyone has the right to freedom of movement and residence within the borders of each State. 2. Everyone has the right to leave any country, including his own, and to return to his country.

Article 14. 1. Everyone has the right to seek and to enjoy in other countries asylum from persecution. 2. This may not be invoked in case of prosecutions genuinely arising from non-political crimes....

Article 15. 1. Everyone has the right to a nationality. 2. No one shall be arbitrarily deprived of his nationality nor denied the right to change his nationality.

Article 16. 1. Men and women of full age, without any limitation due to race, nationality or religion, have the right to marry and to found a family.... 2. Marriage shall be entered into only with the free and full consent of the intending spouses. 3. The family is the natural and fundamental group unit of society and is entitled to protection....

Article 17. 1. Everyone has the right to own property alone as well as in association with others. 2. No one shall be arbitrarily deprived of his property.

Article 18. Everyone has the right to freedom of thought, conscience and religion...[and] to manifest his relig-

ion or belief in teaching, practice, worship and observance.

Article 19. Everyone has the right to freedom of opinion and expression...and to seek, receive and impart information and ideas through any media and regardless of frontiers.

Article 20. 1. Everyone has the right to peaceful assembly and association. 2. No one may be compelled to belong to an association.

Article 21. 1. Everyone has the right to take part in the government of his country, directly or through freely chosen representatives. 2. Everyone has the right of equal access to public service in his country. 3. The will of the people shall be the basis of the authority of government; this will shall be expressed in periodic and genuine elections....

Article 22. Everyone, as a member of society, has the right to social security and is entitled to realization...of the economic, social and cultural rights indispensable for his dignity and the free development of his personality.

Article 23. 1. Everyone has the right to work.... 2. Everyone...has the right to equal pay for equal work. 3. Everyone who works has the right to just and favourable remuneration ensuring for himself and his family an existence worthy of human dignity, and supplemented, if necessary, by other means of social protection.

Article 24. Everyone has the right to rest and leisure, including reasonable limitation of working hours and periodic holidays with pay.

Article 25. 1. Everyone has the right to a standard of living adequate for the health and well-being of himself and of his family.... 2. Motherhood and childhood are entitled to special care and assistance. All children, whether born in or out of wedlock shall enjoy the same social protection. **Article 26.** 1. Everyone has the right to education. Education shall be free, at least in the elementary...stages. Elementary education shall be compulsory. Technical and professional education shall be made generally available...higher education shall be equally accessible to all on the basis of merit. 2. Education shall be directed to the full development of the human personality and to the strengthening or respect for human rights and fundamental freedoms.... 3. Parents have a prior right to choose the kind of education that shall be given to their children.

Article 27. 1. Everyone has the right to freely participate in the cultural life of the community.... 2. Everyone has the right to the protection of the moral and material interests resulting from any scientific, literary or artistic production of which he is the author.

Article 28. Everyone is entitled to a social and international order in which...rights and freedoms...can be fully realized.

Article 29. 1. Everyone has duties to the community in which alone the free and full development of his personality is possible. 2. In the exercise of his rights and freedoms, everyone shall be subject only to such limitations as are determined by law solely for the purpose of securing due recognition and respect for the rights and freedoms of others and of meeting the just requirements of morality, public order and the general welfare in a democratic society.

Article 30. Nothing in this Declaration may be interpreted as implying for any State, group or person any right to...perform any act aimed at the destruction of any of the rights and freedoms set forth herein.

The American Declaration of Independence asserts that "all men are created equal, that they are endowed by their Creator with certain unalienable Rights, that among these are Life, Liberty, and the Pursuit of happiness." It then goes on to declare that securing these rights is the very purpose of government.

The concept of human rights, then, is at the heart of American political thought. More broadly, it provides the ideological foundation for the modern democratic political era. This idea—that human beings have basic rights which governments are bound to respect—informed not only the American and French revolutions but also the scores of colonial revolutions that begat, directly or indirectly, most of the nations of the modern world. As recently as the late 1980s, the concept of human rights helped inspire the national movements that brought about the end of Soviet domination in Eastern Europe.

By far the best and most detailed recitation of these fundamental rights is contained in the Universal Declaration of Human Rights. As described by a later Secretary General of the U.N., Javier Perez de Cuellar, the U.N.'s adoption of the Universal Declaration was "a landmark in the evolution of global life and civilization ... the first time that the international community as a whole accepted the protection and promotion of human rights as a permanent obligation."

Unmarried Mothers

Almost 30 of every 100 babies delivered in the United States in 1991 were born to unwed mothers, reflecting a sharp rise in such births. It compares to a little more than 18 of every 100 in 1980, 11 of every 100 in 1970, and only a little more than 5 of every 100 in 1960—a rise of almost 600 percent in three decades.

Although illegitimacy rates are climbing for most ethnic groups, the rate is highest among African-Americans. In 1990, 65 percent of all black children born were born to single mothers, up from 38 percent two decades earlier. Meanwhile, the illegitimate births among whites climbed even faster, soaring from 6 percent in 1970 to approximately 20 percent by the mid-1990s. If these trends continue, the rate of illegitimacy among whites will eventually catch up and pass that of African-Americans.

Effects on Society

Social scientists and moral leaders alike are alarmed by these figures. High rates of illegitimacy harm not just individuals, but society as a whole. Illegitimacy, for example, is a major contributor to poverty. It is hard for single parents, and particularly single mothers, most of whom are also relatively young and uneducated, to find and keep good jobs while raising children. The burden of providing food and support for the children often falls on taxpayers through the Aid to Families with Dependent Children (AFDC) program. The less than 20 percent of white children who live with only one parent make up more than 45 percent of all poor children in the United States.

Children of unwed mothers often grow up either with no man in the home, or with several of them, one after the other. They have no chance to bond with a father and no consistent male authority in their lives. Even when known to the child, the biological father often refuses to help raise the child or to give the child any financial sup-

port. These factors tend to produce children who get in more trouble and have higher school dropout rates than children from two-parent families.

Causes

There are several major causes of illegitimate pregnancies. One is ignorance. Couples who have sex, but do not wish to have children, do not understand how to prevent pregnancy. Other pregnancies are caused by mutual carelessness, and still others are caused by carelessness or lack of consideration on the part of just one of the sexual partners—the man ignores the request of the woman to use a condom, or the woman indicates that she is taking birth control pills when she is not.

However, many other illegitimate pregnancies are deliberate. Young women sometimes become pregnant to spite their parents or in hopes that the adult world will then take them more seriously. For some teenagers, pregnancy is an excuse to leave an unhappy home situation. Single women, teenaged as well as older, sometimes become pregnant out of loneliness or because they desire to share their life with a child, even though they may not want to share it with a man. Still others become pregnant in hopes of entrapping a man into marrying them.

The above causes of illegitimate pregnancies have always existed, however. Many social scientists believe that there must be some additional causes for the soaring illegitimacy rates of the past few decades. Conservatives like Charles Murray, the author of a controversial book on the welfare system entitled *Losing Ground*, blame the AFDC program. Providing government support for unmarried mothers and their infants encourages immorality and unprotected sex, these conservatives argue. It may even provide a financial motive for some unmarried poor women to deliberately attempt to get pregnant. At the very least, it removes a powerful reason that made many women resist the temptation to take part in unprotected sex in the past: the fear that they would not be able to support the child that might be born as a result.

Another reason often given for the current high rates of illegitimacy is the apparent breakdown of family structure across the social spectrum. Social critics like former Secretary of Education William Bennett blame what they see as a decline in the morality of society in general, starting with the so-called sexual revolution of the 1960s and now fed by ever-rawer sex in popular entertainment.

Furthermore, the social stigma once attached to unmarried mothers and their offspring is no longer as powerful as it used to be. Among some groups in society, including some elements of both the lower and the upper classes, there is no stigma at all. This is a welcome change in some respects. It protects many unfortunate young mothers, and their totally innocent children, from suffering the humiliation and discrimination that used to attach to them. But it also has the effect of removing a powerful restraint that used to discourage single people from having children for whom they could not provide.

For whatever combination of reasons, sexual activity among the young people most likely to have children out of wedlock has soared since the 1960s, sparking the increase in illegitimate births. In 1970, only about 5 percent of 15-year-old girls in the United States acknowledged having had sexual intercourse. By 1980, the percentage had tripled, and by 1988 nearly 25 percent admitted having taken part in sexual activity. Among 18-year-olds, the rate was almost 70 percent. Even the threat of

acquired immune deficiency syndrome (AIDS) apparently has not been enough either to drastically reduce this sexual activity among young American women and men or to prompt them to protect themselves against disease and pregnancy.

There have been some encouraging signs in recent statistics, however. The rate of illegitimate births held steady in 1992, according to the National Center for Health Statistics, and there was a slight (2 percent) decrease in the birth rate for 15- to 17-year-old girls. It is too early to tell whether these figures signal a real reversal of the trends or only a slight blip on a rising chart line.

Can Anything Be Done?

Society is struggling with the question of what can be done to slow the advancing rate of illegitimacy. The state of Wisconsin has pioneered an effort to get at the problem through welfare reform by refusing to provide AFDC payments for the care of new children born to single mothers who were already receiving money from the program. A Planned Parenthood group in Colorado has even offered to pay single mothers for not having more children.

Other proposals include increasing sex education and promotion of abstinence in and out of the schools and making birth control and abortion more available to young people. Some schools around the country have gone so far as to provide condoms to their students, an idea that has caused protest from parents and others who fear that the young people will see such programs as permission to take part in sexual activity.

Ultimately, however, illegitimacy is not caused by sexual activity alone. Nor is it the sole responsibility of the young women who bear the children. As much as anything else, illegitimacy frequently represents a failure of responsibility on the part of the biological father. Too many young men feel free to father children and leave the mother to face the physical, emotional, and economic consequences. Women's rights organizations and others have called for measures to make the fathers of such children legally responsible for supporting them.

"As the answer to teenage pregnancy," says Carolyn Gordon of the Illinois Caucus for Adolescent Health, which supports a variety of birth control methods, "we sup-port programs that address the inequities in access to education, health care, jobs and the absences of comprehensive health and sexuality education and healthy alternatives to early sexual activity that are among the actual causes of...pregnancy."

See also Aid to Families with Dependent Children (AFDC); Single-Parent Families.

Urban Renewal
See Gentrification.

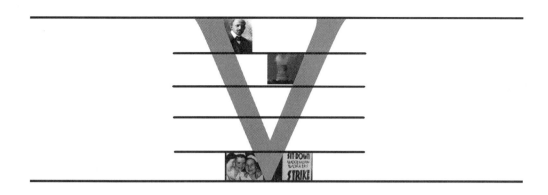

V-Chip

The V-chip—the "V" stands for violence—is a microchip that can be installed in a television set. When activated, the V-chip will block out any program carrying a code that identifies it to the chip as undesirable.

Television violence is of concern to many set owners, but it is especially to parents who worry about the effect such violence might have on their children. They worry that very young children might be shocked, or even traumatized, by particularly graphic violence, and that older children might be desensitized by it, becoming hardened to violence in real life. Another concern is that the *way* violence is sometimes presented in television entertainment programs may make it seem attractive to children and cause them to become more violent themselves.

Parental apprehension revolves not only around children's cartoons and other programming specifically aimed at children, but also prime time network programs, cable programming, syndicated series, and theatrical and made-for-TV motion pictures that may be intended for adults, but which children see as well. Because television is so pervasive in our culture, and because of their own busy work schedules, most parents find that they cannot constantly monitor what their children watch on television. They feel helpless to control even when and where they watch it. The V-chip is seen as at least a partial electronic solution to this problem.

Progress toward implementation of the V-chip was encouraged by U.S. Senate hearings in the mid-1990s. Pressed by concerned senators, including Paul Simon (Democrat, Illinois) and Joseph Lieberman (Democrat, Connecticut), and the threat that censorship might be imposed if they were uncooperative, the major television networks have agreed to have their programming rated and encoded for the V-chip. Exceptions are to be made for news and sports.

Although the original impetus for the V-chip was concern about violence, programs are expected to be rated for sexual conduct and language as well. Initially, at least, the rating system is intended to be age-based, similar to the letter ratings of the Motion Picture Association of America. A further alternative being explored is the possibility of making the rating systems more descriptive of the potentially objectionable materials contained in specific programs, so that parents can make their own decisions as to whether such material is acceptable fare for their children.

As of January 1998, all television sets sold in the United States will be required to have V-chip potential. Parents and other viewers will be able, if they choose, to block programming identified by specific ratings from being received in their homes at times when children might be watching. Adults who wish to watch an encoded program will be able to dial in a private combination that will unblock it.

Industry spokespeople generally accept the V-chip as a desirable alternative to government-imposed censorship. Parents are expected to like the V-chip because it will allow them to prevent their children from watching programs that are unsuitable for them, without depriving the adults of the more mature programming they may prefer for themselves.

Some television producers and artists hope that the chip will actually lead to greater creative freedom. They reason that the makers of adult programming will no longer have to feel constrained by the possibility that their programs will be watched by large numbers of unsupervised children. Other producers, however, fear that the new technology will have a chilling effect on creativity by making network executives wary of buying programming that might be automatically blocked out of large numbers of households.

See also Violence on Television.

Victims' Rights

A growing number of crime victims and their supporters believe that the American criminal justice system ignores their rights and concerns. Defendants, they say, are protected by a variety of procedural and constitutional rights, whereas victims have no such protections.

Defendants, for example, have an inalienable right to be represented by counsel, whereas victims have no right to representation at trial. In many states, they have no standing in the legal process at all. They see this as manifestly unfair. As if the ordeal of the crime itself were not bad enough, many victims are then subjected to another ordeal at the trial. Called as witnesses, they are subjected to severe cross-examination. They have their competency, their memory, and even their honesty questioned by defense attorneys eager to throw any possible doubt on their testimony. Such tactics are particularly painful for victims of rape, who frequently have their own moral character challenged by defense attorneys trying to show that they were, in fact, willing participants in the alleged act.

Victims' complaints frequently involve pre- and post-trial proceedings as much as the trial itself. Traditionally, victims have been denied any part in such procedures. Before trial, prosecutors routinely plea bargain with defendants, dropping or reducing charges relating to some crimes in return for guilty pleas in others. Many victims feel that they are denied justice when a criminal who has committed a serious offense against them is let off with a punishment for a lesser crime. Again, when it comes to sentencing, victims frequently feel that their pain and suffering are devalued by light punishments handed out by judges and juries.

Criminal defense lawyers and other defenders of the current system argue that many victims' complaints stem, at least partly, from a misunderstanding of what the criminal justice system is all about. Victims' rights advocates seem to regard the legal process surrounding a criminal charge as, at least partly, a means for the victim, supported by the state, to obtain retribution. In their view, the victim has been wronged and seeks redress for that wrong. This is not, however, what the criminal justice system was designed to accomplish.

As defense lawyers point out, the criminal justice system was invented as an alternative to private vengeance, not as a means for carrying it out. If the goal is a peaceful and orderly society, in which people are protected from the dishonesty and violence of others, then crime must not be considered merely an offense against individual victims, but against the entire community. Punishment has to be exacted, not by or for individual victims, but by and for the society itself.

Victims tend to make certain assumptions that the law cannot make. The first is that they are, in fact, victims of a crime. The second is that the accused defendant is guilty of that crime. For the victim, then, the legal process is a device for seeing to that the guilty person is punished for the harm they have done to the victim.

The law, however, does not make the same assumptions. In fact, a criminal trial is a means of determining whether or not a crime has been committed and, if so, what that crime was; and then, whether or not the accused person committed that crime. Because a crime is an offense against the peace and order of society, the trial is a dispute between the accused person and society as represented by the prosecution—and not between the accused and the alleged victim.

Supporters of victims' rights refuse to accept the idea that the actual victim of a crime is, or should be, irrelevant to the process. They insist that the individual victims of specific crimes have a special claim on justice. Society can only protect itself, much less avenge itself, by protecting and avenging the victim. If personal vengeance is to be avoided, victims must feel that their need for justice has been satisfied by the criminal justice system. Under the current system, in which the rights of individual victims are frequently ignored, far too many victims believe just the opposite.

Driven by concerns like these, public pressure has been growing to give victims more say in the criminal justice process. Victims' rights organizations have been formed to lobby for this. Judges have become more sensitive to victims' concerns, while an increasing number of lawyers are taking up the cause of crime victims and pressing for their rights in court. Politicians in several states have responded by drafting legislation to give legal standing to victims and their families. In 1995, the U.S. Congress wrote into a major federal crime bill a requirement for convicted criminals to make restitution to victims.

In some states, victims now have the legal right to consult with prosecutors and give their views on prospective plea bargaining arrangements. In some jurisdictions, they also have the right to testify at sentencing hearings about the loss or pain they have suffered as a result of the crime.

For further reading Fletcher, George P. *With Justice for Some: Protecting Victims' Rights in Criminal Trials*. Reading, MA: Addison-Wesley, 1996. Stark, Jerome, and Howard Goldstein. *The Rights of Crime Victims*. Edwardsville, IL: Southern Illinois University Press, 1985.

Video Game Ratings

Billions of dollars' worth of video games are sold in the United States each year, a large proportion of which are purchased or used by young children and teenagers. The violence and sexual content in some of these games has been of growing concern to many parents. Although violence was relatively mild and cartoon-like in early video games, the violence tended to become ever more realistic and gory as the quality of video graphics improved in the 1990s. At the same time, certain games began to feature strong sexual content.

In the past, the content of games was not always apparent from the packaging in which the games were sold. Parents, who rarely if ever played such games themselves, often had no idea of the real nature of the materials their children were spending much of their time with. Consequently, many parents were shocked to find their children manipulating characters engaged in tearing each other's heads off or ripping out each other's hearts while blood gushed and spurted on the screen; or manipulating semi-clothed bodies in explicitly sexual situations or situations that combined sex with violence in sadistic or sadomasochistic ways.

Partly as a result of parental demands and partly as a result of political pressure imposed by such concerned politicians as Senators Joseph Lieberman (Democrat, Connecticut) and Herb Kohl (Democrat, Wisconsin), the video game industry adopted a rating system in 1995. The ratings combine an age-based labeling system (such as K-Adult, meaning suitable for all ages, and T, meaning suitable for teenagers, etc.) with descriptors that indicate the amount or level of potentially objectionable material the game contains.

Some video game manufacturers were reluctant to have their games rated at first, fearing an adverse effect on sales. They worried that some potential customers might refuse to buy games labeled as violent or sexually explicit, while others might be unwilling to buy games rated as acceptable for children, assuming that they were too easy, too tame, or too unsophisticated for older children or adults.

Resistance to the ratings was rapidly broken down when two of the nation's leading retail sellers of video games, Wal-Mart and Toys 'R' Us, announced that they would refuse to carry unrated games. Manufacturers quickly concluded that loss of the huge markets represented by these chains would be much worse for them than any reduction in sales resulting from any negative effects of the ratings.

By the Christmas game-selling season of 1996, the National Institute for Media and the Family announced that most video games available in U.S. stores had been rated and labeled. The institute remained troubled, however, by the finding that video arcade operators often failed to enforce the suggested age restrictions on young customers.

See also Motion Picture Ratings.

Violence, Domestic
See Child Abuse; Domestic Violence; Spouse Abuse.

Violence in American Society
See Crimes against Women; Domestic Violence; Juvenile Crime; Kerner Commission Report; Violence in the Schools; Violence on Television; Violent Crime; Violent Crime Control and Law Enforcement Act (1994).

Violence in the Schools
Violence in and around our nation's schools has become a major concern for students, parents, and school officials alike in many parts of the United States. Schools have always had bullies, but in the 1980s and 1990s, the bullies in many schools started to carry guns.

In cities across the country, scores of students, teachers and administrators alike have been assaulted, stabbed, and even shot to death on school grounds. Although the danger may be more intense in big city schools, it exists in schools of all kinds, including many in prosperous white suburbs. What is more, the threat seems to be spreading. Almost 40 percent of the 600 communities of all sizes surveyed by the National League of Cities in 1994 reported a definite increase in violence over the previous five years. One in four reported at least one incident of school mayhem that resulted in serious injury or death.

Much, though by no means all, of the violence in the schools is gang-related. Almost three-quarters of big city schools in the study cited above reported problems with gangs, along with about half of middle-sized cities, and just over a quarter of the small towns.

The widespread, and in some places commonplace, violence has created a climate of fear and tension in many schools. This is not only unhealthy for the students, who are forced by law to enter this threatening environment each day; it also causes an increasingly oppressive response from school officials. Respect for the privacy and civil rights of students has been diminished, locker and desk searches are becoming commonplace, and uniformed officials patrol the halls of many school buildings.

The most frequent response to violence on the part of school officials has been the beefing up of security measures of all kinds. Schools around the country have hired their own security guards, while some cities have started assigning on-duty police officers to patrol the schools. The perceived threat from lethal weapons has gotten so extreme in some schools that metal detectors are set up at the entrances in an effort to find and confiscate guns and knives from students before they enter the building.

Officials at some schools have become sterner in their discipline of students who exhibit violent behavior, and quicker to expel them. This has produced complaints from civil libertarians who fear that the students' rights are frequently being ig-

nored in the otherwise laudable effort to protect them from physical harm. Some schools have taken a more positive tack, introducing peer-counseling programs and providing intervention programs that are designed to allow students to settle conflicts through communication, negotiation, and compromise.

Although officials at several schools report that these programs have helped to resolve some tensions, critics complain that, however well-intentioned the programs may be, their good effects are limited at best. They are rarely even tried until trouble has already occurred. What's more, they are only useful to the extent that students are willing to make use of them. They require a degree of goodwill and a sophistication in communication that the most violent students rarely have.

Although some critics urge schools to abandon such programs in favor of stronger disciplinary measures, other critics, like the columnist Coleman MacCarthy, urge them to go further. They call for the addition of classes in the peaceful resolution of conflicts, in nonviolence, and in peace studies to the standard curriculum. A handful of schools around the country have introduced such courses. The educators who teach them believe that students need to be shown from a very early age that there are better ways to solve disputes, and to uphold their own self-respect, than through violence.

See also Nonviolence.

Violence on Television

In recent decades, growing numbers of critics, parents, psychologists, and other concerned observers have come to believe that there is a direct correlation between violence in the media—and particularly on the most widely experienced medium of television—and violence in society.

The exact nature of the supposed connection between television and real world violence is unclear. Some psychologists have suggested that excessive violence in the media may desensitize viewers to the horrors of violence, and therefore make them more likely to commit it. Others suggest that a heavy diet of televised violence feeds an irrational fear on the part of many viewers, a view backed up by studies indicating that people who watch a great deal of television tend to be more afraid of crime than other Americans. It has also been suggested that the reliance of many TV characters on violence as a means to resolve their problems may encourage impressionable viewers to look to violence as a means to resolve their own problems in real life.

Whatever the actual effects of televised violence may be, they are likely to be amplified in the future, as more and more television programming becomes available to viewers through the proliferation of cable and satellite reception.

Anecdotal Evidence

Anecdotal evidence has been brought forward that media violence has, in certain specific cases, encouraged individuals of various ages to commit real violence. Children routinely imitate fights and other violent activities they see on television. Several convicted criminals have claimed to have committed their violent crimes, ranging from rape to murder, shortly after watching similar acts on television.

Defenders of television argue that the scientific studies are far from conclusive. Furthermore, they say, the anecdotal evidence is unconvincing. Most children who imitate the violence they see on television do so in a playful and harmless manner.

Playing war and staging mock fights and gun battles were staples of childhood behavior long before television, and the subjective testimony of criminals who attempt to blame television for their own crimes is clearly self-serving. Any adult who imitates a particular criminal act seen on television is clearly predisposed to crime and would likely have committed some form of violent act in any case.

Violence in news and informational programming is generally considered less problematic than violence in fictional or entertainment programming. Some critics argue that the broadcasting of real-life violence may ultimately be the more serious issue, when it comes to the possible desensitizing effects of televised violence.

Violence in Children's Programming

Most problematic of all, in the minds of parents, is the violence that occurs on television shows directed primarily at children. Whatever the negative effects of televised mayhem on adults, they fear that the effects must be much more intense on the young and immature. Studies have suggested that extended exposure to televised violence, whether real or fictional, leads to increased aggressiveness on the part of children.

Although defenders of current children's programming argue that violence has always played a part in popular entertainment, some critics insist that the impact of television violence is inherently different than the impact of other media. This is particularly true, they claim, when it comes to children, many of whom routinely watch several hours of television every day.

Because of these parental concerns, much of the controversy over television violence centers on the Saturday morning time period, which the broadcast networks set aside for cartoons and other children's programs.

Public concern over televised violence came to a head in the late 1980s and early 1990s. This was a period during which network entertainment programming seemed to many viewers to be becoming notably more violent at the same time that news footage was becoming more graphic and cable channels showing violent theatrical films were becoming available in more American homes.

Government Pressures

In 1990, Senator Paul Simon (Democrat, Illinois) began a campaign to lower the level of violence on TV, particularly during hours when children would be most likely to be watching. Combining intensive "jawboning" with the threat of federal action, Simon pressured the television industry to do something about what he perceived to be a serious national problem. When the industry responded that antitrust laws prevented the broadcast and cable networks from getting together to make policies, Simon managed to win a three-year antitrust exemption for the television industry so that it could act in concert to reduce violence on the medium.

The industry remained reluctant to act, however. Violence, of various kinds, was a popular element in many different kinds of shows. The 1993 May sweeps week was pivotal when it came to reforming television executives' attitudes. The networks rely on the ratings taken during the sweeps weeks to measure their viewership and, thereby, to sell advertising time for the next several months. Ratings taken that May revealed declining viewership for some of the most violent programs. This seemed to support allegations that the public was becoming tired of—if not actively upset by—an overabundance of violence. The

networks were shocked into becoming more amenable to the calls for a reduction in the violence level of their programming.

In August 1993, at an industry wide conference on violence, Senator Simon challenged the industry to set up a monitor to document televised violence, under the threat that if the television industry did not begin to regulate itself, the federal government might begin to do so. The ultimate result of this combination of pressures was an agreement between the networks to take certain steps. They committed to reduce the level of violence on their programs, particularly those aimed at children; to label programs for violent content; and to hire an independent monitor to report on the effectiveness of these efforts.

Network Violence Reduced

Studies done over the next few years indicated that the amount and intensity of violence in network entertainment programming did drop markedly. This was true in virtually all time periods. It was noted, however, that, although the number of shows aimed at children that contained what the independent monitor classified as an excessive level of violence had dropped, the handful of Saturday morning shows that continued to emphasize violent content were the most popular.

The reduction of violence on the networks and on cable in general has not been matched by a decline in the violence available on those cable channels, including pay-per-view, which featured motion pictures originally made for theatrical release. Most of those channels do make a practice of identifying controversial content before a program airs, however, and refrain from running films rated R-17 or X.

Demand for further safeguarding against the possible negative effects of televised violence continues. Suggestions range from a more effective rating system, to the banning of all violence during the Saturday morning "children's hours" and in the early evening hours, to electronic solutions like the V-chip. Some critics, including *Los Angeles Times* columnist Tom Plate, have argued that the goal should not be to reduce violence on television, but to eliminate it.

See also Motion Picture Ratings; V-Chip.

Violent Crime

The United States has always had a violent society compared to most other western countries. A historic tradition of "taming" a wild and hostile frontier, combined with a mix of different peoples and the persistence of a large and seemingly intractable underclass, have produced a nation whose rates of violent crime are much higher than those in most of the nations from which its peoples have come.

Public Concern

Crime—and particularly violent crime—is a perennial concern of the American public, although the extent of that concern is subject to drastic swings. In 1992, for example, approximately 3 percent of those people polled by the Times Mirror Center for the People and the Press considered crime to be America's most pressing problem. Two years later, the number of Americans who saw crime as the nation's most serious threat had jumped to more than 25%. This periodic change in the depth of public concern is not fully accounted for by changes in the incidence of crime in the United States.

Instead of following the rise and fall in actual crime, the average citizen's fear of crime seems to respond most directly to the degree of attention paid to the problem by the media and by politicians. In 1994, for example, when the number of Americans naming crime as their major social concern topped 25 percent, the media had been obsessed by a number of highly publicized criminal cases; several reality-based cop shows had become popular on national television; and the question of which candidate was "tougher on crime" had become a key issue in many of that year's congressional election campaigns.

Recent Trends in Violent Crime Rates

The overall national violent crime rate (which includes rapes, robberies, and assaults) actually declined slightly from 1973 to the mid-1990s, and in 1995 even the murder rate declined dramatically.

The reasons for these declines were not entirely clear. Some experts credited tougher incarceration practices, mandatory sentencing, and "three-strikes-and-you're-out" laws, which, they claimed, kept an increasing number of dangerous criminals off the streets for longer periods of time. Others credited demographic changes, particularly the fact that the U.S. population has gotten older with the aging of the so-called baby boomers, whereas most violent crimes are committed by men who are relatively young.

Even with the declines, however, violence remains rampant in the United States. In 1991, the last year for which complete figures are available, there were an estimated 6,427,480 violent crimes in the United States. Although robberies and burglaries have gone down, there has been a dramatic and troubling increase in certain kinds of violent crimes. The incidence of forcible rape rate increased by more than 14 percent during the 1980s, for example. What is more, both the numbers and rates of crimes among certain segments of the population have increased much more drastically than among the population as a whole. Drug-related violent offenses have reached epidemic proportions in many inner cities, while violent crimes committed by and against juveniles have increased almost as dramatically in virtually all classes of society. Most alarming of all are the rates of murder by and of juveniles, which have increased at all economic levels.

Murders

Although the murder rate in the United States has remained extremely high, it has not been historically high in the 1990s. In fact, the murder rate per 100,000 Americans has been at approximately the same level in recent years as it was in 1933, at the end of Prohibition. In both cases, the high rates were associated with the use of illegal substances: alcohol in the 1930s, and drugs in the 1990s.

Although relatively low in the 1950s and early 1960s, the murder rate more than doubled from 1960 to 1975. The rate then dropped slightly until the mid-1980s, when it began to rise to its current levels. In a typical year, approximately two-thirds of the people murdered in the United States are killed by guns. Of the 23,760 murder victims in 1992, 11,175 were African-American and 10,645 were white. (The rest were listed by the FBI as "other.") Approximately 94 percent of the African-American victims and 83 percent of the whites were murdered by members of their own race.

In the past, most victims were killed by people they knew, often members of their own family. In 1994, however, for the first time since such statistics have been kept, more Americans were murdered by strangers than by acquaintances. Most murders are isolated events. There are, however, an average of two mass murders a month. Many of these are random crimes.

Reducing the Violence

A variety of general approaches, as well as many specific measures, have been suggested for curbing violent crime. Religious leaders, in particular, emphasize the need to improve the nation's moral climate and to strengthen the nuclear family. Although these ideas resonate with many Americans, and few would quarrel with their worthiness as goals, most see them as insufficient to solve the practical problem of how to reduce the current levels of violent crime.

The majority of the public favors measures they think of as "getting tough" with the criminals. Longer prison sentences, reduction or elimination of parole, and a greater use of the death penalty all have the support of most Americans polled on the issue. Police chiefs call for more police officers, increased community policing, and greater citizen involvement through neighborhood watch programs.

In the long run, however, the single most effective way to reduce violent crime—in the opinion of many top law enforcement officials, as well as many social scientists—is to reduce drug abuse. The second is to improve the economy, and by doing so, to provide more jobs for Americans, and particularly for those males in their late teenage years and early twenties, who are at highest risk to become violent criminals. Congress passed the landmark Violent Crime Control and Law Enforcement Act of 1994 in response to concern about this issue.

See also Crimes against Women; Death Penalty; Juvenile Crime; Violent Crime Control and Law Enforcement Act (1994).

Violent Crime Control and Law Enforcement Act (1994)

The landmark Violent Crime Control and Law Enforcement Act passed Congress in

August 1994 and was signed by President Bill Clinton on 13 September of that year. The most ambitious crime bill in U.S. history, it marked the assumption of a greater federal role in crime control and prevention than it ever had taken before.

The bill consisted of a plethora of measures, some of which were designed to beef up law enforcement efforts, some to increase the penalties for criminals, and some to help in the prevention of crime.

Perhaps the most controversial of the bill's measures was a ban on certain assault weapons and categories of ammunition, which the government alleged were useful only for military or criminal purposes. Other specific gun control measures included new licensing requirements for gun dealers and a ban on sales of guns to people under a restraining order to prevent family violence.

Several provisions created new federal crimes and stiffened the sentences for old ones. Among the new offenses were many related to drugs, while among the increased-punishment provisions was a new federal three-strikes law mandating life in prison for those convicted of a federal felony who already had two prior major felony convictions.

In a measure decried as draconian by anti–capital punishment activists, some 60 new federal offenses were made subject to the death penalty. Still other provisions of the bill strengthened the rights of victims and required the perpetrators of certain categories of crimes to pay restitution.

The Violent Crime Reduction Trust Fund

The most expensive provision in the bill was the establishment of a $30.2 billion Violent Crime Reduction Trust Fund, to be funded by savings accomplished in the downsizing of the federal government.

The trust fund was to be used for a variety of anticrime measures. Much of the money was to go to law enforcement programs, the most ambitious of which was a community policing effort that supporters claimed would put 100,000 more police on the streets of the nation's cities. Of the remainder, nearly $8 billion was earmarked for prison construction, and almost $2 billion to help states pay for imprisoning criminal aliens.

Approximately $1 billion was set aside for new federal "drug courts," designed, among other functions, to determine which nonviolent drug offenders should be offered treatment and which should be sent to jail. Six billion dollars more was directed to a multitude of crime prevention ventures, including education, drug treatment, antigang and antidrug programs, midnight basketball, and jobs-for-youth programs, among many others. More than $1.5 billion was targeted to fight violence against women.

See also Gun Control; Violent Crime.

War on Drugs

See Drug War.

Watergate Scandal

On 17 June 1972, several men were caught breaking into the offices of the Democratic National Committee in the Watergate building at Washington, D.C. It was soon revealed that at least some of the burglars were Cubans active in the anti-Castro movement in the United States. Some also had ties to people in the presidential administration of Richard Nixon and/or to Nixon's campaign organization, the Committee to Re-Elect the President (sometimes known as "CREEP").

The White House denied any involvement in the break-in, and the event had little direct effect on the presidential contest that was then being waged between the incumbent, Nixon, and his Democratic challenger, Senator George McGovern. Despite Democratic suspicions about a possible White House role in the burglary, Nixon won the election in a landslide.

Thanks significantly to the work of Bob Woodward and Carl Bernstein, two young reporters for the *Washington Post*, interest in the break-in continued past the elections. Investigations of what came to be known as the Watergate scandal were eventually conducted by an appointed special prosecutor, Archibald Cox, and by a Senate select committee. These investigations, along with the journalistic efforts of Woodward and Bernstein, eventually proved extensive wrongdoing by members of the Nixon administration and by others working on their behalf.

Among the transgressions uncovered were a previous break-in at the offices of a psychiatrist in order to gather information about a patient; the solicitation and acceptance of illegal campaign funds; the existence of a secret slush fund used to pay potential witnesses against administration officials for their silence; the maintenance of a political enemies list and the covert use of executive power against some of those whose names appeared on it; and a variety of so-called dirty tricks against the administration's political opponents, including faked documents designed to reflect badly on high-ranking Democrats. Perhaps the most serious charge made against the president himself was participation in efforts to obstruct justice by covering up evidence of White House involvement in the burglary at the Watergate.

Altogether, the Watergate revelations are generally considered the most sweeping demonstration of the domestic misuse of executive power in U.S. history.

The Evolution of the Scandal

The first important hearings on Watergate were convened by the Senate Select Committee on Presidential Activities in May 1973. The committee was chaired by the colorful Senator Sam Ervin of North Carolina, who was considered one of the Senate's leading experts on the U.S. Constitution and on the relationship between the Congress and the president. The ranking Republican on the committee was Senator Howard Baker of Tennessee, who set the goal for the committee with his repeated asking of the question: "What did the president know, and when did he know it?"

A major turning point in the scandal was the testimony of the former White House counsel, John Dean. Dean, who had intimate knowledge of the early days of the scandal from within the White House itself, testified that Attorney General John Mitchell had ordered the Watergate break-in and that President Nixon himself had directed the coverup.

It was Dean's word against the president's and the attorney general's until, on 16 July 1973, another White House aide, Alexander Butterfield, revealed to the Senate committee that Nixon had taped meetings in the Oval Office of the White House. Those meetings, it turned out, included the key conversations to which Dean had already testified.

When Special Prosecutor Cox subpoenaed several of these White House tapes, Nixon refused to produce them, claiming executive privilege on the grounds that the tapes would compromise national security. A U.S. District Judge, John Sirica, turned down the president's claim and ordered him to turn over the tapes to Cox. Eventually, the U.S. Supreme Court would unanimously agree that Sirica's decision had been correct. In the meantime, however, the angry president responded by ordering

his new attorney general, Elliott Richardson, to fire Cox. In a series of events that became infamous as the Saturday Night Massacre, Richardson resigned rather than obey the president's order, as did the deputy attorney general, William Ruckleshaus. Eventually, the solicitor general obeyed the president and dismissed Cox.

Forced by public outrage at the "massacre," the president appointed a new special prosecutor named Leon Jaworski. He also surrendered the demanded tapes, although 18.5 minutes had been mysteriously erased from one of them. What remained, however, proved damaging enough. John Mitchell and six other White House officials were indicted, and the House Judiciary Committee proceeded to launch impeachment proceedings against the president himself.

On 29 and 30 July 1974, the House Judiciary Committee voted three articles of impeachment against President Richard Nixon. As further damning tapes were made public, it became clear that the whole House would vote to send the case to trial in the Senate and that, if the impeachment came to trial in the Senate, the president would be found guilty and removed from office. Rather than face that certainty, on 9 August 1974, Nixon became the first—and, so far, the only—U.S. president ever to resign from office.

Nixon did not acknowledge any serious misconduct on his part. Instead, he claimed to be resigning in order to put the divisive Watergate scandal behind the nation and to allow a healing process to begin.

The next month, Nixon's successor, President Gerald Ford, pardoned the ex-president for any crimes he might have committed while in office. In justifying his action, Ford explained that Nixon was in poor health and had already paid a terrible penalty for whatever he had done. The pardon spared the country the trauma of having an ex-president tried for serious crimes and freed Nixon from the threat of having to join John Mitchell, John Dean, and several other associates in jail had he been convicted.

Contemporary Reactions

Americans were variously shocked, saddened, outraged, or comforted by the Watergate scandal, depending on their political points of view and on their earlier preconceptions about the U.S. government. Only two years before, they had given Nixon one of the biggest landslides in U.S. election history. Now he had been driven from office in disgrace. Some felt betrayed and deeply troubled about the political future of the country. Others took heart from public, press, congressional, and judicial responses to the scandal. In their minds, Watergate proved that not even the president could violate the Constitution with impunity.

For many of Nixon's political enemies, the Watergate revelations said less about the U.S. political system than about the character of Richard Nixon. Although Nixon had won reelection handily, he had never been particularly well-liked by many Americans, and he had always been heartily detested by liberals. Their distrust of him was reflected in the derisive nickname "Tricky Dicky." For them, the Watergate revelations confirmed their darkest fears about him.

Nixon and his supporters believed that the intense reaction to the scandal by the press and Democrats was influenced largely by personal dislike of the president. At first, many Republicans refused to believe the charges against Nixon. Some continued to defend him even after the tapes proved that many of the allegations were true. Nixon may have done some things

wrong, some now admitted, but they insisted he had done nothing worse than many of his predecessors. No previous president, they insisted, would have been driven out of office for such relatively minor transgressions.

Aside from Republican partisans, however, it was widely acknowledged that the offenses committed by the Nixon administration had been far from minor.

Long-Term Effects

Presidents Nixon and Ford hoped that the country would soon leave the Watergate scandal behind. However, the effects of Watergate continued to haunt the nation well into the 1990s.

At the time the scandal broke, the United States had already gone through a series of events that caused many Americans to reexamine their once unquestioning faith in the country and its government: the violent resistance to the civil rights movement; the assassinations of John and Robert Kennedy and Dr. Martin Luther King, Jr.; the controversy over the U.S. role in Vietnam, culminating in the killings of four student protesters by national guardsmen at Kent State University; and, finally, the political and military failures resulting from the conduct of the United States in that war.

Coming on the heels of all this, the Watergate scandal confirmed many Americans' disillusionment with government and distrust of politicians. For them, the multifaceted scandal seemed a final proof that the U.S. government was not only incompetent but fundamentally corrupt.

In retrospect, Watergate led to a new era of bitterness and partisan hostility in American politics. A generation of journalists, inspired by the work and financial success of Woodward and Bernstein, became fixated on uncovering political scandal.

Embittered Republicans, convinced that Nixon had been treated too harshly, looked for opportunities to repay the Democrats. It has been argued that the spirit of animosity that would later inform the House bank scandals, the misconduct of House Speakers Jim Wright and Newt Gingrich, and the financial dealings of President Bill Clinton had its roots in the Watergate affair.

See also Resignation of Richard Nixon.
For further reading Archer, Jules. *Watergate: America in Crisis*. New York: Thomas Y. Crowell, 1975.
Bernstein, Carl, and Bob Woodward. *All the President's Men*. New York: Simon & Schuster, 1974.
White, Theodore H. *Breach of Faith: The Fall of Richard Nixon*. New York: Atheneum, 1975.

"Wealth"

In his famous essay, "Wealth," originally published in the *North American Review* in June 1889, Andrew Carnegie laid down his views on the proper administration of wealth in a capitalist society. Born in Scotland, Carnegie had come to the United States as a young man and accrued vast wealth of his own by building the United States Steel company.

Carnegie wrote at a time when a handful of men who, like himself, had accumulated great wealth and economic power were under attack for unscrupulous business practices and for the incredible self-indulgence with which they spent their enormous fortunes. Carnegie, however, believed that the accumulation of great wealth by individuals such as himself was an indication of their worthiness to control that wealth. "Godliness," he wrote, "is in league with riches." For him, it followed that those who earned great wealth must use it to further godly ends.

His essay might have been self-serving, but it presents a quintessentially American view of wealth and of the role that men of great wealth and achievement ought to play in a society. It is excerpted here because these views are echoed, even today, in the beliefs and opinions of many American conservatives. "Wealth" remains the most influential defense ever written of industrial capitalism and of the economic inequities which inevitably result from it.

The problem of our age is the proper administration of wealth, so that the ties of brotherhood may still bind together the rich and poor in harmonious relationship. The conditions of human life have not only been changed, but revolutionized, within the past few hundred years. In former days, there was little difference between the dwelling, dress, food, and environment of the chief and those of his retainers....The contrast between the palace of the millionaire and the cottage of the laborer with us to-day measures the change that has come with civilization.

This change, however, is not to be deplored, but welcomed as highly beneficial. It is well, nay, essential for the progress of the race, that the houses of some should be homes for all that is highest and best in literature and the arts, and for all the refinements of civilization, rather than that none should be so. Much better this great irregularity than universal squalor. Without wealth there can be no Maecenas. The "good old times" were not good old times. Neither master nor servant was as well situated then as to-day. A relapse to old conditions would be disastrous to both—not the least so to him who serves—and would sweep away civilization with it. But whether the change be for good or ill, it is upon us, beyond our power to alter, and therefore to be accepted and made the best of....

The price we pay for this salutary change is, no doubt, great. We assemble thousand of operatives in the factory, in the mine, and in the counting house, of whom the employer can know little or nothing, and to whom the employer is little better than a myth. All intercourse between them is at an end. Rigid Castes are formed, and, as usual, mutual ignorance breeds mutual distrust.... Under the law of competition, the employer of thousands is forced into the strictest economies, among which the rates paid to labor figure prominently, and often there is friction between the employer and the employed, between capital and labor, between rich and poor. Human society loses homogeneity.

The price society pays for the law of competition, like the price it pays for cheap comforts and luxuries, is also great; but the advantages of this law are also greater still, for it is to this law that we owe our wonderful material development, which brings improved conditions in its train....[W]hile the law may sometimes be hard for the individual, it is best for the race, because it insures the survival of the fittest in every department. We accept and welcome, therefore, as conditions to which we must accommodate ourselves, great inequality of environment, the concentration of business, industrial and commercial, in the hands of a few, and the law of competition between these, as being not only beneficial, but essential for the future progress of the race.

...Objections to the foundations upon which society is based are not in order...The Socialist or Anarchist who seeks to overturn present conditions is to be regarded as attacking the foundation upon which civilization itself rests, for civilization took its start from the day that the capable, industrious workman said to his incompetent and lazy fellow, "If thou dost not sow, thou shalt not reap," and thus ended primitive Communism by separating the drones from the bees...But even if we admit for a moment that it might be better for the race to discard its present foundation, Individualism....This is not evolution, but revolution. It necessitates the changing of human nature itself—a work of aeons, even if it were good to change it, which we cannot know....

The question then arises...What is the proper mode of administering wealth after the laws upon which civilization is founded have thrown it into the hands of the few? And it is of this great question that I believe I offer the true solution....

There are but three modes in which surplus wealth can be disposed of. It can be left to the families of the decedents; or it can be bequeathed for public purposes; or, finally, it can be administered during their lives by its possessors. Under the first and second modes most of the wealth of the world that has reached the few has hitherto been applied...

There remains, then, only one mode of using great fortunes; but in this we have the true antidote for the temporary unequal distribution of wealth, the reconciliation of the rich and the poor—a reign of harmony—

another ideal, differing indeed from that of the Communist in requiring only the further evolution of existing conditions, not the total overthrow of our civilization. It is founded upon the present most intense individualism, and the race is prepared to put it in practice by degrees whenever it pleases. Under its sway we shall have an ideal state, in which the surplus wealth of the few will become, in the best sense, the property of the many, because administered for the public good, and this wealth, passing through the hands of the few, can be made a much more potent force for the elevation of our race than if it had been distributed in small sums to the people themselves. Even the poorest can be made to see this, and to agree that great sums gathered by some of their fellow-citizens and spent for public purposes, from which the masses reap the principal benefit, are more valuable to them than if scattered among them through the course of many years in trifling amounts....

This, then, is held to be the duty of the man of Wealth: First, to set an example of modest, unostentatious living, shunning display or extravagance; to provide moderately for the legitimate wants of those dependent upon him; and after doing so to consider all surplus revenues which come to him simply as trust funds, which he is called upon to administer, and strictly bound as a matter of duty to administer in the manner which, in his judgment, is best calculated to produce the most beneficial results for the community—the man or wealth thus becoming the mere agent and trustee for his poorer brethren, bringing to their service his superior wisdom, experience, and ability to administer, doing for them better than they would or could do for themselves...

Those who would administer wisely must, indeed, be wise, for one of the serious obstacles to the improvement of our race is indiscriminate charity....In bestowing charity, the main consideration should be to help those who will help themselves....

The rich man is thus almost restricted to following the examples of Peter Cooper, Enoch Pratt of Baltimore, Mr. Pratt of Brooklyn, Senator Stanford, and others, who know that the best means of benefiting the community is to place within its reach the ladders upon which the aspiring can rise—parks, and means of recreation, by which men are helped in body and mind; works of art, certain to give pleasure and improve the public taste, and public institutions of various kinds, which will improve the general condition of the people;—in this manner returning their surplus wealth to the mass of their fellows in the forms best calculated to do them lasting good.

Thus is the problem of Rich and Poor to be solved. The laws of accumulation will be left free; the laws of distribution free. Individualism will continue, but the millionaire will be but a trustee for the poor; intrusted for a season with a great part of the increased wealth of the community, but administering it for the community far better than it could or would have done for itself...The man who dies leaving behind him millions of available wealth, which was his to administer during life, will pass away "unwept, unhonored, and unsung," no matter to what uses he leaves the dross which he cannot take with him. Of such as these the public verdict will then be: "The man who dies thus rich dies in disgrace."

Such, in my opinion, is the true Gospel of Wealth, obedience to which is destined some day to solve the problem of the Rich and the Poor, and to bring "Peace on earth, among men of Good-Will."

Wealth (Reconcentration in the Late Twentieth Century)

The 1980s saw a massive reconcentration of wealth in the hands of a relatively small economic elite. It was brought about by a variety of economic and political developments, including a reorganization of the tax code that relieved the relative tax burden of people in the upper income brackets, and a nationwide trend that reduced or limited the payroll costs of American industry while increasing the remuneration of top executives.

A study carried out by economists at the Federal Reserve Bank discovered that by the close of the 1980s, 1 percent of U.S. households accounted for 37 percent of the net worth of all households in the country. That was considerably more than the net worth of the entire lower 90 percent of households. Put another way, this meant that approximately 834,000 wealthy families owned more than 84,000,000 other American families combined. This was a greater concentration of wealth in a smaller number of hands than in any other developed country in the world.

Although the household wealth figures represented assets (which could be inherited as well as earned or achieved through investment), a similarly extreme dispro-

portion could be seen in terms of income patterns. Although most wages went up only moderately during the economic upturn that occurred in the 1980s, and again in the recovery of the 1990s, those of a small percentage of Americans, including top corporate executives, star entertainers, and major-league athletes, went up at a much higher rate.

The combined pay and benefits paid to workers in the United States (as measured by the U.S. Department of Labor's Employment Cost Index) rose a mere 2.9 percent in 1995, or just 0.4 percent more than inflation (as measured by the Consumer Price Index) rose over the same period. It was the smallest increase since the Labor Department started keeping the combined-pay-and-benefit statistic in 1982. In the same year, the typical chief executive officer of a major U.S. corporation was being paid 180 times as much as the lowest paid employee of the same corporation. Twenty years earlier, the ratio had been only 15 to 1, a proportion much more in line with the ratios in other highly developed countries in Europe and Asia in the 1990s.

Welfare Magnet

Welfare is a joint federal, state, and local responsibility. To a great degree, the level of benefits provided to recipients in each state is largely determined by the government of that state. Because of this policy, there have been significant differences in the levels of benefits available in different states. States such as Mississippi and Texas, for example, have traditionally provided much less in the way of benefits to poor families than have more generous states, such as New York or Massachusetts.

There is some reason to believe that the relatively high payments in some states may act as a magnet that draws poor people away from low-paying states and into high-paying states. This is a serious concern for the governments and taxpayers in the relatively high-paying states, and particularly for those that neighbor low-paying states. They complain that the poor emigrants from other states overload their welfare system, requiring the taxpayers of the high-paying state to provide for them.

The evidence supporting these claims is controversial, however. Studies of migration patterns between states indicate that welfare recipients, like other people, are influenced by a variety of factors when deciding whether or not to move from one state to another. The studies show, for example, that significant numbers of poor people move from high-paying states to relatively low-paying states, as well as the other way around.

In order to solve what they perceive as the welfare magnet problem, some states have gone to a two-tier payment system in which welfare newcomers receive a lower level of benefits than do long-term state residents. For the first year that welfare recipients arriving from other states spend in California, for example, they are only eligible to receive whatever payments they would have received in the state from which they came. The U.S. Supreme Court has ruled some two-tier systems unconstitutional but, as of this writing, has not struck down the California law.

A broader solution to the problem, to the extent it does exist, would be to make welfare benefits uniform in all states. This solution has been opposed, however, by a wide range of interests. State governments are not only eager to protect their prerogatives; they argue that uniform benefits would be unfair to taxpayers as well as welfare recipients in many states. Any sort of averaging out of benefits would be unfair to recipients who live in states where

the cost of living is high, while being unfair to taxpayers who live in states where the cost of living is low. The real issue, they argue, is not whether a state's level of payments is relatively high or low, but rather, whether it is sufficient to allow welfare families to survive with some dignity in whichever state they choose.

In any case, the difference in benefit levels between states is likely to increase, rather than decrease, under the welfare reforms passed in 1996, which give more autonomy to individual states to establish their own welfare systems.

See also Aid to Families with Dependent Children (AFDC); Welfare Reform (1996); Welfare State; Welfare System; Welfare Trap.

Welfare Reform (1996)

The 1996 Welfare Reform Act, which was signed into law by President Bill Clinton on 22 August 1996, was more than a simple restructuring of the U.S. welfare system. It marked a major change in the nation's attitude toward welfare itself. In effect, it was a rejection of the idea of an American welfare state. The culmination of a long effort by Republicans to end a half-century of expansion of the U.S. welfare system, the act was so widely popular that it was supported by many congressional Democrats and signed into law by a Democratic president.

In the past, welfare had been a joint federal, state, and local responsibility. Generally speaking, the federal government would set guidelines for the programs and provide half or more of the money. Within the federal guidelines, each state would design and administer its own programs, contributing the rest of the funding itself. Actual operation of welfare programs would typically be carried out by the states and localities themselves. Although keeping the same tripartite structure, the Welfare Reform Act shifted the major responsibilities within it from the federal government to the states.

The most important of the reforms was the termination of Aid to Families with Dependent Children (AFDC), the child-support program that had long been the backbone of the American welfare system. AFDC was replaced by federal block grants, which the states are free to spend more or less however they desire. The program's elimination was heralded as signifying the end of welfare as an entitlement in the United States.

Although transferring significant new authority over welfare measures from itself to the states, the federal government retained considerable authority over state welfare programs. Leaving states relatively free to invent and enact their own programs, it retained the power to restrict eligibility for those programs that were supported by federal grants. Among the federally imposed restrictions was a maximum lifetime limit of five years on an individual's eligibility for welfare and the requirement that most adult welfare recipients be forced to take a job within two years. In addition, benefits available to poor immigrants and other noncitizens were cut or eliminated.

The reforms were met with outrage by advocates for the poor, who predicted that they would lead to a drastic increase in poverty, homelessness, and social unrest. Critics especially objected to the mandatory work requirement after two years, on the grounds that many current and future welfare recipients would be unable to find work. Objections were also made to the five-year lifetime limit, which was below the average length of time most past recipients had been on welfare. The reforms also alarmed many immigrants, who were made ineligible for many of the benefits immigrants had previously received.

See also Welfare Magnet; Welfare State; Welfare Trap; Welfare System.
For further reading Bender, David L., editor. *Liberals and Conservatives: A Debate on the Welfare State*. Anoka, MN: Greenhaven Press, 1982. Cottingham, P. H., and D. T. Ellwood, editors. *Welfare Policy for the 1990s*. Cambridge, MA: Harvard University Press, 1982. Davey, Joseph D. *The New Social Contract: America's Journey from a Welfare State to a Police State*. Westport, CT: Greenwood Press, 1995. Long, Robert Emmet, editor. *The Welfare Debate*. New York: H. W. Wilson, 1989.

Welfare State

Welfare state is the term used to describe a nation in which the government undertakes to ensure that some minimum level of goods and services is provided to all its citizens. Welfare states typically provide medical care, insurance against unemployment and illness, public housing for those who cannot afford to own or rent their own homes, family allowances to offset the expenses of children, and pension benefits for the elderly. In addition, the modern welfare state may include such features as a minimum wage and government-subsidized child care and higher education.

Civilized societies have always acknowledged the need for some help to be given to their most unfortunate members. In some cases, this help was provided by governmental organizations; in others, by religious or other charitable bodies or by acts of private charity. In modern times, however, the governments of many countries have come to accept responsibility for providing such assistance, either as a matter of course to everyone, or in those situations where help is not available from other sources.

In addition to such charitable assistance, however, the welfare state typically provides at least some basic services—such as universal medical care—to everyone, regardless of individual need. This is crucial to an understanding of the welfare state, in which benefits are considered a right of citizenship, rather than a favor done for the unfortunate.

Supporters of the welfare state argue that such universal coverage has many advantages over traditional, charity-based welfare programs. It eliminates means testing, which they say demeans the recipients and makes social programs more complicated, difficult, and ultimately expensive to run. Universal coverage is also valuable, they argue, because it encourages everyone, poor and rich alike, to feel that they have a common stake in the society. Perhaps most importantly, it increases support for welfare programs, because everyone feels that they have something to gain from them. In societies in which only the poor are helped, those who are better off, and who necessarily provide the bulk of the money to pay for such programs, are apt to become resentful. This can not only cause funding problems for the programs; it makes for divisions within the society, creating hostility and bitterness between those in need and those who have to pay to provide services for them.

Opponents of universal coverage argue that providing services to everyone only makes programs bigger and more expensive. Although it may be justifiable, they say, to tax the economically comfortable in order to provide benefits to those in need, it is not acceptable to take their money in order to provide benefits to people as prosperous as—or even more prosperous than— themselves.

The welfare state provides many of the programs and benefits associated with socialist societies. Unlike socialism, however, it is ideologically compatible with modern capitalism. In fact, the early elements of the modern welfare state were developed as a way of undercutting socialism's appeal.

The Development of the Modern Welfare State

Germany was a prosperous industrial country in the late nineteenth century, but its workers were dissatisfied and angry. They had to work very hard for scarcely enough money to provide for themselves and their families. Worst of all, few earned enough money to save for the future. When they got too sick or old to work, they were fired, and they and their family were out on the streets.

Many workers of the time were beginning to respond to the Socialists, who spoke about strikes and revolution. This frightened the German Chancellor, Otto von Bismarck, who knew that the nation needed a dependable and stable workforce to establish itself as the strongest industrial and military power in Europe. In order to placate the workers, he provided them with sickness and accident insurance and pensions for when they got old. These programs—the beginnings of the modern welfare state—were paid for by contributions from the government as well as from the employers and workers themselves.

By the early 1910s, most western European countries had followed Germany's lead. Some had even surpassed it and already had established some form of several programs associated with the welfare state. These included social insurance, funded at least partly by the government; sickness and accident insurance for workers; and old age pensions.

The first more-or-less complete welfare state, providing a full range of social services to all citizens, was set up by the Labour Party government of Great Britain following World War II. Although many of its more sweeping provisions were eventually cut back in the 1980s by the Conservative government led by Margaret Thatcher, the basic elements of the welfare state remain. A similar pattern has been followed in other welfare-state nations, which have found their programs difficult to sustain in hard economic times.

Besides Great Britain and Germany, other major modern welfare states include the Scandinavian countries and New Zealand.

The United States

The United States was one of the slowest of all the developed countries to adopt programs associated with the welfare state. Even while most of the rest of the developed world was adopting welfare-style programs in the late nineteenth and early twentieth centuries, the United States continued to rely on private charity to help the poor and disadvantaged.

It was only when the numbers of poor people increased astronomically during the Great Depression of the 1930s that the federal government began to accept a significant role in providing relief to the destitute. President Franklin D. Roosevelt's New Deal inaugurated a variety of short-term programs designed to cushion the effects of the depression on the people, along with the much more far-reaching Social Security pension system.

By enacting these measures, the federal government implicitly accepted at least some responsibility to provide for the economic, as well as political, well-being of the people. That has been a controversial responsibility ever since, but one that the nation has never relinquished.

Nonetheless, the United States has been reluctant to become a true welfare state. The idea of the government providing assistance to those who can, in fact, provide for themselves goes against the grain of many Americans who highly value self-reliance. Although they are willing to help what President Ronald Reagan called the "truly needy," they balk at subsidizing in any significant way those they consider able to care for themselves.

Today, then, the United States might best be described as a partial welfare state. Although it is virtually the only economically developed western nation that does not provide universal medical care, it does have many of the other features typical of a modern welfare state. These include an all-but-universal form of social insurance, in Social Security, and a large and complex welfare system that provides services, as well as financial assistance, to those in need. Medical care is provided to many of the poor and near-poor through Medicaid, and to the elderly through Medicare.

Although these programs, even taken together, fail to provide the kind of "cradle-to-grave" protection offered by more comprehensive welfare states, they do serve as what politicians often refer to as a "safety net" to stop most citizens from falling below a certain minimal level of subsistence.

See also Aid to Families with Dependent Children (AFDC); Medicaid; Medicare; Welfare Magnet; Welfare Reform (1996); Welfare System; Welfare Trap.

For further reading Bender, David L., editor. *Liberals and Conservatives: A Debate on the Welfare State*. Anoka, MN: Greenhaven Press, 1982.
Flora, Peter, and Arnold J. Heidenheimer, editors. *The Development of the Welfare States in Europe and America*. New Brunswick, NJ: Transaction Books, 1981.
Jansson, Bruce S. *The Reluctant Welfare State: A History of American Social Welfare Policies*. Belmont, CA: Wadsworth, 1988.
Piven, Francis Fox, and Richard A. Cloward. *Regulating the Poor: The Functions of Public Welfare*. New York: Pantheon, 1971.

Welfare System

An elaborate array of programs and agencies has been developed in the past half-century to help Americans meet their basic needs for food, clothing, shelter, and medical care. Some are local, some are state, some are federal, and some are funded and/or administered by a combination of all these levels of government.

Some, like Social Security and Medicare, provide help regardless of economic status. Others are means tested; that is, they are limited to those in economic need. Although programs designed to advance the welfare of the American public might rightfully be considered parts of the U.S. welfare system, it is primarily the means-tested programs that most people think of when they use the term.

Means-Tested Programs

The most important of the means-tested welfare programs are:

- **Medicaid,** which is, in terms of expense, the largest of all the means-tested welfare programs, and which provides certain basic medical assistance to poor people and others unable to pay for the services themselves.
- **State programs,** funded substantially by federal block grants, which replaced Aid to Families with Dependent Children (AFDC) which previously had given financial assistance to families in order to provide for the well-being of children of parents who cannot support them.
- **Food stamps,** which provides federal government vouchers, or chits, to enable people to purchase food they could not otherwise afford.
- **Supplemental Security Income (SSI),** which is a federal program providing direct financial assistance to the elderly, the blind, and the physically or mentally impaired.

- **General relief,** which is the term for those local (whether city or county) programs that serve as a kind of emergency back up to the various state and federal programs by offering immediate help to the poor of the community.

Welfare programs reserved for the poor generally do not raise the recipients out of poverty. Even in a relatively generous state, benefits for a typical family receiving AFDC and food stamps add up to less than 80 percent of the poverty level.

History

In the early nineteenth century, help for the poor came almost exclusively from individuals helping other individuals, or institutions like church groups helping members of their congregations who fell on hard times. By the late nineteenth century, however, a variety of private social and religious charitable organizations had sprung up, most of which provided specific kinds of assistance to specific categories of people in need.

Most of these charitable groups were located in the big cities. Many gave help to alcoholics and prostitutes who promised to reform. Temporary help was offered to new immigrants by settlement houses, modeled after Jane Addams's famous Hull House in Chicago. Besides helping immigrants adjust to their new lives, these institutions fostered a sense of community and pride in many urban neighborhoods. The largest of the private charities working in the cities was the Salvation Army, which had been founded in England but expanded to the United States in 1880, and which gave food and shelter to the downtrodden and homeless. In addition to these private charities, some local governments provided temporary and limited relief to people in great need.

This system—or, more accurately, lack of a system—failed to provide much real help to the great majority of poor Americans. No matter how unfortunate a person might be, he or she had to fall into a particular category of distress in order to even be eligible for help from a particular organization. A great many of those who needed assistance failed to qualify for any at all. And even many of those who did qualify failed to receive help because the charitable institutions of the time were too small to help more than a fraction of those in need.

The Great Depression prompted governments at all levels to get more involved in providing help to individuals than ever before. Even the federal government took up some responsibility, providing some relief through the temporary relief and job provision measures of the New Deal and providing the more long-term retirement assistance in the form of Social Security.

In 1964, President Lyndon Johnson and the Democrat-controlled Congress launched the War on Poverty and established a major new government agency, the Office of Economic Opportunity (OEO), to oversee it. The War on Poverty not only expanded many existing welfare programs, but added the most ambitious collection of new social measures since the New Deal.

The most ambitious of these were Medicaid and Medicare, which provided national health insurance to the poor and the elderly, respectively. Other major War on Poverty programs included Head Start, which prepared poor children for school; an array of Community Action Programs designed to show poor people how they could help themselves in their own communities; and the Job Corps, which trained young poor people in the skills they would need to get a job. Although the OEO and many of its programs were dismantled under later administrations, many of the other programs started during the War on Poverty, including Medicaid and Medicare, remain.

The Constitutional Rationale for Welfare

The Preamble to the U.S. Constitution declares that one of the fundamental purposes of government is to "promote the general welfare." Some scholars and politicians consider this a valid constitutional basis for an American welfare state. Others insist that it is not. The founders, they say, had only the well-being of a free people in mind when they enacted those words, not the kind of government programs associated with modern-day welfare. Certainly, they made no effort to initiate such programs in the early years of the republic.

In the case of *Goldberg* v. *Kelly* (1970), the U.S. Supreme Court affirmed the constitutional basis for welfare, while making clear that welfare had a practical as well as charitable function. "Welfare," proclaimed the Court, "by meeting the demands of subsistence, can help bring within the reach of the poor… opportunities… to participate meaningfully in the life of the community. At the same time, welfare guards against the societal malaise that may flow from a widespread sense of frustration and insecurity. Public assistance, then, is not mere charity, but a means to promote the General Welfare, and secure the Blessings of Liberty to ourselves and our Posterity."

The Cost of Welfare

In the 1995 fiscal year, the federal share of the cost of U.S. welfare programs was $182.6 billion, or approximately 12 percent of the total $1.5 trillion federal budget.

Nearly one-half of the welfare budget, or $87.2 billion, went to Medicaid. The next biggest shares went to food stamps ($25.5

billion), Supplemental Security Income ($23.9 billion), and housing assistance ($22.4 billion). AFDC, the welfare program that arouses the most public controversy, came in at $16.4 billion, while child nutrition and milk programs cost the federal government another $7.2 billion.

The enormous cost of the welfare system has led to a growing dissatisfaction on the part of many Americans. Welfare reform was an important campaign issue in the presidential and congressional election of 1992 and in the historic congressional elections of 1994. It was a major element of the Republican's Contract with America in that year, and the Republican victory in that election put the future of many welfare programs, and perhaps the entire welfare system itself, in jeopardy. That threat was fulfilled, to a limited extent, by the welfare reforms of 1996, which ordered the phasing out of the AFDC program and, in a slogan of the time, "ended welfare as an entitlement."

See also Aid to Families with Dependent Children (AFDC); Head Start; Medicaid; Medicare; Welfare Magnet; Welfare Reform (1996); Welfare State; Welfare Trap.
For further reading Ellwood, David. *Poor Support*. New York: Basic Books, 1989.
Fine, Sidney. *Laissez-Faire and the General Welfare State: A Study of Conflict in American Thought*. Ann Arbor: University of Michigan Press, 1964.
Kronenwetter, Michael. *Welfare State America: Safety Net or Social Contract?* New York: Franklin Watts, 1993.
Trattner, Walter I. *From Poor Law to Welfare State: A History of Social Welfare in America*. New York: Free Press, 1984.

Welfare Trap

The term *welfare trap* was coined by the opponents of the traditional U.S. welfare system to describe what they believed to be the debilitating effects of that system on the people who received help from it.

The term implies that welfare recipients came to rely so completely on their benefits that they found it difficult, and often impossible, to live without them. Once on the welfare roles, the critics charged, families tended to stay on them indefinitely, often remaining on welfare for generation after generation. The critics of welfare argued that, by meeting the recipients' basic needs for food and shelter without requiring them to work, the system robbed them of initiative. This analysis was based on two assumptions: that there was a certain weakness of character among welfare recipients and that the level of benefits made life on welfare more desirable than life in the workforce. Many recipients objected to both assumptions.

Insisting that life on welfare was far from desirable, recipients gave very different reasons for the difficulties they faced in escaping the welfare rolls. Among these were the need to care for infant children, the lack of training for any worthwhile job, and welfare regulations that actually penalized them for working by taking away benefits needed to survive. A typical complaint was that a mother who went to work would lose Medicaid and childcare benefits, even though her job did not pay enough for her to obtain equivalent services.

Defenders of the welfare system as it once existed claimed that welfare was not as much of a trap as the critics charged. Despite the manifold difficulties of finding a job that paid a living wage—and despite the widespread impression to the contrary—few Americans actually spent their lives on welfare.

In any case, the welfare reforms of 1996 attempted to end the so-called welfare trap by requiring adult welfare recipients to work and limiting the total amount of time a family could be on welfare.

See also Welfare State; Welfare System; Welfare Reforms (1996).

White Flight

The phenomenon of relatively prosperous white families leaving the inner cities of the United States as increasing numbers of relatively low-income black and other minority families were moving in has been dubbed "white flight." The process began as an adjunct of the suburbanization that followed World War II, although it was not then seen primarily in racial terms. It accelerated in the 1960s and 1970s, when it took on a more overtly racial character, as the changing racial makeup of the inner cities became increasingly pronounced.

White flight helps to explain why the populations of some U.S. cities, such as New York and Philadelphia, declined between 1960 and 1980. White flight has contributed to a shift in political as well as economic power toward the suburbs. It is also related to the problem of urban decay and the breakdown of the infrastructures in many cities, since it removed much of the tax base on which city governments once relied.

Reasons for White Flight

The term *white flight* can be misleading. Prosperous whites left the cities for a variety of reasons, most of which were not associated with race.

Among the factors that contributed to what became known as white flight were disgust with the corruption of many city governments and with the overcrowding and general discomforts of city life. Many people fled the high crime rates of the cities, while others were attracted to the greater open spaces and greener environments to be found in the suburbs and to the newer homes and infrastructures to be found there. Even more important to those with young families was that the suburbs were considered better places to raise children. The streets were considered safer in the suburbs, and the schools were newer and better staffed. For many Americans, the suburbs seemed to be a step closer to a lost ideal of small-town life.

Race, however, was clearly a major factor as well, particularly after the first waves of black and Hispanic residents moved in to much of the housing surrendered by departing whites. There is no doubt that many whites were prejudiced against African-Americans and Hispanics and welcomed the opportunity to move where they did not have to deal with them as neighbors. Others were primarily discomfited by the changing economic makeup of their neighborhoods.

In many respects, white flight to a great extent was self-accelerating. As the more affluent residents of the inner city neighborhoods left, property values dropped or failed to rise as rapidly as in other neighborhoods. Whether they blamed the declining values on the presence of minorities or simply on the drop in demand caused by an increasing vacancy rate, more residents felt the need to leave before they lost too much of their equity.

The poorer the population of the inner cities became, the more intense became the problem of street crime. At the same time, the more disproportionately black the inner cities became, the more uncomfortable many whites felt living there.

The same things that attracted whites to the suburbs attracted African-Americans, Hispanics, and other minorities as well; and, in fact, many minority families who could afford to do so moved to the suburbs as well. Nonetheless, the movement out of the cities remained a largely white phenomenon for several reasons, perhaps the most important of which was the fact that more whites were financially able to make the move. They had the assets to make down payments on suburban houses and jobs that paid well enough to make the commute into the cities economically feasible.

Still another important factor was the unwelcoming attitude of many suburban communities toward minority families desiring to move into them. Several communities discriminated against minority residents, making it difficult for them to buy real estate and socially uncomfortable for those who succeeded in doing so.

Recent Developments

In recent years, there have been some signs that white flight may have been reversed, at least to some extent; well-off whites, tired of long commutes, are beginning to move back into cities such as New York. Nor are the suburbs as white as they used to be. According to experts at the University of Michigan, minorities made up 17.6 percent of the residents of all U.S. suburban communities in 1990.

See also Suburbanization.

Women and the Church

Feminists complain that most religious organizations discriminate against women in their institutional practices and, in many cases, in their doctrines as well. Islam, Judaism, and various forms of Christianity have all been attacked as being unfair to women in a variety of ways.

Islamic laws, such as those that require women to wear veils in public and that make divorce relatively easy for men, are particularly offensive to western feminists. They see such laws as locking women into what the feminists interpret as an inferior position. Although some Islamic women do chafe under these laws, many others insist that they feel honored and at peace within their traditional role in Islamic society.

Feminists have similar complaints about the Judaic and Christian religions, which they criticize for being excessively patriarchal. Feminists are especially troubled by the prejudicial implications of the account of creation in Genesis, in which woman is created only to be a companion to man, and then proceeds to lead the human race into sin. Other complaints include the once universal, and still common, practice of referring to God as "He."

Special exception is taken to those Christian denominations that emphasize teachings that subordinate wives to their husbands, and to those religions, Christian and otherwise, that refuse to allow women into the clergy. (This is true of most of the world's religions, with the exception of several Protestant sects and some Jewish congregations.) The Roman Catholic Church, the largest Christian denomination in the United States and the world, comes under particular attack from some feminists. Catholicism welcomes women to serve as nuns, or "brides of Christ," but refuses to ordain them as priests and thereby allow them to perform the sacraments, which are the fundamental rites of the Church.

The limitation of the priesthood to men is rooted largely in the apparent fact that Christ chose only men as his apostles, and a belief, expressed by Pope Paul VI in 1977, that "men more perfectly show forth the image of Christ"—a claim that many feminists find outrageous. Most modern Catholic theologians acknowledge that the ban on women priests is not a question of theological doctrine, but rather a matter of discipline. It is, however, a discipline that is enforced with all the authority of the Vatican. As recently as the early 1990s, Pope John Paul II rejected the possibility that women could ever be ordained as priests. The Vatican also rejected the introduction of gender-neutral language into the catechism.

Despite the stubbornness of Rome on such issues, the Church in several countries has tried to reach out to women and to improve their status within the institution. This has been especially true in the United States. In 1994, a committee of U.S. Catholic bishops publicly acknowledged that the Roman Catholic Church has been lacking in its openness to women. "We are painfully aware that sexism… is still present in the church. We reject sexism…." declared the bishops, calling on their fellow members of the clergy to end the authoritarian conduct women have long complained of in church affairs, and to find structures that will make it easier for the Church to recognize and respond to women's complaints and concerns. As first steps, they committed themselves to remove the masculine language from church textbooks and to encourage more women to pursue such traditionally clergy-dominated fields as theology, scriptural studies, and canon (or church) law.

For further reading Lindley, Susan H. *You Have Stept Out of Your Place: A History of Women and Religion in America.* Louisville, KY: Westminster John Knox, 1996.
Wessinger, Catherine, and Frederick Denny. *Religious Institutions and Women's Leadership: New Roles Inside the Mainstream.* Columbia: University of South Carolina Press, 1996.

Women in Politics

For the first two centuries of the United States's existence, government at all levels was almost exclusively the province of men. The few women who did become active in political affairs, such as Susan B. Anthony and other early feminists, were considered at least eccentric, if not actually disreputable. Women did have one significant, if unofficial, role to play in traditional politics, but that was only as the dutiful wives of male politicians. Voters preferred "family men" with supportive wives, and consequently, a political wife was expected to appear at her husband's side, to host his get-togethers, and generally, to play the role of dutiful spouse.

Today, women are no longer confined to such a limited, and secondary, role. Instead, they are active in virtually every aspect of American politics, and at every level—except at the very top. On 23 January, 1997, Madeleine Albright became the highest-ranking woman to serve in the federal government to that point, having been appointed by President Bill Clinton and confirmed by the U.S. Senate to serve as Secretary of State.

Women as Candidates

Although very few women were serious candidates—much less victors—for major elective offices until fairly recently, widows were sometimes appointed to serve out their husbands' terms in various offices. In some states, where officeholders could not succeed themselves, wives of popular politicians sometimes ran in alternate elections, only to serve as surrogates for their husbands.

The first woman to be elected to either house of Congress was Representative Jeannette Rankin of Montana. Not only a suffragette, but a pacifist as well, Rankin was elected to the House of Representatives in 1917, at a time when women were not even allowed to vote in most states. The Nineteenth Amendment, which gave women the right to vote, was not passed by Congress until 1919 or ratified by the required number of states until 1920. Rankin ran for the Senate in 1918, but she was defeated. She would return to the House for another term in 1941, just in time to cast the only vote against the declaration of war on Japan.

The first woman to be elected to the U.S. Senate was Hattie Caraway of Arkansas in 1932. Caraway was already in the Senate at the time, having been appointed to serve out the term of her recently deceased husband, Thaddeus. Helped by the support of Huey Long, the influential senator from Louisiana, she won a surprisingly easy victory. She was reelected in 1938 but lost in a try for her third term in 1944.

It is no longer uncommon for women to run for local, state, or national offices, nor is it rare for women to be elected. Women made up 15 percent of the candidates for the U.S. Senate in the 1994 primary elections, as well as 13 percent of the candidates for U.S. House seats and state governorships. As a group, they did as well, and in some respects better, than the men in those races. They won as high a percentage of the Senate primaries in which they ran as men did, for example, and an even higher percentage of the congressional and gubernatorial primary elections. Even more impressively, every incumbent female senator, representative, and governor who ran for re-election won their party's primary, while several male incumbents lost.

No woman has yet made a serious run at the presidency. Some minor parties have nominated women for president, but so far neither of the two major parties has done so. Of them, only the Democrats, who nominated Geraldine A. Ferraro as Walter Mondale's running mate in 1984, have ever nominated a woman for vice president. Ferraro's nomination was considered a real boon to Mondale's candidacy until ethics charges against her husband, regarding some business dealings, distracted the candidates and seriously damaged the Democratic campaign.

In the eyes of some political observers, Ferraro's problems signaled an unexpected drawback for women candidates. Because more female than male candidates are likely to have spouses with active political or business careers of their own, they are more likely to be vulnerable to scandals or other controversies involving their mates.

Women as Voters

Fifty-four percent of those who voted in the election of 1992 were women. The fact that women make up the majority of the voters gives them an enormous potential for political power. Recognizing this, feminist organizations like NOW (the National Organization for Women) have attempted to marshal this power on behalf of moderate and liberal measures opposing sexual discrimination and upholding gay, lesbian, and abortion rights. Despite the feminists' claim to speak for women politically, the reality is that many women do not share feminists' opinions on all issues, nor do women vote as a bloc.

In recent years, women voters have tended to support slightly more liberal candidates on the national level than men have. In the 1992 presidential election, for example, 46 percent of the women voted for the Democrat Bill Clinton, 37 percent for the Republican George Bush, and 17 percent for the independent Ross Perot. That was not much different from the men, however, who went 41 percent for Clinton, 37 percent for Bush, and 21 percent for Perot. In 1996, this so-called gender gap widened even further.

Women as Activists

The potential political power of women is probably best exemplified by the legions of female political activists who work at all levels of party and special interest politics. Women are active in every significant political movement and most of the minor ones. They are invaluable to the major party organizations and their candidates, particularly at the local level, where they make up the bulk of the volunteer workers who make modern campaigning possible.

Despite the slightly more liberal leanings of women voters, many of the 1990's most prominent women activists are found in conservative political circles. The political strategist Mary Matalin played a major role in George Bush's reelection campaign, for instance. Phyllis Schlafly is the leader of the traditionally conservative Eagle Forum, and Arianna Huffington is a leading spokeswoman for what might be called New Age conservatism. Huffington was also widely reported to be the real power behind her husband's nearly successful campaign for the Senate from California.

See also Gender Gap.

Women in Sports

Women have historically played a secondary role in American sports. Individual star athletes—such as track stars Wilma Rudolph and Jackie Joyner-Kersee, tennis players Billy Jean King, Christ Evert and Martina Navratilova, and the multitalented Olympic medal winner "Babe" Didrikson Zaharias, who was named female athlete of the century in 1950—have gained worldwide fame and admiration. But opportunities for women to play and coach sports, in general, have always trailed behind those of men. This has been (and is still) true at virtually every level of organized sport.

Professional sports, in particular, have always been dominated by men. Women have been largely shut out of most professional sports leagues and other institutions as being too small and weak to compete with men. No women currently play in the major professional baseball, or football leagues. A few have made their way into minor leagues in some sports, but they are given little chance to make successful careers for themselves in the major leagues.

Exceptions to the almost total exclusion of women from the upper levels of professional sports are motor sports and horse racing. In these, women have competed side by side with men on more or less equal terms. But even these sports remain overwhelmingly male-dominated, and the number of women who have successfully infiltrated them is relatively small.

Although there have been women's baseball, hockey, and football teams, golf and tennis remained the only major professional sports with significant women's divisions until two now-pro women's basketball leagues were launched in 1997. The audiences, and revenues, for these women's divisions, however, tend to be small compared to those of their male counterparts. So do the advertising contracts that star athletes in such sports can expect to generate, an important consideration when measuring the economic (as opposed to athletic) success of a modern sports figure.

Amateur Sports

On the international amateur level, most Olympic sports have separate competitions for men and women. With a few exceptions (notably figure skating), the men's divisions usually get more attention. To some extent, at least, the focus on men's sports is a result of social history and athletic tradition. The original Olympic games, for example, were offshoots of the military and were, therefore, all male.

In the nineteenth and early twentieth centuries, differing standards of modesty for men and women worked against female participation in many sports. It was socially acceptable, for example, for men to appear publicly in shorts or tight-fitting leggings that suited them for competition in sports like running or swimming. Women, on the contrary, risked their reputations if they appeared publicly in such costumes.

High School Sports

On the high school level, boys have always been encouraged to take part in team sports, while girls have often been denied participation in any sports program except cheerleading. Teams in many sports, including football, baseball, and hockey, were traditionally reserved entirely for boys. Few, if any, girls' teams were fielded by many high schools. When they were, the girls' teams were usually smaller, and less well-funded and well-supplied, than the boys' teams in the same schools. On the rare occasions when this male domination of high school sports was challenged by female students or their parents, the status quo was typically justified on the grounds that girls were supposedly neither as interested in nor qualified for sports as boys were.

High school sports are no longer all but exclusively male preserves, however. More and more schools are fielding girls' basketball, volleyball, and soccer teams. Girls are even being allowed to try out for, and occasionally succeed in winning spots on, teams in sports like football and hockey that have no girls' teams and were once reserved for boys.

In the 1995–1996 school year, some 2,367,936 high school athletes took part in girl's sports, compared with 3,634,052 boys. Nearly 18,000 other students participated in co-ed sports. In total, girls now make up approximately 37 percent of all high school athletes. Even so, male-dominated sports, such as football and basketball, still receive the most money and attention at the majority of high schools.

College Sports

Participation in college sports is even more unbalanced than it is at the secondary school level. Approximately seven out of every ten college athletes are male, a disparity that is reflected in the smaller amounts of sports scholarship money available for female students. If anything, the physical disparities in strength between female and male athletes are even more pronounced at the college level than at the secondary school level, and the opportunities for a female to make a traditionally male team are even fewer.

Since 1972, federal civil rights legislation known as Title IX has forbidden colleges and universities to discriminate against female athletes. The Office for Civil Rights of the Department of Education standards for determining whether a school is in compliance with Title IX require schools to meet at least one of three tests: Has the school made a real effort to expand athletic opportunities for women? Does the school provide a substantially similar number of intercollegiate athletic opportunities for women as for men, proportional to each gender's enrollment in the institution? And, does the school provide sufficient opportunities for intercollegiate athletics to meet the interests and abilities of its female students?

Pressed by the demands of Title IX, by civil rights suits, and by women's rights advocates, the institutions of the National Collegiate Athletic Association (NCAA) have been working to improve the balance. Progress has been real but falls far short of achieving equity. According to a survey conducted by *The Chronicle of High Education*, women made up 50.8 percent of the student body at 257 large colleges in 1993–1994, but received only 35.7 percent of the athletic scholarship money. The discrepancy in scholarship money is echoed by an even greater discrepancy in overall money spent on major university athletic programs. According to a 1992 study by the NCAA, a typical Division 1 athletic program spends about $4 on men's sports for every $1 spent on women's.

In college, as in high schools, the disparity is exacerbated by the importance put upon football and basketball, two male-dominated sports that tend to receive the biggest chunk of most schools' athletic and sports scholarship budgets. The schools justify the preference given to these sports on the grounds that they are the main revenue-producing sports in college athletics and help to provide funds for the institution's entire athletic program.

Coaching

The ranks of coaches, at all levels, are even more male-dominated than the ranks of players. Not only are 99 percent of the college coaches in men's sports male, so are 54 percent of the coaches in women's sports. At the professional level, the imbalance is even greater.

Women in the Military

Historically, warfare has been a male activity. Although women have often been the victims of war, they have rarely taken a major part in prosecuting it. That, however, has begun to change.

As of the fall of 1994, according to the U.S. Defense Department, there were approximately 200,000 women in the U.S. military: some 72,000 in the Army, 66,000 in the Air Force, 54,000 in the Navy and approximately 8,000 in the Marines. They made up approximately 15 percent of the Air Force, 12.5 percent of the Army, 10.7 percent of the Navy, and 4.4 percent of the

Marines. Altogether, women made up a total of approximately 12 percent of all military personnel.

These percentages of women in the military services have been increasing. Approximately 17 percent of all new members of the U.S. armed forces were women in 1994, including almost one in four Air Force recruits.

Wider Roles for Women

It is not only the numbers of women in the military that have been expanding, but their roles as well. During World War II and the Korean War, women served mostly as nurses, or secretaries, or in other support roles. By the time of Operation Desert Storm, however, women were serving in virtually every military capacity, except as members of ground combat units. Women have been rising through the officers' ranks as well. Elizabeth Hoisington and Anna May Hayes were nominated by President Richard Nixon to become the first women generals in 1970.

In 1973 the Defense Department launched a major effort to open up new opportunities for women in all the services. Progress was slow, however, and it was not until 20 years later that women were allowed to fly fighter aircraft in combat and serve aboard warships. In 1994, Navy Lt. Kara Hultgreen, one of the first two women to qualify to pilot an F-14 fighter jet, became the first woman to die flying one, although her death did not occur in combat. Opponents of women in combat suggested that the accident had been caused by her incompetence and used her death as an argument against expanding the roles of women in the military. Following a complete investigation, however, the Pentagon released a videotape of the incident which proved that engine failure, and not pilot error, had led to the accident.

In 1995, Lt. Colonel Eileen Collins became the first woman to pilot a space craft, when she brought the *Discovery* space shuttle into rendezvous with the Russian *Mir* space station. In 1996 the astronaut Shannon Lucid, a 53-year-old mother of three, set a new space endurance record for an American of either sex by spending 188 days aboard the Russian *Mir* station.

The extent of the activities open to women varies from service to service, from as little as 80 to over 90 percent. The Air Force has been the leader in integrating women into the full range of military duties and opportunities, having already opened almost all its positions to them.

Women in Combat

Even while new military opportunities are opening up for women, others remain stubbornly closed. The most obvious, and still the most controversial, is the opportunity to take part in ground combat. Although women now serve in virtually every combat support job in all of the services, actual battlefield combat remains largely a male province. This is true in most other nations as well. In Canada, the only combat roles women are denied are those in submarines, while in Norway women are allowed in all combat positions in every branch of the services.

Several reasons are advanced for not granting women a larger role in infantry combat. Some are based on society's traditional view of women as needing more protection than men. For example, it is argued that the risk of being taken prisoner, which is inherently higher in ground combat than in most other military activities, is more dire for women than men, since female prisoners would be especially vulnerable to rape.

Most of the arguments against women in combat are predicated on real or imag-

ined differences between women and men. Women are weaker physically, it is said, and therefore less able to haul the heavy loads soldiers need to carry with them. They are emotionally more unstable, and so less able to withstand the pressures of combat. They are more sensitive and compassionate by nature, and therefore more vulnerable to the many assaults on the feelings and sensibilities that are bound to occur in combat. They are less suited, both by nature and training, to withstand the physical hardships combat soldiers have to endure.

Advocates of women in combat challenge many of these assumptions as sexist and bigoted. Even if some or all of them were true, the advocates insist, they are generalizations. They are not true of all women compared to all men. Some women are clearly physically and emotionally stronger and hardier than some men. The fact that a smaller proportion of women may be suitable for combat does not mean that all women should be barred from it. The decision of whether or not an individual of either sex is fit for combat ought to be made on the basis of that individual's strengths and weaknesses, not on the arbitrary basis of their gender.

Eligibility for serving in combat aside, the question remains whether women should be *required* to serve in that capacity, as men in the military are, or only allowed to *volunteer* for combat if they choose to do so. The advocates of greater roles for women in the armed services are divided on this issue. Some say that of course women should be required to take part in combat. They should have exactly the same responsibilities and duties as men, just as they should have the same opportunities. Others feel that, for cultural reasons if no others, it would be wrong to insist that women serve on the battlefield. A poll of military women showed that, although a majority of them believed that they should be allowed to volunteer for combat, only a minority would actually do so.

Sexual Harassment

Despite the efforts to move toward complete integration of women in the military, some distinctions are inevitable, and some special concerns are bound to arise. Like women in other occupations still dominated by men, military women frequently find themselves subject to sexual harassment.

In the early 1990s, this problem was thrust to the center of public attention by an incident that became known as the Tailhook Scandal. The affair was brought to light when a number of female naval officers complained of massive harassment, and even sexual attacks, by their male colleagues at the Tailhook convention, attended primarily by naval flyers, in a Las Vegas hotel.

The widely publicized scandal brought out more harassment complaints by other women in the military, suggesting that the problem was bigger and more widespread than the services had previously acknowledged. As a result of Tailhook, the military adopted a declared policy of "zero tolerance" of sexual harassment. There is some question about how effective this policy has been, however. Female members of more than one armed service have testified before Congress that, far from ending the problem, complaining about harassment has damaged their own careers rather than those of their harassers.

At the same time, the zeal inherent in the "zero tolerance" policy creates pressures of its own. In March 1997, several female recruits at the Army's Aberdeen Center in Maryland who had previously accused drill instructors of sexual harassment retracted their charges. They claimed that, although they had indeed had sex with the instructors, their actions had been voluntary. They had only made their original charges, they said, after being pressured to do so by their superiors. Other instructors were, however, convicted of similar charges later in the year.

Conscription

Conscription is another major question that hangs over the issue of women in the military. For whatever reasons, most countries in which women serve in the military make their service voluntary. Among other nations, only Israel currently drafts women.

In the United States, the question of whether to draft women is only a prospective one, since there has been no actual conscription of people of either sex for many years, and there is no plan to renew the practice. Young men are still required to register with the Selective Service System, however, although young women are not. Some who believe that the sexes should be treated equally when it comes to military service see this discrepancy as unfair. If men are required to register, women should be as well. What is more, if conscription is ever resumed, they believe that women should be required to serve in the same proportions as men.

See also Sexual Harassment.

Women in the Workplace

For centuries, women were thought to be fit only for "women's work." Aside from labor in the home and around the farm, this was limited primarily to single women doing such respectably female jobs as childcare, sewing, cleaning, millinery, and secretarial work. Women seeking other employment were considered eccentric, to say the least. Furthermore, except in times of labor shortages like the one brought about by World War II, there was great social resistance to women entering the workforce in any numbers. "A woman's place," it was generally agreed, "was in the home."

Today, however, women have little trouble getting into the American labor force. In 1992, nearly 58 million women filled 45.5 percent of all the jobs in the United States. In Minnesota, the state with the highest proportion of women workers, just over two-thirds of all women are employed.

The increase in the cost of living over the past few decades, combined with stagnant or dropping real wages and a decline in the standard of living of the American middle class, has made two jobs a virtual necessity for a growing number of families. Furthermore, the growing number of single mothers, who have to provide for children on their own, make it necessary for more and more women to join the workforce.

Approximately 66 percent of all part-time workers are women. Some are second earners who are working primarily for spare income in prosperous families primarily supported by their husbands. But many are single women who need to work to support themselves, single mothers who need to work to stay off welfare, or married women who have to work part-time for their families to make ends meet. A great many women in all these categories work at more than one part-time job or work part-time in addition to holding down a full time job.

Barriers Are Falling

The increasing need for women to work has resulted in a drastic revision of the concept of "women's work." Today, almost 45 percent of working women have college degrees. Barriers that once kept women out of many well-paying fields have been falling left and right. Women are no longer seen as out of their place working as physicians, lawyers, or engineers—or as cab drivers or members of highway construction crews, either. Nor are they any longer seen as unfit to serve in the nation's executive suites in any capacity other than secretarial. The percentage of women serving in the upper management of major American companies rose from less than 1 percent to around 8 percent during the past decade. Barriers have been falling even in such previously macho jobs as fire-fighting, military service, and law enforcement. In 1994, Beverly Harvard of Atlanta became the first woman to be named chief of a major U.S. city police department. Hers was no soft job, either. Atlanta had recently been named the most violent city in the nation according to a prominent magazine.

These changes are not mere tokens, but they are far from achieving equity. Women remain rare exceptions in the upper reaches of law enforcement and the military, and although the percentage of women executives has increased eight-fold, it is still less than 10%. Furthermore, the fact that a woman may get a job does not mean that she will be treated equally in the workplace. Sexual harassment and discrimination of various kinds are common complaints of women in many fields. Perhaps the most widespread, and serious, form of discrimination is that involving wages.

Wage Differences

On average, women tend to earn about 77 percent of what men earn in similar jobs. The difference is greater for older women, and less for younger women, who tend to be better educated. Even in jobs in which they have traditionally dominated, women are disadvantaged when it comes to pay. For example, according to the U.S. Census Bureau, 98.4 percent of all secretarial and typist workers are women; yet, the few men in those fields tend to earn $14 more per week. Of all elementary school teachers, 85.6 percent are women, yet women elementary teachers typically earn approximately $80 less per week than men earn. There are a few fields, however, including nursing and university administration, in which women actually earn more than men. Female registered nurses, for example, earn more than $10 a week, on average, than men.

There are several reasons for the wage gap between men and women. Some are historical. In the days when women made up a much smaller proportion of the work force, those jobs that were reserved for women were among the lowest paid. Consequently, the labor of women in general came to be valued less than that of men. Later on, as more women sought and found jobs in a greater variety of fields, a wage bias operated against them.

Most employers were men who made certain negative presumptions about women workers. Many employers also assumed that women needed less money than men, since they were less likely to have large families relying on them for support. Beyond this, there was a certain resentment on the part of many male workers that women were working at all, and competing with men for jobs. This led some employers to make sure that they received less pay and benefits to keep up morale among male employees, by assuring them that women would be kept "in their place."

Another factor in the relatively low pay received by women was their frequent willingness to work for less than men would work for. Partly, this willingness came from a lack of self-confidence, born of their relative lack of experience in the workplace. Partly, it came from their recognition that there were fewer satisfactory jobs available for them, and that they therefore could not afford to be as choosy as a man might be. Many of the same reasons that kept employers from paying equal (much less higher) wages to women kept them from promoting them. Recognizing that many male employees would be uncomfortable with a female boss, employers tended to appoint men, rather than women, to supervisory positions.

There is still a certain amount of prejudice operating against women in the workforce, although it is greater in some fields than in others. However, the wage gap has closed rapidly since the mid-1980s. At 23 cents per dollar in 1994, it was down 36 percent from the 36.3 cents at which it stood in 1984.

Employers argue that the remaining gap does not result from discrimination of any kind. Instead, they say, it reflects the reality that women, on average, have less training for many positions, and have put in less time on the job, than their male counterparts. Therefore, they are less eligible for promotions and for the kinds of pay raises that follow experience. Furthermore, there tend to be fewer women in several of the professions, and therefore the simple numerical odds are against them achieving many of the highest-paying positions.

As new generations of women enter these professions in greater numbers, and stay in them longer, employers suggest, most of the remaining wage gap should disappear. Although numbers, training and experience may account for some wage differences, however, they hardly seem to account for the disparity that still exists in such fields as elementary teaching and secretarial work.

See also Glass Ceiling; Sexual Harassment; Women and the Church; Women in Politics; Women in Sports; Women in the Military.
For further reading Davidson, Kenneth M., Ruth B. Ginsberg, and Herma H. Kay, editors. *Sex-Based Discrimination: Text, Cases, and Materials*. Minneapolis: West Publishing, 1974.

Woodstock

The legendary Woodstock Music and Arts Fair was a massive rock concert held on a rainy weekend in August 1969 near the small communities of Bethel and Woodstock in upstate New York. Expecting perhaps 200,000 spectators, the organizers were stunned when at least twice that many young people poured onto the farm where the concert was to be held. Estimates ranged from 400,000 to 500,000 attendees, making it the largest such event in history up to that time.

The huge crowd was an unlikely mixture of college students and dropouts, hippies and conservatives, druggies and straights, with some older music lovers and even a few Roman Catholic nuns mixed in. They gathered to hear one of the most stellar lineups of popular music artists ever brought together, including Jimi Hendrix, Richie Havens, the Grateful Dead, Crosby, Stills, and Nash, Janis Joplin, The Who, and The Jefferson Airplane, among many others.

By most standards, the concert should have been a disaster. Heavy rains turned the farm's fields to mud and threatened to wash out the entire event. The sanitary and other facilities provided for the spectators were totally overwhelmed by the massive turnout. Yet, despite the physical hardships, the overcrowding, the disorganization, and the widespread drug use, the weekend stayed not only peaceful but joyous. Everyone seemed to catch the freewheeling and good-natured spirit of the event. The organizers were not even bothered by the fact that many of those who attended never paid. Even the police cooperated by staying away, despite the fairly widespread and obvious use of illegal drugs.

The Woodstock Festival was instantly proclaimed a landmark event by the young people, who saw it as "a celebration of peace and love"—a symbol of the new spirit they believed themselves to represent. It is often contrasted with the disastrous Rolling Stones concert at Altamont, California, which was held only a few months later.

Many of the performances and some of the events of the festival weekend were captured in the popular documentary movie *Woodstock* (1970).

See also Altamont; Counterculture.
For further reading Pollock, Bruce. *When the Music Mattered: Rock in the 1960s*. Holt, 1983.

Worker Layoffs of the 1980s and 1990s

Large-scale hirings and firings of workers typically occur more or less in conjunction with the business cycle, that is, in line with expansions and contractions in the overall economy. With some exceptions, brought about by the particular circumstances of individual companies, employers traditionally cut their workforces in bad times and increase them in good times. As a result, the number of Americans who lost their jobs has typically risen during periods of economic recession or depression and fallen during periods of economic strength, in a more or less predictable pattern.

During the 1980s and 1990s, however, this traditional relationship between employment and the state of the economy has broken down. Following recent recessions, the rate of layoffs in American industry refused to drop as the economy improved, remaining instead at the high levels previously associated with economic downturns. From 1979 to 1996, some 43 million Americans lost their jobs despite the fact that, by standard economic measurements, the economy was doing extremely well during most of that time.

The layoffs of the late 1980s, and particularly those of the 1990s, have differed from those of the past in another key way as well. Although layoffs traditionally hit blue collar workers harder than other employees, these more recent layoffs have affected lower and middle management positions to the same degree, or to an even greater degree, than they affected those employees lower on the wage scale.

Reasons for Noncyclical Layoffs

A number of factors contributed to the high rates of layoffs in the closing decades of the twentieth century and to the unusually high percentage of supervisory and lower managerial jobs that were lost. The most obvious factors were the downsizing and outsourcing trends in which most U.S. industries were engaged. Company after company instituted drastic plans for restructuring their operations and reducing their workforces. A key provision of most such plans was the elimination or drastic reduction of middle management and supervisory positions.

Much of the unprecedented downsizing was made possible by new technologies, including advanced computer systems and robotic machinery that allowed companies in some industries to reduce their human workforces with no reduction in output. At the same time, new theories of management encouraged companies to experi-

ment with innovative organizational arrangements that called for fewer managerial and supervisory positions.

Still another factor that contributed to disproportional job losses in the United States was the movement of many companies' operations from their traditional bases. Company headquarters and aging factories were closed down, and the activities that had been conducted there were shifted to new facilities. These shifts were often to places where cheaper labor was available. Many were to foreign locations, a trend that was encouraged by the North American Free Trade Agreement (NAFTA) of 1993 and other international developments.

Lower payrolls were not the only reasons companies moved. Other factors included the desire to take advantage of lower energy costs, lower state or local taxes, a more suitable labor force, a closer proximity to raw materials, or a better access to markets for the companies' products.

Within the United States, some state and local governments deliberately enticed businesses to move from other places by tempting them with special tax concessions or right-to-work laws that helped companies secure a nonunion workforce. Companies that moved their operations abroad frequently did so, at least partly, in order to comply with foreign regulations requiring businesses that hoped to sell their products in the country to manufacture them there.

Whether the new manufacturing locations were within the United States or abroad, the effects on the abandoned communities, and on the workers who had been employed there, were sometimes catastrophic. Some of the fired workers were unable to find new jobs for long periods. Others could find only part-time employment, lower-paying work, or jobs without benefits, resulting in a lower standard of living for the community. Many of those who lost their jobs were forced to relocate in search of work, leaving extended families, friends, and civic relationships, disrupting not only their personal lives but the life of their community as well.

Labor leaders believe that the negative effects of all these factors on American jobs was exacerbated by the decline in the power of unions that had taken place over the previous decades. The weakened state of the unions left threatened workers with little leverage to use in combating corporate plans to close down plants, downsize, outsource, or move.

The Future

It is unclear whether the breakdown in the traditional relationship between employment and the business cycle is per-

manent. Industry spokespersons insist that downsizing and globalization—the two main contributors to the increasingly noncyclical layoffs—are necessary for companies to compete in the modern economy and to take advantage of an increasingly international marketplace. In the long run, they say, these changes in traditional employment practices will make American-based companies and the American economy stronger. Labor representatives complain that, although such developments may temporarily help the balance sheets of the companies involved, they will inevitably undermine the prosperity of the American middle and working classes.

See also Corporate Responsibility; Downsizing. **For further reading** *New York Times. The Downsizing of America.* New York: Times Books, 1996.

Bibliography

A Clash of Arms: The Great American Gun Debate. Upland, PA: DIANE, 1994.

Aggarwal, Arjun P. *Sexual Harassment: A Guide for Understanding and Prevention*. Charlottesville, VA: MICHIE, 1992.

Anti-Slavery Reporter. London: Anti-Slavery International, yearly editions.

Archer, Jules. *Watergate: America in Crisis*. New York: Thomas Y. Crowell, 1975.

Bannister, Robert C. *Social Darwinism: Science and Myth*. Philadelphia: Temple University Press, 1988.

Bartlett, Peggy F. *American Dreams, Rural Realities: Family Farms in Crisis*. Durham: University of North Carolina Press, 1993.

Bawden, Lee, editor. *The Social Contract Revisited: Aims and Outcomes of President Reagan's Welfare Policy*. Washington, DC: Urban Institute, 1984.

Beane, James A., and Richard P. Lipka. *Self-Concept, Self-Esteem, and the Curriculum*. New York: Teachers College Press, 1986.

Bedau, Hugo A. *Civil Disobedience*. New York: Pegasus, 1969.

———. *The Death Penalty in America*. Chicago: Aldine, 1982.

Belth, Nathan C. *A Promise to Keep: A Narrative of the American Encounter with Anti-Semitism*. New York: New York Times, 1979.

Bender, David L., editor. *Liberals and Conservatives: A Debate on the Welfare State*. Anoka, MN: Greenhaven Press, 1982.

Bernstein, Carl, and Bob Woodward. *All the President's Men*. New York: Simon and Schuster, 1974.

Blackstone, William T., and Robert Heslep, editors. *Social Justice and Preferential Treatment*. Athens: University of Georgia Press, 1976.

Boucher, David, and Paul Kelly, eds. *The Social Contract from Hobbes to Rawls*. London: Routledge, 1994.

Bremner, Robert H. *American Philanthropy*. Daniel J. Boor, editor. Chicago: University of Chicago Press, 1988.

Brilliant, Eleanor L. *The United Way: Dilemmas of Organized Charity*. New York: Columbia University Press, 1993.

Brown, Joe David, editor. *The Hippies*. New York: Time, 1967.

Castro, Barry. *Business and Society: A Reader in the History, Sociology and Ethics of Business*. New York: Oxford University Press, 1996.

Chase, Naomi Feigelson. *A Child Is Being Beaten: Violence against Children, An American Tragedy*. New York: Holt, 1975.

Cookson, Peter W., Jr. *School Choice: The Struggle for the Soul of American Education*. New Haven, CT: Yale University Press, 1994.

Cottingham, P. H., and D. T. Ellwood, editors. *Welfare Policy for the 1990s*. Cambridge, MA: Harvard University Press, 1982.

Council on Economic Priorities Staff, et al. *Rating America's Corporate Conscience*. Reading, MA: Addison-Wesley, 1987.

Davey, Joseph D. *The New Social Contract: America's Journey from a Welfare State to a Police State*. Westport, CT: Greenwood Press, 1995.

Davidson, Kenneth M., Ruth B. Ginsberg, and Herma H. Kay, editors. *Sex-Based Discrimination: Text, Cases, and Materials*. Minneapolis: West Publishing, 1974.

Deats, S. M., and L. T. Lenker, editors. *The Aching Hearth: Family Violence in Life and Literature*. New York: Plenum, 1991.

DeJasay, Anthony. *Social Contract, Free Ride: A Study of the Public Goods Problem*. New York: Oxford University Press, 1991.

Dellinger, Dave. *Revolutionary Nonviolence*. Garden City, NY: Anchor Books, 1971.

Dietz, Robert. *Willful Injustice: A Post-O. J. Look at Rodney King, American Justice, and Trial by Race.* New York: New Press NY, 1995.

Dobson, James. *The New Dare to Discipline.* Wheaton, IL: Tyndale House, 1992.

Elkins, Stanley M. *Slavery.* Chicago: University of Chicago Press, 1975.

Ellwood, David. *Poor Support.* New York: Basic Books, 1989.

Fine, Sidney. *Laissez-Faire and the General Welfare State: A Study of Conflict in American Thought.* Ann Arbor: University of Michigan Press, 1964.

Flanders, Stephen A. *Capital Punishment.* New York: Facts on File, 1991.

Fletcher, George P. *With Justice for Some: Protecting Victims' Rights in Criminal Trials.* Reading, MA: Addison-Wesley, 1996.

Flora, Peter, and Arnold J. Heidenheimer, editors. *The Development of the Welfare States in Europe and America.* New Brunswick, NJ: Transaction Books, 1981.

Fuller, Bruce, et. al., editors. *Who Chooses? Who Loses? Culture, Institutions, and the Unequal Effects of School Choice.* New York: Teachers College Press, 1996.

Garrow, David J. *Bearing the Cross.* New York: William Morrow, 1986.

Gelles, Richard J., and Denileen Leseke. *Current Controversies on Family Violence.* Thousand Oaks, CA: Sage, 1993.

Ginger, Ray. *Six Days or Forever? Tennessee* vs. *John Thomas Scopes.* New York: Oxford, 1974.

Goldberg, Jacob. *The Disappearing American Farm.* New York: Watts, 1996.

Greider, William. *Who Will Tell the People?* New York: Touchstone, 1992.

Gwaltney, John Langston, editor. *Drylongso: A Self-Portrait of Black America.* New York: Random House, 1980.

Harris, Fred. *America's Democracy; The Ideal and the Reality.* Glenview, IL: Scott, Foresman, 1980.

Henderson, David L. *The Case for School Choice.* Stanford, CA: Hoover Institution Press, 1993.

Herbert, Carrie M. *Talking of Silence: The Sexual Harassment of Schoolgirls.* Bristol, PA: Taylor & Francis, 1989.

Hofstader, Richard. *Social Darwinism in American Thought.* Boston: Beacon Press, 1992.

Hutchinson, E. P. *Legislative History of American Immigration Policy, 1798–1965.* Philadelphia: University of Pennsylvania Press, 1981.

Hyman, Ronald T., and Charles H. Rathbone. *Corporal Punishment in Schools.* Nos. 48 and 48A. Topeka KS: Nolpe, 1993.

Jansson, Bruce S. *The Reluctant Welfare State: A History of American Social Welfare Policies.* Belmont, CA: Wadsworth, 1988.

Jaworski, Leon. *The Right and the Power: The Prosecution of Watergate.* Houston: Gulf, 1976.

Johnson, Andrew. *Factory Farming.* Williston, VT: Blackwell, 1991.

Jurinski, James J. *Religion in the Schools.* Santa Barbara, CA: ABC-CLIO, 1997.

Kaufman, Johnathan. *Broken Alliance.* New York: Macmillan, 1988.

Kelly, Dean M., and Richard D. Lambert, editors. *The Uneasy Boundary: Church and State.* Philadelphia: American Academy of Political Science, 1979.

Kennedy, Gail, editor. *Democracy and the Gospel of Wealth.* Boston: D. C. Heath & Company, 1949.

Kennedy, John F. *A Nation of Immigrants.* New York: Harper, 1964.

Konvitz, Milton R., editor. *Bill of Rights Reader: Leading Constitutional Cases.* Ithaca, NY: Cornell, 1973.

Koss, Mary, et al. *No Safe Haven: Male Violence against Women at Home, at Work, and in the Community.* Washington, DC: American Psychological Association, 1994.

Kronenwetter, Michael. *Capital Punishment.* Santa Barbara, CA: ABC-CLIO, 1993.

———. *How Democratic Is the United States?* New York: Watts, 1994.

———. *Welfare State America: Safety Net or Social Contract?* New York: Franklin Watts, 1993.

Kruschke, Earl R. *Gun Control: A Reference Handbook.* Santa Barbara, CA: ABC-CLIO, 1995.

Laurence, John. *The History of Capital Punishment.* New York: Citadel, 1960.

Lee-Wright, Peter. *Child Slaves.* London: Earthscan Publications, 1990.

Lindley, Susan H. *You Have Stept Out of Your Place: A History of Women and Religion in America.* Louisville, KY: Westminster John Knox, 1996.

Long, Robert Emmet, editor. *The Welfare Debate.* New York: H. W. Wilson, 1989.

Low, W. Augustus, and Virgil A. Clift. *Encyclopedia of Black America.* New York: McGraw-Hill, 1981.

Luker, Kristen. *Abortion and the Politics of Motherhood.* Berkeley, CA: University of California Press, 1984.

Masur, Louis P. *Rites of Execution: Capital Punishment and the Transformation of American Culture, 1776–1865*. New York: Oxford University Press, 1989.

McCamant, Kathyrn, and Charles Durrett. *Cohousing: A Contemporary Approach to Housing Ourselves*. Berkeley, CA: Ten Speed Press, 1994.

McClellan, Grant S. *Immigrants, Refugees, and U.S. Policy*. New York: H. W. Wilson, 1981.

McMillan, Richard C. *Religion in the Public Schools: An Introduction*. Macon, GA: Mercer University Press, 1984.

Meltsner, Michael. *Cruel and Unusual: The Supreme Court and Capital Punishment*. New York: Random House, 1973.

Mercurio, Joseph. *Caning: Educational Rite and Tradition*. Syracuse, NY: Syracuse University Press, 1971.

Murphy, Jeffrie G., editor. *Civil Disobedience and Violence*. Belmont, CA: Wadsworth, 1971.

National Association for the Advancement of Colored People Staff, et al. *Beyond the Rodney King Story: An Investigation of Police Conduct in Minority Communities*. Boston: Northeastern University Press, 1994.

New York Times. The Downsizing of America. New York: Times Books, 1996.

Newman, Graeme. *Just and Painful: A Case for the Corporal Punishment of Criminals*. Albany, NY: Harrow & Heston, 1995.

Payton, Robert, et al. *Philanthropy: Four Views*. New Brunswick, NJ: Transaction Press, 1988.

Piven, Francis Fox, and Richard A. Cloward. *Regulating the Poor: The Functions of Public Welfare*. New York: Pantheon, 1971.

Pollock, Bruce. *When the Music Mattered: Rock in the 1960s*. Holt, 1993.

Potter, Beverly A., and J. Sebastian Orfali. *Drug Testing at Work*. Berkeley, CA: Ronin, 1990.

Raines, Howell. *"My Soul Is Rested": The Movement Days in the Deep South Remembered*. New York: G. P. Putnam's Sons, 1977.

Resenthal, John K. *To Spank or Not to Spank: A Parent's Handbook*. Kansas City: Andrews & McMeel, 1994.

Rose, David. *Home, School, and Faith: Towards an Understanding of Religious Diversity*. Bristol, PA: Taylor & Francis, 1992.

Rosenfeld, Michael. *Affirmative Action and Justice: A Philosophical and Constitutional Inquiry*. New Haven, CT: Yale University Press, 1990.

Rossetti, Stephen J. *Slayer of the Soul: Child Sexual Abuse and the Catholic Church*. Mystic, CT: Twenty-Third, 1990.

Russell, Francis. *Tragedy in Dedham*. New York: McGraw-Hill, 1971.

Rutland, Robert Allen. *The Birth of the Bill of Rights*. Boston: Northeastern University Press, 1991.

Sammons, Jeffrey. *Beyond the Ring: The Role of Boxing in American Society*. Champagne: University of Illinois Press, 1988.

Scott, George R. *The History of Capital Punishment: Including an Examination of the Case for and against Capital Punishment*. New York: AMS Press, reprint of 1950 edition.

Sheleff, Leon Shaskolski. *Ultimate Penalties: Capital Punishment, Life Imprisonment, Physical Torture*. Columbus: Ohio State University Press, 1987.

Sitkoff, Harvard. *The Struggle for Black Equality, 1954–1980*. New York: Hill & Wang, 1981.

Stark, Jerome, and Howard Goldstein. *The Rights of Crime Victims*. Edwardsville, IL: Southern Illinois University Press, 1985.

Stevens, Leonard A. *Death Penalty: The Case of Life and Death in the United States*. New York: Coward, McCann & Geoghegan, 1978.

Straus, Murray. *Beating the Devil Out of Them: Corporal Punishment in American Families and Its Effects on Children*. New York: Free Press, 1994.

Szumski, Bonnie, et al., editors. *The Death Penalty*. St. Paul, MN: Greenhaven, 1986.

Thompson, William N. *Legalized Gambling*. 2d ed. Santa Barbara, CA: ABC-CLIO, 1997.

Thoreau, Henry David. *Walden and Civil Disobedience*. New York: NAL-Dutton, 1943.

Trattner, Walter I. *From Poor Law to Welfare State: A History of Social Welfare in America*. New York: Free Press, 1984.

U.S. Department of Labor. *By the Sweat and Toil of Children: The Use of Child Labor in American Imports*. Washington, DC: U.S. Department of Labor, 1994.

van den Haag, Ernest, and John P. Conrad. *The Death Penalty: A Debate*. New York: Plenum, 1983.

Van Scotter, Richard D. *Public Schooling in America*. Santa Barbara, CA: ABC-CLIO, 1991.

Wessinger, Catherine, and Frederick Denny. *Religious Institutions and Women's Leadership: New Roles inside the Mainstream*. Columbia: University of South Carolina Press, 1996.

White, Theodore H. *Breach of Faith: The Fall of Richard Nixon*. New York: Atheneum, 1975.

Wolf, Leonard, editor. *Voices from the Love Generation*. Boston: Little, Brown, 1968.

Index

For Reference

Not to be taken from this room